Introduction to Education Studies

Second Edition

Education Studies: Key Issues Series

In the last fifteen years or so Education Studies has developed rapidly as a distinctive subject in its own right. Beginning initially at undergraduate level, this expansion is now also taking place at masters level and is characterised by an increasingly analytical approach to the study of education. As education studies programmes have developed there has emerged a number of discrete study areas that require indepth texts to support student learning.

Introduction to Education Studies; Second Edition is the core text in this series and gives students an important grounding in the study of education. It provides an overview of the subject and introduces the reader to fundamental theories and debates in the field. The series, 'Key Issues in Education Studies,' has evolved from this core text and, using the same critical approach, each volume outlines a significant area of study within the education studies field. All of the books have been written by experts in their area and provide the detail and depth required by students as they progress further in the subject.

Taken as a whole, this series provides a comprehensive set of texts for the student of education. Whilst of particular value to students of Education Studies, the series will also be instructive for those studying related areas such as Childhood Studies and Special Needs, as well as being of interest to students on initial teacher training courses and practitioners working in education.

We hope that this series provides you, the reader, with plentiful opportunities to explore further this exciting and significant area of study and we wish you well in your endeavours.

Steve Bartlett and Diana Burton
Series Editors

Education Studies: Key Issues Series

Steve Bartlett and Diana Burton: *Introduction to Education Studies; Second Edition* (2007)

Stephen Ward and Christine Eden: *Key Issues in Education Policy* (2009)

Diana Burton and Steve Bartlett: *Key Issues for Education Researchers* (2009)

Alan Hodkinson and Philip Vickerman: *Key Issues in Special Educational Needs and Inclusion* (2009)

Introduction to Education Studies

Second Edition

Steve Bartlett and Diana Burton

SAGE Publications
Los Angeles ▪ London ▪ New Delhi ▪ Singapore

First published 2007

SAGE Publications Ltd
1 Oliver's Yard
55 City Road
London EC1Y 1SP

SAGE Publications Inc.
2455 Teller Road
Thousand Oaks, California 91320

SAGE Publications India Pvt Ltd
B1/I1 Mohan Cooperative Industrial Area
Mathura Road, Post Bag 7
New Delhi 110 044

SAGE Publications Asia-Pacific Pte Ltd
33 Pekin Street #02–01
Far East Square
Singapore 048763

British Library Cataloguing in Publication data

A catalogue record for this book is available from the British Library

ISBN 978-1-4129-2193-0
ISBN 978-1-4129-2194-7 (pbk)

Library of Congress Control Number: 2006939008

Typeset by Pantek Arts Ltd, Maidstone, Kent
Printed in Great Britain by The Alden Press, Oxford
Printed on paper from sustainable resources

Contents

Dedication

To our dear, long-suffering sons, Tom, Dan, Eddy and George with love.

What is education studies?

The first chapter will introduce you to the study of education. We examine the appeal of the subject for students and explain its rapid recent growth. Whilst the significant contributions of the related disciplines of sociology, psychology, history and philosophy are discussed, we argue that it is the positioning of education as the central focus that provides education studies with its own identity. The chapter also introduces comparative education as an area of study, pointing to some of the advantages and problems of comparing education systems and processes.

The new 'education studies'

FIRST ENCOUNTERS

Many students, like yourself, are surprised by their early encounters with education studies. You have all experienced several years within formal systems of education either recently or in the more distant past. It is likely that you have gone through formal education without really questioning what was happening and it is unlikely that you were encouraged to probe the nature of the process as opposed to the content of study. In schools pupils study history, maths, science and other subjects but not usually the education process itself. You may therefore be unsure of what to expect when beginning your study of education as a subject in its own right. Some of you will assume education studies is an uncomplicated study of a clearly defined process. Perhaps it will involve accounts of how to teach, how schools or colleges should be organised, how to revise and get good results. Many students express surprise that education is so 'political' with so much argument and no absolute answers. They may not previously have looked at education in a critical manner nor realised that research into education takes place across such diverse fields of study. There is much more, then, to the study of education than the schooling of 5–18 year olds.

In your other subject degree studies you are likely to have experience of the subjects' content and methodologies, having studied them at school. This is not the case with education studies. Whilst the education process is something that we all have experience of it has not actually been a focus of study for us unless we have taken sociology and psychology at school or college and studied aspects of education within these. For many students with no previous experience of the subject embarking on an education studies course can be an unsettling time and they may feel insecure. This is perhaps because they are questioning something which they had previously regarded as one of the fixed entities in their lives. For others, of course, it may be a relief to find alternative accounts and analyses of education which align with their own feelings about the difficult times they spent in educational institutions.

You will be directed to many interesting journals and books from the beginning of your course but generally these assume a level of understanding and knowledge which you are unlikely to have at this stage. Thus, whilst there are many texts suitable for the knowledgeable student, there are very few which may be used by the novice as an introduction to the field. This present book aims to introduce the study of education and to provide a starting point from which to progress. It outlines several major areas of education studies and the key issues therein. In the text we refer, wherever possible, to current literature which you should be able to access. We are also aware that to deal with the overarching questions and issues in such a short space can actually do them a disservice and cause distortion by oversimplification. We want therefore to emphasise that the purpose is to introduce the study of education, outline the theoretical arguments and encourage deeper exploration.

THE DEVELOPMENT OF THE 'NEW EDUCATION STUDIES'

In the past education(al) studies has been seen as very much part of the education/training of teachers (Burton and Bartlett, 2007). The study was effectively invented during the period of expansion in education post-Second World War, which created a demand for more high quality teachers. To meet this demand the teacher training courses at the colleges of education were lengthened and the Robbins Report (1963) declared an intent to develop teaching into an all-graduate profession. This heralded the creation of the new B.Ed. degree, which comprised both theoretical and practical study of education. As McCulloch (2002) pointed out, the content of these new B.Ed. courses was largely created from a range of subjects already in existence at the validating universities. Thus the academic study of education came to be made up primarily of the sociology, psychology, philosophy and history of education.

Rather than becoming a unified subject these disciplines generally remained as discrete units and were taught separately. For many students they were presented in isolation and did not sufficiently link with the other parts of their professional training courses to make them appear worthwhile. For such students their prime focus was on the subjects they were going to teach, the teaching practice itself and, particularly, aspects of classroom management and control. In an effort to make the theoretical and academic study of education more relevant to the needs of the student teachers, many B.Ed. programmes began to create a more integrated approach. This involved the development of what became known as curriculum, professional or even educational studies. In hindsight this can be seen as a significant point in the development of a specialist study of education.

As a result of political and economic pressures in the 1970s and 1980s the theoretical study of education as part of teacher training courses fell into disrepute. Teacher education was criticised as being too removed from the classroom. It was perceived as largely ignoring the practical nature of teaching whilst also promoting progressive ideologies of education. It was from the 1980s onwards that the nature of teacher education changed drastically. With the emphasis becoming firmly placed on training, any traces of academic education(al) studies were removed from Initial Teacher Training (ITT) programmes. However, shortly after the critical study of education disappeared from teacher training courses, new programmes, called education studies, began to develop in the rapidly expanding sector funded by the Higher Education Funding Council for England (HEFCE). We suggest a number of reasons for the rapid growth of this subject and its popularity amongst the student population (Bartlett and Burton, 2006a).

The increase in student numbers entering higher education (HE) and the concomitant development of modular degree programmes, allowing more flexibility in the choice of subjects studied, meant that education studies came to be seen as an important partner for a number of combinations. Thus students combine education studies with sports science, English, drama, religious studies, geography and the like. It took on a special significance for students planning careers that involved working with people in a variety of contexts. Teaching is often the first that springs to mind but there are also personnel management, welfare and health services, retail, publishing and a range of others.

The recent trend for many students who intend to become teachers to take a first degree and then a PGCE rather than the traditional B.Ed. has made education studies a more attractive part of that first degree. This changing landscape of teacher training has led to many schools of education seeking actively to diversify their portfolios making education studies an obvious addition from an institutional point of view.

THE NATURE OF EDUCATION STUDIES

Whatever your eventual career decisions as an education studies student, you have chosen education as an academic area of study and will need to approach it in a critical fashion. You will be seeking answers to key questions such as: What is education and what are its purposes? How does learning take place and how far is achievement dependent upon natural ability or social factors such as income, life chances, gender and ethnicity? Your attention will also be drawn to educational policy and political issues surrounding education and to ways of researching these phenomena.

With the resurgence of the academic study of education, and an increasing number of students with education studies in their degree title, the significance of the traditional disciplines from which it draws once again becomes apparent. Aspects of education are studied within various disciplines, specifically philosophy, psychology, sociology and history, as part of their particular interest in the human condition. However, education is also seen as a legitimate area of study in its own right by the Quality Assurance Agency (QAA) which considered that:

> Education studies is concerned with understanding how people develop and learn throughout their lives. It facilitates the study of the nature of knowledge, and a critical

engagement with a variety of perspectives, and ways of knowing and understanding, drawn from a range of appropriate disciplines. Education studies courses … all involve the intellectually rigorous study of educational processes, systems and approaches, and the cultural, societal, political and historical contexts within which they are embedded. (QAA, 2000: 4)

This means that education is at the centre of the study and therefore draws on the other disciplines as appropriate in an eclectic manner. Thus, while psychology students will study aspects of education as appropriate, for instance, in relation to cognitive development, education studies students will study some aspects of psychological theory when looking at the process of learning within schools or colleges. It is interesting to consider the status relations between these older and newer subjects, the longer standing disciplines having a better developed theoretical base to consider as their own.

A recent study by Davies and Hogarth (2004) was unable to identify a clear consensus about the nature of education studies, suggesting that there would be some value in exploring what might constitute its broad parameters.

Some features we would argue characterise the subject are that:

- it is 'young' and developing
- it takes a critical, analytical and 'resistant' approach to the study of education
- it grapples with fundamental, contested concepts
- it explores a range of perspectives, not just those of teachers and schools
- it deals with multiple rather than singular explanations of phenomena.

Thus, the way in which education studies facilitates a critical engagement with educational phenomena contrasts sharply with the 'technical–rational' approach to teacher training described earlier. Even within non-teacher training programmes education studies is circumscribed to some extent by this pervasive culture since it must examine and describe extant education processes and systems in order to analyse them. However, the power to critique and rethink educational policies and processes is available to students of education studies in a way that is denied to ITT students. Education studies provides a set of analytical discourses that generate insights into educational phenomena as bodies of knowledge and societal conditions shift, develop and wane.

Whilst the Education Studies benchmarks (2007) provide a guide to those designing new courses, the structure and content of education studies programmes varies enormously. At the heart of all of these courses lies a critical analysis of key issues such as the nature of education, the content and development of curricula, teaching and learning, the relationship between ability, opportunity and success, and the policy issues impacting on all of these.

Some people make the mistake, perhaps due to its historical connection to teacher training, of seeing education studies as essentially school focused. This is certainly not the case as all areas and aspects of education can be included. The subject has enormous scope from the development of young children, through learning in HE, to the workplace and the third age – a true study of lifelong learning.

We now turn to the interest education holds for a number of significant disciplines concerned with the study of people and society. The discussion will illustrate how the approaches and theories developed within these disciplines may be used by those students whose main concern is the study of education itself.

The traditional disciplines and education studies

Fundamental to any society, education and the processes it involves are of great interest to fields of study concerned with the human condition. In particular we refer in this book to philosophy, sociology, psychology and history.

PHILOSOPHY

The philosophy of education illuminates the ideas which underpin action and thought in education. The questions philosophers ask concern the nature and purposes of education, such as what makes an educated person, how knowledge is organised and what should be learned. They are primarily interested in the beliefs, morals and values which permeate education. These are very important questions which are at the heart of the whole process and therefore appear in every aspect of the study of education. They are key to discussions of the nature of curriculum which derives from different ideological positions on education and the structure of knowledge. Such questions are also apparent when analysing how beliefs are translated into policy or when looking at issues of individual development and progression.

SOCIOLOGY

The sociology of education examines the wider social influences upon the individual in education and analyses the processes of socialisation. Sociologists ask questions about the influences of social class, ethnicity and gender upon achievement and these are seen in relation to various ideologies which shape education. Sociological analysis is concerned with power operating at different levels in society and how this influences outcomes. This explains the sociologist's interest in the creation of education policy and its implementation. To understand modern education systems it is vital to study the relationship between prevailing ideologies and the societal structures and values they shape through the process of education.

PSYCHOLOGY

The psychology of education is mainly concerned with how people learn and develop. As such it asks questions about our maturation, intelligence, personality and motivation, as well as about the learning process itself. It is interested in the relationship between nature and nurture and the way they interact to influence individual development and achievement. A psychological analysis also involves philosophical issues of the nature of knowledge and understanding and shares an interest in sociological issues since the individual is seen to be part of wider social groups. An examination of pedagogy from a psychological perspective further reveals the link between psychological and sociological theory as well as the ideological perspectives which have influenced it.

HISTORY

The history of education may suggest causal explanations for changes which punctuate the political and social timelines of educational development. It helps us to understand the evolution of the educational system and structures to date. There are key dates and events within the development of the English education system that reflect the significant political and social issues of the time. While the scope of education has changed radically since the late nineteenth century, the pastoral, disciplinary and knowledge distribution functions of schools and other education establishments remain significant in modern Western societies.

RELATING THE FOUR DISCIPLINES TO EDUCATION STUDIES

Each of these four disciplines brings its own specific perspective to the study of education and each is interested in particular aspects as they relate to their own concerns. It is also clear that their areas of interest overlap. It is interesting that these four disciplines were the ones included in the initial B.Ed. teacher training degrees (McCulloch, 2002). Others may have been incorporated. The economics of education, for instance, would look at the importance of education and training in the creation of a valuable, high skills labour force, or at the benefits of state education systems compared to competitive provision of schooling in the light of economic theories of monopoly and market forces.

When education itself is the focus for the student, as in education studies, it is important to draw from these disciplines as appropriate. This eclectic view can provide a richer picture of the whole process and may produce new forms of knowledge and new ways of understanding. Take, for example, comparative education which has been an area of study for many years and which, in recent years, has grown in importance as an aspect of education studies.

Comparative education

WHY COMPARE EDUCATION?

Reader reflection

The academic study of comparative education has grown enormously since the middle of the twentieth century showing the increasing interest in education in many parts of the world. Think about what the reason for this might be.
Reasons for this growth of interest include, for example:

- post-industrial nations wanting to improve their existing systems in order to remain competitive
- impetus for newly emerging European Union states to modernise quickly
- developing countries wishing to overcome disease and poverty.

Education is of central concern in all of these examples so comparing and learning from others facilitates better understanding and further improvement.

Comparative education means comparing aspects of education, looking for reasons that may account for any similarities and differences. It is usually applied to the broader comparisons of one nation's education (or aspects of this) to those of another.
Arnove (2003) sees three dimensions to comparative education.

1 The scientific dimension (called by some the academic approach)
   This is about theory building and understanding about the working of education systems and how they interact within different societies.
2 The pragmatic dimension
   This is about studying other systems in order to discover what can be used to contribute to improved policy and practice at 'home'. The pragmatic dimension has been referred to as education 'lending' or 'borrowing' (Altbach, 1998). The pragmatic dimension can lead to adapting what others do or even to straight copying.
3 International education: the global dimension
   Arnove sees this dimension as contributing to international understanding and peace. Comparative education will become more important 'as processes of globalisation increasingly require people to recognise how forces from areas of the world previously considered distant and remote impinge upon their daily lives' (2003: 8).

These three dimensions can be seen as separate but overlapping reasons for the study of comparative education.

PROBLEMATISING COMPARATIVE EDUCATION

Whilst clear advantages exist for studying comparative education there are also significant pitfalls of which students need to be aware. For instance, McLean (1992) outlines certain inherent perils involved in comparisons made in too simplistic a manner.

He warns of cultural superiority, the assumption that education in developed (our) countries is superior to foreign practices which may be seen as backward. When developed countries become involved in the economy and education systems of the 'underdeveloped' they are open to accusations of cultural imperialism. The European Union and British Council have long had schemes for supporting transference of pedagogical developments from 'Westernised' states. Burton and Robinson (1999) found that cultural and educational imperialism was writ large in a European project designed to update the pedagogy within a Belarussian psychology curriculum and that this was exacerbated by the severe economic differentials between the participants.

Nguyen et al (2006) refer to the need for *culturally appropriate pedagogy*, a pedagogy that focuses on educational competence in a global context, and which addresses the cultural context of learners and teachers. Their study in Confucian Heritage Culture (CHC) countries such as China, Vietnam, Japan, Korea, Singapore, Taiwan, Hong Kong and Malaysia found that Western-style group learning is not always as appropriate as earlier research studies had suggested since traditional CHC lecture-based education often generates higher achievement. Thus, Nguyen et al counsel that it is critical to conduct research on how culturally appropriate methodologies can be implemented instead of relying on imports that ignore the complexities of cultural learning environments.

McLean (1992) also notes the way in which politicians may use comparisons as a means of justifying ideologically based policy and education reform. Often these comparisons are only partial, are quickly conducted and their validity is highly suspect. There is a rather dangerous assumption that education directly influences economic performance and so improving education is likely to increase efficiency and hence lead to greater competitiveness. When an economy begins to have problems it is easy to blame the education system.

This same assumption suggests that if you wish to improve economic production you should look at other countries and find out why their education systems are producing more effective employees. This approach is facilitated by the availability of comparative assessment data such as that provided by the Trends in International Mathematics and Science Study (TIMSS) which compares data on the mathematics and science achievement of US students with that of students in other countries (www.nces.ed.gov/timss). TIMSS data has been collected in 1995, 1999, 2003 and 2007. The Progress in International Reading Literacy Study (PIRLS) is a large international comparative study of the reading literacy of young students. PIRLS 2001 was the first in a planned five-year cycle of international trend studies in reading literacy and is coordinated by the International Association for the Evaluation of Educational Achievement (IEA). The PIRLS study focuses on the achievement and reading experiences of children in 35 countries in grades equivalent to fourth grade in the USA. The study includes a written test of reading comprehension and a series of questionnaires focusing on the factors associated with the development of reading literacy (http://nces.ed.gov/search).

A comparative study might look at pupil performance, teaching methods and assessment in, for example, maths and language. Once the successful formula has been identified, it can be copied or at least adapted for use in other countries. This approach led in the 1990s to overseas visits and surveys being conducted by British politicians and school inspectors (HMI and Ofsted). Many changes in pedagogy and curriculum have been justified by such international comparisons. Evidence to support politicians' opinions is often cited whereas alternative examples can be ignored or explained away. Britain, for example, has increasingly developed structured pre-school education and assessment but this would not appear to be based on comparisons with other countries since it is not the practice in many economically and educationally successful countries. Conversely, a concern for the reading development of primary age children led the government to import the Reading Recovery scheme from New Zealand. Reading Recovery provides daily one to one teaching with a specially trained teacher for children making the slowest progress in literacy learning after a year at school. It is supplementary to classroom instruction and is designed to significantly reduce the number of children with literacy difficulties in schools. Developed in New Zealand, Reading Recovery is now widely implemented in English speaking countries throughout the world (www.readingrecovery.ac.nz/).

There are, of course, flaws in adopting an overly simplistic comparative approach. Only parts of the systems are examined rather than the whole picture and these are usually seen in isolation. Wider social and cultural influences are not taken into account. We will see as we progress through this text just how important such contextual parameters are in explaining how each education system develops. Ignoring these renders it difficult to claim clear cause and effect relationships for educational initiatives.

Comparisons of educational systems and practices, then, can be useful but only if they are made within the broad context of understanding whole cultures. Attempts to find 'quick fixes' become even more attractive in our current context of technology-enabled instantaneous communication but developing an awareness of how systems work and interact with society is essential.

Conclusion

In this chapter we have outlined how students first encounter education studies as a subject and the way in which critical engagement with the subject brings new understandings. We have seen how the study of education has developed, we have outlined its key features as a subject and how its constituent elements might be described. Finally, we have introduced the idea of comparative education and how this, in keeping with all aspects of education that we will explore, is inextricably linked to its socio-economic and political context. This, you will find, is a feature throughout the book.

Student activities

1 Find the education studies benchmarks on the QAA website (www.qaa.ac.uk) and read through the statements. How useful do you find these in outlining the subject of education studies? How do your experiences of education studies relate to them?

2 Visit the TIMSS website (www.nces.ed.gov/timss) or the PIRLS website (www.nces.ed.gov/surveys/pirls). Describe what the charts on international comparisons of achievement show. What different explanations can be given for these results? Search through past editions of the education and popular press from the time of the first publication of these statistics. In what different ways have they been presented and interpreted?

3 Visit the Eurydice website (www.eurydice.org). This site is run by the European Commission and provides information on the organisation of the education systems and current policy developments of member states. Compare the structure of the education systems of several different countries in Europe. Note the similarities and variations in how these countries choose to educate their citizens. Note, particularly, differences in when children start their formal education, how young children are educated, the structure of compulsory education, the provision for vocational education. This is also a useful task for Chapters 5 and 10.

Recommended reading

Alexander, R. (2002) *Culture and Pedagogy*. Oxford: Blackwell. This volume gives a detailed outline of a number of education systems from around the world including the English. It is a very good text for students of comparative education.

Kubow, P. and Fossum, P. (2003) *Comparative Education: Exploring issues in International Context*. Columbus, Ohio: Merrill Prentice Hall. This text introduces the student to comparative education outlining various theoretical approaches and frameworks that can be used. It applies a comparative approach to four areas; the purposes of schooling, educational access and opportunity, education accountability and authority, and teacher professionalism. This is helpful in illustrating the construction of comparative accounts.

The nature of education

This chapter considers the complex nature of education as an area of study, looking at the meaning of the term itself. It moves on to a discussion of the purposes and processes of an education system that can be seen from a number of different sociological perspectives. The key educational ideologies are outlined and a typology of ideologies is considered along with the component features which are said to characterise any ideology. The chapter concludes by emphasising the importance of a critical approach to the study of education.

The meaning of education

Education is an activity we all feel that we know something about, having had practical experience of it. In a systematic study of education, however, two fundamental questions will be posed:

1 What do we mean by education?
2 Why is education important?

Finding the answers to these two questions is a complex endeavour. As students of education, the answers we give are likely to vary over time. Thus the meaning of the term 'education' and its purpose is not universally fixed and is not the same for all of us.

Personal resonances of the term 'education' are shaped by a number of individual experiences such as coming top of the class, passing examinations, going on school trips, being made fun of by pupils or teachers, or being in the bottom set. Various groups of people are usually positioned differently in relation to education and its purposes. Political leaders, parents, pupils at school, university students, teachers, the police, factory managers will all espouse different views. These groups might themselves be differentiated, for instance parents may be classified by income levels, marital status, age group, number of children in the family and so on. More specific questions about education help to elicit a deeper analysis.

Reader reflection

- **Is education a process?** Is it something which we go through over a period of years? Does this process vary over time? For instance, how is education for 4 year olds in nursery different from that for 20 year olds at university?
- **Is education a product to be consumed?** Can it be quantified? Is the product defined as what someone can do at the end of it, i.e. a demonstration of competence at something, or is the product about exam passes? Where does intellectual development fit in here? Does the product vary? For instance, is the education of an unskilled worker different from that of a nation's leaders? Should it be different?
- **What does education involve?** Is it about sitting at desks, learning important facts and answering questions? Does it mean being absorbed by interesting tasks or solving challenging problems? Should it make us happy or serious and should we be put under pressure and 'extended' to our limits?
- **Where does education take place?** Is it mainly in schools, colleges and universities? Can we do it at home using ICT and learning packages delivered 'on line'? Does it carry on throughout life beyond school, college or university?

It is interesting to analyse our perceptions of education using such questions. Yet the range of responses, when we compare our views to those of others, can also be disconcerting. The complexity of the area of study becomes very apparent. Deciding what education is about may mean thinking of it as a process, as something to be consumed, or as a result or product. All of these possibilities are emphasised in various ways by different people when looking at the meaning of the term 'education'. We also need to ask if education has to be intended or if it can happen by accident in an unplanned and sometimes, perhaps, unrecognised manner.

Peters (1966), a significant modern education philosopher, was well aware of the problems in attempting to define 'education'. He suggested that the term had been used in many different ways and, as such, was difficult to capture in any precise definition, though he was able to outline a range of 'normative' and 'cognitive' aspects associated with it. For Peters, education was deeper than just learning facts or how to do something. This more superficial approach he associated with training. Education involved a linking of concepts by the learner to gain a wider understanding of the world. In his view, for something to count as education it had to be regarded as worthwhile. In this way it was inseparable from judgements of value. It should also be learned in a morally acceptable manner; it should not involve coercion or brainwashing. This implies some agreement by the learner to take part (Peters, 1967). This view of education could certainly cause us to question some of our own experiences within compulsory education.

Consider the life histories of convicts and the questions one could ask concerning their education. What has their education involved? Could it be that they learned different things than the teachers intended? What skills have they developed? Once in prison what do convicts learn and from whom? Do they go to education classes and listen attentively to the advice of the warders or do they 'pick up tips' from listening to and being with other inmates? Using Peters' view of education unreformed convicts would see their learning of how to be criminals as useful. They entered into this voluntarily and so it is morally acceptable from their position, unlike their experiences at school where they had perhaps been chastised. It also fits with their wider view of the world and how they can survive in it.

In its broadest sense education is normally thought to be about acquiring knowledge and developing skills and understanding – cognitive capabilities. It can be claimed that as humans, we are identified by our capacity to learn, communicate and reason. We are involved in these things throughout our lives and in all situations. From the earliest times people have learned from one another in family and social groups. As society became larger scale and more complex, so systems of education became formalised and expanded. We still learn from those around us but the education system now also plays a large part in all of our lives.

Formal education developed first for the elite minority and, over time, became compulsory for all. This is not to say that schools for the elite and those for the masses gave the same education or had the same purposes. Those being groomed to rule and those subject to being ruled have traditionally been educated in different ways and with different expectations. Steadily the time spent in educational institutions increased as children started younger and finished older than their predecessors. This trend of an increasing number of years spent in formal education continues today. The development of post-16 and higher education in recent years is testament to this whilst, at the same time, nursery and pre-school provision is also rapidly expanding.

Education has become a large industry employing many thousands of people in Britain alone. It is supposedly an important part of ensuring future economic development yet it also imposes a major financial cost. It is presented by politicians as an investment in our future, the 'our' referring to the nation as a whole as well as to the individual. Thus education plays a central role in society and also in all of our lives.

Sociological perspectives on the purposes of education

We may accept, then, that it is appropriate to take a broad view of the meaning of education. Turning our attention to why education is important may help us to understand more fully the meaning of the term. When looking at the purposes of education we are generally referring to the purposes of the education 'system'. It should be apparent from the previous discussion that this is likely to exclude a great deal of interesting material. Whilst a wide detour may be made into education at the 'university of life', space does not permit this here. We will limit our concern to the 'official', or 'formal', processes of education.

THE FUNCTIONALIST APPROACH

The functionalist perspective views society as a system where interconnected parts function in relation to an integrated whole. Functionalism depends on the idea that social systems are significantly determined by fundamental human need. In this way it tends to be seen as a 'conservative' ideology. Functionalism also works with the idea of functional prerequisites: some social phenomena are simply there as they are necessary for the society to work for the benefit of all its different members. Some needs are common to all societies implying the idea of a general human condition independent of cultural differences (consider the work of sociologists such as Davis and Moore, 1967; Durkheim, 1947; Parsons, 1964). Thus, education is seen alongside other social institutions as working to create and maintain a stable society. The functionalist analogy compares society to a machine or a living organism. The different social institutions, such as the forces of law and order, the political system and also education, function to maintain the whole society. In the same way that the different parts of a machine or a body contribute to the working of the whole, if any of the parts does not function properly then this affects the whole society and may even lead to a breakdown. The main functions of education may be listed as follows.

Development of basic academic skills

In order to participate in a modern society certain skills are seen as very important. Most notably we need to be able to read, write, perform basic arithmetical tasks, reason and problem solve. These are needed in all areas of modern life. Consider how many times you use reading skills in any one day. You could conclude that life as we know it is virtually impossible to live without them. It is amazing to think that some people do actually survive without highly developed reading skills but they are at a distinct disadvantage and need to seek help frequently. This is not easy for them because of the social stigma attached to an adult being unable to read proficiently. The ability to use ICT is now also regarded as an essential skill. The importance of, and increasing emphasis on, the acquisition of what are variously called 'transferable', 'key' or 'core' skills is part of the rhetoric surrounding the development of an adaptable, flexible workforce for the 'skills economy'. Thus interpersonal, communication, problem solving, literacy and numeracy skills have been promoted up the educational agenda particularly within post-16 learning.

Socialisation

Functionalists see this as the way in which we become human. It is a process which begins at birth when we start effectively as blank slates. We develop our 'selves' as we learn what we need to know to live and operate with others in social groups. This includes language, right and wrong, expectations of ourselves and others, how to behave in different situations and so on. It is, of course, a matter of debate as to how much our development depends upon social learning or biological processes.

Socialisation is a process of induction into society's culture, norms and values. This ensures a level of social cohesion necessary for society to be sustained. It is a process which continues throughout life but which is certainly of central importance in our early years. Thus the family and schooling have a crucial role in the socialisation process.

Social control and maintaining social order

For us to live our lives and for established social life to exist we must be assured of a level of order and safety as we go about our daily business. This involves the rule of law but also certain expected ways of behaving. These may be seen as norms of behaviour or manners. Consider how we behave in an orderly manner for much of our lives without really thinking about it. We queue up for things in shops or when waiting for public transport. We say 'please' and 'thank you' in appropriate circumstances. In public places we walk without bumping into or touching other people. We maintain appropriate eye contact and distance when conversing with others depending upon who these others are. These norms are learned and education helps in this process. Control mechanisms may be overt and show outward force, as in the case of riot police quelling trouble on the streets. Control may, however, be more covert and subtle when compliance is expected, as in the case of a disparaging look from a teacher when work has not been completed.

Preparing for work

In small-scale and self-sufficient societies children would learn about survival from adults. In these communities adults are multi-skilled and can satisfy most of their wants by using their own abilities. There may be only a few specialist roles such as healer or midwife in such groups. As forms of employment diversified and became specialised, increasingly specific training needed to take place. Payment, in the form of wages, generally reflected the level, scarcity and importance of the skill required. General qualities needed for employment such as those expressed in the transferable skills can be developed at all levels of education. Job specific training is likely to be workplace based but also to involve further and higher education.

The functions of education may be seen to overlap. The preparation for work involves the developing of minds and learning of important skills. Socialisation is an important part of preparing for adulthood and elements of internalised social control form part of this. Different functions may be to the fore at certain times during a pupil's education. Whereas it may be appropriate to stress the development of the mind and individual freedom to experiment at particular stages, it may be important to stress discipline and the need for self-control at others. Each of these functions can be seen to be appropriate but, taken together, there are potential tensions between them. For example, developing minds means encouraging a questioning attitude. The image is of a learner exploring and experimenting. However, the need to maintain social order involves pupils showing obedience to authority and 'correct' behaviour. This could be interpreted as the creation of accepting, rather than questioning, individuals.

Pupils may be encouraged to question within the topics chosen by a teacher. Much primary work, for instance, involves investigations by pupils into the world around them. The children may ask questions to do with friction, life cycles, different materials and so on. They carry out investigations designed to find the answers. However, other areas of school life must not be questioned beyond a superficial level: 'Why must we wear this uniform?' 'Will all of this homework help our progress?' 'Why are we studying "this" as opposed to "that"?' Obedience is an important part of any pupil's schooling. When the characteristics of a 'good' school leaver are listed they include independence and initiative, yet prospective employers also look for a willingness to obey instructions and for a neat (in other words, conforming) appearance.

It seems there is a need for both self-development and self-control. The difficulty is striking a balance. We can see the importance of order, direction, control and discipline but not to the extent that it prevents questioning and individual development. This balance is a judgement which rests upon beliefs about human nature, the working of society and, thus, the purposes of education.

The stress placed upon the different functions of education may be different depending upon the pupil. Some pupils may be pushed academically whilst others may be prepared for low level employment. Indeed some functionalists, such as Davis and Moore (1967), saw the sifting of talent and allocating of individuals to appropriate roles in society as an important function of a formal education system. Some pupils may be given freedom to express themselves whereas for others the emphasis may be on modifying their behaviour. Chapters 6–9 examine this potential for treating pupils differently and posit some explanations for it.

The rhetoric of consensus

When considering the functionalist perspective on education we need to ask for whose purposes education exists. One main criticism of functionalist perspectives is the way that they see social structures according to a hidden logic of cause and effect. By saying that education functions for the whole society it is assumed that what is good for the society is good for us all. The implication is that we all have the same needs and wants and also that there is equality of opportunity to benefit from such a system. In short it takes a consensus view of society and ignores the fact that significant differences and conflicts of interest may exist. Inequality, in terms of income or wealth, is actually seen as something which itself performs a function of encouraging us to better ourselves and, in the process, benefits the society as a whole. Vital questions about conflict and difference in societies are explained away by functionalist perspectives.

The rhetoric of consensus also ignores the power differentials between separate sections of society and how these can be used to maintain superior positions. Children from certain groups are significantly more successful in education and it has been posited that this is a reflection of their economic and social background (Bourdieu and Passeron, 1977). Research has also shown that the labelling which attaches to children in lower socio-economic groups serves to further disadvantage them (Hargreaves, 1967). Functionalist theories tend to be 'monologic'. Social phenomena are seen as having single and simple, surface causes. Social conflicts are minimised and the normative elements of social life are emphasised.

Functionalists assume that the system must be maintained if the society is to survive. By reinforcing the status quo these functions actually benefit those who are in the best positions. They maintain stability and thus it is easier for those at the top to ensure that their children follow in their footsteps. Those at the bottom are, by and large, kept there. It is pointed out that it is largely their own fault for not taking the opportunities on offer. Thus inequality is perpetuated and regarded as the 'natural' order of things. Education is seen as an important part of the unifying process needed to help maintain a level of consensus within society. Functionalist theories can be valuable in describing how societies and their various elements work together in coherent patterns but are less successful in accounting for change and conflict.

CONFLICT THEORIES

From our early years we are encouraged to see education positively, as offering benefits to all. But what if, as some social theorists and education researchers have claimed, education is more about promoting dominant ideology and dividing populations into different class and occupational segments? Conflict perspectives propose that schools perform certain social functions but not necessarily to the benefit of all. Some have suggested that they serve the system well but that the system they serve is based on inequalities that schooling or education in general should be challenging. Rather than the consensus envisaged by functionalism, conflict theorists, Marxists for example, see education as reinforcing a class system.

Marxism perceives a conflict of values in society with those of the capitalist ruling class being dominant. The education system, by operating as an agency of the state, serves to reinforce these values. It helps to keep the working class in their place whilst preparing the middle-class pupils to 'legitimately' take over the powerful positions held by their class. Althusser (1984) formed the concept of Ideological State Apparatuses (ISAs), a development of the concept of government and class relations. ISAs are significant in terms of maintaining ruling class ideology and are an important part of the means through which the capitalist state maintains control. Bowles and Gintis (1976) saw a close correspondence between how schools treat pupils and the later experiences they can expect at work. This plays an important part in preparing working-class youth for menial forms of employment. Bourdieu and Passeron (1977) used the concept of cultural capital to explain how the middle classes are able to maintain their position in the process of social reproduction whilst making this inequality legitimate.

Gramsci (1985, 1991) claims that ownership of the means of production cannot be enough to guarantee class rule. The ruling class must also work for 'hegemony', a key concept signifying the cultural rule of their dominant ideas and values. The ruling class need to actively win the support of other members of society and ruling class concessions have to be made. Gramsci puts great emphasis on civil institutions and cultural practices as fields for political action and intervention. This implies a broad idea of the state, political power and authority as being located in everyday practices and ideas. Hegemony is achieved by continual negotiation and has to be constantly worked at. Thus we see the importance of the education system. By claiming to be a meritocracy, in other words where individuals prosper by their own efforts, the education system helps to keep social order and perpetuate the existing inequalities. This is, for the classic Marxist analyst, the purpose of formal education.

Some conflict theorists would consider it possible for subversive elements to work within the system. Gramsci, for instance, suggests that the dominant class can never totally monopolise power as beliefs and ideas are constantly being contested in everyday practices (in schools and universities for example). As a consequence, social change (revolutionary action) can be located in existing institutions and everyday social practices. Others, however, see capitalism as too powerful to be overthrown by individuals. Idealists working within education to change society will, in the long term, become incorporated into the system themselves. In fact, by helping individual working-class pupils to succeed, these teachers may ultimately be perpetuating the myth of a meritocracy. They are in the end legitimating the very education system which is helping to sustain the existing structural inequalities. In the novel *A Kestrel for a Knave* by Barry Hines, an English literature reader for many 14 and 15 year olds in the 1970s and 1980s, the teacher who befriends and guides the poor, badly treated working-class pupil makes no difference to the overall order of things.

Thus it might be argued that both functionalism and Marxism conceive of the purposes of education as maintaining the current order of society but from very different standpoints.

Sociological perspectives on the process of education

Other sociological perspectives are key to an understanding of how the process of education works. So far we have considered structural theories which place a clear emphasis on how structures relate to the outcomes of education in terms of the reproduction of society's institutions. Now we turn to theorists who approach the effect of education from the perspective of the individual and their interactions within it.

SYMBOLIC INTERACTIONISM

Social interactionists emphasise the actions of members of society as the source for understanding social phenomena and institutions rather than overarching structures. Weber (1958,

1963) was interested in uncovering the meaning behind social actions. The perspective of 'symbolic interactionism' comes out of the development of Weber's thinking and US sociological traditions. George Herbert Mead is often cited as the 'founder' of symbolic interactionism. According to Mead (1934), human beings interact through symbols which define the world and the roles of social actors. (The term 'actors' is used by symbolic interactionists to refer to people playing their roles in society.) This position emphasises the importance of culture in social formations, institutions and practices such as education. Culture specifies roles, symbols and interpretations of symbols. Symbolic interactionism is a 'superstructural' theory par excellence. Symbols enable the social actors to make sense of their world. While symbols in social interactions must be shared, individuals interpret the actions, meanings and intentions of others. Social life involves an ever active role. Mead emphasises the critical importance of role-taking and interpretation in the development of the 'self'. The idea of the coherent self is learned and cultivated. Social institutions such as schools are composed of many roles. These roles can be chosen to some extent and are interpreted and adapted by the actor, for example parenting can be carried out in many ways. Thus culture is not monolithic and constraining. Subcultures exist and are constantly changing. Cultural meanings often indicate possibilities rather than requirements. Social roles are dynamic and, to some extent, fluid.

While Marxism emphasises *structures* as the dominant forces determining the shape and form of institutions and behaviours, interactionists emphasise *agency* or the freedom and ability of the individual to decide. In recent times, the sociologist Antony Giddens (1985) has argued for a theory of social action that sees structure and agency as interdependent: 'structuration' relates structures to action. Giddens writes of the 'duality of structure'; structures do exist but have no existence outside the consciousness of the agents (actors) who act upon them and define them in everyday activity. Language provides Giddens with a model for 'duality of structure'. Language must be rule governed and therefore structural. It depends for its existence on the utterances of individuals who make it happen.

POST-STRUCTURALIST AND POSTMODERN PERSPECTIVES

Some powerful and influential ideas about culture and society come in the form of theories referred to as 'post-structuralist' and 'postmodernist', though neither of those terms can be used in a completely straightforward sense. The importance of these ideas within education is that they challenge dominant discourses and practices by suggesting that, while these things may be fixed in behaviour and institutions, they are at another level provisional. They also indicate the importance of culture, language and identity – key features of the inequalities that operate through education.

Post-structuralism provides opportunities for rethinking the school as an institution. It considers the nature of knowledge, and how this changes through history and according to culture. It is also aware of how knowledge works in relation to different forms of subjectivity. Discourses of knowledge position subjects, exert power and are force fields of power at the same time (see Derrida, 1987; Foucault, 1977b, 1988a). Post-structuralism is critical of the deep-seated ideas that infuse education systems and traditions. On the whole it is anti-essentialist and anti-traditionalist. It is suspicious of ideas like truth and aware of the historical 'contingency' of ideas and 'systems of thought'. With its emphasis on the importance of language and culture, post-structuralism provides the means for examining all the mundane practices of institutional life and posing questions of them, from what texts are read in English lessons to how discourses of science and knowledge represent gender.

Differing social perspectives, such as those described in this section, are important in the study of education. It is vital to work towards some idea of the relations between the social structure and the institutions of education and the education system itself. Tracking these relations is complex and problematic but important.

Educational ideologies

Systems of broad beliefs and values about the nature of the world are termed 'ideologies'. They are relevant to all areas of life and are often related. Thus understandings about human nature may be linked to beliefs about law, order, political life, the economic system, the purposes of education and so on. We have explored the purposes of education from a largely sociological perspective. There are, however, other ideologies which analyse both the purposes and nature of education slightly differently. Carr and Hartnett (1996) recognise that the education system has a purpose of social reproduction in terms of cultural, economic and political life, but they also identify its purpose in relation to social transformation. This, they explain, leads to tension between the need for stability and the desire for change. It is apparent that education is based on beliefs about the things that need to be socially reproduced and those that need transforming. They suggest that, as education is to do with the creation of the 'good society', there is a strong link between political philosophy and educational theory.

Reader reflection

There are many differing positions on the human condition. These lead to alternative visions of what is desirable and what is humanly possible in the organisation of society. These views have tended to be presented as polarised alternatives which offer differing perspectives on the purposes of a formal education system and its concomitant structure.

How do you think society should be organised in a perfect world? How close do you think we can get to your ideal?

PLATO AND HOBBES

Plato argued that humans are naturally predisposed to perform certain tasks. In the Greek State he identified three levels of society – workers, soldiers and leaders. Society will be 'in balance' when people are performing the tasks for which they have a natural disposition. Thus the purpose of the education system is to prepare different pupils in the most appropriate way for their future roles. This means different teaching methods and content as appropriate. Plato saw traditional, high status knowledge being appropriate for some people only and practical instruction appropriate for others; everyone 'in their place' doing what they do best leads to a stable society. It is interesting to compare this view of society with the tripartite education system set up in post-war England (see Chapter 4).

In Plato's analysis, to go against this natural order is to threaten the whole existence of society. Encouraging those not suited to rise above their station will cause social unrest, instability, disobedience and civil strife. Ultimately this must be put down by force or it will lead to revolution, anarchy and a total breakdown of the social fabric. In this way everyone in the society will suffer. Thus, for Plato, order was important for the maintenance of society (see Carr and Hartnett, 1996, for a very lucid account of the views of Plato; also Cooper, 2001).

In the seventeenth century Hobbes suggested that we all have natural desires which we wish to satisfy. Humans in this respect are no different from other animals. Survival is of the fittest and life can be seen as potentially 'nasty, brutish and short'. We are, ultimately, all on our own trying to satisfy our needs and live in a totally hostile world; a dog eat dog existence. Humans do thrive in larger social groups where trade and cooperation can take place. However, the constant pressure to revert back to our natural state needs to be guarded against. Thus for social life to be made possible there need to be rules, laws and sanctions which are rigorously enforced. So, for example, to take a life or to commit a crime against property leads to severe punishment.

Hobbes explained that parameters of behaviour need to be clear and enforcement strict. Anything less, any sign of weakness, will threaten the superficially stable and secure lives of us all. The line between a well ordered society and a state of brutal chaos is slim. Respect and fear of the law is what enables a society to exist (see Olssen et al., 2004; Parsons, 1970, for an account of Hobbes and the problem of social order). For Plato and Hobbes the importance of education in maintaining order and thus the existence of society is clear. People need strict guidelines to operate within and discipline needs to be instilled in mind and body. Order is of central importance if society, and the individuals within it, are to have a chance to prosper.

ROUSSEAU

An alternative view of human nature is put forward by the 'romantics'. In the eighteenth century Rousseau took the view that, far from maintaining society, power in the hands of the few will lead them to reinforce their position which itself results in tyranny. He saw this increasing oppression as leading to violent uprisings from the oppressed in their struggle for freedom. In his view what was needed was to educate all citizens fully. This involved encouraging the development of questioning minds and giving everyone the widest of educational experiences. As our intellects develop we can all contribute to the evolution of society by continuous discussion and reason. Rousseau saw the development of a 'social contract' whereby to maintain their own freedom people respected the rights of others. This would only happen when all felt involved in the society and it would be the height of democratic development. The common good is presented as the 'general will' of the people (see Carr and Hartnett, 1996; also O'Hagan, 2001).

Thus self-discovery and individual development form the basis of education, for Rousseau, leading to a more liberated society. Without this freedom there would always be oppression based on physical force. These freedoms were the very things that Plato saw as dangerous to the fabric of society. On the one hand there is the view that education should be about individual development and fulfilment. All citizens will then be able to play an active part in social life resulting in tolerance of the views of others. This will lead to a 'better' and more just society. On the other, there is the belief that this freedom will lead to instability due to the innate selfishness of human nature. What is needed is social order and a structure which will enable us to lead our lives without fear and within which we can earn our living. A prime purpose of education is to develop individual discipline with a respect for authority and tradition which will ensure this. These opposing views can both be detected when examining political developments in recent education policy (see Chapters 4 and 10).

We can see how our own experiences in schools, colleges and universities mirror one or other of these sets of beliefs. When thinking of our secondary schooling we may recall the ways order was enforced: lining up outside classrooms, detentions, threat of exclusion. Rules were enforced even down to the way work had to be laid out in exercise books. Whilst being critical of the exercise of control over our freedom, we are also aware of what it is like to be pupils in a classroom where order has broken down and the teacher has lost authority. This situation is often regarded by pupils as being fun at first but quickly turns to boredom and frustration at the lack of any constructive activity and direction. A desire grows for a return to an orderly learning environment as pupils themselves begin to complain to wider authorities. The majority of school children, without openly admitting it, welcome the structure and direction a teacher is able to give. Often, however, learning involves both individual choice and external direction and control. Most adults can recall important learning experiences which have affected their personal development, such as a moving poem or story read with feeling by another pupil or a teacher, a word of encouragement from a form tutor, finishing a piece of craftwork and taking it home. Such experiences are generated as a result of this complex interaction between self-determination and teacher control.

A TYPOLOGY OF IDEOLOGIES IN EDUCATION

The views of Plato and Rousseau apply to the whole of society and social life. Now let us consider education specifically. Meighan and Siraj-Blatchford define ideologies of education as:

the set of ideas and beliefs held by a group of people about the formal arrangements for education, specifically schooling, and often, by extension or implication, also about informal aspects of education, e.g. learning at home. (2003: 191)

There have been various attempts to classify ideologies in education and Meighan and Siraj-Blatchford outline the dichotomous approach which uses polarised types such as teacher-centred versus child-centred, authoritarian versus democratic and so on. The juxtaposition of only two ideologies may prove rather simplistic, especially when examining long lists of polarised opposites which may or may not be related to other 'pairs' on the list. Meighan and Siraj-Blatchford suggest that other more complex typologies attempt to go beyond this.

Lawton (1992) pointed out that ideologies are used at different levels of generality. There is the broad level which is about the nature and purposes of education within a wider society, such as those of Plato and Rousseau considered above. There is the interest group level, which is concerned with how the system should be organised, for instance whether education provision should be a totally free market where schools offer and charge for a service and the customer pays according to what is on offer, or a totally comprehensive state system for all with no choice. Then there is the teaching or pedagogic level which is concerned with the organisation and delivery of the curriculum at classroom level. This involves what should be taught and how it should be taught.

Lawton (1992) suggests that these different levels are very much linked and overlapping. For instance, views on the nature and purposes of education are influential when it comes to considering the organisation of schools, colleges and universities. They will also be significant in deciding what is the most appropriate content and methods of teaching to be applied. How individual teachers view content and teaching methods will, in turn, be linked to how they see the purposes of what they are involved in. For this reason Meighan and Siraj-Blatchford (2003) prefer to use the concept of a network of ideologies to show how they operate between, as well as at, these different levels.

Throughout this book there are issues concerning the nature of education, how the system should be organised, what should be taught and how. The relationship and overlap between the three levels of ideology identified by Lawton will be continually stressed. One level cannot be considered without reference to the other two levels.

Ideologies of education may be categorised in many permutations (see Silcock, 1999; Trowler, 2003). Scrimshaw (1983) suggested organising educational ideologies in terms of their stress upon the individual, knowledge or society as a useful means of categorising such a wide range of ideas. Morrison and Ridley (1989) also use these three headings to neatly summarise clusters of educational ideologies in the following way.

Ideologies which emphasise the individual

Under this heading they place ideologies labelled variously as progressivism, child/student centredness and romanticism. The emphasis is on individual development with the needs and interests of the learner being central. The learning process is seen as vital with discovery and experimentation being at its heart. Learning is held to be rewarding in itself and pupils/

students maintain high motivation because of this. The emphasis is on development at different rates with students following their own learning programmes according to their interests. Learning is individualised and lifelong and the concept of failure is not appropriate as it only applies to set courses and fixed parameters of progress. Formative purposes of assessment are favoured over summative ones.Thus student portfolios are regarded as more valid in showing progress than mass exams at the end of the year.

The child-centred approach had made some headway in the 1960s, with the Plowden Report (Central Advisory Council for Education,1967) doing much to endorse these ideas, particularly in primary schools. The development of this approach was a reaction partly to the notion which influenced much post-Second World War education policy that intelligence and aptitude were largely innate. There was a growing belief in the significance of environmental influences on the development of the individual (see Chapter 6 for theories of development and Chapter 10 for changes in education policy).

Various questions and issues are raised concerning the practicalities of this 'romantic' approach which puts pupils, with their interests, needs and wishes, to the fore. In an age of mass education the development and management of individual programmes becomes difficult if not impossible. There is the issue of the pupil who does not particularly want to progress. For instance, the child in the reception class may be very happy playing and not wish to leave the sandpit. It may be felt that, if the pupil is not to be disadvantaged in later life, the accomplishment of some essential skills should not be left to chance. Can we trust that all children will turn to reading and writing when they are ready or should we give them formal teaching?

This then turns the focus onto the teacher. In a child-centred classroom to what extent should teachers intervene and how much can be left to the initiative of the pupil? It is difficult for a teacher to allow experimentation in some areas which may not be seen as socially appropriate. As adults we do more than just discourage young people from trying smoking, drinking alcohol and casual sexual experiences. It is also the case that clear teaching and being 'fed' existing information can save time. The need for every pupil to reinvent the wheel by exploration and experimentation is therefore questionable.

Critics of the 'progressive' approach suggested that the emphasis on individual freedom leads to an increase in permissiveness and a lowering of academic standards. It has been suggested (Cox and Dyson, 1969a, 1969b) that this is what happened in the 1960s. A period of full employment and increasing affluence led to the indulgence of the individual and the development of a more 'permissive society', which allowed the social and economic problems of the 1970s to occur. Remember the warnings of Plato and Hobbes?

Ideologies which emphasise knowledge

Ideologies labelled variously as classical humanism, conservatism and traditionalism are placed here by Morrison and Ridley (1989). These emphasise the importance of formal knowledge arranged in subjects. In its more classical form there is respect for what is seen as high status knowledge. Pupils/students need to start by learning basic facts and then progress through increasingly complex levels. This is done through formal, traditional, tried and tested methods. Assessment is also formal, it indicates success and it enables the selection of an elite. Discipline is an important part of the academic process. The learner is under close supervision in the early stages and only becomes more autonomous when reaching the higher levels of academic study. Thus, in the classroom in early secondary education the whole class is likely to be involved in the same exercises. Students gain more autonomy as they move from General Certificate of Secondary Education (GCSE) to more advanced level study. There is even more autonomy for an undergraduate at university whilst at the postgraduate level students, as well as having higher status, are much more in control of their studies. The pinnacle of independent academic success is found at university professorial level where individual decisions are made about what research to pursue.

The practicality of subjects is less important than high academic achievement in classical humanism. The public school epitomises the elitism, discipline and academic standards of this ideology. There is also a strong adherence to the traditional values which have been seen to be those that make a nation great. The criticisms of the more classical forms of humanism concern its elitism and defence of privilege. These may be said to maintain inequality and, in Rousseau's view, would mean the continued use of repressive means to subdue the underprivileged. The belief in tradition leads to lack of adaptability and innovation which is likely to result in economic decline when in competition with modern world economies.

The more liberal form of humanism also stresses knowledge but in a less traditional format. The emphasis is on a core curriculum for all, with elements of choice, as pupils move through the school system. Providing equality of opportunity is seen as important, in addition to maintaining academic standards. A tension is felt between setting by ability to allow the able to progress fully and not appearing to be elitist. This is a dilemma currently faced by Labour politicians when attempting to raise standards in the state system (see Chapter 10).

Ideologies which emphasise society

These are again divided into two by Morrison and Ridley (1989). Ideologies including instrumentalism, revisionism and economic renewal form one group. These ideologies are looking to develop, improve and modernise the economy. The emphasis is on producing workers to enable this to happen. This can mean developing adaptable, thinking, problem solving, high quality individuals as well as placing value on the traditional worker qualities of reliability and hard work. Education here has a practical purpose which teaching and assessment should reflect. Competencies become important and the vocational element is stressed. The nature of individualised programmes associated with vocationalism have shades of the student-centred approach but with more external direction.

The second group includes 'democratic socialism' and 'reconstructionism' both of which emphasise the power structures in society. Democratic socialism sees education as important in the creation and protection of equal opportunity for all and the development of all sections of society. The aim is to reform society from within and education must play a significant part in this process. Reconstructionists take this further and point to the possibility of totally reconstructing society through education. Education is seen as a revolutionary force through the enlightenment of the populace and the application of a critical approach to existing structures of social inequality. This is using the education system in the struggle to overthrow existing structures of inequality. Such a revolutionary stance is not generally tolerated by a system it seeks to undermine. The establishment has always been deeply suspicious of teachers who may be seen as potential revolutionaries and in a position to influence the vulnerable young. This ideology was a 'popular' part of the left wing political movements of the late 1960s and early 1970s and is shown in works such as *Teaching as a Subversive Activity* by Postman and Weingartner (1969).

THE VALUE OF TYPOLOGIES

Typologies of ideologies can never be more than generalisations, which at times appear very sweeping, of sets of beliefs that are linked together. They are useful in that they help us to understand the actions of groups of individuals but they are never total explanations because of the existence of variations. This can be seen when looking at the ideologies associated with the two major British political parties, Labour and Conservative. There are disagreements between the two and also arguments within each. It should also be noted that at times there is agreement between Labour and Conservatives on certain issues.

> Meighan and Siraj-Blatchford (2003) outline 11 significant 'component theories' which when put together make up an educational ideology and distinguish it from others.
> Each ideology possesses a theory of:
>
> - discipline and order
> - knowledge, its content and structure
> - learning and the learner's role
> - teaching and the teacher's role
> - resources appropriate for teaching
> - organisation of learning situations
> - assessment that learning has taken place
> - aims, objectives and outcomes
> - parents and the parent's role
> - locations appropriate for learning
> - power and its distribution. (Meighan and Siraj-Blatchford, 2003 p. 197)

Each ideological grouping outlined by Morrison and Ridley (1989) can be analysed according to Meighan and Siraj-Blatchford's 'component theories', which reveal how sets of beliefs and values, in the form of ideologies, exist in education. Students take courses, have lessons and are assessed in ways which take a recognisable ideological stance. Different ideologies can coexist within the same institution, even operating alongside each other. Thus schools emphasise the future employment of pupils as well as academic knowledge. Subjects are taught differently and teachers of the same subject may have very different teaching styles. Although often taught in large classes, pupils are treated as individuals by their teachers as well as being classified into sections within the class.

Marsh (2004) states that the schooling which pupils receive is a result of the decisions and actions of many individuals and groups. These are both professional and lay persons who may be operating at national or local levels as well as within the school. Thus it would be misleading to assume that one dominant ideology has total control. Marsh suggests that it is worth considering the impact of different groups, which he identifies as decision makers, stakeholders and wider influence groups, upon the classroom. This illustrates the many influences on the actual education received by pupils and also the power possessed by those involved in varying capacities. Even when given a formal national curriculum teachers will decide what each lesson will include. However, they are unlikely to ignore the concerns of stakeholders such as parents, as these are close to their daily activity and can directly affect classroom life. They will also take into account wider influences such as local employers who can offer different kinds of support in lessons and to pupils. Teachers must also pay close attention to the regular school inspections by the Office for Standards in Education (Ofsted) and the increased scrutiny of their work resulting from the publication of league tables of GCSE examination and National Curriculum test results. Thus teachers are very significant in the education process but they are not, and perhaps never have been, totally autonomous.

Kelly points out that, in examining the development of schooling and the curriculum, one can see the compromise which inevitably results from the constant tensions between competing sets of beliefs:

> which might be broadly polarised as a conflict between the claims of society and those of the individual, the vocational and the liberal, the economic and the humanitarian, a national investment and the right of every child, the instrumental and the intrinsic, what education *is for* and what it *is*, elitism and egalitarianism, and perhaps, in general, between the possible and the desirable, between reality and idealism. (2004: 163)

In conclusion we can say that there are various theories concerning human nature and that these provide alternative views of how society can be organised and, in turn, of the purposes of education. The education system reflects the differing values of the society in which it exists as well as helping to shape its future. As Young put it:

> The history, the social divisions and the many competing interests and value systems found in a modern society are expressed in the school curriculum as much as they are in its system of government or its occupational structure. Likewise, curriculum debates, implicitly or explicitly, are always debates about alternative views of society and its future. (1998: 9)

Ideologies are central to the development of education which is not an objective enterprise. Questions concerning its nature and purpose are returned to again and again throughout this book.

Conclusion

Some would argue that too much time is spent looking at questions concerning the nature and purposes of education. There has been a tendency to criticise and decry theorising by academics as being removed from the 'real' issues of education. Her Majesty's former Chief Inspector for Education, Chris Woodhead, wrote in his annual report for 1998/99 (Ofsted, 2000):

> We know what constitutes good teaching and we know what needs to be done to tackle weaknesses: we must strengthen subject knowledge, raise expectations, and hone the pedagogic skills upon which the craft of the classroom depends ... Why, then, is so much time and energy wasted in research that complicates what ought to be straightforward ... If standards are to continue to rise we need decisive management action, locally and nationally, that concentrates attention on the two imperatives that really matter: the drive to improve teaching and strengthen leadership ... The challenge now is to expose the emptiness of education theorising that obfuscates the classroom realities that really matter. (2000: 21)

Woodhead's apparent rejection of alternatives could be interpreted as an attempt to close down debate and to silence dissenting viewpoints. In returning to this position statement a number of years on it would be reassuring to find that a new official view had emerged. Whilst there is greater sophistication in relation to the presentation of such views and greater care is taken not to upset education professionals, in essence the establishment view remains largely the same. This can be seen in a number of the policies and practices systematically pursued by government which, as Chapter 10 explains, are manifestly the product of a well-developed ideological position. Education, not least because of its ideological basis, will always be important in the political arena and for those who study politics and policy.

Education is a central part of any society. It is to do with helping to shape the future in terms of developing individuals and the promotion of ideas. Politicians, parents, teachers, employers, taxpayers and pupils all have their own views of the purposes of education and what it should involve. The interaction of these sometimes competing interests renders education a fascinating area for study.

Student activities

1 In order of priority compile a list of the ten most important things a school should include in the education of its pupils. Compare your list with those of other students in the group. To what extent are ideologies apparent in these lists?
2 Choose three significant learning experiences that you remember from lessons when you were at school. These may have been isolated incidents or they may have occurred regularly over a period of time. How do these relate to the ideologies of education considered earlier in this chapter? Compare your analysis with others in your group.

Recommended reading

Kelly, A.V. (2004) *The Curriculum. Theory and Practice*, 5th edn. London: Sage. This is a significant academic analysis of curriculum development and the underpinning ideologies. Suitable for the more advanced student, this is a detailed and challenging volume.

Meighan, R. and Siraj-Blatchford, I. (2003) *A Sociology of Educating*, 4th edn. London: Cassell. A good book to read after this one, this is an interesting account of the different aspects of the educational experience and the sociological perspective on education. An easy to follow discussion of ideologies provides an excellent typology to use in analysis. As the title suggests, this book is also useful reading on how social factors influence success in education.

Trowler, P. (2003) *Education Policy*, 2nd edn. London: Routledge. This is a very accessible text that analyses political and educational ideologies and illustrates, through the use of case studies, how they have shaped policy.

Researching education

In this chapter we aim to show the importance of research in developing an understanding of the field of education. The relationship between research paradigms and notions of reality are explored. We discuss how the beliefs inherent in the different paradigms inform the whole research process from the selection of issues regarded as worthy of research, the purposes of the research and questions of validity, to the status of different forms of data and the relevance of different methods of data collection. Qualitative and quantitative methods of data collection are briefly outlined and related to the discussion of paradigms. Research is presented as an integral part of the process of education itself and, as such, is argued to be central to individual and professional development. Action research, school effectiveness research and school improvement research are critiqued in terms of both their methodological features and their contribution to the study of education.

Introduction

Chapters 1 and 2 established that education is a broad area of study involving a number of disciplines. Research from within these disciplines may provide discrete lessons for the student of education or it may overlap and interweave in a complex manner. The questions which interest education researchers often relate to these specific disciplines. For example, some are interested in the individual, how learning takes place and the cognitive processes involved while others may wish to examine social issues such as the ways in which ethnicity, gender and class continue to be significant in terms of 'success' in education. Yet others decide to examine the policies of successive governments and the influence these have had on practice in different sectors of education. The skills to investigate and gather information in pursuit of these research foci require a working knowledge of the research process. This chapter will consider research in relation to the study of education. It should be read in conjunction with specific methodological texts (for example Burton and Bartlett, 2005) for practical details of how to construct research projects and devise particular research instruments.

The nature of educational research

WHAT IS RESEARCH?

Formal research may seem daunting to the novice but we are already used to gathering data in many ways on a daily basis. The methods we typically use to find things out include observing situations or particular events, listening to the radio, asking different people, looking things up in books or surfing the web. All of this normal activity is data collection. We do it to make sense of the world in which we operate. The goal may be simple and straightforward such as to find out what the weather will be like the next day. It may involve gathering data from several sources, which is perhaps typical of a school homework task where pupils are required to find something out about their neighbourhood. They may need to use newspapers, ask some local people, find a map. Another data gathering task is when we carefully question several friends to find some interesting, perhaps controversial, information, for instance what happened at a social event we missed. We realise, of course, the subtle differences that asking such friends individually, or in certain combinations, would make to the information gleaned. As new information becomes available to us in our daily lives we are constantly checking, modifying, refining and developing what we know. Local opinion, regional newspapers and international news are all useful but for different interests and purposes. Clearly, then, different methods of gathering information are appropriate to different situations.

It is also apparent that the skills of the researcher are very significant to the achievable outcomes and that these skills improve with practice. We are all researchers in that we have to make sense of our world. Our personal research methods are in permanent use. We become skilled at analysing and evaluating data, making decisions as to its validity or truthfulness. Our skills usually depend on previous experience. Some information received carries more weight than alternative sources of evidence. Within conversations do we believe a particular person's account more than someone else's? When watching something happening we probably ask ourselves if this is what usually happens. Are the people involved putting on an act or perhaps showing off? Do we believe the headlines of certain Sunday newspapers or are they rather exaggerated? We are aware that information gathered may vary and even conflict. So we may expect to hear different accounts, for instance, of how efficient the local bus service is when listening to a driver or a passenger in the rush hour. Using both accounts will help provide a broader understanding of the situation.

Information is received from a wide range of sources. Some of this is even portrayed as research findings. In a typical evening's television viewing, for example, information about political conflict and war, economic developments, garden design, possible holiday destinations or the benefits of particular washing powders may be presented to us. We evaluate and store or disregard all information presented to us. Different types of research results are presented to help inform our opinions and enable us to make decisions about, for example, smoking or not smoking, drug and alcohol use or which trainers to buy. We accept some data more readily than others and though we enjoy certain adverts, such as for a particular deodorant, we do remain sceptical of its claims for increasing our sexual magnetism. Presentation impacts differently on people and is a major concern of the advertiser. This is worth remembering when we begin to look at how academic or formal research is presented. This chapter will thus suggest that we must consider many ways of looking at things and maintain a healthily critical approach to all research findings. No research into aspects of education, no matter how detailed, extensive and apparently objective, can tell the whole story. All research is positioned.

FORMAL RESEARCH

The process of academic or formal research has come to be seen as something which others (usually very learned or expertly trained) do. What does the term 'research' mean when used in relation to academic study?

Let us begin by considering some definitions of research.

Reader reflection

Consider the different aspects of research that these three definitions emphasise:

1 All types of research should be 'planned, cautious, systematic, and reliable ways of finding out or deepening understanding' (Blaxter et al. 2001: 5).
2 'Research is not just about gathering information, it is also about analysing and *interpreting* that information and using it to make predictions or to build theories about the way the world works – or parts of it at least!' (Evans and King, 2006: 131)
3 'Here ... we focus on formal research: research in which we intentionally set out to enhance our understanding of a phenomenon and expect to communicate what we discover to the larger scientific community.' (Leedy and Ormrod, 2001: 4)

Verma and Mallick (1999) suggest that research has attained a high degree of respectability and that educators, politicians, business people and others turn to researchers when seeking information on which to base decisions. Most advanced societies have evolved a research-oriented culture, or are in the process of moving in that direction. Formal research, then, would appear to be the systematic gathering, presenting and analysing of data. Actually, some research methods are more systematic than others. Some research methods are more formalised than others. The process can appear mysterious to 'outsiders', making researchers seem special and somehow different. It is important to 'demystify' the process in the rest of this chapter since we are all players of the research game.

Academic research essentially refines the information gathering practices of daily living. Watching other people becomes observation, asking questions becomes interviewing. If the questions are written down they are called questionnaires. The difference is that these information gathering practices are carried out in a more conscious manner. They become more structured, rigorous and deliberate. The findings are recorded systematically and with care. The research methods are formalised for a number of possible motives: to make more 'scientific', to make larger scale, to make more authoritative, to 'prove', to inform action, to take further than individual experiences. Research, however complex or formally presented, is simply a part of the process of finding out and understanding phenomena.

PURPOSES OF RESEARCH

Clough and Nutbrown (2002) explain that all social research is persuasive, purposive, positional and political and these are the reasons why it is conducted. The need to persuade someone or a group of people about something underlies all research, whether it is persuading customers to buy a particular product or persuading teachers of a particular teaching method. Research is purposive in that it attempts to produce something such as the solution to a problem. Research is positional because it is imbued with the perspective of the researcher and the research funders and is derived from a set of circumstances where a problem was defined necessarily from a particular viewpoint or position. As Clough and Nutbrown observe:

> Research which did not express a more or less distinct perspective on the world would not be research at all; it would have the status of a telephone directory where data are listed without analysis (2002: 10).

Finally, research is political because it seeks to make a difference within a policy context. Practitioner researchers, for instance, may seek to change the behaviour policy of a school based on research they have conducted into the efficiency of sanctions.

TYPES OF RESEARCH

We can never dissociate the motives for, and context of, our research from the types of research methodologies we employ. There are a great many types of research defined either by their context, for example, market research, or by their approach. Verma and Mallick developed the following typology of research which highlights 'critical differences between research that is oriented to the development of theory and that designed to deal with practical problems' (1999: 11).

- **Pure or basic research** This is concerned with the development of theory and discovery of fundamental facts to extend the boundaries of knowledge.
- **Applied or field research** This is the application of new knowledge to everyday problems. Though more practical, it usually employs the same rigorous methodology as pure research.
- **Action research** Research into specific practical situations is carried out by practitioners to solve clearly identified problems in order to improve them. As such it is continuous and cyclical. (Action research is discussed in more detail on page 49.)
- **Evaluation research** This is carried out to assess the effectiveness of specific projects to see if the original aims have been achieved. Many government funded projects allocate a proportion of their budgets for evaluation.

Hammersley (2002) suggests a distinction between what he terms *scientific* and *practical* research. The criteria of validity and relevance are important to both types of research but are given different weight and interpreted differently within each. Hammersley further divides scientific enquiry into:

- *theoretical scientific research*
- *substantive scientific research.*

Practical research subdivides into:

- *dedicated practical research* the goal of which is to provide information to a specific group
- *democratic practical research* that provides information for anyone interested in a particular issue
- *contract-based practical research* where the project is commissioned to produce information on a specific issue
- *autonomous practical research* when researchers are autonomous in how they approach an issue of interest.

Both Hammersley and Verma and Mallick's typologies highlight the key point that there are different types of research with different purposes. Each have particular strengths and weaknesses and, whilst these types of research are complementary to each other, 'criticism arises, in part at least, from the impossibility of satisfying, simultaneously, all the criteria by which research findings can be judged' (Hammersley, 2002: 124).

RESEARCH PARADIGMS

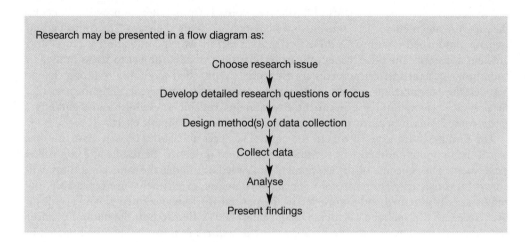

Research may be presented in a flow diagram as:

Choose research issue

Develop detailed research questions or focus

Design method(s) of data collection

Collect data

Analyse

Present findings

Research appears here as far neater, more orderly and more controlled than it actually is. The influence of personal values on the process is also ignored. Every stage in the process can turn out differently if alternative choices are made by the researchers. Just as the whole notion of education is informed by different beliefs and values, so too is the way we study and research it. The education researcher has to make decisions throughout the process which will reflect their ideologies and beliefs concerning both education and research.

This leads us to examine research paradigms. This term describes models of research which reflect general agreement on the nature of the world and how to investigate it. Within a paradigm there would be a general consensus on the research methods that are appropriate and acceptable for gathering data and also those that are not, or are at least less, acceptable. A paradigm then:

> is a network of coherent ideas about the nature of the world and of the functions of researchers which, adhered to by a group of researchers, conditions the patterns of their thinking and underpins their research actions (Bassey, 1990: 41).

In social sciences research is often divided into two major paradigms, the positivist or quantitative and the interpretivist or qualitative. These are perhaps best seen as characteristics clustering into two general groups rather than as clear extremes.

Positivist paradigm

This paradigm developed in the nineteenth century with the apparent success of the natural, or physical, sciences in advancing human understanding of the world. Scientific advances had led to improvements in many areas of people's lives, notable examples being in the field of health and medicine, and had contributed to increased standards of living (see Hitchcock and Hughes, 1993).

The scientific approach consists of testing a hypothesis (initial idea, unproved theory) by the experimental method. This often involves having two identical groups. The control group remains untouched – nothing is done to it and all factors which could affect it (variables) are kept constant. The other group, the experimental group, is subject to some change in conditions (certain specific variables are altered in a controlled way). Any resulting change between the experimental and the control group must be due to the change in the variables made by the scientist in the experiment. Experiments are able to establish cause and effect relationships. Altering a particular variable has a particular, measurable effect.

The findings from experiments in the natural sciences are said to be objective, in other words the opinions and hopes of the researcher cannot influence the results of a controlled experiment. The outcome of the experiment, if carried out under the same conditions, will always be consistent. Thus natural science is systematic, experiments are repeatable, the results are documented and knowledge of the natural world is incremental being built up over time (see McNeill and Chapman, 2005; Yates, 2004). Research in the natural sciences thus has high prestige and the findings are treated with respect. Inevitably pure research in the natural sciences, over time, became an area of applied research, which had the potential to inform future policy. Such a status was regarded as desirable by those interested in the social world and thus an interest grew in developing the social sciences.

The positivist belief is that the approach of the natural sciences could be applied to the social world. It assumes that the social world exists in the same way as does the natural world (Evans and King, 2006; Yates, 2004). Individual behaviour is continually influenced by various pressures upon us. These may be internal pressures, such as biological and psychological, and/or external pressures, such as the norms and values held by the social groups to which we belong. As a result, regular and predictable patterns of behaviour can be said to be displayed by individuals and groups in society. In such a way social forces may be seen to exist both as external and as internalised constraints. As individuals we operate within these internalised constraints and influences which derive from our interaction with the wider society.

Positivists believe that the structures which create the apparent order in social life can be discovered by research. They contend that society can be investigated in the same objective way as the natural world. The approach is empirical in that it shows something exists through observations, that is, data. Going beyond theory and debate, positivist researchers attempt to show that what is being discussed in the theories actually exists because it has the status of the external; it is not just hypothetical. The purpose is to uncover the 'social facts' which make up our world (see the work of Durkheim, 1964; 1970).

To be objective, the positivist social science researcher would ideally like to conduct experiments, in the same way as the natural scientist. Some educational research is able to use this method, for instance certain psychological experiments. However, for much social research it is not possible to create experimental and control groups and to alter variables in a controlled way. People need to be studied in their usual environment if they are to act 'naturally'. Much of the seminal work of the Swiss psychologist, Piaget, was based on experiments conducted with his own children in 'laboratory' conditions which have since been criticised for their inappropriateness. There are also moral objections to treating people in certain ways, so although it might appear to be interesting to deprive babies of human affection and see how their personalities develop, it would not be allowed in our society.

In order to show relationships between variables researchers frequently use the comparative method. This is where groups are compared and differences are noted (McNeill and Chapman, 2005). The purpose is to identify significant variables which explain the differences between the groups. The aim ultimately is to show cause and effect relationships. This strategy is felt to be more reliable the greater the numbers used in the comparison. Thus the sample size and its representativeness of the whole population being studied are important factors for the positivist. The findings become more significant when the amount of data collected is larger and can be presented in ways that aid categorisation and comparison. It is important that the researcher maintains an objective standpoint and keeps personal 'contamination' of the data collection process to a minimum. The most effective positivist research is able to be replicated by others, as with experiments in the natural sciences, or at least compared closely with other similar studies. For these reasons positivist researchers prefer structured methods of data collection which can be carried out on a large scale (macro studies). The data favoured is quantitative, usually presented as statistical tables. This enables others to see how the data has been interpreted and allows for more accurate comparisons. It also attempts to minimise the effect of the particular researcher. The aim is to be able to generalise from the findings.

Certain criticisms have been levelled at the positivist paradigm and the use of statistics in social science research:

1 Statistics may show trends but they do not explain why people have done or said certain things. They are unable to yield detailed accounts of people's reasons thus the meanings obtained from statistical data remain superficial. Statistics of truancy, absence or examination success may show interesting trends but it is the stories behind them that explain these trends. In this way statistics may be seen as impersonal. Positivist methods may ignore the richness of detailed individual accounts.

2 Statistical correlations should not be confused with causality. There may be statistical relations between social deprivation and lack of educational success but we need to go further than statistical analysis to see if the link is real and to seek explanations.

3 Statistical tables and analysis appear to be objective but the significance of individual researchers in their compilation must not be overlooked. A researcher decides what to look for, designs and asks certain questions yet ignores other possibilities. The statistics have to be collected and the answers interpreted and categorised. It would be dangerous to assume that this whole process is unaffected by human contamination (see Cohen et al, 2000).

See Edwards and Usher (2000) for an exposition of strong theoretical grounds for challenging the objectivity and scientific claims of positivist approaches to education research.

Interpretivist paradigm

This is an umbrella term for many social perspectives, notably phenomenology, symbolic interactionism, ethnomethodology (see Denscombe, 2003 and Flick, 2002, for a discussion of these). This paradigm does not see society as having a fixed structure, hidden or not. The social world is created by the interactions of individuals. There are norms and values but these do not exist as clear-cut entities. They are used and changed by people as part of their daily lives. People, termed actors by some interpretivists, interpret events and act in response. Though there are external pressures upon individuals we are not seen to be controlled by some external system. Weber (see Cuff and Payne, 1984; Hammersley, 2006) maintained that actions must be seen as meaningful at the level of interaction. By this he meant that action is taken to be deliberate and meaningful to those involved and the interpretivist paradigm seeks to understand the meanings behind these actions.

The interpretivist tries to show how choices are made by participants or 'actors' in social situations within the process of interaction. For the interpretivist there is no one objective reality which exists outside of the actor's explanations, just different versions of events. Pupils, the classroom teacher, other teachers at the school, parents, all have a view of 'what goes on' and act according to how they interpret events. The researcher in this paradigm seeks to 'understand' these actions.

Interpretivists prefer more 'naturalistic' forms of data collection, making use of individual accounts and biographies and often including detailed descriptions to give a 'feeling' for the environment. Methods favoured in interpretivist studies are informal interviews and observations which allow the situation to be as 'normal' as possible (Hitchcock and Hughes, 1995). These methods are often reliant upon the ability of the researcher to be reflexive in the research process. Interpretivist studies tend to be small scale (micro) aiming for detail and understanding rather than statistical representativeness. Whilst it is not possible to generalise from such studies researchers in this paradigm do attempt to be as rigorous as possible.

Woods suggests that qualitative research focuses on natural settings and is 'concerned with life as it is lived, things as they happen, situations as they are constructed in the day-to-day, moment-to-moment course of events' (1999: 2). The researcher seeks to understand and to portray the participants' perceptions and understandings of the particular situation or event. Interaction is ongoing and there is a continuing chain of events which gives insight into how people live and the research emphasises this process. Woods (1999) also cites the important part played by inductive analysis and grounded theory in qualitative research. The term 'grounded theory' comes from the work of Glaser and Strauss (1967) who suggested that in qualitative studies the researchers do not begin hoping to prove or disprove a set hypothesis. They may have ideas on how 'things will go' but the theory comes from the data they have collected after the research has begun. It is 'grounded' in the data and the experiences of the researcher rather than being imposed upon the research before commencement.

In summary, Yates says that qualitative research attempts to do one or more of the following:

- achieve an in-depth understanding and detailed description of a particular aspect of an individual, a case history or a group's experience(s)
- explore how individuals or group members give meaning to and express their understanding of themselves, their experiences and/or their worlds
- find out and describe in detail social events and explore why they are happening, rather than how often
- explore the complexity, ambiguity and specific detailed processes taking place in a social context. (2004: 138)

Inevitably there are criticisms of qualitative research and these have found particular expression within a policy context intent on 'driving up standards'. Policy makers felt that interpretivist approaches failed to provide clear-cut solutions, presenting instead an overly complex analysis of educational issues (Nisbet, 2000, cited in Greenbank, 2003).

Ethnography

This is a research strategy sometimes adopted by interpretivists which developed from anthropological studies of small-scale societies. Scott (1996) suggests that the spread of this approach can be seen as a reaction to the dominance of positivism in social science. Ethnography is characterised by 'thick' descriptive accounts of the activities of particular groups studied. Accounts focus on the micro, spending much time looking at small groups and particular institutions.

For Walford (2001), ethnography takes into account the wider cultural context in which individuals or groups exist and live, as part of seeking to understand their behaviour and values. Fieldwork takes numerous forms and researchers gather data from many sources, with particular reliance on 'naturalistic' interpretive methods, such as participant observation and informal interviews. This is to develop a multidimensional appreciation of these cultures and individuals. The researcher must have a long-term engagement with the situation to observe developments first hand and to experience the culture. Paradoxically the researcher should also attempt to view cultures dispassionately and to step outside their situation at times. This has been termed as viewing situations as 'anthropologically strange' (see Hammersley and Atkinson, 1995). Thus Walford (2001) sees ethnographic researchers developing their theoretical accounts over time as they conduct their ethnography. The aim is to construct an account that gives a deep and rich appreciation of the people who have been studied. Central to the description and analysis in ethnography are the views and perceptions of the actors.

This research strategy, then, studies groups and individuals in their natural settings, considers the perspectives of those involved and the culture they are living in, uses a wide range of methods to develop a deep understanding and produces accounts which both actors and researchers recognise.

Approaches to the research process and the type of data considered acceptable very much depend upon how those carrying out the research see the world. Much falls within and between the two paradigms of positivism and interpretivism but sometimes this dichotomy proves to be rather too simplistic ignoring a multitude of variations (see Pring, 2004). Several proponents of action research suggest that this two-paradigm view of research emanates from a traditional academic approach and they are critical of its application to professionally based research. McNiff and Whitehead (2005), for instance, suggest critical theoretical and living theory approaches as being more appropriate. Clough and Nutbrown suggest that research studies often move between these paradigms selecting the most appropriate for different parts of the study:

> The issue is not so much a question of which paradigm to work within but how to dissolve that distinction in the interests of developing research design which serves the investigation of the questions posed through that research. (2002: 19)

Reader reflection

Below is a comparison of the positivist and interpretivist paradigms. How easily do you think research falls into one or the other?

Positivist	**Interpretivist**
Natural science	Naturalistic
Objective	Ethnographic
Macro	Micro
External structure	Created by actors
One reality	Multiple realities
Qualitative data	Quantitative data
Questionnaires and structured methods	Unstructured interviews and observations

---

Research methodologies

There are many ways in which information can be obtained and a list of the most common might include:

- experimental test scores
- interviews

- questionnaires
- observation – structured or ethnographic
- diaries by researchers
- diaries by respondents
- photographs
- video recordings
- content analysis (of student work or texts)
- documents
- official records and statistics
- student examination results.

Each of these can be subdivided many times to show variations in structure. In deciding which methods to use the researcher will acknowledge the relative data collection time and associated expense of each different method. Some methods may not be possible because of the particular circumstances of the study, for instance the researcher may not be allowed access to observe certain confidential interviews between the headteacher and parents or other members of staff. Researchers are likely to prefer particular forms of data and thus favour certain research methods over others depending on the paradigm they are working within. They may have to make difficult compromises but ultimately will have to decide what is appropriate in terms of the type of research they wish to conduct. It may seem sensible to take an eclectic approach. However, this can only be acceptable up to a point. 'Mixing' data can be useful but it may be inappropriate to use quantitative methods when a qualitative approach is what the researcher favours and vice versa.

Space does not permit a detailed examination of each research method here. Reference to a specialist methodology text is advisable for this. We will now examine briefly three of the more popular methods of gathering data as well as important research concepts.

QUESTIONNAIRES

This is a useful method, if carefully planned, for obtaining large numbers of responses relatively quickly and, as such, may be seen as providing quantitative data. It is more difficult to obtain in-depth personal responses by this method and so it is less useful for the qualitative researcher. A questionnaire is simply a list of questions. These can be presented to the respondents in different ways: they may be read out by the researcher who writes the answers, they may be sent by post with a stamped addressed envelope for the reply, they may be given out and collected later by the researcher (Bell, 2005).

Strengths of questionnaires in data collection:

1 It is possible to gather large amounts of data relatively quickly.
2 The researcher can compare the responses to particular questions by individuals or between different groups of respondents.
3 The data can be expressed statistically. It is thus possible to make comparisons with other studies.
4 The research may enable overall statements concerning the population to be made, for example the percentage who left school at 16, the percentage who gained certain qualifications, the numbers who felt that they were bullied at school.

Weaknesses of questionnaires:

1 Questions about complex issues are difficult to compose. Respondents may not find it easy to place their responses into specific categories.
2 The short responses required often fail to reflect the varying depth or complexity of people's feelings.
3 It is the researcher who sets the agenda of questionnaires not the respondent. The questions may create attitudes by asking the respondents to comment on things which they may not previously have considered. Alternatively the questions may not give enough emphasis to areas which the respondents see as important.
4 The researcher may attempt to overcome the above problems by adding open ended questions. Answers to these will need to be codified by the researcher which can lead to the very subjectivity which the questionnaire may well have been chosen to overcome.

Munn and Drever (2004) give useful practical advice on questionnaire design.

INTERVIEWS

Interviews may take many different forms. They can vary from being highly structured and very formal to being unstructured and so informal that they appear to be little more than conversations between respondent and researcher (for a detailed overview see Bell, 2005, or Cohen et al, 2000).

In the more structured interview the researcher follows a set format with fixed questions. How much they are able to adapt each interview to varying circumstances is decided beforehand but it may be very little. This approach allows for a team of interviewers to interview a large number of respondents and for the results to be standardised. This really is a further development of the questionnaire and is likely to provide quantitative as well as some qualitative data.

Where the researcher prefers the emphasis to be on the respondent's account, a less structured approach is likely to be taken, perhaps relying on a few fixed questions and prompts.

The interview may be very informal so it becomes, to all intents and purposes, like a normal conversation. Here the respondents may be very open but the researcher must be careful not to lead them. These less structured interviews are favoured by the qualitative researcher. The most 'natural' interactions between the researcher and the respondent may take place during participant observation or a chance meeting during a case study.

Before carrying out interviews several considerations must be addressed from the form of the interview and the role of the interviewer to how the data will be recorded and analysed. Crucially the interviewer must determine who to interview. Burgoyne (1994) described this as 'stakeholder analysis'. For example, are the views of the headteacher more significant than those of a Year 7 pupil? Certainly the head has more power within the school but it depends upon what is being researched. Ball (1990), when looking at the making of national education policy, had to interview those who he felt were most influential in making that policy.

Strengths of interviews in data collection:

1 They can be adaptable to different situations and respondents.
2 The interviewer can 'pick up' non verbal clues which would not be possible from questionnaires, for example annoyance or pleasure shown by the respondent over certain topics.
3 The researcher can 'follow hunches' and different unexpected lines of enquiry as they come up during the interview, for example issues of bullying may become apparent that had not been mentioned or suspected before the start of the study.
4 The researcher can obtain detailed qualitative data expressed in the respondent's own words.

Weaknesses of interviews:

1 The interviewer may significantly affect the responses. They may influence or lead the respondent.
2 Interviews can take a great deal of time and may be difficult to set up. This will restrict the number it is possible to carry out.
3 The more unstructured they are the more variation there is between interviews. This makes comparing data more difficult.

OBSERVATION

The type of phenomenon to be observed and the perspective of the observer will be key factors in determining the methods of observation selected. The observation may be formal and overt as in many psychological experiments where the researcher notes the reactions of respondents to certain stimulations. Similarly, though separate and at the back of the room,

Ofsted inspectors, with their clipboards, are observing the lesson overtly. Observation may also be formal and covert with those being observed unaware of the observer. Here the 'action' may be observed through CCTV cameras, two way mirrors, or the observer may just not be noticed in the crowd. The observer may take part in the proceedings with the subjects of the observation sometimes knowing they are a researcher and sometimes not. Teacher researchers may 'help' in another teacher's classroom whilst unobtrusively observing. Ball (1981) posed as a teacher whilst collecting data in Beachside Comprehensive.

The techniques employed in the collecting of data is very important in this approach. The observer may be noting events as they occur openly or they may have to remember them to be written up as soon as possible afterwards. The more formal the observation the more detailed a tally chart is devised. The Flanders observation schedule, for instance, is very detailed and will yield quantitative data to be analysed. The schedule proposed by the Quality Assurance Agency to observe teaching in Higher Education has fixed categories that the observer has to write in. With the more informal observations the schedules become looser in outline until, in full participant observation, the observer is making mental notes under broad headings to write up later.

Thus observation may be formal or informal. It may yield certain amounts of quantitative data or it may concentrate on qualitative descriptions. Much depends upon how the observation is designed by the researcher. Ethically the researcher must be sensitive to the situation. It is less appropriate, for instance, to use overt formal observation methods when researching the counselling of pupils than it is in a formal lesson.

Any research method can be analysed in similar ways to the three we have outlined. Fundamentally research design is a creative activity in which the researcher crafts an approach which is determined by their perspective as well as by the answers to the host of questions raised above. The outcomes of any research are a result of the approach of, and decisions made by, the researcher.

IMPORTANT RESEARCH CONCEPTS

We now turn to a discussion of the importance of reliability and validity, fundamental concepts of great significance, in education research. Triangulation is outlined as a significant strategy that can be applied in order to increase the validity of the findings.

Reliability

Reliability describes the extent to which a research instrument or method is repeatable. It is an assessment of the consistency of any method. Thus for Pole and Lampard (2002) the reliability of a measure is the extent to which respondents will consistently respond to it in the same way. Corbetta (2003) says that reliability marks:

> the degree to which a given procedure for transforming a concept into a variable produces the same results in tests repeated with the same empirical tools (stability) or equivalent ones (equivalence).

Strengths of observation in data collection:

1 It is possible to see how people behave in 'natural' situations.
2 The researcher can see whether the subjects in the observation act as they say they do.
3 An observer can gather large amounts of data in a short time.

Weaknesses of observation in data collection:

1 Gaining access to situations which would be useful to observe can prove difficult, for example bullying takes place secretively or only when the observer has 'infiltrated' the group; outside observers are not normally allowed into confidential discussions such as teacher appraisal interviews.
2 It is difficult to observe and record at the same time, for example Flanders' observation analysis used by Ball (1981) in Beachside Comprehensive requires recordings to be taken every three seconds.
3 Sometimes it is difficult to categorise behaviour if schedules are being used. It is not always possible to understand actions by observation alone, for example why a teacher treats children differently. A follow-up interview may be needed. This may actually turn a weakness into a strength by providing a fuller analysis.
4 The observer may affect the situation. Did we behave as usual when the inspector was in the lesson?
5 There are ethical issues of observing people if they do not know that they are being observed. It can be seen as a form of spying.

In other words the more reliable the method of data collection the more likely it is to give similar results in subsequent administrations. An unreliable measure will yield different results every time it is administered (Anderson, 1998).

Positivist researchers who wish to carry out large-scale research are most concerned with reliability. The methods need to be capable of being applied to large numbers of respondents in order to generate the data required. To be able to make the desired statistical comparisons the collection of data needs to be consistent, i.e. reliable. In contrast, the interpretivist researcher is likely to be more concerned with the suitability of the methods for eliciting qualitative, accurate and detailed accounts from each respondent. Thus the emphasis on reliability varies according to the paradigm of the researcher.

It should be noted that a high level of reliability of a data collection instrument does not necessarily mean that it is accurate. For instance, if a tutor asks students to evaluate the course by named questionnaire and they are aware that the tutor will shortly be marking their assignments, this is likely to concentrate their minds. Not surprisingly the tutor will have positive student feedback. Whilst this method can be said to be reliable, in that its questions are similarly understood by successive cohorts of students and thus it is always measuring the same thing, its accuracy in terms of the truthfulness of the student responses is certainly suspect.

Validity

Validity and its measurement plays an important part in determining the appropriate methodology to employ. Validity refers to the 'truthfulness', 'correctness' or accuracy of research data. If results are to be considered accurate the research instrument must measure what we claim it to measure. Thus 'an indicator is valid to the extent that it empirically represents the concept it purports to measure' (Punch, 1998: 100). For instance, tests of mathematical ability might actually be producing results which are indicative of the ability to read the questions rather than of mathematical prowess. If the methods are at fault then the findings will be invalid and the research worthless. In aiming to increase validity positivists emphasise the standardisation of data collection whilst using as large a sample as possible. Thus the piloting of any method for accuracy is very important.

Another approach to validity, more associated with an interpretivist approach, places emphasis on the final account and how the researcher is able to defend the interpretations they make from the data (Punch, 1998). In other words the researcher needs to show on what evidence they base their findings. This can be done in a number of ways such as giving full explanations as to how data was gathered; member checks (Maykut and Morehouse, 1994) whereby research participants are asked if their accounts have been recorded accurately; reducing researcher bias by giving a colleague samples of all data collected to verify the analysis and conclusions drawn by the researcher (as suggested by Miles and Huberman, 1994). In action research the openness of the findings to scrutiny and discussion by fellow practitioners is seen as a significant part in ensuring the validity of what is often small-scale research carried out by researchers who are themselves part of the research project (McNiff, 2002).

Triangulation

Triangulation is a navigational term which means to fix one's position from two known bearings. This process is carried out by researchers to increase the validity of their research and it means checking their findings by using several points of reference. In effect, the researcher is approaching the object of the research from as many different angles and perspectives as possible in order to gain a greater understanding (Cohen et al., 2000). Researchers can triangulate by using a number of different fieldworkers in the collection and analysis of data; by seeking the contribution of varied groups of respondents such as pupils, teachers and parents; by using a range of research methods; by considering qualitative and quantitative data and so on. Miles and Huberman pointed to triangulation as a way of life. If findings were consciously checked and double-checked using different sources of evidence then verification would be built in:

> ... by seeing or hearing multiple instances of it from different sources, by using different methods and by squaring the finding with others it needs to be squared with. (1994: 267)

The positivist would hope to show congruency of results from triangulation. The interpretivist would use the different sources of data to give greater depth to their analysis, corroborating or leading to discussion of variation in the findings (Woods, 1999). Thus for Hammersley and Atkinson:

> What is involved in triangulation is not the combination of different kinds of data per se, but rather an attempt to relate different sorts of data in such a way as to counteract various possible threats to the validity of our analysis. (1995: 232)

Certainly both paradigms would suggest the use of triangulation to increase the validity of their findings but would use it in slightly different ways. In order to produce a more thorough and rigorous piece of research several research methods are often used in conjunction with one another. The main methods, in fact, often complement each other. For instance, what has been seen during observations can be raised in interviews by the researcher. This will give an understanding of why something happened as well as a descriptive account. Triangulation is likely to appear as almost a natural process to practitioners who are used to considering different viewpoints and obtaining data from several sources in order to more fully understand particular incidents or aspects of their daily work.

Case studies

The case study approach is not a methodology as such but a research strategy where the researcher aims to study one case in depth. Work in the legal and medical professions is very much based upon case studies (see Hammersley and Gomm, 2000, for a discussion of the use of cases in varying contexts). Here particular cases are examined, usually in order to produce a solution or cure to the issue in question. Each case is unique, which is what makes them so interesting. However, the professionals involved are able to draw upon their knowledge of previous similar cases in order to understand the one currently being examined and to help them decide upon an appropriate ruling or action. For instance, since the law recently allowed parents to be prosecuted for truancy the first test case which resulted in a mother being imprisoned has provided case law for similar prosecutions to be tested against.

Thus practitioners, in these fields that are looking at case studies, draw upon their own previous experience and documented accounts of previous cases to help them to analyse, explain and where appropriate suggest action. Their own findings can in turn be added to a growing body of case histories. What actually constitutes a case is defined by the researcher and can vary enormously in size. Thus the case could be a local education authority (LEA), a school, a class or a particular pupil.

By concentrating on a particular case or cases, data is usually collected by using several methods. Blaxter et al. (2001) suggest that in this way the case-study approach is ideally suited to the needs and resources of a small-scale researcher. Anderson (1998) suggests that most case study research in education is interpretive, seeking to bring a case to life. He states that it often, but not exclusively, occurs in a natural setting with the researcher employing qualitative and/or quantitative methods and measures as fit the circumstances. As Yin (2003) notes, the forms that the data collected will take essentially depend upon the nature of the particular case to be investigated. In this way triangulation automatically takes place thereby increasing the validity of the study.

A major criticism of case studies is that they lack representativeness of the wider population and thus researchers are unable to make generalisations from their findings. However, proponents claim the importance of the case study approach is the in-depth analysis and the understanding gained. For these researchers, the strength of this research approach lies in the 'relatability' of the findings (Bassey, 1990). By this term Bassey is suggesting that although each case may be unique there are sufficient similarities to make the findings from one study useful when seeking to understand others.

Case studies often provide fascinating reading due to the richness of the data. Examples of the use of case studies in education research include the seminal work of Ball (1981), and Lacey (1970), both of whom explored particular schools, and Willis (1979), who studied a group of teenage boys within a school. Bartlett and Burton (2006b) examined cases of individual teachers' own classroom research.

ETHICAL CONSIDERATIONS

There are always ethical considerations that must be addressed before embarking upon a research project and also taken into account whilst the project is ongoing. Researchers may find themselves in a potentially powerful position socially when they have been gathering data in a particular community and care needs to be taken that they do not abuse this privileged position. Researchers should also be aware that the questioning and probing involved in data collection during research can have significant effects on the respondents' daily lives. The British Educational Research Association (BERA, 2003a) suggests 'that all educational research should be conducted within an ethic of respect for:

- the person
- knowledge
- democratic values
- the quality of educational research'. (2003a: 3)

BERA set out guidelines concerning the researcher's responsibilities to participants in the research, to sponsors of research and to the wider community of educational researchers. Key ethical considerations include:

1 securing the consent of those involved
2 the openness of the researcher and the research process
3 access to findings by those who have been involved in the research
4 possible effects of the research on participants during the project and in the future
5 ensuring the anonymity of those involved.

Those working and researching in fields such as education, social work and medicine are continually presented with ethical dilemmas. For instance, discovering through interviews information concerning the drug use, sexual activity or other deviant behaviour of pupils has always presented the researcher/teacher with the dilemma of protecting confidential sources or reporting such activity to parents and the 'authorities'. It is important that all researchers take an ethical stance in their research and only act in a way that they can morally justify even though this may not always be easy (see Oliver, 2003 for a discussion of this).

Research methodology: some conclusions

- Many research methods can be used to collect data. Even within particular method types there is enormous variation.
- The researcher may use or adapt an existing research instrument. In many cases the researcher designs their own instrument.
- Researchers make decisions concerning the methodology to be used in the light of the type of data they require.
- Practical constraints, such as time, money and the nature of the respondent group, will be significant factors to be taken into account when designing the research.
- The data collected will be a reflection of the decisions made by, and the skills of, the researcher.
- Researchers aim to be as rigorous as possible but inevitably their beliefs and assumptions can affect research.
- Large-scale research projects are not necessarily better than small-scale projects.
- The researcher needs to address ethical issues including the confidentiality of data collected and gaining consent as appropriate.

The design of a piece of research is thus highly significant to the data obtained. Some central influences on this design are the perspective of the researcher, the decisions made due to the nature of the group to be studied, and the resources available to carry out the research. We will now consider, briefly, some recent significant research 'movements' in education.

Educational research movements

ACTION RESEARCH

The development of action research

The development of action research is often attributed to the work of Kurt Lewin (1946) who was seeking ways of increasing productivity in industry by involving a larger proportion of the workforce in decision-making. He also saw what became termed the action research approach as a way of tackling many of the post-Second World War social problems. He developed a spiral of action that involved fact finding, planning and execution. This act of professionals conducting research in order to solve professional problems could be easily applied to many areas, education being a prime example.

The action research 'movement' in education in Britain has been greatly influenced by the work of Lawrence Stenhouse at the Schools Council (1967–72). The Schools Council was the forerunner of various government curriculum agencies but, unlike the subsequent National Curriculum Council and the Qualifications and Curriculum Agency, Council members were drawn from academic educationalists and teachers. Stenhouse felt that teachers needed to be at the centre of curriculum development if it was to be effective. Therefore it was essential that teachers reflected upon practice, shared experiences and evaluated their work if the education of pupils was to improve. For Stenhouse, each classroom could be seen as a laboratory and each teacher a member of a research community.

Stenhouse found the 'objectives model' of curriculum design to be uneducational as it assumed knowledge as a given and discouraged wider questioning and individual development whilst encouraging passive acceptance of the facts as presented. For teachers to appear authoritative and to present subject content as beyond doubt was a misrepresentation encouraged by many in education. He viewed knowledge and its structure as inherently problematic and contestable. For this reason Stenhouse favoured a process model of curriculum design that was based upon learners questioning and exploring in order to gain their own understanding. Teachers themselves, whilst having knowledge about what they are teaching, are cast in the role of learners alongside their students. For Stenhouse it was this continual questioning and learning by teachers that gave them more to offer their students. In this way learning itself is a research process and research is seen as the basis for teaching (Stenhouse, 1983).

Stenhouse believed in the professional desire of teachers to improve education for their pupils and so benefit society. For this reason he considered teachers the best judges of teaching. By working in research communities they would be able to reflect upon and then improve their practice. Other interested members of the community, such as parents and employers, would in turn be drawn into this research process. In this way a social democratic ideology ran through the work of the Schools Council. Curriculum reform was visualised as happening at the grass roots level and involving all those with a stake in education. Action resulting from the reflective process was regarded as a means of empowering practitioners and therefore central to the professional development of teachers. It is noteworthy that an abhorrence of the notion of empowering teachers and viewing them as education experts was what led to the eventual demise of the Schools Council under the Conservative government of Margaret Thatcher.

This development of action research fitted Schon's (1983) view of the reflective practitioner where discussion of practice is shared with both clients and colleagues. Resulting from this, modern professional communities reflect upon, discuss and learn from each other's work. It also ties in with Hoyle's (1980) view of extended professionals who were likely to be involved in action research as a 'natural' part of their professional development.

Action research grew in part out of disillusionment with traditional forms of educational research that were conducted by the universities during the 1960s and 1970s. These were felt to adopt an academic approach to research and to be of little practical use to those working in classrooms. They took a disengaged stance and offered no help in terms of the practice of teaching. Also, much influential academic research of the time had promoted a view that either innate factors (Jensen, 1973) or wider social circumstances (Douglas, 1964) largely determined overall educational achievement. It was as though schools did not make a difference to pupil attainment and it was the influence of wider social forces on the pupil or natural ability that were seen as the key factors. If anything, schools only reinforced these existing inequalities acting as processing agencies in which teachers were unwitting players (Bowles and Gintis, 1976). Such research gave little encouragement to teachers about how to change or improve things.

Though closely linked with higher education institutions that provided mentors who were a valuable source of support, action research was seen as a new approach to research carried out by professionals. It was thus rooted in practice and it moved away from the traditional academic approach based upon the major research paradigms. McNiff (1988) spoke of a wish to create a study of education that was grounded in practice and developed by those involved. Thus teachers were to develop their research skills to evaluate their practice. The process needed to be rigorous and critical if it was to create effective change. Thus injunctions to become more critical meant far more than simply evaluating practice for many proponents of action research (Carr and Kemmis, 1986). The development of critical theory was seen as a questioning of the whole purpose and techniques employed by teachers. It involved asking fundamental questions about why things are done in a certain way and why other processes are not used. This would encourage further research, experimentation and, ultimately, change. There would be a linking of theory and practice alongside the development of research for action.

Defining action research

According to Elliott, a lifelong proponent, action research is 'the study of a social situation with a view to improving the quality of action within it' (1991: 69), and 'theorising from the standpoint of action in order to act with "understanding" of the practical situation' (2003: 172). Altrichter et al (1993) suggest that action research starts from practical questions that fit in with the working conditions of the teachers. Methods of data collection are tailored to suit the circumstances. Each research project is designed for a specific set of circumstances and so is unique.

These definitions indicate that action research starts with a problem, issue or set of questions arising out of professional concerns. Initial research is carried out to collect data that clarifies the situation. A plan of action is devised in the light of this evidence. This is put into place and the effects carefully monitored. This is likely to lead to further refined questions and so further developments which will, in turn, be implemented and researched. However, what is critical for Elliott (2003) is that the action part of improving practice is an integral part of the teacher's construction of new knowledge and understanding of the problem. The action research process has frequently been shown in diagrammatic form as some form of developmental spiral.

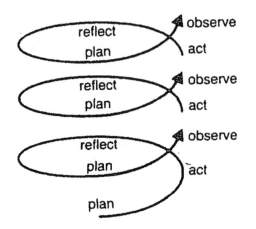

Figure 3.1 *McNiff's original model*
Source: McNiff, 2002

Action research is curriculum development at the classroom level. It is concerned with how to improve education practice and it is practitioners themselves who carry out the research in examining and developing their teaching. The nature of this form of practitioner research means that it is carried out in the teacher's own place of work and so the case study approach is the most common. Ideally, an eclectic view of data collection is taken with the researcher using a variety of methods to examine the particular issue. The process whereby researchers are able to use their own understandings to interpret the situations they are investigating is termed *reflexivity*. This is an important aspect of action research and it is expected that the reflexivity of the researchers will be heightened as they develop their research skills.

Increased validity is aimed at through a rigorous approach to the research coupled with tri-angulation and openness at all stages of the process. Though it is not possible to generalise from the findings of such small-scale research, its strength, according to Bassey (1990), lies in its relatability to similar situations. Validity is also strengthened as communities of researchers in schools examine and discuss each other's findings, an activity described by Elliott (1993) as 'discoursive consciousness'. This process would involve others and develop a wider understanding of the nature of education as part of the social democratic process. Kemmis and Wilkinson (1998) also stress the participatory nature of action research. They see action research itself as a social and educational process that is part of the development of a professional community.

Criticisms of action research

The use of diagrams showing action research as a continuous process of development has been criticised as inadvertently promoting a rigid approach to research (Carter and Halsall, 1998). Dadds, for instance, realised that 'the tidy action research cycle was never that tidy in the practices of research' (Dadds and Hart, 2001: 7). Diagrams that indicate stages in a research cycle may encourage the view that these are the 'correct' order in which to conduct action research. This may create problems when any new researcher finds that they are deviat-

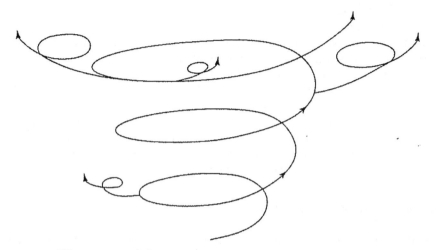

Figure 3.2 *McNiff's new model*
Source: McNiff, 2002

ing from these prescribed stages. The diagrams themselves may appear daunting and even confusing to the novice (Hopkins, 2002). In fairness, many of those who designed action research diagrams, such as Elliott (1991), only intended them to be used as guides. More recently McNiff (2002) has developed her original model, which she accepts could be seen as rather prescriptive, to show how the action research process can take many turns.

Action research for the twenty-first century

There have always been different interpretations of what action research actually involves (Bryant, 1996). For many of the proponents of the late 1970s and early 1980s it provided a whole philosophy of the future development and control of education linked to the social democratic movement in the wider society. Thus according to Carr and Kemmis:

> … it comes out on the side of the control of education by self-critical communities of researchers, including teachers, students, parents, educational administrators and others. Creating the conditions under which these participants can take collaborative responsibility for the development and reform of education is the task of a critical educational science. Educational action research offers a means by which this can be achieved. (1986: 211)

An evangelical approach to action research that sees it as a quest for personal and professional fulfilment can still be seen in the work of many educationalists (see McNiff, 2002; McNiff and Whitehead, 2006). However, for others it remained at the level of problem solving for teachers. They were not concerned with developing a new educational science, nor did they take a critical stance on the basic values and actions in their practice. This second, rather narrow approach to teachers as researchers may be seen in the utilitarian approach taken by many politicians and managers.

Throughout the late 1980s and 1990s when teachers were subject to increasing pressure and a rising number of directives from central government, many critics saw action research as too micro in scale and somewhat insular. Thus, as teachers appeared to be losing control over the curriculum, action research seemed increasingly irrelevant in the face of wider political pressures. The assumption that teachers had the power to change their practice rather than being constrained by wider pressures now appeared rather naive (Avis, 2001). The underpinning social democratic ideology being promoted in the curriculum developments of the 1960s, 1970s and even the early 1980s was replaced by that of neo-liberalism and competition (see Chapter 10 for an outline of these developments). Certainly, the image of the extended professional does not sit comfortably within an environment of increasing central control and the development of market forces that has taken place in education over the last 20 years.

SCHOOL EFFECTIVENESS RESEARCH

The adoption and development of managerialist strategies in the 1980s with their aim of increasing efficiency by improving results and reducing costs led to a growth of interest in what became known as school effectiveness research. As its title implies, this approach sought, by using quantitative analysis, to identify what led to the creation of effective schools. Perhaps the first significant study in Britain using this approach that caught the public imagination was *Fifteen Thousand Hours* by Rutter et al (1979). Using statistical techniques comparisons of schools were made that identified the factors that set more successful schools apart from the less successful. Over the years lists of these characteristics have been added to and refined by a number of studies (see Creemers, 1994; Reynolds et al, 1994; Sammons et al, 1995; Teddlie and Reynolds, 2000). These lists tend to be very similar, usually citing strong and effective leadership, high expectations of pupil achievement and behaviour, an orderly atmosphere with an emphasis on learning, monitoring of pupil progress and clear enforced discipline with positive reinforcement of success.

However, various criticisms have been levelled at school effectiveness research (see Carter, 1998; Elliott, 1998; Thrupp, 2001; Willmott, 1999). The data collected was statistical and there were issues concerning the accuracy of its measurement. Indeed it was questionable as to whether an agreed definition could even be arrived at for many of the factors, such as 'an orderly atmosphere' or 'effective leadership'. The term 'effective' is itself a value laden term when applied to education. There are different opinions as to what constitutes an effective school, or effective teaching. Many felt that this research considered effectiveness from a managerial perspective only. It became tied to measurable outcomes and these were then taken as important outcomes of education. Thus exam results and truancy figures may be used to judge effectiveness but not the happiness of pupils or the job satisfaction of the teachers. Many of the factors linked to effective schools by this research were not startling in themselves and were already regarded as important issues in schools. The difficulty for schools was to actually develop the traits that were seen as linked to effectiveness. So, whilst identifying and developing lists of what could be seen as almost common sense factors linked to school effectiveness, this research gave no indication of how schools could work towards these. As this research was carried out by 'outside' researchers rather than teachers, the findings often appeared as another presentation of management ideology being passed down from above. The result was that they were often treated with cynicism by those working in schools.

SCHOOL IMPROVEMENT RESEARCH

The disillusionment with the positivist approach of school effectiveness research and its associated ideology was countered by the development of the 'school improvement movement'. This has the individual school at its centre and through a research approach seeks to develop and implement strategies that will lead to improvement. It encourages a more eclectic approach to data collection and can therefore take a less restricted view of what is meant by school improvement. School improvement research sees the school as a community and recognises the importance of those with a 'stake' in the findings being involved in the research (see Hopkins, 2002, 2001; Hopkins and Harris, 2000). It is through school improvement research that the notion of teachers as researchers, developed initially within the action research movement, was maintained throughout the 1990s. Thrupp and Lupton (2006) suggest that, whilst school improvement research does acknowledge that schools operate in different environments, it still needs to give more prominence to their particular contextual circumstances in order to avoid drawing misplaced generalised conclusions. This would allow the impact of local factors such as the nature of housing, employment opportunities and cultural diversity to be taken into account.

Carter (1998) noted the emergence of a more eclectic approach to school research that encouraged the use of aspects of both the school effectiveness and the school improvement approaches to research on schooling. Others, however, held that effectiveness and improvement research are predicated on different ideologies of education that make any future merger of the two approaches impossible (Elliott, 1996, 1998; Halsall, 2001).

PRACTITIONER RESEARCH AND EVIDENCE-BASED PRACTICE

'Practitioner research' is a more recently used term to describe the process whereby professionals, such as teachers, conduct research into their own practice. Evidence-based practice is when professionals base how they act upon evidence of what is successful. Whilst the notion of teachers as researchers seemed increasingly out of place in the Conservative administrations from 1979 until 1997, the climate changed somewhat under the 'New Labour' government. Research continued to be focused on school improvement perspectives but talk of partnerships in education with all stakeholders working together to raise standards became the norm. There was also a re-examination of the professional nature of teaching. The Labour government appeared to recognise the importance of teachers developing their classroom skills and how this might be achieved through reflective practice. The promotion of teachers researching their own classroom practice was formally encouraged through DfEE funding of

Best Practice Research Scholarships (DfEE, 2001). However, the focus of this research has been firmly in the classroom and on raising (largely measurable) standards. Funding made available through government agencies has tended not to encourage wider questioning of the purposes of education or where these standards have come from. As such this research has done little to create communities of teacher researchers and has promoted largely restrictive professional development (Bottery and Wright, 1999).

Such policy-driven outcomes have been referred to by Patrick et al as the dual ambiguity of autonomy–performativity (2003: 239). In other words, government is deploying the language of empowerment and professional autonomy whilst using funding to coerce a focus on measurement of performance. This narrow focus on classroom and pupil performance may explain why practitioner research and evidence-based practice is presented as a new initiative with the broader vision of many action researchers from the past not mentioned. We contend, however, that to some extent a Stenhousian approach will be revived as teachers gain more confidence in their new research skills and begin again to ask questions about the purposes and nature of learning (Bartlett and Burton, 2006b; Burton and Bartlett, 2005).

The importance of freedom in research

Academic research in education has been criticised for a number of reasons in recent years. In the Teacher Training Agency Annual Lecture of 1996, David Hargreaves, an influential UK educationalist, highlighted what he saw as the failure of educational research to serve those working in education. He called for teaching to become a research-based profession similar to medicine. He suggested that teachers at that time made little use of research evidence to inform their practice, through no fault of their own but because researchers were not producing findings that supported practice. Hargreaves suggested that current educational research was poor value for money and that it inadequately served the teaching profession. He called for the setting up of a National Education Research Forum 'which would shape the agenda of educational research and its policy implications and applications' (1996: 6). He also suggested that funding should be redirected from academic researchers to agencies committed to evidence-based practice and to fund teachers as researcher-practitioners.

Both the Tooley Report (Tooley and Darby, 1998) funded by Ofsted, and the Hillage Report (Hillage et al, 1998) funded by the DfES, also raised questions concerning the quality and usefulness of educational research. Elliott (2001) and Hammersley (2002) argue that these criticisms, Hargreaves' in particular, all take a rather simplistic view of how research is able to inform practice. They assume that causal relationships can be revealed by research and that findings can be easily applied to all schools. This would mean that variables can be identified and allowed for, ignoring the complexity of what actually happens in classroom situations (Thrupp and Lupton, 2006). Both Elliott and Hammersley maintain that what is essentially a positivist approach suitable for medical research is inappropriate in educational investigations. They also suggest that there is a values dimension to education that a natural scientific methodology looking for absolute answers fails to recognise. Clark acknowledges that educational research is logically tied to practice but notes that 'the quest for scientifically-proven knowledge of "what works" is either incoherent, or at best reflects the attempted ascendancy of a particular unstated and undefended ideology' (2005: 290).

If, as Hammersley (2002) and others argue, there are different forms of research that are carried out for different purposes, it could be claimed that their outcomes should be evaluated differently because they offer complementary strengths and weaknesses. However, there is a danger that this could exacerbate the 'hierarchy' of research outputs that already exists. Greenbank (2003) points to how policy makers hold quantitative research in higher esteem simply because of the way it is presented. There also exists a hierarchy in terms of where educational research is disseminated. 'Academic' peer-reviewed education journals of national or international repute do not publish professionally oriented research – this finds expression through professional publications, conferences and in-service courses. Since Hargreaves (1996) questioned the relevance of 'academic' educational research to teachers, the complexity of the debate has been revealed, imbued as it is with political tensions around research funding policies and the hijacking of so-called professional, accessible research in pursuit of the ill-defined populist agenda of raising standards. Notwithstanding the differences in emphases of different types of research, there is every reason and every need, in our view, to assign parity of status to 'professional' and 'academic' research.

Conclusion

The research process is complex yet, like the questions involving the purposes of education, is often presented as falling within two perspectives: positivism and interpretivism. The positivist believes in the need for scientific research, the purpose being to uncover facts to permit an explanation of reality. The focus is on large-scale, quantitative methods, carried out in an objective manner. The interpretivist, on the other hand, sees multiple realities which are created by the actors themselves. Interpretivists prefer small-scale, qualitative methods involving 'rich' accounts and description to the impersonal statistics of the positivists.

The ideological underpinning of data collection becomes apparent when particular groups of researchers, or 'schools of research', are analysed. Ideologies of education link in a complex way with the types of research carried out. Thus action research, developed by practitioners, emphasises qualitative methodologies, seeking to understand what is happening in order to change and improve it. Education is characterised as a constantly developing process.

School effectiveness research is also concerned with improving education but takes a much more positivist approach. The aim is to collect quantitative data in an objective manner so that comparisons can be made using large numbers of statistics. By using various statistical techniques factors which influence outcomes can be isolated and measured. Findings can be used to alter the practice of teachers. The emphasis on objectivity fits with a view of education as a product which can be measured. The school improvement approach takes a more qualitative view of school development and a more eclectic approach to data collection.

Thus there are differing approaches in education research because beliefs and values both predicate and are a part of the research process.

Student activities

1 Design a small-scale research project using the following headings:
   - Issue or area to be researched
   - Research questions
   - Data collection methods.

2 Choose a piece of published research and analyse it. Make particular reference to:
   - the paradigm of the research
   - methods of data collection used – appropriateness, strengths, weaknesses
   - validity and reliability
   - relationship of findings to the data
   - presentation of findings.

Recommended reading

Every degree course has some form of methodology section concerning the particular area of study. Education and the social sciences are no exception and as a result there are a multitude of high quality texts available.

Bell, J. (2005) *Doing Your Research Project. A Guide for First-Time Researchers in Education, Health and Social Science.* 4th edn. Maidenhead: Open University Press. This book has been recommended for initial research methods courses for a number of years. It is a well-written, easy to understand guide on how to carry out a research project. In this respect it is ideal for undergraduates preparing for a research dissertation.

Cohen, L., Manion, L. and Morrison, K. (2000) *Research Methods in Education.* 5th edn. London: RoutledgeFalmer. This volume is also highly recommended by many tutors of research methods courses. Whilst giving a clear account of different research methods, it also considers the underpinning philosophy of research in detail. It gives a useful outline of different research paradigms and considers the whole nature of research in relation to notions of truth and reality. As such it is more academically advanced than the other three texts.

Oliver, P. (2003) *The Student's Guide to Research Ethics.* Maidenhead: Open University Press. This text introduces the reader to ethical issues that occur in research. It considers every stage of the research process from design to writing the final report. This is a very accessible volume that covers an area that must be addressed by all researchers.

Yates, S. (2004) *Doing Social Science Research.* London: Sage, Open University Press. This book is useful for those new to the research process. Written as a general text for social science students, it provides an introductory overview of the research process. It offers a clear explanation of the main research paradigms and their associated methodologies. Many interesting readings are used as illustrative examples.

4 A modern history of schooling

The study of education systems, structures and processes cannot be complete without an understanding of their histories. Any attempt to account for education in the here and now, to describe its structure and its particular concrete reality, can be enhanced by reference to its history, how it came to be what it is (Hunter, 1994).

A knowledge of the history of the education system provides a very powerful means of understanding why things in education are as they are. It is possible to trace the processes whereby the present order of things has become established. We can detect the ideas and policies that motivated educational change and the development of practices that now have the status of common-sense wisdom and are accepted as necessary elements (Donald, 1992).

This chapter will explore briefly the period leading up to the introduction of state education as we know it and will chart developments since World War II including the establishment of comprehensive schooling.

Introduction

The history of modern education has been dominated by the period from 1870 since this was a symbolic 'moment' of huge transition, leading to the present order of things. We begin our overview in the period prior to 1870 when the foundations of the state education system were being laid. The history of this modern period in education can be divided roughly into the following phases:

- 1800–70: towards state education
- 1870–1902: the first stages of elementary schooling
- 1902–44: establishing secondary schools and local education authorities
- 1944–65: universal secondary education
- 1965–88: comprehensive schooling
- 1988–present day: diversity and competition.

Each of these phases represents a significant stage in the development of education, though some contemporary historians would be wary of thinking in terms of progressive development. These phases are not completely discrete either (see Brooks, 1991). The phase belonging to the comprehensive school does not, for instance, represent the unequivocal triumph of comprehensive schooling. One problem with describing the history of education in phases is that it implies linearity, or a sequence of interlinking events and developments. Some models of history would challenge the idea of a smooth narrative and would also challenge the centrality given to matters of education policy, claiming that the big narrative accounts necessarily omit the countless other stories, struggles and events. They might also complain that linear policy history actually deals with only a small and not necessarily important segment of the history of education. Contemporary history of education may review the history of the school as an institution (Copeland, 1999) by asking what the effects were on the populations of schooling, how these effects can be gauged, what of the untold stories of countless thousands who passed through schooling and whose lives were marked with its traces. An ethnographic account of classroom practices, looking back at former teaching approaches, conducting interviews with former pupils and teachers and so on, would furnish a very different kind of history from that which charts changes in legislation and in the formal arrangements of schooling.

The idea that education is a human right is a relatively recent historical idea (Porter, 1999). It can be traced through the rise of nation states in the eighteenth and nineteenth centuries. Legislation appeared during the nineteenth century to control the employment of children, to protect children from sexual abuse and from exploitation as cheap labour. This process has been described by some as the construction or invention of childhood (Aries, 1962). Along with the intervention of the state into questions of the rights of children came an increasing concern with the idea of education as being appropriate for all levels of society and especially appropriate for the young. Given that, during the nineteenth century, education was to be experienced by total populations, these questions took on, and still retain, very considerable force and significance (Green, 1990).

1800–70 Towards state education

Since the Middle Ages the Church had provided some form of rudimentary education to many poor children within charity schools and orphanages as well as more formal education within monasteries and public schools for a small, relatively privileged section of the population. During the early years of the nineteenth century large numbers of children in the new urban centres were working in factories while those remaining in rural areas worked in agriculture or cottage industries of various kinds. The early 'poor' schools of the 1800s were voluntary and funded by philanthropists and religious groups. Intended for urban working-class children they were essentially 'drill' schools, concerned with strict training in literacy and numeracy for large numbers of pupils as quickly as possible, given the uncertain nature of the clientele and the duration of their school life (Donald, 1992).

Designed to manage the learning of large numbers via a rank-and-file ordering of all its pupils in a single space, monitorial schooling promoted a monolithic version of learning via repetition. It was the proud boast of these schools that they could effect learning for large numbers of pupils with the presence of a single instructor. The *monitorial system* organised pupils by ability and broke down the learning into small elements to be learned by rote. The teacher selected a number of the most able pupils as monitors who instructed small groups of children whilst the teacher disciplined them and examined their work before they could progress to the next element. The problem with this system was that it concentrated on the learning of facts and made no allowance for the different rates at which children worked and the different ways in which they learned.

The monitorial system fell into decline in the second half of the nineteenth century but the government began to grant-fund voluntary schools, which were almost exclusively run by the Church, from 1833. The *ragged schools* established by John Pounds to educate destitute children free of charge were supported and extended by Lord Shaftesbury since there was a need to civilise the masses. Shaftesbury was concerned about girls in mining districts who drank, swore and fought and felt that education was the way to deal with such behaviour. In order that parents could go to work in the increasingly labour intensive city factories some form of social control and respectable values had to be instilled in children. Ragged schools were governed by elected boards of prominent citizens and this formed the governance model for the elementary schools that were to follow.

As elementary schooling began to gain pace there was more time in school to fill and more pressure on the authorities of education to ensure that schooling was meaningful for the various interest groups or stakeholders concerned (Horn, 1989; Hurt, 1979). The *Revised Code of 1862* laid down conditions for school managers to claim grants for children attending. To be eligible for these grants children had to attain one of six standards in reading, writing and arithmetic. Each standard in each subject was stated in terms of a precisely defined skill to be demonstrated, rather like contemporary National Curriculum attainment targets. This imposed a concentration on the basics and became known as 'payment by results' (Martin, 2004). Thus, even before universal elementary education was legislated for, its foundations were well established.

1870–1902 The first stages of elementary schooling

Modern education systems across Europe evolved out of various needs that came together through the large transformations of society that took place during the eighteenth and nineteenth centuries. Within a more industrialised society the factories needed literate and numerate workers, especially as Britain's economic position in the world began to be challenged by Germany and the USA. Key political changes had led to most working-class men being granted the right to vote in 1867 so it was important to ensure that their education enabled them to understand what they were voting for.

The *Education Reform Act of 1870* was designed to legislate for subsidised elementary education for all up to the age of 13. Education reform had been on the agenda since the government started to provide grants to schools in the 1830s. However, opposition from a number of different interest groups delayed it. The establishment of elementary schooling was fraught with contentious issues. Firstly, there were the widespread concerns amongst the upper and middle classes about the possible consequences of educating large numbers of people, their worries being that an educated population would not obey its 'superiors' and that workers would leave their menial jobs. There was also a deep-seated resistance among laissez-faire liberals, conservatives and working-class activists to the idea of state-funded compulsory education. They were suspicious of the state's efforts to control education on different grounds. Those who believed in laissez-faire values argued that state intervention and funding in education would endanger freedom of thought, reduce personal initiative and, if it involved no cost to people, would be perceived as having no value.

A further set of concerns and political lobbying came from the very powerful voice of the Church, which had dominated schooling for centuries with most education for children delivered through Church of England schools. The importance of educating the masses in Christianity could not be underestimated since it came with a clear message about the lower classes' place in society and a fear of what would happen in the afterlife if good behaviour within that place was not maintained. The Church had the physical and financial means to deliver schooling because people in whose interests it was to educate people in this way, landed gentry and important industrialists for example, supported it. There was also reluctance on the part of government to spend money on education.

Various religious conflicts arose about education. The Church of England wanted to maintain control of its schools so refused to cooperate with government inspectors. Catholics and others wanted single denomination schools. Radicals and non-conformists wanted secular education. These conflicts continued from the 1840s through to the 1860s and delayed agreement on the provisions in the Act. Eventually, as its power declined, the Church of England's ability to influence the education agenda diminished, leading to a universal agreement that public funds would be required if large-scale education was to be developed. This in turn had ramifications for the curriculum because if public rates and taxes were to pay for part of the education a partial withdrawal from religious instruction was possible.

The *Forster Elementary Education Act 1870* required partially state-funded board schools to be set up to provide primary (elementary) education in areas where existing provision was inadequate. Board schools were managed by elected school boards. Children still had to pay a small fee to attend. Though the 1870 Act did not make education compulsory to begin with, by 1880 all children between the ages of 5 and 10 were required to attend school (Martin, 2004). In 1891 the *Free Education Act* provided for the state payment of school fees up to ten shillings per week so by the end of the century most children were attending schools and were in some form of full-time education for a significant segment of their early lives. The school leaving age was increased to 11 in 1893 and 12 in 1899. The emergence of state education with the rapid development of the school as a central institution of civil society represented a massive change in social order.

Reader reflection

In the early phase of the elementary schools (1870–1900) the curriculum was largely concerned with the teaching of values, virtues, literacy, numeracy, personal hygiene, physical maintenance, domestic skills and rudimentary knowledge about the world and the nation's considerable influence within it. The pioneers of state education had seen the emergent school as the potential instrument of moral transformation, especially important in relation to urban populations that were deemed to be threateningly amoral and disorganised. The school could be a key instrument in the training of populations and in the construction of the idea of community.

What are the ideological underpinnings of this early curriculum?

Early urban state schools can be seen to have this socially symbolic function in their dramatic and often cathedral-like architecture. The powerful, conservative nineteenth-century idea that education for the working classes was potentially dangerous and might give the proletariat ideas above their station was evident in the limitations of the early elementary school curriculum. Early state educators believed that education was necessarily about making the nation cohesive, fostering and cultivating national identity. There was little embarrassment about the political function of that ideological effort.

Thus the elementary school emerged in the nineteenth century as a new form of institution with a newly formulated social mission. The school as we know it is closely related to this recent ancestor. These 'new' elementary schools that appeared like 'beacons of the future' over the urban landscapes of the industrialised nation were quite different from the 'monitorial' schools that had successfully drilled working-class children in the basics of literacy and numeracy. They were often constructed using a grand architectural design,which strongly resembled the nineteenth-century factory buildings dominating the post-industrial revolution skylines of urban industrial centres. Indeed, these were conceived of and developed as responses to urbanisation and industrialisation, as responses to the problems of population management. They became complex institutions for the governance *and* for the transformation of populations (Hurt, 1979). The schools represented a new form of aspiration for mass urban populations and, architecturally, presented a socio-cultural symbolism in their (early) grand designs and were structured and embellished accordingly (Donald, 1992; Lowe and Seaborne, 1977).

They also operated a more subtle pastoral and disciplinary regime than the monitorial system with its huge drill rooms. In the elementary school the teacher was brought closer to the pupils in smaller classrooms and the culture of the children met with the supervisory gaze of the teacher in the playground. The collective space of the hall could be utilised for the promotion of collective identity and moral guidance. Elementary school was to be the basis for the development of an entirely new kind of 'human technology' capable of producing responsible and self-governing citizens. This self-governing aspect of the school's characteristic way of working remains very powerful. It is deeply embedded in the work ethic that prevails in schools and in the contemporary drive to develop a self-managing, self-governing citizenry through state-funded education.

The development of the school as a key component of civic life, particularly in urban centres, transformed the nature of society and the 'citizen' (Hunter, 1994). In its early phases (from 1870) the school was primarily designed to produce this new form of 'citizen' who was basically literate, was trained in certain disciplines of conduct and had learned some basic facts about the world (Donald, 1992). It was during this period that the many still relatively new urban centres in Britain became governed and ordered locally. Amenities and systems for cleanliness and health were provided, for example public baths, drainage systems, new technologies of hygiene and waste disposal. It is possible to see the school as one very important manifestation of this civic concern. It is certainly important to recognise the extent to which the early elementary school represents a vast extension of government in the name of both social control and social improvement (Wardle, 1970). The early education system was thus concerned with the moral, physical and spiritual condition of the population. Domestic economy and the civic virtues of cleanliness and personal self-management could be taught and some of the negative effects of urban poverty could be dealt with by health care and large-scale feeding programmes managed through schools (Horn, 1989).

1902–44 Establishment of secondary schools and Local Education Authorities

When, in 1897, voting rights were extended to every male householder living in a borough constituency and those earning over £10 in lodgings, the need to educate for democracy was further strengthened, leading to expansion of the school system. With society having become more accepting of state intervention the *Balfour Education Act of 1902* legislated for the development of grammar and secondary schools and developed the free place system, which provided funded scholarships for a few able but poor children to attend grammar school. Despite this, only 10 per cent of children had secondary school places by 1944. Secondary schools were for the fee-paying middle classes. For the remaining 90 per cent elementary schools up to the age of 14 were all that was available.

The 1902 Act also replaced the school boards of the 1870 Act with local education authorities (LEAs). The government's Board of Education would now only deal with 318 LEAs instead of 2,500 school boards and over 14,000 voluntary schools. The act was particularly significant because it legislated for all schools, including denominational schools, to be funded through rates.

In 1904, two years after the 1902 Education Act had laid the basis of the compulsory education system, the Board of Education published an *Elementary Code* and regulations for secondary schools. This continued the tradition of the elementary school stressing conduct and discipline with minor emphasis on subject knowledge. The Act itself spoke strongly in terms of 'self-sacrifice', 'respect for duty', 'respect for others', 'instinct for fair play', 'loyalty to one another' and other qualities that emphasised the personal, moral dimension of the curriculum. More secondary schools emerged after 1904. They mostly tended to borrow the academic curriculum of the private schools, which had modified classical curricula. The Act specified: English language and literature, at least one language other than English, geography, history, mathematics, science and physical exercises (Jenkins and Shipman, 1976). It added the proviso that girls' schools should include 'house-wifery'.

After the First World War, state-funded education in Britain was regarded as important in improving the quality of life of the oppressed classes. Social reformers and revolutionaries saw it as a mechanism for enabling class inequalities to be challenged and swept aside. A number of forces and factors combined to pressure for the idea of a type of schooling different from the well-established elementary school system. The war exposed the deficiencies in British scientific and technical education so the *Fisher Education Act, 1918* made secondary education compulsory up to the age of 14 and gave responsibility for secondary schools to the state. Under the Act, many higher elementary schools and endowed grammar schools sought to become state-funded central schools or secondary schools. However, most children attended primary (elementary) school up until age 14, rather than going to a separate school for secondary education.

Early primary schooling developed in a learner-centred direction. The Hadow Report of 1926 was an influential document recommending a free two-stage education system to meet post-war demands for more education for older learners. It gave guidelines on primary schooling for the general direction of the curriculum: 'Its aim should be to develop in a child the fundamental human powers and to awaken him [sic] to the fundamental interests of a civilized life so far as these powers and interests lie within the compass of childhood' (Jenkins and Shipman, 1976: 29).

At this stage access to proper secondary education for working-class children was strictly limited. The vast majority of children finished their education at 13 or 14. It was only exceptionally that successful working-class children could gain access to full secondary schooling and higher education. As the urban populations threatened to become self-organised and a force for radical political change, governments became increasingly concerned to counter political ideals with social values and new opportunities realised through the school. Public debates about the need to change education often took the form of a tension or conflict between ideas about the health and wealth of the nation – education as a means towards economic growth, stability and improvement – and education as a social right. Clearly a major shift in the public idea of education was taking place during this period. At the same time, thought was being given to the kind of curricula that were suited to different groups within the population. Sir Cyril Norwood had read Classics at Oxford and had been Head of Bristol, Marlborough and Harrow public schools. He believed the world was divided into 'men who know … and men who don't know' (Carr and Hartnett, 1996). The Norwood Report of 1943 identified three types of curriculum.

- The first type is academic in orientation and pursues knowledge for its own sake – having an indirect relation to 'considerations of occupation'.
- The second type of curriculum is directed to 'the special data and skills associated with a particular kind of occupation'. This curriculum would always have a limited horizon and would be closely related to industry, trade and commerce 'in all their diversity'.
- The third type of curriculum balances training of mind and body and teaches the humanities, natural science and the arts to a degree which enables pupils to 'take up the work of life'. While practical in orientation it would appeal to the 'interests' of pupils and would not have as its immediate aim the preparation for particular types of work.

The Second World War seriously disrupted educational services and developments. The evacuation of children from the cities to the rural areas led to school closures and discontinuity of experience for pupils. One of the consequences of the Second World War was a public demand for the post-war world to be better than the pre-war world (Carr and Hartnett, 1996). There was concern to encourage the 'spiritual, mental and physical' well-being of the community.

1944–65 Universal secondary education – the tripartite system

In 1944 the *Butler Education Act* established a Ministry of Education with the power to influence LEAs and created a universal system of secondary education for the first time. The Act defined the modern split between primary and secondary education at age 11 and created the opportunity for a *tripartite* hierarchical system of grammar, technical and secondary modern schools as proposed by the *Norwood Committee* in 1943. The Norwood Committee had recommended that consideration be given to general needs that would pertain to all: 'in spite of differences all pupils have common needs and a common destiny; physical and spiritual and moral ideals are of vital concern to all alike' (Silver, 1973: 82). Explicitly different types of curriculum were deemed to be relevant for these pupils. The civil servants who had forged this new version of the education system drew their authority from the division of humanity expressed in Plato's *Republic*: 'You are all of you in this land brothers. But when god fashioned you, he added gold in the composition of those who are qualified to be rulers; he put silver in the auxiliaries and iron and bronze in the farmers and the rest' (1955: 160).

The moment of the 1944 Education Act is often represented as *the* defining moment in the history of modern education. Chitty suggests that the Act 'owed much to a growing appreciation among policy-makers, administrators and teachers of the importance of state education to economic advance and social welfare' (2004: 18). Secondary education was to be provided for all according to the age, aptitude and ability of each pupil. This was to be a right for all pupils, rather than being based on ability to pay, as had largely been the case before the Second World War. The Act established a nationally funded education system, which was overseen by the Ministry and administered by LEAs.

Labour won the post-war election promising a new welfare state. In a radical agenda of social transformation, nationalisation accompanied a fresh vision for social welfare and social mobility. Thus it was a Labour administration that encouraged the creation of the tripartite system under legislation passed by the previous coalition government. Labour ministers denounced those who took issue with them for promulgating a social philosophy based on three types of schools. They claimed that by abolishing fees in maintained schools they had ensured that entry to the various types of schools would be on the basis of merit. Education was made compulsory up to age 15 in 1947. The number of young people attending universities was also expanded and there was the expectation that working-class children would have access to education of the most 'complete' kind as well as of the highest quality. This advance was seen as essential as much on the grounds of realising the nation's economic and industrial potential as on grounds of social justice. A new vision of the nation as cohesive and purposeful with common goals seemed to be on the verge of realisation.

Influenced by thinking at the time that intelligence was relatively fixed and could be measured (see Chapter 6), and being given the legal responsibility to provide a suitable education, the LEAs developed the tripartite system of education in many areas. In this system pupils went to a primary school until the age of 11 where they were inducted into the school system and began learning the basic skills of the three 'Rs'. This was seen as an important time when the intelligence and aptitude of the child began to develop. In their final year of primary school, pupils took the 11-plus, an intelligence test designed to show both their ability and aptitude. Based upon the results pupils were sent to one of three types of secondary school.

1 *Secondary grammar schools* were for the more intelligent pupils with an academic aptitude. The emphasis was on traditional subjects and knowledge. It was expected that these pupils would be suitable for a university education in the future or would take a career in the minor professions or the white-collar sector.
2 *Secondary technical schools* were for pupils with a practical aptitude. Their curriculum would be based on craft and technical skills. It was envisaged that these pupils would be suited to future careers as skilled workers and engineers in industry after taking apprenticeships.
3 *Secondary modern schools* were for pupils who did not fit either of the above categories and were suited to a more general education to prepare them for their future lives as citizens and (largely unskilled) workers.

Throughout the 1940s and 1950s the Labour Party continued to defend the tripartite system but the system gradually lost credibility. Concerns were raised about the validity of 11-plus tests, especially since sociological studies revealed that social factors played a powerful role in determining which type of secondary school pupils went to. The new education system was fraught with problems. While it certainly did have the effect of enabling more working-class young people to gain access to an expanded higher education system, it remained shot through with inequalities. Statistics produced by large-scale studies of social differences in educational attainment grimly revealed that significant numbers of working-class children were failing to succeed, either by not passing the 11-plus examination which determined whether they went to secondary modern or grammar school, or by being unable to capitalise on opportunities that were on offer if they were given a place in a grammar school through a lack of financial and cultural resources (Halsey et al, 1980). The capacity for working-class children to take advantage of the opportunities that were apparently being placed freely before them became the crux of big debates about the state of education. Questions centred on where failure was to be located: the children themselves, the parents and their lack of educational nous, the school system or the whole of working-class culture which became increasingly significant in the discussion (see Douglas, 1964). There were at the same time large-scale popular 'parental' concerns over inequalities in the tripartite system that the comprehensive school was at least partly designed to confront (see Jackson and Marsden, 1962).

Criticisms of the tripartite system began to emerge and pressure to change the system grew throughout the 1960s. Though the three types of school set up in most LEAs were supposed to have 'parity of esteem' this was not the case in practice (Jones, 2003). Grammar schools were academic and therefore seen as superior. Certainly parents who had career aspirations for their children needed them to take the General Certificate of Education (GCE) O level examinations, an examination in each subject at 16 which preceded the GCSE. It was designed for the top 40 per cent of pupils and led on to A levels taken in school sixth forms which only the grammar schools offered. Increasing parental pressure was put on pupils, especially middle-class pupils, to gain a place at grammar school. Children were coached for the 11-plus and it was soon realised that this was not an accurate measure of innate ability as had at first been supposed. The whole notion of intelligence being fixed and pupils falling into one of three types became highly questionable. Academically able pupils were often also very practical and technically minded. Likewise lack of academic ability was not necessarily made up for in practical aptitude. The pressure to obtain a grammar school place affected the primary school curriculum which was increasingly based on preparation for the 11-plus.

Very few technical schools were built. Those that were came to be seen as for those too bright for secondary modern school but not good enough for grammar school. Secondary modern pupils often felt labelled as failures at 11 as they had, from the time of selection, effectively been rejected as lacking in intelligence. These schools became regarded as 'sink' schools with pupils often seeing little reason to work hard. Some secondary modern schools began to copy the grammar school curriculum by developing examination streams to enable some of their pupils to take GCE O levels. The argument that separate schools were required to provide different curricula for different abilities began to be seriously undermined. There appeared to be a great wastage of talent caused by the poor development of pupils placed in secondary modern schools. This feeling was reflected in the growing unease concerning the validity of the increasingly discredited selection procedure (see Young, 1998). The argument for abolishing the 11-plus grew. This was especially strong among middle-class parents becoming anxious at their children's chances of entering grammar schools. The more radical versions of this view were expressed by left-wing demands for the eradication of public schools in England and Wales and for the institution of a new 'comprehensive' school system (CCCS, 1991).

Walford (2001) suggests that, as a result of the problems generated by the tripartite system, the pressure for the development of comprehensive education came from a range of groups with different interests and ideologies. By 1965 the idea of the comprehensive school was well established in public consciousness. It was conceived of as a major political breakthrough in the development of the principle of equality of opportunity.

1965–88 Comprehensive schooling

The move towards the comprehensive school was designed to heal the divisions of the tripartite system; it was an attempt to provide a form of education that would cater for all. In comprehensive schools entrance is not by ability as pupils are accepted across the whole range. In the first instance these secondary schools were often neighbourhood schools, taking all pupils from a particular geographical area in which they were situated. The 11-plus was abolished in those areas which introduced comprehensive education. This immediately reduced the pressure on pupils in their final year of primary school and also on their parents. Primary schools were now more able to follow the progressive recommendations of the *Plowden Report* (CACE, 1967). Pupils were no longer clearly stigmatised as failures at 11. They were not divided up into separate schools according to ability and they could not be identified in the street by a secondary modern or grammar school uniform.

Some of these schools were new and were built to cope with expanding numbers of pupils now entering secondary education. They were large and able to offer economies of scale. The raising of the school leaving age to 16 in 1970 meant that the curriculum had to be rethought to be more inclusive (Jenkins and Shipman, 1976). This led to increased choice and diversity in the curriculum with more extra-curricular facilities available. A generation of 'ROSLA' (Raising of the School Leaving Age) children caused significant pedagogic issues for teachers who suddenly had to devise educationally justifiable but life relevant experiences for young people who in many cases wanted to be at work. Schools developed a vocational curriculum for such pupils offering courses in car maintenance, keeping allotments, child care and hair and beauty. There were also differing ways of organising the teaching in these schools. Some used setting, some streaming and, increasingly, in the 1970s, classes were of mixed ability. It is interesting to note that primary schools had always been comprehensive schools in the way this term was now being applied to secondary schools. Pupils in primary schools had also usually been taught in mixed ability classes.

Although it was never the case that there existed a single and unitary form of the comprehensive school curriculum, there were a number of tendencies that appeared to make the curriculum more relevant to the newly extended school population (Chitty and Dunford, 1999; Jenkins and Shipman, 1976). This sometimes meant the inclusion of vocational areas of study for the non-academic, but it also meant that subject boundaries began to be less rigidly adhered to. Integrated humanities and integrated science courses appeared, for example. New, open forms of assessment came into being through the Certificate of Secondary Education (CSE) examination and began to infiltrate the socially and academically prestigious General Certificate of Education (GCE). In 1985 these two different systems were unified into the General Certificate of Secondary Education (GCSE) and forms of assessment became much more liberal, flexible and open. Continuous assessment through coursework and module tests came to have equal status with end of course examinations.

'Comprehensivisation', though, was not to make a dramatic break with the thinking and practice of the time. Whilst there was the development of mixed ability teaching in a number of comprehensive schools, the majority were still to be streamed according to 'ability' (DES, 1965) though the divisions between differently labelled pupils would be more fluid and open to movement. It would appear that, while the goal of social mobility dominated, the desire to relinquish ability-based organisational structures was more muted. The comprehensive school was, however, intended to enable greater flexibility and opportunity to those whose fate had hitherto been determined at the moment of the 11-plus examination.

The project of comprehensive education, involving a break-up and reformation of the previous 'tripartite' system, was never in fact complete. Comprehensive schools were not universal, though in some areas they became the dominant form of state provision.

Reader reflection

Jones (2003) points out that during the period 1965–88, selective grammar schools remained powerful magnets in many areas and the private/public school system was largely untouched by developments in the state sector, leaving the question about inequality and an elite system open and unanswered.

There is continuing debate as to whether selective or comprehensive schooling is the most effective form of secondary education. In considering the arguments put forward for each assess the dominant underpinning ideologies. Where do you stand on this issue?

1988 – present day: Diversity and competition

Following the 1979 general election, when the Conservative party regained power, they implemented two key policy changes. New vocationalism was expanded. Labour had made some efforts beforehand, but the Conservatives expanded it considerably through initiatives such as

TVEI, the Technical, Vocational and Educational Initiative, which existed to advise schools on relevant curriculum changes. There was scepticism that the true reason for this scheme was one of a series of attempts to reduce the power of LEAs, which the Conservative government felt had too much control at a local level (Phillips, 2001). Initiatives such as Youth Training Schemes were devised ostensibly to improve the vocational training of 16 year olds but also, of course, to reduce the high youth unemployment, which was regarded as one of the causes of city riots in the late 1970s. The Conservatives also introduced the Assisted Places Scheme in 1980 which allowed 'gifted' children who could not afford to go to fee-paying schools to have free places if they passed the school entrance exam.

By the 1980s the political ideology that drove the Conservative government, that is, competition through market forces alongside a desire to return to traditional values, began to spawn a series of policies which were to dramatically change the face of modern education in Britain. These became manifest mostly through the *1988 Education Reform Act* which introduced both structural and curricular changes. These were aimed at creating a 'market' whereby schools competed with each other for 'customers' (pupils) and ensured a traditional subject-based curriculum for all pupils. The (rather crude) theory was that, in exposing the achievements of schools through close inspection of a tightly controlled National Curriculum and league tables of examination results, weaker schools would lose pupils to the good schools and would be forced to improve or close.

At this point we leave our historical overview and pick up the story of present day competition and diversity within Chapter 10 because the policy initiatives that have shaped English education since the 1988 Reform Act need careful and thorough examination within prevailing political and socio-economic influences.

Conclusion

This historical appraisal reveals huge ideological shifts and conflicts that can still be felt in contemporary values and ideas about education and the proper identity and function of the curriculum (Silver, 1973). We have seen how nineteenth-century concerns about education for the working classes being dangerous have given way to powerful, often socialist, pressures to make education accessible to the people and to reconstruct the curriculum along more inclusive and liberal lines. The seminal 1944 Act seems to have instigated many of the themes that still haunt debates about education. A central issue remains the provision of differentiated schooling. While liberally providing education for all, the Act ensured that differentiation of provision would be structurally established, a legacy that remains powerful. The contemporary curriculum, with its tensions between academic knowledge and life skills, liberal conceptions of learning and vocational training, bears something of the unresolved tensions of that history (CCCS, 1981).

We can conclude that, since the Second World War, industrial societies have seen the development of education systems in terms of the social democratic ideals of social equality. Schools and the processes of schooling are viewed as instruments of social advancement.

Expansions of the higher education system during the late 1940s, the 1960s and the 1990s represent significant phases in the development of this ideal. During these periods the school was increasingly seen as a route towards the social advancement that higher education appeared to offer. This represents a very significant change from the situation before the Second World War under the elementary school system. The transition to the tripartite system and later to comprehensive schooling was designed to enable greater numbers of working-class children to make progress through the school to higher education and thereby to social advancement. The education system, at least in the state sector, was being redefined in this process as ostensibly meritocratic. Reay (2006) has argued that this meritocracy was never realised and remains a powerful myth that helps hold the social hierarchy in place. Little change then from the power that church schooling exerted to keep the working classes in their place one hundred years earlier. This issue is examined in detail in Chapters 8 and 10.

In this chapter we have taken a fairly standard chronological approach in which we have looked at the large-scale legal and societal changes that have impacted on the school system. There are, of course, other ways of viewing this history. Important areas of educational history have been opened up by a cultural-studies oriented approach where questions might be asked about specific histories in the field of education. The role of women in the management of early board schools, for example, is one instance of a study concerned to uncover the unwritten gender politics of a small but significant segment of the history of education. Exploring the practices of schooling after the First World War in the cultivation and promotion of ideas of the nation and empire, for example, might necessitate doing some archaeological or genealogical research into textbooks, recorded events, ethnographic work with the elderly and so on. Recent historical studies include accounts of the education experiences of refugee populations in England and Wales, studies conducted of teachers' roles in resistance in Europe during the Second World War, analyses of early school photographs, and studies of the cultural and social implications of school architecture. Thus different historical studies provide different perspectives on the complex interactions of policy, institutions, practices, individuals and social groups within the field of education. Overarching histories of education may still provide useful accounts of larger movements, surface trends and changing legislative frameworks for education.

It seems self-evident, perhaps, that the study of history should be central to education studies. Understanding the processes, pressures, events, stages, linkages, ruptures and so on that give rise to the contemporary scene must be useful and productive for students of education. Studying even what may appear now as remote examples may provide useful points of reference to review and rethink contemporary dominant practices.

Student activity

It is interesting to research the history of schooling through individual case studies. Find out what you can about the history of one particular school. Evidence consisting of statistics, written accounts and pictures can be found in local and national archives, newspaper records, public libraries and perhaps from the school itself. Relate any data you find to broader social and economic events of the time and also to the history of the education system.

Recommended reading

Jones, K. (2003) *Education in Britain: 1944 to the Present*. Oxford: Polity Press. This book describes and analyses changes in education in Britain from 1944 to the early years of the 'New' Labour government. It carefully links these to wider economic, political and social developments that have occurred over this period.

Lawson, J. and Silver, H. (1973) *A Social History of Education in England*. London: Methuen and Co. Ltd. Though published many years ago this remains a very interesting and detailed text on the history of English education from Anglo-Saxon times up until the late 1960s.

5 Curriculum

Chapter 5 considers the meaning of the term curriculum. There follows an epistemological analysis that considers differing views of the nature and organisation of knowledge. These views are significant in that they are closely linked to perceptions of the world. Thus understandings of knowledge, education and the processes of research are closely related. The chapter goes on to examine curriculum frameworks that involve an analysis of aims, content, pedagogy and assessment. The significance of beliefs about the purposes and nature of education in the creation and development of any curriculum is then illustrated with reference to the National Curriculum.

Introduction

The idea of the curriculum is one of those fundamental constructs that have an embedded and taken for granted status. One of the functions of a study of education is to open up these central, and apparently given, ideas and to make them available to rethinking. If we start to ask basic questions the apparent unity and simplicity of these ideas dissolves and we can begin to probe them more critically (Foucault, 1988b). The curriculum of educational establishments such as schools, colleges and universities has a powerful legal basis and represents an important social requirement, which is regulated and kept under strict control by various institutions. Changing the curriculum can be a difficult, long-winded and bureaucratic process. All of this indicates that the curriculum and the view of knowledge and learning it embodies are regarded as important matters for governments and for the processes of governance that occur in the various institutions of education – schools, colleges and universities.

The regular and regulated curriculum that we are familiar with embodies a set of ideas and practices that have evolved. Different subjects on the curriculum have their own different histories, the traces of which can be seen in their present forms. Subjects have a 'life of their own' that is expressed in textbooks and in traditions of practice and is written into the very language of professional discourses (Ball, 1993). Subjects are 'authorised' and gain legitimacy, so they accrue institutions and embedded practices around themselves. Examination authorities such as the (English) Qualifications and Curriculum Authority (QCA) significantly influence the form and shape of curriculum subjects and the subject practices of teachers.

Teachers interpret the curriculum within the context of their own situation. Thus teachers, and therefore teaching, can be differently oriented in terms of their subject and general professional practices according to their own preferences, the culture of the department and the general ethos of the school (Jones, 1990). This represents a significant power of control by teachers but at the same time they are constrained by their role in the school and required to behave in certain ways and to subscribe to certain values. There is always a tension between a teacher's capacity to act on their individual judgement and to conform to external constraints. As Reay (2006: 292) points out:

> Teachers do not simply deliver the national curriculum and enact a positive discipline policy, they also confront contextual circumstances such as dilemmas over levels and distribution of resources, acts of violence and aggression, complex patterns of interpersonal and group relationships, power struggles for control and dominance, disputes over achievement, and issues about what constitutes 'really useful knowledge' for different groups of students. All these multi-faceted dilemmas facing teachers are imbued with gender, ethnicity and social class.

The nature of the curriculum

'Curriculum' is a term frequently used in a variety of ways by those involved in education and its meaning is often taken for granted. Hayes (2006) suggests that it is in fact difficult to find agreement on this apart from perhaps 'the sum total of what pupils need to learn' (p. 57). However, even here it is unlikely that a consensus can be reached over what pupils do actually *need* to learn. Sometimes the term 'curriculum' is used to refer to the content taught on a course. However, this is more properly called a syllabus. A curriculum is more than this and according to Jenkins and Shipman:

> A curriculum is the formation and implementation of an educational proposal to be taught and learned within the school or other institution and for which that institution accepts responsibility at three levels: its rationale, its actual implementation and its effects (1976, p. 26).

Lawrence Stenhouse expressed his idea of curriculum differently, as:

> An attempt to communicate the essential principles and features of an educational proposal in such a form that it is open to critical scrutiny and capable of effective translation into practice (1975: 53.)

The curriculum is often referred to as though it were a collection of subjects that appear on the timetable of education institutions such as schools. Kelly (2004) suggests that this is very limiting and that a broader way of looking at the curriculum is in terms of all the experiences that the school provides.

Reader reflection

How well do you think the following definition of the curriculum offered by HMI in 1985 encapsulates school life?

A school's curriculum consists of all those activities designed or encouraged within its organizational framework to promote the intellectual, personal, social and physical development of its pupils. It includes not only the formal programme of lessons, but also the 'informal' programme of so-called extracurricular activities as well as all those features which produce the school's 'ethos', such as the quality of relationships, the concern for equality of opportunity, the values exemplified in the way the school sets about its task and the way it is organized and managed. Teaching and learning styles strongly influence the curriculum and in practice they cannot be separated from it. (DES, 1985a: 11)

A whole curriculum will be a particular way of organizing these different elements. What is taught, how it is put into a particular arrangement of learning experiences, the kind of teaching methods used to 'deliver' the curriculum, and how the learning of pupils is assessed: all these things are factors in what the curriculum is. This means that the curriculum is a complex and multi-faceted 'thing' rather than just a collection of different subjects. Subjects may be important but they make up just part of the whole curriculum. Understanding the curriculum involves exploring what is taught, why it is taught and how it is taught (Husbands, 2004).

Kelly suggests that there needs to be awareness of the differences between the planned curriculum, what is intended, and the 'received' curriculum, what is actually experienced and happens. He also refers to the formal curriculum, what is timetabled, and the informal curriculum, what happens outside of the timetable and could be called 'extracurricular activities' (2004: 7). The informal curriculum should not be confused with what has been termed the 'hidden curriculum'. The hidden curriculum refers to the messages implied by school rituals: learning how to be obedient, how to cope with long periods of boredom and inactivity, and learning to remain silent in certain formal social contexts (see Bowles and Gintis, 1976; Willis, 1979). The hidden curriculum includes all the 'unofficial' learning that happens, for example the social and emotional exchanges between pupils, which for adolescents often constitute powerful motivation for school attendance with the formal curriculum at times simply being background noise. Thus it is essential that a study of the curriculum looks at the unintended experiences as well as those that are official and planned (the significance of the hidden curriculum is looked at in more detail in Chapter 7).

The curriculum is not a given but is a selection from a range of possible choices and it will therefore always represent a particular view of knowledge and learning (Hartley, 1997). The curriculum will define what is important in terms of knowledge and learning (Goodson,

1994; Helsby, 1999). Moreover, the curriculum is made. It is a social construction that sits at the very heart of the education system and gives shape and form to much of what happens in schools. Decisions based upon ideological beliefs are made at every stage in the development and delivery of any curriculum that determine what kind of knowledge is contained in the curriculum, how it is delivered, assessed and so on.

In modern state education systems, the curriculum is likely to derive from a complex amalgam of different ideologies rather than from one completely consistent, clearly defined paradigm. The official curriculum can also be considered as a public statement about what is significant knowledge. In the curriculum, ideas about knowledge are not just expressed; they carry considerable legal, social and moral force. The curriculum says, in effect: 'This is the kind of knowledge that really counts. It may determine your social future, your capacity to earn, your right to participate in social institutions at various levels.' To control the curriculum is to exert considerable power. Hence, we might assume the desire of governments to intervene in the nature of the school curriculum. The curriculum should be seen as a site for contest rather than as something given and complete in itself (Aronowitz and Giroux, 1986).

When considering English schools, for example, a number of stakeholders can be identified who all have varying influence on the official and delivered curriculum.

- Civil servants drew up and politicians voted upon the legal framework of the curriculum and this remains at the centre of political debate and policy.
- Ofsted inspectors influence how the curriculum is taught because inspection grades affect public league table position which in turn impacts on parents' choice of school.
- Employers are involved with schools through governance, attendance agreements, work placements and so on, passing opinions on to headteachers, governors, and local and national politicians.
- Local authorities (previously local education authorities) support schools in their authority offering professional development courses for teachers and other school personnel as well as support services for pupils with a range of needs.
- Parents have a vested interest in the school and the quality of the learning experiences for their children.
- Teachers deliver the curriculum and pupils will respond to this in different ways.

Thus there are many different groups that can influence how the curriculum is made manifest and how it evolves.

The structure of knowledge

EPISTEMOLOGY

Epistemology (theory of knowledge) is concerned with questions of knowledge, how we know what we know and how we may orient ourselves to what we don't know. Epistemologists may ask questions of knowledge, its sources, its history, its 'provenance', its claims to authority and where these derive from. Issues about the relations between the knower and the known, between teaching and learning, between individuals and institutions would also concern them. Enlightenment or modernist epistemology can be characterised by a certain kind of faith in progress. It is associated with the rise of scientific knowledge. Descartes (1596-1650) is most frequently cited as the first thinker of the modern period to confront the question of knowledge and consciousness, responding to the question: How can I be sure that I know what I know?

Descartes could only be certain of anything because he could be certain of himself as a thinking subject. For Descartes it is self-consciousness that guarantees knowledge. Immanuel Kant (1724–1804) was fascinated by the critique of knowledge proffered by the sceptics of the eighteenth century who pursued a line of thinking that meant that certainty about anything could not be guaranteed. His philosophy is an elaborate attempt to confront that uncertainty and scepticism with a thoroughly logical account of human understanding and knowledge. Kant's ideas, though radical at the time of their introduction into European thought, are now so deeply embedded that they can be said to be fundamental to Western thinking. Rationality was seen as the very stuff of thought and, through conflicts between different ideas, new knowledge and ideas come into existence which are themselves transformed and surpassed by others (Hegel, 1770–1831). This rationalism came to dominate thinking, for example Darwin detected progress in the order of beings in nature through his law of natural selection.

We are born into a world of knowledge and meaning that pre-exists the individual. We don't each of us have to find out everything for the first time. We draw on existing and established forms of knowledge held by others and this raises the question of authority and power in the process of knowledge acquisition. Children may be encouraged to explore the world around them for themselves. Some models of education emphasise the investigative nature of learning but children must also acquire established skills and knowledge, like reading, for example, which they cannot make up for themselves. This always requires the submission to a prior authority, an order that precedes the individual. Our knowledge of the world is the product of a complex network of factors: family background, formative experiences, cultural identity, social class, gender and language are all contributory to our sense of who we are but also our sense of what the world is like and what constitutes significant knowledge. Different ways of life and belief systems will inevitably produce different knowledge and different orientations towards it.

Knowledge comes not just as a body of 'facts' about the world; it comes packaged in a certain style. Official knowledge as expressed, for example, in the school curriculum may clash with alternative forms of knowledge that may belong to the lifestyles and belief systems of different cultural groups (Eagleton, 2000). In recent times the awareness of cultural difference and of its impact on schooling has increased. In the USA this has produced some quite fierce debate about the language of schooling and the cultural exclusion of African American children in particular (Delpit, 1995; Smitherman, 2000).

KNOWLEDGE – ABSOLUTE OR PROVISIONAL?

We may tend to think that knowledge is not tied to beliefs and values and that the square on the hypotenuse is really, in some incontestable way, the sum of the squares on the two opposite sides. After all, it has been proven to be the case and it would seem very strange now to argue that the world is really flat. Its roundness has been long established. It is the case, though, that knowledge, no matter how well established scientifically, cannot be totally fixed and absolute. It is always, in some way, relative and contingent, even though for the practical purposes of living we must behave as though certain knowledge is simply true and reliable.

Clearly there are degrees of provisionality here. We would be deeply unhappy if we thought, for example, that the science of aerodynamics relating to flight engine technology was a kind of open-ended affair dependent upon opinion and belief. But even this kind of hard scientific technical knowledge rests on premises about matter, about physics and so on that are changing all the time. Thankfully the form of practical knowledge that enables aeroplanes to be effectively managed through take-off, flight and landing is secure (although conditions do change above the speed of sound). Aerophysics is changing constantly and revisions are being made to knowledge in this area, hence new technologies of flight have come into being over the past one hundred years. We may, for good reasons, think of medicine as a well-established field of contemporary research and knowledge. We are aware, however, of the developmental nature of medical knowledge and that new discoveries and technologies of treatment are emerging all the time. Scientists frequently argue about the precise nature of the tiniest particles of matter and whether they are particles or waves of energy, just as historians argue about the precise methods for the dating of archaeological evidence. Thus scientific, medical truth is not absolute at any time, but it is often represented as such or at least as unquestionably authoritative.

ORGANISING KNOWLEDGE AS SUBJECTS

Influential educational theorist, Basil Bernstein (1995) considered the organisation of knowledge in the medieval period, giving an account of two different and specialised types of knowledge in the medieval university. Mental knowledge is classified, Bernstein explains, into two different systems: the trivium and the quadrivium. Briefly, the trivium is concerned with logic, grammar and rhetoric; the quadrivium is concerned with astronomy, music, geometry and arithmetic. The trivium is studied first and the quadrivium follows. The quadrivium cannot be studied without the trivium. In effect, what Bernstein is describing is how knowledge came to be divided up in the medieval period in Europe and organised into a system. Bernstein goes on to examine the changing classifications of knowledge that occur in the modern period between the nineteenth and the twentieth century. Here he writes about singular forms of knowledge giving the examples of physics, chemistry, sociology, psychology and how they come to be reorganised into new formations: medicine, architecture, engineering, information science or education, for example. In these knowledge regions, different singulars may come together and mingle to produce quite new forms and orders of knowledge. What

Bernstein is describing here is the historically changing patterns of knowledge and the curriculum.

The idea of the curriculum as the organisation of knowledge into separate subject areas has developed powerfully through state education systems (Bourdieu and Passeron, 1977; Bowles and Gintis, 1976). It was Paul Hirst, as recently as the 1970s, who believed that the curriculum could be related to universal 'forms of knowledge', distinct areas that have their own concepts. These must be testable against experience and they each have particular criteria for establishing this relation with reality. Hirst (1975) divided knowledge into the following seven forms: mathematics, physical sciences, human sciences, history, religion, literature and the fine arts, philosophy and moral knowledge. In order to be fully educated we need to study all of these forms. It is this view of knowledge which structures the present day curriculum in schools and which still exerts powerful influence over subject divisions in other academic institutions like sixth form colleges and universities, for instance. Fields of knowledge exist which cut across these forms. These are created by borrowing from several forms. Examples of fields would be business studies or geography. Knowledge is deemed to inhere in specific subjects that fit within a particular form. They may relate to one another but also have their own discrete and different sets of ideas, practices and contents. These are not just collections of facts but include ways of looking at things and modes of understanding. Each subject follows its own rules and practices with its own discourse.

Counter to the idea that knowledge is fixed, complete and knowable is the idea of knowledge as constructed through social activity. Different social practices, engaged in by different groups of people, will necessarily give rise to different types of knowledge and different ways of knowing. Foucault (1977b) sees knowledge systems as shifting according to the dominant 'episteme' or regime of knowledge. These systems are not progressive and may differ radically from one historical period to another. More recently Henri Giroux and others have challenged the forms of knowledge and pedagogy inherent in contemporary state and national curricula as limited and excluding (Aronowitz and Giroux, 1986).

Young (1971) considered how knowledge can be organised through the curriculum and teaching groups to exercise control over pupils. He was interested in the way that only some pupils are given access to high status knowledge, i.e. those in the top sets who are seen as the most able. Those in the lower sets are given watered down versions of subject knowledge. They are often channelled into low status subjects with a vocational emphasis. Thus teachers are 'gatekeepers' to knowledge, allowing or denying access to pupils. These issues are dealt with in more depth in Chapter 8.

POSTMODERN PERSPECTIVES ON KNOWLEDGE

Postmodern views of the curriculum characterise it much more as a provisional social construct rather than as the expression of functional and intrinsically important knowledge. In the postmodern world, knowledge is at the centre and controlling it is a means to exercise power. Knowledge in this view is always contested and what we take for progress, the steady march of science, for instance, towards more inclusive and more powerful explanations of the world, is really the victory of one set of ideas and one kind of knowledge over others (Harvey, 1991; Lyotard, 1986). Education institutions are endowed with the power to grant social status on individuals, to award them credentials, and to authorise ideas and practices with the status of socially significant knowledge. Individuals receive status through accreditation systems that validate their knowledge at different levels, thus producing a knowledge hierarchy.

In contemporary global conditions, knowledge is rapidly changing shape and form, largely under the influence of new, electronic means of storage and distribution. Some knowledge becomes commercially very significant and its circulation increases via new technologies. Knowledge becomes more fragmented and more specialised. Hybrid forms of knowledge are produced (as with cultural studies, for instance). The conventional institutions of knowledge – schools, colleges, universities – become subject to the logic of performativity, required to be more cost-effective and more productive and measured against performative criteria (Lyotard, 1986).

In summary, this brief look at knowledge has indicated that some thinkers within the functionalist tradition have espoused the singular view that the conventional curriculum of schooling (as in the case of the National Curriculum in England and Wales, Australia, New Zealand and South Africa) follows the shape and logic of knowledge itself. Against this position is the idea that the curriculum is actually shaped by a number of forces, many of them having little or nothing to do with education or knowledge. We have seen it claimed, from a critical sociological position, that the curriculum embodies what has been set as knowledge by powerful groups in society. It has also been argued that knowledge is actually always a contested field, that the value of what is learned is of less importance than the social authority that learning in institutions carries with it. It has been suggested that discourses of knowledge are historically 'contingent', that they appear and hold authority according to the social pressures that give them legitimacy rather than according to their 'scientific' truth.

Having considered the nature of knowledge, how it is organised and how certain forms of it gain ascendancy through ideological positioning, we can now examine the structure of curricula.

Curriculum frameworks

Marsh (2004) suggests the use of frameworks – a list of significant headings – to help design and also to analyse existing curricula. Thus when analysing a curriculum, or even a part of a curriculum, it is useful to consider it under headings such as: aims and purposes, content, teaching and learning principles (pedagogy), and assessment of learning (adapted from Marsh, 2004: 21).

AIMS AND PURPOSES

There are many forms curricula can take and these reflect the different aims they were designed to achieve. The current National Curriculum in English schools, for example, aims to provide a broad and balanced education for all pupils in state schools between the ages of 5 and 16. This involves promoting their spiritual, moral, cultural, mental and physical developments and preparing them for adult life (see page 88). The effectiveness of the curriculum can thus be judged in terms of how well it does these things.

Other curricula may be much more specific in their aims. Much vocational training, for instance, has a clearly defined set of practical skills and knowledge in which trainees are expected to demonstrate competence to successfully complete the programme. It is very important to consider aims and purposes as we would expect these to greatly influence the content, methods of teaching and learning, and forms of assessment that make up a curriculum.

CONTENT

Many considerations govern the content of a curriculum and these stem from its overall aim or purposes. What kinds of knowledge should be taught? What values do they represent? How useful are they? How relevant is this knowledge? Practical relevance, of course, is not the only criterion for establishing the value of knowledge. There may be powerful cultural reasons for learning certain things. Subjects like French and German provide good mental exercise and require the application of discipline in learning and applying rules so it is unimportant whether or not the subject content is pertinent to the needs and demands of modern life. The training involved in conjugating French verbs is transferable to any kind of learning whether academic or worldly. It could be said to be about training in the acceptance of authority and as such is a way of averting more creative kinds of learning. Others might say that the kind of learning embodied in the declining of Latin nouns or reading Shakespearean texts is actually about joining a learned caste, becoming a member of an elite social group who may recognise and relate to one another through their common heritage of 'useless' but socially powerful knowledge.

The characteristic content of the school curriculum is defined in terms of subject knowledge but also in terms of the kinds of thinking and related skills – literacy and numeracy, for example – that might be deemed to be appropriate for learning. Subject organisation implies different and discrete areas of knowledge. The National Curriculum for England and Wales had ten specified subjects when it was first introduced. It named three core subjects (English, mathematics and science) and seven foundation subjects (history, geography, technology, music, art, physical education and, at secondary level, a modern foreign language). This selection of subjects indicates a particular view of knowledge and learning. The terms 'core' and 'foundation' suggest a hierarchy of knowledge with all the concomitant tensions which that implies (Skilbeck, 1994).

One of the issues with basing a curriculum around subjects is that a significant decision has to be made by someone about which subjects to include and which to leave out. Even when a subject has been included it should not be assumed that the content within it is in any way a given. At first sight, deciding what to teach in mathematics and science may appear unproblematic. In reality, however, what is included in these subjects and how the material is taught and learned are hotly contested issues (see Patmore, 2006 and Walton, 2006 for a discussion of maths and science curricula). Such struggles over prioritisation of content take place in all subjects. What aspects of history, for example, should be taught? History looks very different when presented from different perspectives. The Scots, English and French do not necessarily interpret British and European history in the same way. How we teach about the slave trade or the rise and fall of the British Empire can be very contentious. When teaching geography what regions do we give preference to? Do we consider our own part of the world to be more relevant or important than other regions? Such decisions about content and its presentation relate to all subjects to a greater or lesser degree.

There are various ways of organising curriculum content. These may not be subject based, but instead organised around key experiences. Several commentators on the modern school curriculum have looked at the idea of moving away from strict subject boundaries and have advocated that learning, teaching and assessment be structured around critical themes where a number of different conventional subject areas can meet. Stenhouse for instance, working for the Schools Curriculum Council in the 1960s, advocated a more integrated approach to curriculum design that centred on themes or issues rather than separate subjects. He developed the Integrated Humanities Project that aimed to make the content more relevant to the learners. He felt that subjects created artificial boundaries that made understanding more difficult. In an integrated curriculum when learning about their local environment, for example, a pupil would look at aspects of history, geography, and social and moral education. Pupils would collect information, measure, count, present results and produce written accounts. They would be 'doing' different subjects simultaneously and learning the appropriate skills in an applied way. Whilst these applied methods of empirical work endure in the way pupils are taught today, Stenhouse's ideological position on curriculum organisation conflicted with the more traditional view of subjects held by those who drew up the National Curriculum in the 1980s.

This discussion has centred on the school curriculum and we must remember that this is just one area of education. In vocational learning the organisation of knowledge is often more clearly combined with the development of practical skills. Consider, for instance, how curriculum content and knowledge can be organised very differently in apprenticeships, nursing courses and teacher education.

PEDAGOGY

Pedagogy, or the science of teaching, is concerned with the methods of teaching and learning. It involves structural features such as the learning environment, the classroom and a mode of practice, for example a teacher giving instructions or asking questions. Pedagogical ideas are in part developed from theories about how people learn. Different and contradictory accounts of how learning takes place exist and conflict with one another. (See Chapters 6 and 9 for more detailed discussion of psychological theories of learning and for further information on pedagogical trends.)

There are many different traditions of learning. In Europe, for example, there is much more emphasis on pedagogy as a distinctive branch of educational knowledge. Pestalozzi,

Montessori and Frenais have been associated with different versions of pedagogy. The challenge to institutions of learning to construct an effective and inclusive pedagogy was made by J.S. Bruner in 1972 when he claimed that any aspect of any subject could be made accessible and taught to anybody at any age. In the UK the influential Plowden report (1967) stimulated an emphasis on child-centred learning. This stressed creativity, spontaneity and individuality in an effort to draw out what was there already in the child. More recently, interest among theorists of pedagogy has turned to socio-cultural activity, using social constructivist theory that derives from Vygotsky (Engestrom, 1993). These theorists see individual learning as structured mental development. Learning is always a development of the self; it is always social and cultural. This implies a different way of organising the experiences of learning from that of child-centred approaches. Vygotskyans tend to believe that teaching must take the child forward, must be concerned with new concepts, new hierarchies of ideas and ever more complex forms of mental operation. The emphasis on subject knowledge in the National Curriculum lent itself to more traditional methods of whole class teaching and formal classroom settings but the pedagogic approaches of social constructivism have become very influential in UK schools (see Chapter 7 for an elaboration of Vygotsky's ideas).

Methods of teaching and learning give rise to questions about autonomy and authority. We might consider what are the 'best', most productive, most relevant and socially desirable forms of practice. How much should teaching and learning within a curriculum be concerned to cultivate the development of autonomy, initiative, critical awareness and other qualities that might be thought of as central aspects of citizenship? How much should it be about developing discipline of thought and acquiring important formal knowledge? Once again the answer depends upon the particular curriculum but also on how we perceive the nature and purposes of education.

Teaching and learning can take many forms. The emphasis may be on practical applications, experimentation, didactic teaching, or open learning. Even within a particular course the teaching methods can vary greatly. For instance, students learning a modern foreign language may have a very different experience from peers taking the same subject in the next room. One teacher may emphasise an interactive, oral approach to language development whereas another may stress writing and rote learning as ways of extending the students' vocabularies.

The following learning situations are commonly experienced by students:

- mass lectures
- whole class work
- small group investigation and discussion
- individual learning.

Learning activities can include making notes, use of stimulus material presented by the teacher/lecturer, investigation in learning centres and libraries, searching through electronic sources, group discussion, practical activity such as experiments or making artefacts, problem solving individually or in groups. There are many possibilities and combinations (Cowley, 2004; Petty, 2004; and Pollard, 2005 outline a range of these).

The form teaching and learning takes depends upon the particular curriculum, the nature of the knowledge, the preferences of the teachers and, sometimes, of the learners. Consider, for instance, how you might organise a learning programme for a foreign language or the history of England. Promoting learning within these programmes would be approached very differently because of the nature of the subject content in each. Furthermore, the teacher's preferred method may be experiential, active learning involving the pupils in investigative tasks. Alternatively, the teacher may have a didactic style where the students are told what to do and are given a large amount of written dictation. The methods and activities employed in learning experiences that we undertake in our daily lives will be very different again. Learning to drive a car, for example, is likely to involve practical driving activity and didactic instruction though even here the 'style' of individual instructors can vary enormously.

In summary, then, decisions on appropriate pedagogy depend upon the purposes of the learning, the type of material to be taught and the ideological views of the 'best' methods held by those 'delivering' the curriculum.

ASSESSMENT

There are many ways in which educational progress and achievement may be judged (assessed). These vary from the formal to the very informal and each provides different kinds of information from statistical results to verbal feedback.

Purposes of assessment

Assessment is conducted for a variety of reasons.

1 **To monitor progress** Here assessment will indicate how the student is progressing. This is often referred to as formative assessment or assessment for learning (see Assessment Reform Group, 2002, for an outline of the principles of assessment *for* learning). Formative assessment may be ongoing, for example regular feedback on coursework, or it may be periodic as with regular tests. It can form part of a diagnostic process providing a basis for decisions on future learning and for developing a record of progress. Assessment is seen here as an integral part of the learning process rather than as something that just happens at the end (Gipps and Pickering, 2006).

2 **To indicate a final level of achievement** After completing a course a final grade or level is often awarded as part of the certification. This is referred to as summative assessment or assessment *of* learning and is done by judging practical, oral, written or graphic course-work and examinations either against a set of specified criteria (criterion-referenced

assessment) or in relation to the achievements of a group of people (norm-referenced assessment). It is a final assessment and judgement about individuals' achievements in relation to established standards and norms (DES/WO, 1989). These assessments can of course be very significant in gaining entry into other educational institutions such as sixth form colleges and universities or for employment purposes.

3 **To evaluate the teaching and learning process** Through assessment teachers can determine which aspects of the learning students find most difficult and also the effectiveness of different pedagogical approaches. This can be done whilst the curriculum is being taught using the results from formative assessments. An end of course evaluation can be conducted that also uses the summative assessment results.

4 **To enable comparisons of achievement by external agencies** External agents such as local authorities, Ofsted, politicians and parents are able to use the results of national assessments, such as GCSE results and National Curriculum scores, to compare education institutions. This is particularly the case when league tables are compiled with this purpose in mind.

Types of assessment

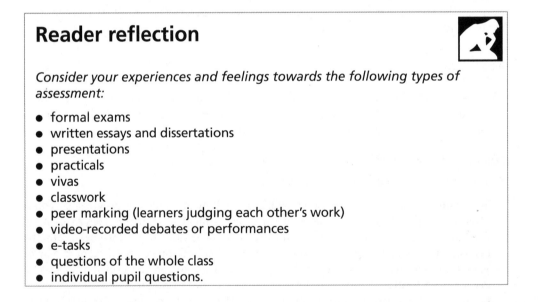

Reader reflection

Consider your experiences and feelings towards the following types of assessment:

- formal exams
- written essays and dissertations
- presentations
- practicals
- vivas
- classwork
- peer marking (learners judging each other's work)
- video-recorded debates or performances
- e-tasks
- questions of the whole class
- individual pupil questions.

The type of assessment used will depend upon the reasons for the assessment, the nature of the learning and also the ideological beliefs underpinning the curriculum. The list above moves from more formal to informal modes of assessment or from 'harder' to 'softer' forms. Formal mechanisms tend to elicit more quantitative data on performance, allow easy comparison between individuals and whole cohorts of pupils/students and may appear more objective. Those forms of assessment that provide 'hard' data may be more valued. However, whilst appearing more accurate, their validity may actually be open to question. Often the most difficult and complex issues cannot be answered through simple multiple choice type questions and so longer accounts have to be given that must be interpreted when marked. This leads to human error. It may also be open to question as to how much understanding and ability an examination is actually able to measure. The softer, more informal modes of assessment, such as discussing work with a student, may reveal the full extent of an individual's understanding. However, making comparisons of large numbers of students is impossible by such a method. Thus different forms of assessment each have their strengths and weaknesses and are compatible with different purposes.

Assessment issues in relation to the curriculum are many, complex and varied. Assessment has important public functions and can dominate curriculum processes and practices. The curriculum may be assessment-driven and risk losing sight of its broader objectives. Hall and Sheehy suggest that 'assessing learning is not a neutral or value-free activity – it is always bound up with attitudes, values, beliefs and sometimes prejudices on the part of those carrying out the assessment and on the part of those being assessed' (2006: 346). The purposes of the assessment will have a significant effect upon how both the assessors and the assessed perceive the process. For instance, formative assessment can be done in a relaxed manner that is open and honest. Both assessor and assessed may feel it to be a positive process. However, a final summative assessment, when results are to be used as part of an accountability process, is likely to be a much more anxious process for those being assessed. Because of these potential conflicts the purposes of assessment need to be clear from the outset. It is difficult, if not impossible, to devise one form of assessment that is able to fulfil all of the possible assessment functions.

It is appropriate now to consider how the elements that make up a curriculum become manifest in practice.

The National Curriculum: a case study

BACKGROUND TO THE NATIONAL CURRICULUM

Since the Second World War, and before the 1988 Education Reform Act, central government had no direct hand in controlling or defining the curriculum of schools. In the 1944 Education Act only religious education was specified as a compulsory subject and even in that case parents had the right to opt out on behalf of their children. Otherwise the curriculum was left to the control of local authorities and schools (in association with governing bodies after the 1986 Education Act). Of course this does not mean that the school curriculum was a free for all before the 1988 Act. In reality it was subject to many constraints and shaping factors that tended to ensure a degree of uniformity across schools and across the country, including external examinations such as GCE Ordinary (O) and Advanced (A) levels, school culture and well-established professional habits.

Prior to comprehensivisation, secondary modern schools had a practical and vocational orientation whilst grammar schools had a more academic curriculum, dominated by a conventional array of subjects up to 16 plus including English, mathematics, modern foreign languages, the sciences and the humanities. Comprehensive reorganisation led largely to the emulation of this grammar school curriculum throughout secondary schools. During the 1980s the secondary school curriculum in England and Wales had been broadly divided up into English (13 per cent), maths (13 per cent), science (16 per cent), design and technology (4 per cent), foreign language (5 per cent), history and geography (10 per cent), art, music, drama and design (7 per cent), PE (8 per cent) with the remaining 10 per cent taken up by other subjects (DES, 1987). Talk of the 'entitlement curriculum' (HMI, 1994), which would provide a broad and balanced diet for all pupils, had existed since the emergence of *Curriculum 11–16* (HMI, 1977). In primary schools, where there was little concern with external examinations, the curriculum was more open and could be quite varied from school to school in terms of both content and style.

We will now analyse the National Curriculum using a curriculum framework of purposes, structure and content, teaching and learning, and assessment to help us to understand its implementation and development.

PURPOSES

The National Curriculum was introduced by the Conservative government of Margaret Thatcher in the Education Reform Act of 1988 after a period of criticism of educational standards in schools (see Chapter 10 for an account of the build up to the 1988 Reform Act). The dominant political ideology of the government, termed the 'new right', comprised a combination of traditionalism and belief in the importance of market forces. This was reflected in the development of a national curriculum that emphasised a traditional approach to education and, when coupled with other Tory education reforms, promoted competition between schools. The aim of the school curriculum as stated in the first section of the Act and quoted in the implementation document, 'From Policy to Practice' (DES, 1989a) should be to provide a curriculum that is balanced and broadly based and which:

a. promotes the spiritual, moral, cultural, mental and physical development of pupils at the school and of society; and
b. prepares such pupils for the opportunities, responsibilities and experiences of adult life.
   (Education Reform Act quoted in DES, 1989a: 2)

These aims were restated in the 1996 Education Act (section 351) and are currently the values underpinning the school curriculum (see National Curriculum online, http://www.nc.uk.net). These aims are very broad, as is appropriate to a curriculum that was designed for all pupils in compulsory state education from the ages of 5 to 16. They are able to encompass all ideologies of education, as outlined in Chapter 2, since they are concerned with the individual, knowledge and preparation for a role in society.

It is in the actual structure and implementation of the curriculum that the traditional (classical) humanist influence becomes increasingly apparent.

Deriving from these aims the four main purposes of the National Curriculum are:

- to establish an entitlement for all pupils.
- to establish standards that can be used to set targets and measure performance.
- to promote continuity and coherence.
- to promote public understanding of and confidence in the work of schools. (National Curriculum online, http://www.nc.uk.net)

THE STRUCTURE AND CONTENT OF THE NATIONAL CURRICULUM

The curriculum was introduced as a legal entitlement (requirement) for all pupils in state education from the ages of 5 to 16. The teaching and assessment of the National Curriculum is divided into four key stages as follows:

- key stage 1 – up to age 7 (Years 1 and 2)
- key stage 2 – up to age 11 (Years 3–6)
- key stage 3 – up to age 14 (Years 7–9)
- key stage 4 – up to age 16 (Years 10 and 11).

The National Curriculum in England was divided into the following subjects for the first two key stages, with the first three designated as 'core' and the rest as foundation subjects: **English, mathematics, science,** information technology, design and technology, history, geography, music, art, physical education. At key stage 3, a modern foreign language is included in the requirements. At key stage 4, history, geography, music, art and a modern foreign language are no longer compulsory but have to be available for pupils to choose as part of their entitlement. All of these subjects have to be taught according to their programmes of study laid out in the National Curriculum documents. The specific requirements concerning each subject vary according to the age of the pupils.

Citizenship was added to the curriculum with voluntary subject guidance at key stage 2 and statutory guidance (meaning it has to be followed) at key stages 3 and 4. Religious education has to be provided throughout all the key stages along with sex education and careers education at key stages 3 and 4 and work-related learning at key stage 4. Schools also have a requirement to cater for the personal and social education (PSE) of their pupils.

The primary curriculum is 'supplemented' by the literacy and numeracy strategies outlined in the non statutory documents covering literacy (DfEE, 1998a) and numeracy (DfEE,

1999a). Though not a legal requirement these strategies prescribe both content and methods of teaching for English and maths in the primary school and the majority of primary schools follow them, sometimes with their own modifications, as school inspections focus particularly on pupils' achievements in literacy and numeracy.

The Education Act 2002 included the foundation stage as part of the National Curriculum. This made the following six areas of learning in the foundation stage the statutory curriculum for children aged 3 to 5:

1 personal, social and emotional development;
2 language and literacy;
3 mathematical development;
4 knowledge and understanding of the world;
5 physical development;
6 and creative development.

The early learning goals set out what most children are expected to achieve by the end of the foundation stage (National Curriculum online, http://www.qca.org.uk). Whilst many early years teachers welcome the recognition that the foundation stage brought to this phase of education, criticism has been levelled at how young children are being subjected to an increasingly formalised curriculum at the expense of exploration and play. It is felt that this may actually hinder their intellectual and emotional development (Moylett, 2003).

It is interesting to compare National Curriculum subjects with the subject regulations for 1904 and 1935 (Mayes and Moon, 1994: 248):

1904	1935
English language	English language
English literature	English literature
One language	One language
Geography	Geography
History	History
Mathematics	Mathematics
Science	Science
Drawing	Drawing
Due provision for manual work and physical exercise	Physical exercises and organised games
(Housewifery in girls' schools)	Singing
	(Manual instruction for boys, domestic subjects for girls)

The National Curriculum is not intended to take up all of the time pupils are in schools but there are no statutory regulations about how schools should divide up their time. The Dearing Report of 1993 made some recommendations indicating that English should occupy

14 per cent, maths 12 per cent, Science 13 per cent, technology and foreign languages, RE and PE 5 per cent each, and that the remaining 43 per cent should be discretionary but should include a balance of other specified subjects (Dearing, 1994).

TEACHING AND LEARNING IN THE NATIONAL CURRICULUM

Decisions about how to teach the curriculum were left to the teachers. However, the content that was prescribed in detail for all subjects when the curriculum was first introduced had to be taught to all pupils. All pupils were to be assessed, as described in the next section, and the results made public in the form of performance tables for each school. The 1993 Education Act saw the creation of the Office for Standards in Education (Ofsted) which was to inspect every school at least once every four years. These factors put great pressure on teachers to ensure that they covered all aspects of the curriculum and left them little time to deviate from it. Effectively they had to 'teach to the test' in order to ensure the highest possible pupil scores in the assessments. Clearly this pressure led to a narrowing of the range of pedagogic methods teachers could employ and to some extent stifled the creativity of both teachers and pupils.

ASSESSMENT IN THE NATIONAL CURRICULUM

It was the assessment framework that gave shape to the National Curriculum, drawing criticism that the assessment tail was wagging the curriculum dog (Gipps and Stobart, 1993). The framework was established by the report of the Task Group on Assessment and Testing led by Paul Black (DES, 1989b). It represented a major break with the school-based assessment traditions of the past as it established national, externally marked tests at ages 7, 11 and 14. The programmes of study for each subject are set out in booklets published by the Department for Education and Employment and the Welsh office (some together and some separately). Each subject is divided into different attainment targets, as illustrated here for the core subjects of English, mathematics and science.

Table 5.1 *Attainment targets for English, mathematics and science*

English	Mathematics	Science
En1 Speaking and listening	Ma1 Using and applying mathematics	Sc1 Scientific enquiry
En2 Reading	Ma2 Number and algebra	Sc2 Life processes and living things
En3 Writing	Ma3 Shape, space and measures	Sc3 Materials and their properties
	Ma4 Handling data (KS 2 – 4)	Sc4 Physical processes

For each attainment target in most subjects nine successive levels of attainment are identified. Each of these has level descriptions. In effect this means that the National Curriculum sets out how pupils should make progress in each subject area from the very beginning of their studies at age 5 to the end of key stage 3 at age 14. These levels do not coincide directly with key stages as there is recognition that children may differ in their rates of progress. However, it is specified that by the end of each key stage, the vast majority of pupils should have levels of attainment within the following ranges:

- end of key stage 1 – levels 1 – 3
- end of key stage 2 – levels 2 – 5
- end of key stage 3 – levels 3 – 7.

There is also a level 8 for 'very able' pupils and a ninth unnumbered level for 'exceptional performance' at key stage 3. These levels of achievement do not apply to key stage 4 when pupils will be taking GCSE, nor do they apply to art, music or physical education at any stage. These subjects have end of key stage *descriptions*, setting out the achievements expected of most pupils at the end of each of the four key stages.

CRITICISMS OF THE NATIONAL CURRICULUM

So it was that the National Curriculum, a historical milestone in the history of education in England and Wales, came into being. It was attacked in many ways and on many grounds at the time (Bash and Coulby, 1989; Lawton and Chitty, 1988; Pring, 1989). In the years following, the National Curriculum has continued to receive critical treatment from educationalists many of whom agreed with the principle of a National Curriculum but deplored the process of its implementation and development, lamenting the unimaginative form it has taken (Lawton, 1999). Complaints included the absence of a clear educational purpose, its disregard of recent debates about curriculum and the failure to engage in detailed and sustained consultation with teachers and other education professionals. There was early pressure to reconsider the curriculum as originally established.

The original National Curriculum was critiqued on the following grounds:

- It was too bureaucratic.
- It centralised control of education.
- Private schools were exempt.
- The curriculum was felt to be too traditionalist and too conventionally academic in orientation.
- There was an enormous amount of content to be covered that left little time for exploration outside of the formal curriculum.
- Testing at 7 and 11 was felt to be dangerous in terms of labelling.
- The theoretical ideas underpinning the notion of cumulative achievement within all subjects was challenged (Gipps, 1993).

The testing regime put great pressure on pupils and teachers alike. It was felt that the National Curriculum worked against the spirit of comprehensive reform that had envisaged the development of a school curriculum based on the idea of a common culture (Lawton, 1975).

Some critics (Ball, 2003) have claimed that the National Curriculum favours certain (middle-) class groups above others. It has also been accused of working against the cultural orientations of ethnic minority groups in its historical, cultural and linguistic biases (Gillborn, 2001). Thus the history syllabus was primarily British (English) history that stopped at the end of the Second World War. It took no account of more recent world conflicts such as the Middle East crisis, the cold war, the decline of the British Empire. In English the literature studied was British and all pupils had to study Shakespeare. The emphasis given by the National Curriculum to Christian religious traditions has also been noted as symptomatic of cultural bias (Troyna and Carrington, 1990).

It was in the introduction of national standards that the National Curriculum was felt by some commentators to be most likely to accentuate class differences. The introduction of standardised age-related testing has been represented as meaning that children will be ranked and ordered as never before and that their value to the school, in the labour market and in the sphere of education will vary accordingly. For some this means that the National Curriculum is a massive machine for differentiating children against fixed norms – a very powerful, pervasive form of control. The decision to publish test results exacerbated these fears at a school level on the grounds that it could further disadvantage schools operating in deprived areas. In some schools these league tables of results led to the organisation of pupils on ability grounds, a policy later encouraged by the Labour government (see DfES, 2005). Even at primary level this is now commonplace. Known as setting, this approach has been criticised on grounds of equality of opportunity but sits well within a differentiated school system with grammar schools, city technology colleges and later specialist schools, academies and trust schools.

Increasing pressure from teachers and parents provoked a review of the National Curriculum and the arrangements for testing in 1993 by Ron Dearing. This made some relatively small changes to the structure of the National Curriculum but could not achieve the radical rethink that some called for. Nor could it provide the kind of ideological rationale and professional support for the curriculum that it lacked from the outset (Chitty and Dunford, 1999). In the main, subsequent changes have been in the form of cutting subject content requirements, making some subjects optional thus allowing increasing specialisation at key stage 4 and limiting national assessment to the three core subjects.

FINAL OBSERVATIONS ON THE NATIONAL CURRICULUM

Whilst there were significant problems initially in terms of the sheer volume of content, assessment and bureaucracy associated with the National Curriculum, these have been steadily ironed out over time. When first introduced, the curriculum was very traditional and as such only reflected the beliefs of a small ideological base. The appeal of the curriculum has broadened under pressure from different stakeholders. It has become increasingly flexible with the introduction of more vocational learning and the creation of subject options, particularly in older year groups. Whilst still remaining largely traditional, the curriculum now has a wider ideological appeal. Having been in place for nearly 20 years the National Curriculum is all that current pupils and a substantial proportion of teachers have known, the subject content and assessment being regarded as 'normal'. What we need to remember is that this curriculum is just one possible structure. It reflects the dominant ideologies that introduced it and the political power of the different groups who have helped to shape it.

Conclusion

The impact of different ideologies and beliefs on the creation, positioning and structure of a curriculum has been illustrated. We have seen that the nature of knowledge and views on what it is important to 'know' play a central part in the design of any curriculum. Knowledge can be structured and presented in different ways. In the context of modern schooling, traditional subject knowledge may be seen as important or knowledge may be presented thematically. Thus teaching and learning can take many different forms depending upon the purpose of the curriculum and the beliefs of the teachers. Assessment is a fundamental element of the curriculum and can take many forms. These different forms of assessment reflect what those designing and delivering the curriculum see as important in terms of student outcomes. They are tied very much to the purposes of the curriculum and beliefs concerning the nature of education.

The structural features of the curriculum are thus influenced by the purposes and beliefs of the teachers, course designers, examination boards, government ministers and established discourses. The final delivered curriculum is often the result of a complex interaction and power struggle between the various interested parties.

Student activities

1 Look at the DfES website and find the National Curriculum online: http://www.nc.uk.net. Read the section entitled 'Values, aims and purposes' and identify the key words and any important contrasts that are set up. To what extent do these concepts inform the subject-based curriculum that is available on the same web pages?
2 Look again at the National Curriculum online website. Examine the section, 'Learning across the curriculum'. Comment on this section considering why it is included and defining your own thoughts and reactions to it.
3 Some critics have suggested that the curriculum should be rethought, and that the traditional subject-based curriculum is moribund and anachronistic. What might be included in a radical rethink of the curriculum, in terms of contents, experiences, teaching and learning, assessment? Is it possible to define a new programme for learning? What would be the basis for this new curriculum and how would it meet the needs of contemporary conditions and people?

Recommended reading

Marsh, C.J. (2004) *Key Concepts for Understanding Curriculum*. 3rd edn. Oxon: RoutledgeFalmer. As the title suggests this is a basic text on curriculum. It covers all areas of curriculum development including defining, planning, assessing and managing as well as discussing significant ideological issues. This is a very useful book for education studies undergraduates.

Moon, B. (2001) *A Guide to the National Curriculum*. 4th edn. Oxford: Oxford University Press. This guide provides a comprehensive outline of all aspects of the National Curriculum giving details of the content and mechanics involved.

White, J. (ed.) (2003) *Rethinking the School Curriculum: Values, Aims and Purposes*. London: RoutledgeFalmer. This book considers the aims and purposes of the National Curriculum. Each of the component subjects is examined in turn thus providing a useful overview of the curriculum.

6 Individual achievement: major psychological theories

Chapter 6 focuses on the individual and achievement from a psychological perspective. It examines briefly the influence of philosophy on ideas about how the mind works and explores the concepts of self, intelligence, cognition, personality, creativity, motivation and metacognition. The major perspectives on learning are outlined including behaviourism, Gestalt theory, Piaget's cognitive-developmental theory and the information-processing approach.

Introduction

A focus on the individual points us in the direction of psychological research since it is concerned with individual *cognition*, that is knowing, understanding, remembering and problem-solving. It is also able to illuminate our understanding of human behaviour, motivation, achievement, personality and self-esteem. Throughout this book we maintain that perspective influences the explanations we develop for phenomena. Psychology is no different so it is important to briefly chart the most significant influences from within philosophy from which different views about the way mental processes work have been derived. We will also give an overview of the seminal work of the earliest psychologists and of classic twentieth-century psychological research which is relevant to education.

Leaving a long-established legacy are:

- the debates of seventeenth- and eighteenth-century philosophers about rationalist and empiricist explanations of human understanding
- the earliest psychological investigative approaches of introspection and functionalism
- behaviourist theory with its emphasis on external stimuli for learning
- gestalt theory which developed principles of perception grounded in the brain's search for 'wholeness'

- personality theories – psychoanalytic, psychometric and humanist explanations
- motivation theories – instinct, drive/need and cognitive explanations
- creativity and intelligence theory – the impact and controversy of IQ testing
- cognitive-developmental theory – Piaget's maturational explanation of human development and learning
- cognitive psychology: schemata and concepts; information-processing theory – processes of attention, perception and memory.

The influence of philosophy

The French philosopher Descartes' seventeenth-century notion of the *dualism* of mind and body still prevails as a common-sense explanation of the mechanistic, material body existing in parallel with something quite non-material, the mind. The work of neuroscientists shows us, of course, that the mind is just as material as the body but to think of it so mechanistically does not sit comfortably with most ordinary people.

Think, for example, how easily we use expressions like 'in my mind's eye'.

Similarly, the seventeenth- and eighteenth-century argument about whether knowledge exists outside of human reasoning and experience is still played out today. *Rationalists*, like Descartes, believed that there is knowledge beyond experience, the existence of God for example, or of abstract ideas like 'triangle'. *Empiricists*, on the other hand, maintained that all knowledge derives from experience. Thus Locke, a late seventeenth-century English philosopher, believed children were born with a blank slate for a mind on which all learning and experience is imprinted. He advocated individualised instruction and control of self through reward and punishment. In contrast, in the eighteenth century the Swiss Romantic, Rousseau, believed that talent and genius were inborn along with an innate sense of right and wrong. He advocated a free, unrestrained environment which the child would explore, learning at their own pace. These ideas could be found over a century later within the progressive movement of Montessori education for example.

What follows from these differing perspectives are very different accounts of the way the mind works. Thus empiricists see the mind as an information-processing device which applies processes of attention, sensation, perception and memory to each new stimuli (experience). Conversely, rationalists, and a subsequent related group of thinkers, *nativists*, governed by their belief that some ideas are innate, maintain that the mind is similarly preprogrammed with an inherent structure of concept development and language acquisition. Researchers within these opposing traditions necessarily take different approaches to psychological study, with the starting point of empiricists being objective, experimentally acquired data on human behaviour from which theories about mental processes are developed. Rationalists and nativists will start from their theories of a priori knowledge and innateness of mental structures and explore how these are manifest within human behaviour. Three centuries on, the nature/nurture debate is still alive and well with much research data now available to support both sides of the argument.

Brook (1999) describes Immanuel Kant, the eighteenth-century philosopher, as the single most influential figure of pre-twentieth-century cognitive thinking. A rationalist for most of his life, he was strongly influenced by David Hume, the British empiricist who distinguished between ideas and impressions and gave an early account of concept formation. Kant theorised that mental representation requires concepts *and* sensations. In other words, we need information to make judgements about, but we also need to be able to discriminate (Brook, 1999: 427). *Representationalism* held that thoughts are intermediaries between the physical objects or abstract ideas we experience and the internal mental structures of our minds.

> *If you think about 'kindness' you are representing a socialised act that you have experienced using the mental structures of concept formation and discrimination.*

Much more recently a parallel theory was developed by Fodor (1975). Fodor espoused a Language of Thought, a mental language through which we are able to think and reason. Kant was the first theorist of the modern era to suggest that the mind was a system of functions, a position which continues to spawn much research.

Early psychological ideas

The earliest psychologists did not emerge until the late nineteenth century. Darwin's (1859) work on origins of species was influential in establishing child psychology as a scientific discipline. Preyer, a German researcher interested in ontogenesis (the origin and development of individual beings), is sometimes said to be the father of modern psychology. The earliest psychologists used methods of *introspection* – reporting on one's own feelings and thoughts – to find out how minds worked. Wilhelm Wundt established the first psychological experimental laboratory in Leipzig in 1879 where he studied behaviour through experimentation and systematic self-observation methods. He believed that ultimately the only way to systematically study the differences in societies' beliefs, language, personality and social cognition was to detail everything about those societies.

Around the same time William James was working in the USA, on the first modern psychology textbook (James, 1890). He was very interested in states of consciousness and took a phenomenological approach to their analysis; in psychology *phenomenology* holds that each person's perception of events or experiences is unique and determines how the person will react, therefore the study of psychology should be these individual perceptions. Like John Dewey, James developed a *pragmatic* or *functionalist* explanation for phenomena – that words and thoughts are only meaningful in relation to the purpose to which they are put.

> *Thus a school is not defined conceptually in terms of its physical properties as a building but in relation to its purpose as a community of learning.*

Similarly, mental processes were seen as adapting to the function in hand and, as such, functionalists stressed the need to examine mental phenomena within natural contexts. Influenced by Darwin's new theory of adaptive evolution, they also believed that mental processes transcend species such that, for example, the processes involved in moving from one place to another would be fundamentally the same whether within human or animal because their function or goal is identical. This signalled a move away from introspective methods which could not be used to examine the behaviour of other species.

In contrast to functionalism, other early psychologists were interested in the structure rather than the function of mental activity. Ebbinghaus (1885) used introspective methods to study memory systematically; he memorised hundreds of nonsense syllables and then studied the rate of memory loss at recall. He established the importance of *associations* in learning, that is, adding to what is already known. The modern day version of this is *connectionism* in which a cognitive architecture of ever-increasing neural connections is proposed as an explanation for thinking and understanding.

BEHAVIOURIST THEORY

Introspection had obvious drawbacks in terms of reliability because of its first person perspective; nevertheless, the contribution of these early psychologists was fundamental to the discipline's development. Approaches concentrating exclusively on observable behaviours emerged in the early part of the twentieth century through the work of the Russian physiologist, Pavlov (1927) and of Thorndike (1911) in the USA. Pavlov trained dogs to salivate through the association of external stimuli (a buzzer) with food and Thorndike measured how long it took cats to escape from puzzle boxes, outside of which their food lay. This behaviourist school of psychology was developed further by two US psychologists, Watson (1913) and Skinner (1957), who revealed laws of stimulus–response, conditioning and reinforcement. Watson famously claimed that he could teach a child anything. These psychologists realised that *classical conditioning*, where new signals are acquired for existing responses, could be contrived to create associations or 'learning'. An example of this can be presented as:

Unconditioned stimulus Teacher instructs pupils to work quietly.	**Unconditioned response** Pupils work quietly on tasks.
Conditioned stimulus with additional stimulus Teacher instructs pupils to work quietly while putting her fingers to her lips.	**Unconditioned response** Pupils work quietly on tasks.
Conditioned stimulus Teacher puts her fingers to her lips.	**Conditioned response** Pupils work quietly on tasks.

You will probably be able to recall situations in which your behaviour has been classically conditioned. For people of the authors' ages, for example, the sight of a dentist's chair can evoke fretful behaviour! Sometimes unpleasant experiences become irrationally associated with particular places, colours, odours or even people. A teacher who is constantly carping at pupils while teaching them mathematics might condition pupils to dislike the subject.

Operant conditioning is when rewards and punishments are used within teaching. Instructional programmes and schemes designed to help learners with special educational needs use a simple, incremental design wherein a small step in learning, for example forming a letter of the alphabet or adding a simple sum, is followed by the positive reinforcement of being correct. Primary schools have for many years adopted the use of stickers, smiley faces and merit stars to reinforce pupil learning. Positive teaching schemes which train teachers to use praise, ignore poor learning behaviour and reward good learning behaviour were developed in the 1980s by Birmingham psychologists, Wheldall and Merrett (1985) (Merrett, 1998). An assertive discipline scheme (Canter and Canter, 1977; Kavanagh, 2000) also became very popular in schools in many countries during the 1990s. Since then such systems have become more sophisticated with a greater emphasis on the social aspects of behavioural improvements. Nevertheless, all such schemes are external to the learner, encouraging and reinforcing learning behaviour, so they do not reveal knowledge of the learner's cognition. Although achieving results in the short term, teachers will be mindful that external reinforcers have a limited life expectancy, for example, with a recalcitrant, self-conscious 14 year old or a 9 year old who has received her fiftieth smiley face.

The challenge in education is to harness the external reinforcer to an intrinsic desire to learn through a sense of personal achievement. Albert Bandura (1977) thought that reinforcers were not always necessary because children learn from watching or listening to others – *observational learning*. Society encourages parents and teachers to model good behaviour, attitudes and values for children to learn from. The strength of peer modelling has been noted for some time and there is concern that a 'laddish' ethos among boys encourages them to feel that working hard in school is not 'cool' or masculine. In the USA Luiselli et al (2005) reported favourably on a positive behaviour scheme based on 'the application of positive behavioural intervention and systems to achieve socially important behaviour change' (Sugai et al, 2000: 133). Positive Behavioural Support (PBS) models include the design of individual student behaviour support plans but have, as a primary goal, the implementation of prevention practices that target the entire school population.

Stimulus–response theory was predicated on a very simplistic form of *associationism* wherein each response becomes the stimulus for the next, thus forming an associative chain. Although attractive, this explanation does not account for the creativity which individuals bring to their thinking.

> *If somebody says the word 'egg' to you, multiple chaining is possible because you might associate egg with omelettes but also with ornithology or Easter.*

Wilson (1999) contended that the external processes of behaviourism must have corresponding internal processes which generate them and vice versa. In other words, we are not reinforced in a way of behaving unless we have reasoned, even at some basic level, about the consequences of consistently performing that action. In its most extreme form, behaviourism seems not to concern itself with these internal cognitive processes. Noam Chomsky (1965) criticised the principles of behaviourism for their failure to explain complex human behaviour such as language and communication. Chomsky argued that there are pre-existing mental structures including an innate language structure that has a latent grammatical structure which develops as an individual matures. Behaviourism dominated psychology during the first half of the twentieth century and, as we have seen, its influence is still felt; it was not until the 1960s and 1970s that the focus on mental processes begun in the nineteenth century was revived.

GESTALT PSYCHOLOGY

An alternative view to behaviourism, 'gestalt' psychology, was developed simultaneously in Germany by Wertheimer (1923), Koffka (1935) and Kohler (1940). They were disdainful of behaviourism and associationism for their treatment of sensory experiences as independent segments of experience. Gestalt psychologists maintained that animals and humans perceive things and events in their most simple, unified form as a coherent whole, 'that the whole is greater than the sum of its parts' (Gavin, 1998: 14). They used perceptual experiments which indicated that people tend to reorganise information to impose order on it, for example by extracting an image from its background (figure/ground principle), by grouping things together if they are in close proximity (principle of proximity) or by completing missing lines to create a whole picture where, for instance, a triangle shape is drawn with a break on one side (principle of closure).

> *Think about what happens when look at a sentence which has one word missing – you perceive the word to be there in order to allow you to make sense of the sentence. Now read that sentence again!*
> *Have you spotted the missing word that you inserted?*

These principles can guide teachers towards appropriate ways of presenting information to pupils to aid their understanding. Whereas behaviourists explained that trial and error led to the solving of problems through the development of associations, gestalt psychologists believed that animals and humans developed insight in order to determine the solution. These views were influential within research into the perceptual processes of cognition but were criticised for *describing* rather than *explaining* perceptual activity (Hayes, 2000).

Social psychologists emphasise the importance of seeing cognition embedded in its context – personal, social and environmental. Personality development, social cognition and motivation have all to be understood if an individual's education is to be maximised.

Personality theory

There are a number of distinct approaches to personality; we will deal with the main three – psychoanalysis, psychometrics and humanism. Looking back briefly to how the Greeks explained personality differences by reference to bodily fluids gives some idea of the diversity of views in this field. The Greeks associated:

- a *melancholic* personality – pessimistic, suspicious, depressed – with black bile
- a *sanguine* personality – optimistic, sociable, easygoing – with blood
- a *phlegmatic* personality – calm, controlled, lethargic – with phlegm
- a *choleric* personality – active, irritable, egocentric – with yellow bile (Child, 2004).

While the association with bodily fluids might be hard for us to accept, we will all recognise the personality descriptors used.

PSYCHOANALYTIC THEORY

Freud's (1901) psychoanalytic theory has influenced psychological study because of his ideas about the unconscious processing of information. Freud denied the supremacy of a single governing self-will and, like early cognitive psychologists, contended that behaviour derives from the interaction of complex internal systems. He proposed that personality development depended on stages of psychosexual development. While many of Freud's ideas have been opposed, the notion of stages of development governing personality was pursued further by Erikson (1980) who proposed eight stages of conflict resolution which people go through during a lifetime. Erikson's stages of psychosocial development explain the way in which an individual's self-concept develops. For instance, adolescents go through a role identity conflict which must be resolved in order to progress healthily to young adulthood. In schools teachers often encounter, and try to deal sensitively with, the identity confusions young people experience. Harter's research (1985) has since indicated the significance of teacher–pupil relationships for pupils' feelings of self-worth in relation to learning competence. Davies and Brember's (1999) eight-year study showed significant correlations between self-esteem and attainment scores. Garaigordobil and Perez (2005) conducted a study to assess creative behaviour and creative personality traits with 139 children aged 10 to 11 years. They found that creative children display many positive social behaviours and few negative ones – high self-concept, ability to analyse emotions, empathy and high intelligence.

Psychoanalytic explanations of personality development are known as *idiographic* because they are concerned with how the features of individuals contrive to shape personality behaviour.

PSYCHOMETRIC APPROACHES TO PERSONALITY

In contrast, others, most notably H.J. Eysenck and R.B. Cattell, were interested in *nomothetic* explanations – the comparison of individual features with those of the averages or norms of the rest of the population. This approach had already been used within the psychometric method of intelligence testing. The emphasis of behaviourist approaches on the search for objective evidence also impacted upon the development of personality theories. Thus Eysenck (1947) developed self-report measures which sampled an individual's responses to situations which were said to reveal underlying personality traits. Through factor analysis Eysenck revealed two independent dimensions of personality: extraversion–introversion and neuroticism–stability. In 1976 he added a third dimension: psychoticism–normality. Since these qualities were thought to be normally distributed throughout a population, the average person would score at the midpoint of each dimension. Only exceptionally would an in dividual be found to be extremely introverted or neurotic and so on but variations would be found along the three dimensions. Behaviour traits were said to be associated with certain personality types, for example the more extraverted person would present as outgoing, lively and gregarious. Interestingly, Eysenck found the personality types outlined by the Greeks to be fairly accurate. When integrating the characteristics of his two dimensions, it can be seen that a stable extravert, for example, corresponds well to the description of a sanguine personality (Hayes and Orrell, 1998).

The criticisms of Eysenck's approach are first, that in isolating just three personality dimensions there is an oversimplification of a complex phenomenon and, second, that self-report measures are unreliable in that they are affected by mood and context at the time of completion. Eysenck (1967) postulated that the inheritance of features of the nervous system could account for basic personality type differences. He explained that the cortical arousal system required different levels of stimulus in extraverts from that needed by introverts. Similarly, he thought that people who inherited a strong automatic nervous system – the part which deals with stress – were likely to react more to emotional situations, in other words to exhibit more neurotic behaviour.

Reader reflection

Considering the biological basis of personality in this way can be helpful to teachers in understanding something of why pupils behave or present as they do. Eysenck developed questionnaires for use with adults and separate ones for children.

If too much stimulus is known to be counterproductive for introverts or too little stress affects neurotics adversely, teachers can try to create different conditions according to individual personality traits.

Obviously this cannot be achieved individually for each person in a class of 30 but the teacher can be sensitive about expecting introverts to thrive on a lot of noise or neurotics to fare well without a certain amount of drama in their lives.

How much cortical arousal do you thrive on? Do you notice differences in this regard between yourself and others in your peer or study group? Do the different levels seem to fit the personality types of yourself and your peers as Eysenck suggested?

Raymond Cattell (1970) also developed a trait theory of personality, using factor analysis of questionnaires to determine 16 source traits of personality. He developed a test known as the 16PF which is widely used, especially in the selection of people for certain jobs. Often headteachers and others in education management are given the 16PF at interview to examine whether they exhibit the right profile for the post. The test provides a profile of an individual's personality across the 16 dimensions. These include, for example, expedient–conscientious, timid–venturesome, relaxed–tense. Cattell's theory has been criticised for oversimplification and for ascribing too rigid a set of characteristics which does not fully capture the range of human personality behaviour.

One personality assessment instrument that retains favour in both education and work settings is the Myers Briggs Type Indicator (MBTI)/(Myers Briggs et al, 1998). The MBTI is a self-report questionnaire based on Carl Jung's personality types. The MBTI assesses people across four scales: sensing–intuition; extraversion–introversion; thinking–feeling and judging–perceiving. Fallan (2006) used this instrument with business studies students in Norway, concluding that the student's personality type affects both the most effective mode of learning and even the student's selection of major areas of study. He found the most dominant personality type among business students is the sensing and judging (SJ) student. SJ students select subjects where facts, procedures and sequential learning are the usual mode of learning. Hough and Ogilvie (2005) explored how cognitive style, as measured by the MBTI, affects strategic decision-making of senior executives. They found that sensing/feeling types used time to see if their decisions were considered socially acceptable, which led to the lowest number of decisions and the lowest perceived effectiveness of all. Extraverted managers were perceived as being more effective than introverted managers when, in fact, the extraverts were no more decisive than introverts.

With all self-report instruments, the issue of whether people give what they feel to be socially acceptable responses and whether different situations or frame of mind would spawn different answers has to be considered when using the test. It is probably safest to take the view that these tests may provide a skeletal guide to personality types but that only a deeper knowledge of the individual concerned will flesh out the story.

HUMANIST THEORIES OF PERSONALITY

It is helpful to briefly examine studies from social psychology which elaborate the influence of social interaction on personality and behaviour. In 1902 Cooley wrote about the 'looking-glass self' in describing the socially interactive nature of self-perception. The critical role of significant others in this analysis was also a feature of Carl Rogers' (1983) view of personality which was grounded in the notion of the developing self-concept. Rogers believed that every individual has an inbuilt need to reach their potential, that is, to *self-actualise*, and an equally important need for approval from others. The centrality of this led Rogers to argue that the personality could not be perceived as separate traits as the psychometric approaches proposed but as a coherent whole (Hayes and Orrell, 1998). In order for self-actualisation to be successful the individual has to have experienced unconditional approval, usually from parents, in order not to worry about how their views and talents will be regarded and therefore be free to pursue and develop them. Where children have been granted approval which is always conditional on good behaviour, they tend constantly to seek approval from others. This can sometimes manifest as deviant school behaviour as they strive for approval from their peers. It can also appear as setting very high standards for themselves that they almost always cannot reach. The healthy development of the self-concept is therefore fundamentally important and teachers are now taught to appreciate this in their dealings with young people (Lawrence, 2006).

Mboya (1995) investigated the relationship between perceived teacher behaviours and adolescents' self-concepts with 874 students from four high schools in Cape Town, South Africa. Perceived teacher support, interest, encouragement and expectations were found to be positively related to adolescent self-concepts. The relative significance of teachers is dependent less on their perceived status than on the organic nature of their relationship with individual pupils. Lawrence (2006) has suggested that teaching is more effective where the teacher is able to establish a close relationship with pupils. A differentiated classroom, where a choice of tasks increases the pupils' ownership and direction of the learning, may enable the pupil to define the parameters of teacher and peer involvement. The extent to which a teacher or peer is significant to the pupil will be a factor in this definition. In a more tightly structured, 'closed' classroom environment which relies on greater teacher input and direction, the pupil's control over who shares in the learning process is restricted. Thus a pupil for whom the teacher is not significant may have little commitment to either the task or the guidance. If significant others affect an individual's learning, framing a context where the pupil can control this would suggest a greater potential for learning, for instance the organisation of group work could, on at least some occasions, pay heed to pupil friendship groups.

PERSONAL CONSTRUCT THEORY

George Kelly's personal construct theory (Kelly, 1955) does not fit into any of the three traditions described above. His is a phenomenological approach which explains the uniqueness of personality development and learning behaviour by reference to the personal constructs which people use to make sense of new situations, information and so on. Kelly believed that we react not to a stimulus but to what we interpret the stimulus to be (Child, 2004). He developed a technique known as *repertory grid method* which reveals bipolar constructs held by individuals in relation to significant others. Thus an individual may hold a construct such as sensitivity–brashness; another person might see sensitivity juxtaposed with strength (for a full description of the technique and its applications see Ravenette, 1999). Differences in pupils' behaviour and responses would be deemed a product of the various theories they have to explain events, which are in turn a product of their previous experience and analysis of it. Theories or *constructs* are progressively refined as more interactions occur. Sets of constructs held by pupils about learning in a particular subject will therefore differ, as will the teacher's. If the teacher holds a construct which defines reticence of oral response as lack of understanding rather than as uncertainty of the context or shyness, they might adapt their instruction in a way which is inappropriate to the learner's needs. The pupil's construct of oral response may include a perception that the ownership of the vocabulary lies with the teacher, or it may be shaped by cultural and ethnic reference points at variance with those of the teacher.

Henderson-King and Smith (2006) researched the meanings that undergraduate students ascribe to their education and how these meanings relate to their understanding of the constructs of academic motivation and values. Ten meanings emerged including career preparation, independence, making social connections, changing the world, stress and escape. It would be interesting to conduct this same research with their tutors to explore the extent to which their meanings converged with those of the students.

Given that there is a limit to which teachers and learners can clarify their constructs within their interactions, it would seem best to foster a learning situation in which the individual constructs of all participants can be accommodated (see Burton and Anthony, 1997, for a case study example). Such a situation would involve pupil-centred learning, peer interaction, individualised learning and self-monitoring. Opportunities for testing and extending these constructs, that is opportunities for learning, might thus be liberated from the framing effect of the teacher's constructs so that pupils, with access to resources and support, could interpret the task and develop their learning according to their own frames of reference. In so doing, they might construe the situation more inventively such that the constructs are altered through what Kelly calls 'constructive alternativism'. (See Crozier, 1997, for an account of personality differences in education.)

Motivation

Healthy self-esteem is fundamental both to learners' academic performance and to their emotional well-being since it affects motivation. Leo and Galloway (1996: 35) found that recent developments in the study of motivation highlighted a range of cognitive-based processes such as children's attributions for their successes and failures, perceptions of control over their own learning processes, metacognitive processes, self-perceptions of ability and beliefs about the utility of effort (Dweck, 1991; Nicholls, 1989; Weiner, 1979; 1992). Reviewing studies in this area, they warned that:

> the National Curriculum and resultant pedagogic practices could serve to foster debilitating cognitions in primary children about their abilities if, in practice, comparisons among primary children become more salient. School-level practices that emphasise, and focus upon, ability comparisons can interfere with classroom-level practices that foster task-related or mastery goals (Maehr and Midgley, 1991), thus undermining task-oriented classrooms. Orienting classrooms and pupils towards individual and not ability evaluations has been claimed to increase and sustain motivation. (Elliott and Dweck, 1988: 41)

Within education it has traditionally been thought that a certain amount of competition between individuals increases motivation. The dangers in such an approach are, however, clear. Inevitably, differences in ability impact on the outcomes of a competitive learning situation and, in order for some to win the competition, others have to lose. Covington (1998) has exposed the detrimental effects of competition on motivation, pointing to the tendency of learners to avoid the risk of failure by not attempting things and to the demise of learner integrity which is encouraged by competitive practices. Neither can a competitive approach to learning be reconciled with some of the current influences on education. The collaborative approaches suggested by social constructivists, for example, would be antithetical to a competitive learning environment.

High levels of motivation to learn among students must be the holy grail as far as teachers are concerned. The differences between teaching a self-motivated adult and a recalcitrant 15 year old are well known and theories of motivation are helpful in explaining these differences.

Child (2004) provides a useful examination of motivation theory, noting the early twentieth-century instinct theories derivative of Darwin and Freud, the drive and need theories of the 1930s and 1940s, and the cognitive theories of the 1950s and 1960s. To these might be added behaviourist theories since Skinner's ideas about reinforcement of behaviour highlight the effect of praise and punishment on motivation to learn. Instinct theories emphasised the animal urges and instincts humans are born with, for example instinctive fight and flight responses. Drive and need theories differentiate between the basic survival needs of hunger, thirst and warmth, and the secondary or social needs such as the need to achieve, to dominate, to affiliate with others and so on. A very well-known drive or need theory is Maslow's (1954) hierarchy of needs which explains that basic needs must be satisfied before the drive for the higher-level needs of love and belonging, high self-esteem and, finally, *self-actualisation* or the achievement of one's full potential can be aspired to. In some cases pupils come to school with some of their basic needs not met as they arrive hungry or poorly clothed. Others may feel unloved. If Maslow is accurate in saying that these needs must be attended to first before the child can begin to be interested in any form of self-actualisation through learning, teachers need to be very sensitive to individual differences. Given that these needs *are* met, teachers have an important role to play in creating the circumstances which will facilitate self-actualisation. Pupils need to feel safe and valued in class, they need to be listened to and empowered to make decisions about their learning.

Cognitive theories give weight to the role of thinking within motivation, which it is contended plays a greater part than instinct and need/drive theories allow. They also point to the effect of an imbalance or cognitive dissonance between normal performance and unexpected performance (Festinger, 1957). For example, if a pupil normally passes tests quite easily but one day fails, this could either motivate them to try harder to redress the failure or it could lead to avoidance of that particular subject. An example of a cognitive theory is Rotter's (1966) *locus of control* theory in which those with strong internal control believe that it is by their own efforts and talents that they will succeed and those with strong external control believe that any success or progress they make is down to luck or other external factors such as task difficulty. This was developed further by Weiner (1972) into *attribution theory*. As well as attributing their successes and failures to internal or external factors, Weiner argued that learners attribute them to stable causes like ability or unstable causes such as effort. This attribution affects how future tasks are then approached, for example if a pupil attributes failure to unstable causes or internal locus of control they are more likely to persist in the face of failure (Child, 2004). Conversely, attribution to stable causes and external locus of control will lead to minimal effort because responsibility for the failure is being attributed outside of the learner.

Covington claims that many minority pupils 'exhibit an external locus of control. They feel like pawns of fate, buffeted by forces beyond their control' (1998: 63). Most of our readers, as adult self-determining learners, will of course attribute their success or failure within education studies to unstable, internal causes such as effort levels! It can be a major challenge, however, to encourage adolescents to take responsibility for their own learning. Child points out the link to McClelland's (1955) theory of *achievement motivation*. Pupils with a high need to achieve usually attribute any failure to internal causes of lack of effort while low-need achievers attribute their failure to external factors. McClelland's work was developed further by Atkinson (1964) and shows the complexity of the dynamic between success, failure and motivation. Repeated failure, unsurprisingly, does not motivate learners to achieve; a mixture of success and failure can be productive; fear of failure is usually destructive because it leads to safer, lower-order tasks being chosen. Covington explains that it is not so much the event of failure that disrupts academic achievement as the meaning ascribed to the failure. 'Thus, rather than minimising failure, educators should arrange schooling so that falling short of one's goals will be interpreted in ways that promote the will to learn' (1998: 75).

Capel and Gervis (2005: 122–3) provides a useful chart comparing the theories since the 1950s, which we have looked at above. They also include McGregor's (1960) *Theory x, Theory y* ideas about managers. This is relevant because teachers manage learning and learners. Theory x managers assume the average worker is lazy, lacks ambition, is resistant to change, is self-centred and not very bright, while *theory y* managers assume the worker is motivated, wants to take responsibility, has potential and works for the corporate good of the institution (Capel and Gervis, 2005: 123). Relating this to teachers, they explain that a theory x teacher externally motivates pupils with controlling actions while theory y teachers encourage intrinsic motivation through self-development. Phillips and Lindsay (2006) in a recent small-scale study with 15 gifted 14–15 year olds in England found that both intrinsic and extrinsic motivation were important to student achievement. Intrinsic motivation in learners is clearly more productive than extrinsic motivation, not least because it does not require reinforcement through external rewards and punishments. Sometimes, however, teachers will provide these external reinforcers initially with the aim of encouraging task success in learners which will in turn create intrinsic motivation as a product of the pleasure derived from that success. This behaviourist approach to motivating learners could be seen in Wheldall and Merrett's (1985) positive teaching programmes which advocated positive teacher reinforcement for good learning behaviour. Motivation is a complex area of study because it involves personality factors, social and environmental factors, previous experience, the developing self-concept, physical well-being and so on. The interplay of these influences on human behaviour inevitably results in a very individualised picture of learner motivation.

Intelligence and creativity

Individual differences in human competence and performance have always provided a rich research ground for psychologists, the fruits of which are invariably controversial. Francis Galton (1869), a British psychologist of the second half of the nineteenth century, was interested in the hereditariness of genius, advocating the need to measure individual differences. His work laid the foundations of what has developed into probably the most contentious explanation of individual differences, intelligence testing theory, or psychometrics, which seeks to measure the ultimate intellectual power an individual has. The first test was devised for the French government by Alfred Binet and Theodore Simon in 1905. It is important to note that right from these early beginnings the intelligence test was devised for the practical purpose of determining how well a child might do in school. Not surprisingly, then, the test contained items which resembled school tasks, such as comprehension of facts and relationships, vocabulary measures, and mathematical and verbal reasoning (Bee and Boyd, 2007). Soon afterwards Lewis Terman of Stanford University modified and extended the test, developing the Stanford-Binet which has tests for each age of child and can be used from around age 3. Terman (1924) derived the child's 'intelligence quotient' by dividing the mental age the child had achieved in the test by its chronological age and multiplying this by 100. Nowadays an individual's score is compared with the scores of a huge standardised sample of children of the same age. The average score is still 100, however, with the majority of children scoring between 85 and 115. The very few who achieve very high scores of above 145 are said to be

Reader reflection

Intelligence testing is attractive because it enables us to categorise and pigeonhole people and, despite years of critique of its theoretical foundations and its methodological weaknesses, some version of intelligence quotient (IQ) testing is still used in many schools today to indicate potential. One of the major problems is being sure that it tests what it purports to.

If school type tasks are included, can training in those tasks help?
Does reading ability play a part in the outcome?
Do different cultural and linguistic experiences affect an individual's performance on the test?

In fact, it is very difficult to isolate underlying competence because the individual's experience, disposition, motivation and health on the day of the test will all impact on the outcome.

'gifted' and those with scores below around 55 are said to have moderate to profound 'retardation' (Bee and Boyd, 2007: 185). A score of 115 was said to be the threshold for passing the 11-plus examination to attend grammar school (Child, 2004).

Thus, to some extent, an IQ test is a test of achievement. Nevertheless, Bee and Boyd (2007) cite research which indicates a fairly strong correlation between IQ score and school achievement grades. In terms of stability of test results, Bee et al (1982) found that a typical correlation between a Bayley mental test score of a 12 month old and the score of the same child at age 4 on the Binet test was only .20 or .30. While this does indicate a significant correlation, it is a long way from a perfect correlation of 1.

At the heart of the controversy over IQ testing is the question of whether it tests some innate, immutable ability. Hebb (1949) distinguished between Intelligence A – innate potential entirely dependent on neurological facilities – and Intelligence B – interaction of Intelligence A with the environmental influences upon an individual. In this analysis Intelligence B can vary while Intelligence A cannot (see Child, 2004). Child notes that neither is directly testable and that the best we can manage is indirect sampling of some aspects of intelligent behaviour using standardised tests.

A number of intelligence theories were developed during the twentieth century. Charles Spearman (1927) believed two types of intelligence could be identified by IQ tests – g factor (general ability) and s factors (various mental abilities detected in different degrees by different tests). Cyril Burt's *Hierarchical Group-Factor Theory* proposed group factors of intelligence as well as g and s factors because many tests involved a number of skills at the same time, for example verbal ability together with a specific ability (Child, 2004). General ability was thought to govern a series of abilities such as verbal, spatial, practical and numerical skills which themselves interacted with specific abilities measured by each test item. Thurstone (1938), a US psychologist of the 1930s, felt that g and s abilities should be compounded to give a range of factors known as *primary mental abilities* which provided a broad profile of abilities rather than an overall measure. These included verbal comprehension, number ability, word fluency, perceptual flexibility and speed, inductive reasoning, rote memory and deductive reasoning. Guilford (1950) proposed a model of the intellect which had 120 mental factors derived from three independent aspects of intelligent acts. The individual carries out *operations*, such as remembering or thinking, using *content* like symbols or figures, in order to *produce* outcomes, for example relations or implications. Albert and Runco (1999) point out that Guilford's seminal work on creativity challenged the simplicity of intelligence testing which sought to locate people along a single dimension. Guilford (1967) suggested that measuring intelligence and creativity was far more complex than this. He posited two forms of thinking: convergent, wherein a single correct answer is sought, and divergent, which produces a whole range of possible answers. Cattell (1963) defined two types of intelligence. *Fluid* intelligence includes reasoning and memory processes and spatial performance, and Cattel thought it to be hereditary; measures of it vary according to the individual's processing speed at the time of measurement. *Crystallized* intelligence reflects the accumulated products of processing carried out in the past and can be tested by general knowledge and vocabulary questions; Cattell maintained that it is influenced by environment and is therefore likely to increase with education and experience (Salthouse, 1999).

In 1955 Cyril Burt, the British psychologist, claimed to have found high correlations between the IQ scores of 53 sets of identical twins who had been brought up in different environments. These findings were very influential because they seemed to indicate the relative lack of importance of environmental factors to intelligence. The English education system paid great attention to Burt's conclusion that there should be different types of education depending on innate intelligence. His argument supported the separation of children into grammar and secondary modern schools. In 1976, however, Burt's findings were exposed as fraudulent. As Hayes noted, 'this is an important case, because it shows how ready people were to believe that IQ is inherited' (Hayes, 1993: 146). Burt's figures were also used as the basis of further studies, for example Jensen's (1969) controversial race studies. Jensen argued that intelligence was 80 per cent inherited and 20 per cent environmental. However, as Chapter 8 explains, Labov's work on linguistic/cultural differences in relation to educational achievement debunked the myth of black unintelligence.

Reporting on research studies which throw light on the relative influence of hereditariness and environment, Bee and Boyd (2007) cite Bouchard and McGue's (1981) studies of the few pairs of identical twins reared apart which found a strong correlation of between .60 and .70 in their IQ scores. However, more detailed analysis of the cases revealed that the less similar the environmental circumstances the less correspondence is found between twins' IQ scores. The nature/nurture argument is more productively approached, then, by examining the interaction of heredity with environment. Weinberg (1989) proposed that genes establish a *reaction range* for IQ which can vary as much as 25 points depending on the environmental conditions the child grows up in. Thus findings that black children score lower on IQ tests than do white children by as much as 15 points can be accounted for within Weinberg's suggestion of an environmentally determined 25 point range. The debate about genetic intelligence was revived in the mid-1990s by the publication of the highly controversial book *The Bell Curve* by Herrnstein and Murray (1994) in which it was reported that African-American children consistently score lower than Euro-American children on IQ tests. Despite the 12-point gap falling within the accepted Weinberg reaction range and despite substantial evidence of differences in the environmental conditions of the two groups, Herrnstein and Murray argued that the findings signified fundamental genetic differences in intelligence. Their claims created a furore and a spate of research studies emerged to categorically refute them (see Cooper, 1999, for an account of the research).

Nettelbeck and Wilson (2005) concluded from their review of intelligence theories that there is evidence of a general ability that can be tested by IQ tests. They cautioned, however, that such tests should sample a broad range of different intellectual domains in addition to general ability. In Chapter 7 the issue of intelligence is picked up again as the interest in this phenomenon is still intense and newer theoretical positions have been developed.

Cognitive-developmental theory

PIAGET'S MATURATIONAL THEORY

The concept of maturation (genetically programmed sequential pattern of changing physical characteristics) was developed by Arnold Gessell in the USA in the 1920s (Gessell, 1925). The concept of maturation was applied to cognitive growth by Jean Piaget, a Swiss psychologist of the twentieth century, whose work has enjoyed very wide influence within education. Piaget (1932; 1952; 1954) explained cognitive growth as being driven by an internal need to understand the world. He saw intellectual and moral development as sequential with the child moving through stages of thinking. Piaget's theory is one of maturation in which the learner's stage of thinking interacts with his experience of the world in a process of *adaptation*. Piaget used the term *operations* to describe the strategies, skills and mental activities used by the child in interacting with new experience. Thus adding 2 and 2 together, whether mentally or on paper, is an operation. Discoveries are made sequentially, for example adding and subtracting cannot be learned until objects are seen to be constant. Progress through the sequence of discoveries occurs slowly and at any one age the child has a particular general view of the world, a particular logic or structure that dominates the way they explore and manipulate the world. The logic changes as events are encountered which will not fit with the *schemata* (sets of ideas about objects or events) the child has constructed. When major shifts in the structure of the child's thinking occur, a new stage is said to be reached. Central to Piaget's theory are the concepts of *assimilation* – taking in and adapting experience or objects to one's existing strategies or concepts – and *accommodation* – modifying and adjusting one's strategies or concepts as a result of new experiences or information (see Bee and Boyd, 2007, for a full outline of Piaget's theory).

Table 6.1 *Piaget's stages of cognitive development*

Stage	Age	Description
A.		
B. Sensorimotor	Birth–2 years	The baby 'understands' the world in terms of what they can do with objects and of their sensory information. A block is how it tastes, feels to grasp, looks to the eye.
C. Pre-operational	2–6 years	By about 18–24 months, the child can represent objects to themselves internally and begins to understand classification of objects into groups and to be able to take others' perspectives. Fantasy play appears, as does primitive logic.
Concrete operational	6–12 years	The child's logic takes a great leap forward with the development of powerful new internal mental operations, such as addition, subtraction, class inclusion, and the like. The child is still tied to specific experience but can do mental manipulations as well as physical ones.
D. Formal operational	12 years +	The child becomes able to manipulate ideas as well as events or objects in their head. They can imagine and think about things that they have never seen or that have not yet happened; he/she can organise systematically and exhaustively and think deductively.

Source: Bee, 1985: 228

The application of Piaget's theory to education

The neatness of Piaget's theory rendered it appealing to educationalists. The 11-plus test fitted well, for example, with the age at which children were thought to begin abstract or formal operations. Investigative and experiential methods, often referred to as 'discovery learning', were readily inferred because they provided cognitive conflict – the jarring of cognitive structures or schemata to promote new learning. The Plowden Committee, which reported in 1967 on primary education, was influenced by such maturation theory, advocating child-centred, experiential approaches to learning. It is easy to see, however, that a theory which specifies stages of capability can set up expectations about learning readiness – that children only learn effectively if their educational experiences are suitably matched to their current level of understanding. This can then determine the content and pace of instruction. If a child has not reached the anticipated stage the teaching will be too advanced. If the child has gone beyond it the teaching could constrain potential achievement. In the same way that intelligence testing can establish an arbitrary ceiling on learning, the rigid application of Piaget's theory could also place limits on achievement. Nevertheless Piagetian principles are still influencing research. A study in Slovenia, for instance, by Krnel et al (2005) into the development of the concept of matter asked children aged 3–13 to describe objects and substances placed in front of them. Children's responses were coded and explored for patterns indicating development with age and analysed from a Piagetian perspective, which hypothesises that the epigenesis of concepts takes place through children acting on the world. The study found that through their actions children gradually develop more elaborated schema that enable them to distinguish between extensive and intensive properties, and hence between object and matter.

Criticisms of Piaget's work

Many have argued that there are problems with Piaget's theory. It says nothing about individual differences, social context or modes of learning. The child is viewed as a system of developing logic, not as a social, emotional being. The importance of language to thinking, a significant component in any model of human development, is underplayed: other psychologists, such as Vygotsky and Bruner, demonstrated language and socio-cultural linguistic differences to be fundamental to learning, as we shall see in Chapter 7.

Piaget used clinical, decontextualised methods with a very limited sample of middle-class children including his own children. When experiments were repeated with account taken of the importance of context, the power of children's thinking was found to be in advance of Piaget's claims (Donaldson, 1978; Hughes, 1975; McGarrigle and Donaldson, 1974). The success rates among 4–6 year olds were much better when tasks were not disembedded from the context, were made relevant to children's experience and when the children understood what the experimenter wanted. These findings called into question Piaget's claims about young children's egocentricity, revealing a more precocious ability to decentre (to see things from another's point of view in space and time), and about their ability to 'conserve', understanding, for example, that the volume of a liquid remained the same despite its movement to a differently shaped vessel.

Piaget's theory of stages has been seriously challenged too. Although he conceded that the structures or operations (coordinated principles, rules or strategies that are applied across problems or tasks) do not develop all at once, he did imply that all learning could be approached at the same operational level. However, we know that while, like now, we operate at a formal operational level dealing with abstract ideas, we very often operate in our day-to-day lives at a concrete level, needing actual objects or events to work our logic on, for example the use of diagrams. Bee (1992) claimed that the information we have does not show that children are very consistent in their level of performance across tasks. She cites much research to support her (Bee, 1992: 273).

Piaget's legacy

John Flavell, a one-time student of Piaget, concluded that human cognitive growth is generally not very stage-like (in Bee, 1992). He did, however, attest to the sequential nature of learning, saying 'sequences are the very wire and glue of development. Later cognitive acquisitions build on or are otherwise linked to earlier ones, and in their turn similarly prepare the ground for still later ones' (Flavell, 1982: 18). Within any given task, then, there seem to be predictable sequences shared by most children. The key task for teachers is to examine the progress of individuals in order to determine readiness to deal with increased intellectual demand.

Piaget's work can be said to have influenced the ideas of some other psychologists. Kohlberg (1976) posited links between children's cognitive development and their moral reasoning, proposing a stage model of moral development. Selman (1980) was interested in the way children make relationships, describing a set of stages or levels they go through in forming friendships. The stress on the idea of 'stages' in Piaget's theory has thus been quite far-reaching but a rigidly staged model of development is probably less helpful than the features of development the various stage theories describe.

Cognitive psychology

Despite the pre-eminence of behaviourism in the USA during the first half of the twentieth century, an interest in cognitive psychology was maintained by European psychologists such as Frederick Bartlett (1932) who developed the notion of schema. The value of Bartlett's work was not recognised until 1975 when Minsky, a computer scientist, read his book and developed from it the notion of frames of knowledge within artificial intelligence (Brewer, 1999). Rumelhart and McClelland (1986) later related these connectionist models of schema and concepts to psychology. The correspondence between how computers and the human mind process information had fascinated researchers since the 1960s when the *information-processing* approach to explaining cognition became the dominant view. Connections had already been drawn between cognitive processes and neural mechanisms, and there was a renewal of interest in the processes of attention, perception and memory which paralleled the huge advances in computer intelligence. As early as 1943 the British psychologist, Kenneth Craik, likened the brain to a computer. Essentially information-processing theorists proposed that sensory experience (sounds, sights, tastes, smells and tangibles) is perceived and selectively attended to, depending on the individual's motivation, other distractions or emotional state, analysed within a short-term memory and stored within a long-term memory. This process is usually presented graphically as:

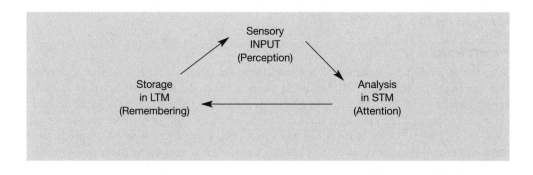

SCHEMA AND CONCEPT DEVELOPMENT

Bartlett (1932) introduced the important idea of *schema* to account for the fact that we do not reproduce facts when we recall them, rather we reconstruct them. Schemata are the organising vehicles which we have built up in our minds from previous experience and knowledge which we then use to analyse new information. If you are presented with a new concept within your studies your tutor will probably attempt to explain it by reference to something you have already studied within that area, thus allowing you to employ the relevant schema. The material held in the long-term memory is stored as 'schemata' ('schema' is the singular) – mental structures abstracted from experience. They comprise sets of expectations which enable us to categorise and understand new stimuli. For example, our schema of higher education includes expectations of students, lecturers, students' union and so on and is refined as we gain more experience and more information is categorised. Everyone's schemata are different, for instance, a teacher's schema of school will include expectations about hierarchies, pupil culture, staffroom behaviour and so on, while the experiences of parents are unlikely to have refined their schema of school to this extent.

A range of work on schema development and concept formation has been conducted since the 1950s. Collins and Quillian (1969) developed the notion that we store concepts hierarchically with general, overarching concepts being subdivided into more specific ones.

Reader reflection

Think about how, from an early age, you developed the concept of 'animal'.

We define this concept by a range of criteria such as four legs, no language and so on. At this crude level our concept of animal does not differentiate between types of animal.

Have you noticed, for instance, how small children sometimes refer to cats as 'doggies'?

As we gain more experience we learn to discriminate between types of animal – we notice that cats are furry and dogs are hairy, cats purr and dogs bark.

Animal is a superordinate concept to which dog and cat are subordinate.

Other models postulate linkages between concepts which are triggered via a logical association which is not necessarily hierarchical, for instance brainstorming a topic produces many related ideas. Sometimes this is referred to as concept mapping. Anderson and Bower's (1973) model claimed that knowledge was stored as propositions about the world. Linkages between these propositions would constitute learning. Teachers encourage concept differentiation through comparison of objects or ideas and they usually introduce new ideas by reference to concrete examples. Even adults find new ideas easier to grasp if given concrete examples of them.

Schemata are thought to differ from concepts because they deal with larger phenomena like discourse structure and events which consist of their own particular concepts and interrelations. If you are presented with a bizarre drawing of a familiar object you will employ your schema of that object to make sense of it even though it does not conform entirely to the set of expectations the schema contains.

Think, for example, of a bicycle drawn without handlebars and saddle and missing the back wheel. Although unrideable, you would still recognise it as a bicycle!

Similarly, when we see clouds which appear to be making recognisable shapes our schema are being involuntarily pressed into service to make sense of the shapes.

Implications of concept development for learning new knowledge

Psychologists interested in education have long argued that new knowledge should be linked to what is already known (Ausubel, 1968). The work of both Gagne (1977) and Ausubel indicated the need for material new to the learner to be structured in a hierarchical way which reflects the inherent conceptual structure of the topic, skill or information in order for assimilation to be effective. Ausubel distinguished between *reception* and *discovery* learning, explaining that most school knowledge is of the former type because there is so much to learn that there is not time for pupils to discover everything anew. However, a certain amount of discovery is involved in learning even prepackaged information because the learner must engage with the material, by reading it or listening to it, and then make new connections with existing knowledge. The use of sequential procedures, moving from the general to the specific, and the recall of key words and ideas from previous lessons to cue the learner are all strategies which can aid retention and recall.

Chyriwsky (1996) argued that mathematical knowledge should be worked through hierarchically. In mathematics we move from the general concepts of addition, subtraction and multiplication to more specific computations like calculating area, solving equations or estimating probabilities. If the teacher has given instruction based on the inherent hierarchical structure of the material, the assimilation and accommodation of schemata will be achieved at varying levels by learners. It could therefore be profitable to create cognitive environments which stimulate new and unique reconstructions of the taught material by individual learners through the use of open-ended tasks.

The clarification and extension of declarative or factual subject knowledge (facts, vocabulary, formulae) has traditionally taken precedence over the learning of procedural knowledge specific to each subject, for example the mechanics of performing calculations in mathematics, the process of writing for different genres in English or the steps taken to set up an experiment in science. Latterly, however, procedural knowledge has been recognised as important in school learning; tasks which facilitate the learning of procedural knowledge are likely to be of an investigative applied nature, possibly involving open-ended role-play or problem-solving.

An emphasis on structure and sequence is evidenced in the learning of modern foreign languages (MFL). Mitchell found that foreign language teachers generally adhered 'to a bottom-up language learning theory, with an emphasis on the recognition and acquisition of discrete vocabulary items, and the subsequent construction of spoken and written sentences' (1994: 56). Knowledge from other subject areas which falls into this category is that of a formulaic nature, such as the periodic table from chemistry or logarithms from mathematics. Information of this kind is traditionally learned by rote but knowledge acquired in this way can have limited retention and is a rather uneconomic means of storing information. Material learned meaningfully, where the essence of something read, seen or heard is abstracted from the whole experience, is stored substantively rather than verbatim in the memory. Combining concrete examples with abstract instruction can assist this learning (Anderson et al, 1996), for instance the use of practical or visual 'props' in the teaching of languages or mathematics.

Rote learning is not inherently meaningful so cannot be stored in LTM with other related information. Rather it must be stored in its full form, taking up a lot of space in the memory.

Reader reflection

We can employ an example now to illustrate the difference between meaningful and rote learning. If you are asked the four times table you will probably recite 'one four is four, two fours are eight' and so on.

You probably will not explain the mathematical principle of multiplication by a factor of four. If, however, we ask you the meaning of the term 'standard deviation', you are unlikely to recite a verbatim answer.

Instead, your short-term memory (STM) searches your long-term memory (LTM) for your 'schemata' of statistical terms and relationships. You then articulate your abstracted understanding of the term.

The intellectual challenge involved in articulating the second answer is greater although knowing one's tables can be very useful.

It is analysed only superficially in STM because the pupil does not have to make connections with other pieces of information.

In the context of information-processing theory the teacher's role is to help learners apply their knowledge and skills by finding new ways of recalling previous knowledge, solving problems, formulating hypotheses and so on. Montgomery (1996) promoted the use of games and simulations because they facilitate critical thinking and encourage new connections to be made between areas of subject knowledge or experience.

UNPACKING INFORMATION PROCESSING

Perception

Perception is deemed to be the first part in the information-processing mechanism. It is the interpretation by the brain of the signals received by the senses. As we have seen, gestalt psychology had revealed some important principles about perception and much research into visual illusion has helped elucidate our understanding of perceptual processes. Gibson (1979) emphasised the functional aspects of perception through his research into pilots landing aircraft. He identified the perceptual phenomenon of a constant aspect approach where the pilot sees the landing point as motionless with the land around it pulling away from that point. Thus the perceptual process assists the perceptual function to which it is harnessed. Neisser (1976) postulated a perpetual cycle of perception in which what we expect to see affects what we do see. The notion of 'perceptual set', where we can be predisposed to perceive something in a certain way, is of particular note to education. A simple illustration of this is when we cannot see the other interpretation within an ambiguous drawing, for example Rubin's vase/faces. When applied to more complex situations this perceptual set can inhibit or advance learning. Often our emotional state can precipitate perceptual set, for instance if a child associates a certain interpretation of an event with a dissatisfied response from a parent or teacher they may be unable to perceive it in that way again. Conversely, a teacher may contrive perceptual set among a class of pupils in order that they are ready to learn a certain topic; if the topic is three-dimensional drawing in the natural environment pupils might be shown in previous lessons a number of artworks in which the three-dimensional perspective is particularly well drawn.

Attention

Broadbent (1958) developed a model of attention which held that stimuli are selectively filtered out because of the limited capacity of the short-term memory to analyse incoming stimuli. The effect of interruption, doing two things simultaneously and dividing one's attention have been the focus of research in this area (see Gavin, 1998). The level of familiarity we have with a task will determine the extent to which we can be interrupted and still perform the task well. If you are a seasoned knitter you will be able to simultaneously engage in quite detailed discussion; not so for the novice! You may well be quite practised in the art of listening to two conversations at once, but in fact we do this by tuning in to one or the other at intervals and while attuned to one we can only register very superficial signals from the other.

In learning environments gaining the attention of the learner is very important – huge tracts of guidance have been written for training teachers on this topic! Younger children are more susceptible to distraction; it is fascinating to note just how much more incidental learning they achieve than do adults. This is learning that derives from attending to stimuli to which the teacher has not directed them.

Reader reflection

You can do a simple experiment to show this.

Show a group of 5 year olds an interesting, lively picture for a couple of minutes and a group of fellow students the same picture for one minute (time varies to account for adult competence).

It might be a picture of some animals in a farmyard. Tell them to concentrate on what the animals are doing. Afterwards ask them what the animals were doing and a series of unrelated questions based on other information within the picture, such as: 'What was the farmhouse made of? How many windows did it have? What were the children doing? What colour was the farmer's jumper?' You will probably find the children are better able to answer the questions relating to incidental learning than the students are.

Teachers generally want their pupils to focus on the matter in hand rather than on incidentals, so they have to use cueing signals to direct attention, develop learning materials and tasks that are stimulating and interesting, use strong colours and sounds, and maintain variety of task and approach.

Memory

While Atkinson and Shriffin (1968) contended that incoming sensations were analysed in a short-term memory and the organised or abstracted idea deposited with the relevant schema within the long-term memory, Craik and Lockhart (1972) suggested that it was the level of processing of the stimuli which determined the degree of permanence with which it was stored. Miller (1956) revealed our ability generally to remember chunks of information up to seven, plus or minus two. Studies have also shown that recalling later items in a list is more difficult when earlier ones have been learned and recall tested. The finding that we tend to recall the first and last sets of items heard when a list is read out is explained by the most recently heard items being retrieved from STM and the least recent items from LTM. The ones in the middle of the list tend to be lost because they have not been processed for storage in LTM and have been subject to decay from STM. Interference theory (Long, 2000) explains that the retrieval of newly learned information can be affected by its similarity to previously stored material. These and other findings have obvious implications for teaching and learning: the value of repetition, rehearsal and mnemonic strategies such as acronyms, rhymes or imagery, the danger of studying too much information at once and the need to organise material in a conceptually coherent way which aids retrieval.

Tulving (1972) postulated two types of memory: episodic and semantic. Episodic memory is when we recall actual events and experiences, replaying conversations verbatim or 'seeing' actions that occurred. It often applies to major events, for example many of you will be able to recall precisely where you were and what you were doing when the news of Princess Diana's death or the 9/11 tragedy were announced, but we also have episodic memories of non-significant occurrences, such as feeding the cat or eating a meal. These fade within days as we have more and more experiences of a similar type but the episodic memories of significant events can remain for a very long time. If you talk to old people, although they might have become very forgetful, they will often be able to recount vivid descriptions of what they were doing at times of significant events which marked autobiographical, national or international historical turning points even if they occurred 50 years ago. Semantic memory stores the abstractions from our experience, so if you read a book you will not recall its contents verbatim but will have a precised account of its meaning within your memory. Sometimes we can retrieve episodic memories which then enable us to retrieve a stored semantic memory. A huge amount has been written about memory which is quite fascinating and of obvious consequence for educational practitioners, but we do not have space to deal with it here (see Baddeley, 1997, or Tulving and Craik, 2000, for comprehensive texts). Ultimately, for the teacher and the learner, strategies for retention and recall are of primary importance.

Conclusion

This chapter has provided an overview of key psychological theories which illuminate our understanding of how educational attainment can differ from individual to individual. The legacy of ideas such as those of Piaget, of the behaviourists and of the cognitive psychologists is powerful and we have seen how their theories have impacted upon pedagogical trends. These psychologists give different explanations of mental ability and individual development. The emphasis of behaviourist theories on external stimuli to learning contrasts sharply with the maturational patterns revealed by Piaget or the information-processing approaches of cognitive psychologists. Certainly there has been heated discussion about how much of an individual's character and ability is due to genetic inheritance (nature) and how much to socialisation and environmental factors (nurture). The type of education deemed suitable has depended to a large extent on whether ability was considered to be innate or determined by experience. This rather simplistic dichotomy of nature/nurture has been rendered more complex by psychological studies of the past 30 years which we will look at in Chapter 7 when we focus on how the interaction of these two influences affects learning development.

Student activities

1 Look at some of the experiments which Piaget used (Bee and Boyd, 2007). Try some of these with a couple of children you know. If possible, choose children of different ages so you can cover at least two of Piaget's stages. Discuss your results with a tutor or other students. Do you think the experiments are useful? Would you/did you alter them in any way?
2 Refer to a text which describes personality measures (Child, 2004, for instance). Most take the form of some sort of inventory of characteristics against which the subjects rate themselves. You might like to have a go. Discuss with other students the value of such inventories. Are there any problems with self-report measures?

Recommended reading

Bee, H. and Boyd, D. (2007) *The Developing Child*, 11th edn. Boston, USA: Pearson Education. This excellent, readable text covers all aspects of human development. The latest edition of this classic brings the research right up to date.

Child, D. (2004) *Psychology and the Teacher*, 7th edn. London: Continuum. This comprehensive, accessible text covers all aspects of educational psychology.

Education and psychological research: contemporary influences

In this chapter influential psychological developments since the 1970s are examined, including social constructivism, multiple and emotional intelligences, situated cognition and metacognition. The growth of interest in individual learning styles, strategies and preferences is explored, so too the growing body of research into brain functioning.

Introduction

Psychologists' interest in how the mind works and how education affects individuals is as vibrant now as it has ever been. It might be argued that the theoretical and empirical work described in Chapter 6, although revealing a great deal about mental processes, also opened new avenues of enquiry. This chapter will examine psychological research which has become influential since the 1970s within education, including:

- constructivist theory which urges a focus on learners' existing conceptions
- social constructivist theory which stresses the importance of social interaction and scaffolded support in the learning process
- metacognitive theory which demonstrates the value of learners understanding and controlling their learning strategies
- learning style theories which imply not better/poorer distinctions between ways of learning but the matching of learning tasks to a preferred processing style
- learning preferences and the implications for conducive environmental conditions for learning
- multiple intelligence theory which suggests a multidimensional rather than a singular intelligence
- emotional intelligence theory which emphasises the potency of the learner's emotional state
- situated cognition theory which explains all learning as context-bound
- the growing knowledge of brain functioning.

Interest in explanations for pupils' differential success rates in learning, which go beyond notions of static intelligence and learning readiness, has never been higher than at the present time. This interest coincides with calls for learning opportunities to be 'personalised', to match work to pupils' needs (Miliband, 2004a). These pedagogical trends are examined in more detail in Chapter 9. As we have seen in Chapter 6, individual differences have traditionally been conceptualised as differences in intelligence as measured by IQ tests. In the contemporary context, however, richer explanations exist for how pupils learn. We begin by looking at research which stresses the individualised nature of constructing meaning.

Constructivism

Constructivism is predicated on the idea that people make their own sense of things in a unique way. It attaches great importance to the individualised nature of learners' conceptions. Information-processing theorists would probably attribute the differences between individuals' conceptions to the different ways stimuli are perceived or represented in their minds. But Driver and Bell (1986) argued that stimuli, or knowledge, are not that straightforward. New information is problematic for the learner, who must examine it in relation to prior conceptions and experiences and see to what extent it fits. Driver refers to these as alternative frameworks (Driver et al, 1996). Little emphasis is placed on the role of instruction. Rather the teacher must create situations which facilitate individuals constructing their own knowledge. If pupils harbour misconceptions they must be helped to take them apart at the root since long-held conceptions are very difficult to shake off and are resistant to change even when teachers and others explain the error. Constructivism emphasises the need to give learners responsibility for directing their own learning experiences. It is in the science subject area that constructivist ideas have been most influential. Naylor and Keogh (1999) developed work in this area, devising concept cartoons which strike at the very heart of learners' misconceptions about scientific ideas in an effort to help them rethink the problem.

Social constructivist theories

VYGOTSKY

Since the 1970s educators have increasingly recognised the importance of the ideas of Lev Vygotsky, the Russian psychologist. Vygotsky's work dates from the 1920s and 1930s but did not become available in the West until the 1970s, which explains why his publications date from after this time despite his early death from tuberculosis in 1934, aged 38. The sociological ideas of Durkheim, Wundt's emphasis on cultural psychology, gestalt psychology, the early works of Jean Piaget, and the new modernist theories of linguistics and literary theory emerging in the USSR in the 1920s influenced Vygotsky. This eclecticism was denounced as anti-Marxist and Vygotsky's work went into oblivion. After the political rehabilitation of his work in the USSR and its delayed discovery in the West, his seminal work on the relationship between language and thought spawned studies of major importance in the former USSR and in the West. Cole and Scribner's (1974) studies, focusing on Vygotsky's view that children's learning of scientific concepts depends on the interaction between these and the child's own spontaneous everyday concepts, revealed that school-based cognitive skills become more important where there is an increased demand for scholastic-type activities outside school.

Kozulin juxtaposed Piaget's and Vygotsky's theories, explaining their 'common denominators as a child centred approach, an emphasis on action in the formation of thought, and a systematic understanding of psychological functioning' and their biggest difference as their understanding of psychological activity (Kozulin, 1998: 34). For Vygotsky (1978), psychological activity has socio-cultural characteristics from the very beginning of development. Theoretical concepts are generative from a range of different stimuli, implying a problem-solving approach for the learner and a facilitator role for the teacher. Whereas Piaget (1959) considered language a tool of thought in the child's developing mind, for Vygotsky language was generated from the need to communicate and was central to the development of thinking. Vygotsky emphasised the functional value of egocentric speech to verbal reasoning and self-regulation, and the importance of socio-cultural factors in its development. In 'inner speech' the sense attached by the individual predominates over meaning but speech forms originating in external dialogues have to be internalised and internal thoughts translated into a form of speech comprehensible for others. Vygotsky likened this to there being two co-authors, where one accommodates their thoughts to the pre-existent system of meanings and the other immediately turns them into idiosyncratic senses, in simultaneous outbound and inbound conversations.

In communicative talk, then, the development is not just in the language contrived to formulate the sentence since the process of combining the words to shape the sentence also shapes the thought itself. Thus Vygotsky's work highlights the importance of talk as a learning tool. Reports of some eminence reinforced the status of talk in UK classrooms, highlighting its centrality to learning (Assessment of Performance Unit, 1986; Bullock Report, 1975; Norman, 1992). The encouragement of pupil talk for the learning of both declarative and procedural knowledge has been increasingly acknowledged to be of value since it allows learners to refine what they know through the articulation of their thoughts (Withers and Eke, 1995).

The concept of 'psychological tools' was a cornerstone of Vygotsky's theory: 'symbolic artefacts' such as signs, symbols, texts, formulae, and graphic symbolic devices which help learners accomplish their own 'natural' psychological functions of perception, memory, attention and so on. They serve as a 'bridge between individual acts of cognition and the symbolic socio-cultural pre-requisites of these acts' (Kozulin, 1998: 1). Naturally existing signs, such as tracks, are replaced by artificial versions of the same and are dependent on the social environment. Vygotskyan theory holds that intercultural cognitive differences are attributable to the variance in systems of psychological tools and in the methods of their acquisition practised in *different* cultures.

Kozulin explored the work of Feuerstein et al (1991) who developed Vygotsky's notion of the human mediator in the interaction between child and environment. Charting the philosophical and sociological antecedents of mediated interaction, Kozulin cited Hegel's description of work as a mediated activity and Mead's view that the interaction between the individual and the environment is always mediated by meanings which originate through social relations. For Vygotsky, psychological tools mediate humans' own psychological processes. Feuerstein developed mediated learning experience (MLE) theory working with culturally different groups, culturally deprived individuals and learning-disabled children. Mediated learning experience is achieved by the involvement of an adult between the stimuli of the environment and the child with the intention of modifying 'learner deficiencies'. This appears to be a deficit model of learners but Kozulin claims it can reveal hidden learning potential and can reorient parents and teachers from passive acceptance of children's 'deficiencies' to active modification of them.

BRUNER

Jerome Bruner, a US psychologist who has contributed a huge amount in a variety of areas of psychological research since the 1950s, also placed an emphasis on structured intervention within communicative learning models. He formulated a theory of instruction, central to which is the notion of systematic, structured pupil experience via a spiral curriculum where the learner returns to address increasingly complex components of a topic as they develop over time. Learners construct new ideas or concepts based upon their current/past knowledge. Thus in Year 5 at primary school tackling the problem of fractions will be approached using many more concrete examples than when it is returned to in Year 7 at secondary school. For Bruner, learning involves the active restructuring of knowledge through experience with the environment. The learner selects and transforms information, constructs hypotheses and makes decisions, relying on an internal and developing cognitive structure to do so. Cognitive structure (schema, mental models) provides meaning and organisation to experiences and allows the individual to go beyond the information given.

As far as teaching is concerned, good pedagogy should try to encourage students to discover principles by themselves. The instructor and student should engage in an active dialogue, asking questions, presenting and testing hypotheses. Thus Bruner advocated discovery methods rather than the provision of prepackaged materials. The teacher's job was to guide this discovery through structured support, for example by asking focused questions or providing appropriate materials.

THE INFLUENCE OF SOCIAL CONSTRUCTIVIST THEORIES

The pedagogical implications of the work of Vygotsky and Bruner centre on the role of communication and structured intervention in thinking and problem-solving. Essentially, if pupils discuss with others what new ideas mean to them, further thinking is generated with more complex links between ideas afforded. The role of the teacher in facilitating learning situations involving talk is of critical importance. Judicious grouping of pupils for such talk is important. Brown (1994) espoused the notion of learning communities which operate like research seminar groups. Taking a Vygotskyan approach she argued that 'students navigate by different routes and at different rates. But the push is towards upper, rather than lower, levels of competence' (Brown, 1994: 7). Homogeneous grouping and pairing has been considered to have advantages in fostering learning, particularly in its promotion of argument and sharing of complex ideas (Gillies and Ashman, 2003; Rogoff, 1990; 1998). Research reviewed by Scott-Baumann (1995) indicated that when 10 year old pupils were paired according to their similar levels of functioning, they worked best and were often faster at solving chemical problems than when they worked alone. A separate study revealed similar findings when pairs of 11–13 year olds worked on computers. However, both studies indicated that the initial gains in understanding made by pairs were not sustained when pupils were tested individually later. This might suggest that strategies for individual consolidation of learning following pair work need to be encouraged by the teacher. Fazey and Marton (2002) explain that one of the reasons why helping children to talk about their learning is so productive is that individual learners tend to assume that the reality which they experience is the reality that others experience too. Greenfield (1997) has shown how even the perceptions and interpretations of the same experiences by identical twins lead to unique sets of memories.

Bruner's ideas about the power of systematic and well-structured pupil experiences to promote cognitive development are fundamental to a social constructivist approach.

Reader reflection

Maybin et al (1992) used Bruner's (1983) ideas of 'scaffolding' in relation to classroom talk. The ideas of pupils emerging through their talk are scaffolded or framed by the teacher putting in 'steps' or questions at appropriate junctures.

A group of pupils might be discussing how to solve the problem of building a paper bridge between two desks. The teacher can intervene when they hear an idea emerge which will help pupils find the solution, by asking a question which requires the pupils to address that idea explicitly.

You may wish to try this if you have a placement in a school.

Is it easy to work out when to intervene?
How far does the influence of an idea reflect the strength of the pupil's personality or the validity of the idea?
How should a teacher handle this without demotivating the pupil/pupils?

Bruner argued that the scaffolding provided by the teacher should decrease in direct correspondence to the progress of the learner. Wood (1988) developed Bruner's ideas, describing five levels of support which become increasingly specific and supportive in relation to the help needed by the pupil:

- general verbal encouragement
- specific verbal instruction
- assistance with pupil's choice of material or strategies
- preparation of material for pupil assembly
- demonstration of task.

Thus, having established the task the pupils are to complete, a teacher might give general verbal encouragement to the whole class, follow this up with specific verbal instruction to groups who need it and perhaps target individuals with guidance on strategies for approaching the task. Some pupils will need physical help in performing the task and yet others need to be shown exactly what to do, probably in small stages.

Some researchers favour slight differences between partners in order to encourage cognitive conflict through interaction. However, the research findings are by no means clear so it is not possible to conclude whether pupils matched on the basis of similar or of different previous performance is most advantageous; this is likely to vary according to the task and the learners. The issue of how well teachers can determine the prior understanding of their pupils and, in turn, match work to individuals, is itself controversial.

The Vygotskyan notion of 'zones of proximal development' has application here. These zones describe the gap between a pupil's current level of learning and the level they could be functioning at given the appropriate learning experience and adult or peer support. Teachers are well aware of the extent to which these zones vary from pupil to pupil even if they do not use Vygotskyan terminology; indeed it is the extent of this variation which constitutes the challenge for the teacher. This challenge can turn to frustration as teachers seek to homogenise these zones in an effort to utilise a directive teaching style. There is often an element of fear of the unknown in moving to a more pupil-centred, discursive pedagogy because a degree of control transfers to the pupils. Pressures of fulfilling curriculum requirements can exacerbate this fear, thus constraining an often genuine desire to incorporate such methodology.

Metacognition

The process of coming to know more about one's own learning strategies, such as strategies for remembering, ways of presenting information when thinking, approaches to problems and so on, is known as metacognition. It has become fashionable to refer to this as 'learning to learn' with researchers suggesting that this concept has potential for moving learning away from a curriculum and assessment dominated education system (Hall et al, 2006). If pupils are helped by their teachers to become more metacognitively aware, they are more able to take control of their learning. Being metacognitively aware can be likened to having a commentator in the learner's mind who analyses and comments upon the methods they are using to learn a new concept or skill while the learning is happening. Flavell claimed that 'a person's awareness of his or her own cognitive machinery is a vital component of intelligence' (1979: 907, in Montgomery, 1996: 15). Learners should be encouraged to explore their own ways of knowing and remembering, to experiment with learning strategies, to appreciate teaching and learning techniques which help them learn best and to monitor their own learning. Anderson et al (1996) reported that studies show that transfer of learning between tasks is enhanced where the teacher cues learners into the specific skill being learned and encourages them to reflect on its potential for transfer.

Quicke and Winter (1996) found that, in a small-scale study with a mixed ability Year 8 class, engaging pupils in a metacognitive dialogue about 'good' learning enhanced their understanding of learning processes. Kramarski and Mevarech (1997) showed that metacognitive training helped 12–14 year olds draw better graphs in mathematics. The role of the teacher is to provide the 'scaffolding' for the pupils to think for themselves. Montgomery (1996) described such an approach as 'cognitive process pedagogy' wherein the emphasis is on critical thinking through games and simulations, problem-solving tasks, study skills, collaborative learning and experimental learning. This approach is informed by a view that hierarchically ordered levels of thinking can be determined (and therefore striven for) in children's learning in the way that Benjamin Bloom's (1956) *Taxonomy of Educational Objectives* theorised.

Bruner (1966) argued that difficult ideas should be seen as a challenge and that, if properly presented, can be learned by most pupils. Adey and colleagues developed a system of cognitive acceleration in science education (CASE) which challenges pupils to examine the processes they use to solve problems (Adey, 1992; Shayer and Adey, 2002). In doing so it is argued that pupils are enhancing their thinking processes. The activities are designed to create 'cognitive conflict', that is, 'a dissonance which occurs when a child is confronted with an event which s/he cannot explain when using his/her current conceptual framework or method of processing data' (Adey, 1992: 138). Pupils are given problem-solving tasks which require them to justify their conclusions. The teacher's role is to carefully question pupils so that each one rethinks the basis for their conclusions. Adey has argued that the activities are appropriate to mixed ability classes because, although undifferentiated, they make intellectual demands at a range of levels. To substantiate this he cited the results of the project as being equally successful with both high and low scorers on initial measures of cognitive development. He claimed that a two-year programme of fortnightly CASE lessons with Year 7 and 8 pupils led to substantial gains for those pupils in science, mathematics and English GCSE results in Year 11.

The apparent transfer of higher-order cognitive skills beyond science suggests that a focus on pupils' metacognition is worthwhile. The CASE project is premised, then, on the notion of an underlying set of intellectual processes rather than domain-specific thinking skills. It is argued that, through discussing their views of, and solutions to, problem-solving tasks: 'students become accustomed to reflect on the sort of thinking they have been engaged in, to bring it to the front of their consciousness, and to make of it an explicit tool which is then more likely to be available for use in a new context' (Adey, 1992: 141). Applying a Vygotskyan explanation, Adey has claimed that the encouragement of pupils to describe reasoning patterns using appropriate terminology, even when they do not fully understand the terms, aids their ability to reflect on how they are thinking because the more the terms are used and discussed with peers, the greater meaning they accrue.

A number of studies across the world indicate learning gains as a consequence of metacognitive training. Namrouti and Alshannag's (2004) research in Jordan identified statistically significant differences in seventh grade students' achievement in science. Black et al's (2002) study in London, in which mathematics and science teachers were trained to use structured questioning and to encourage pupils to discuss their understanding of concepts, led to pupils of all abilities scoring higher in their national assessment tests or GCSEs than pupils in ordinary lessons. Marcantonio et al (2006) found that taking a metacognitive approach with social science undergraduates reduced the tendency for their test anxiety to lead to a surface approach to their learning.

Learning styles, strategies, approaches and preferences

Research into learning styles and strategies has grown apace since the 1950s and some of the more easily understood categorisations have been popularised within both education and management studies. A currently fashionable way of identifying 'learning style' is to refer to learners' preferences for visual, auditory and kinaesthetic ways of working (Burton, 2007). Contrary to popular belief, however, this categorisation is just one way of describing learning style. Whatever construct of style we use, identifying a learner's habitual way of processing information is not a simple case of fixing on one descriptor within the construct to the exclusion of the others, for example identifying someone exclusively as a visualiser, because we know that learning requires the use of different strategies according to the task and the context.

Curry (1983) developed a model which grouped learning style measures into strata which resemble the layers of an onion, distinguishing between a habitual and involuntary underlying feature of personality, the individual's intellectual approach to assimilating information and their instructional preference or choice of learning environment. Since Curry's model was presented, a great deal more research has been done. It is therefore helpful to define what is meant by the four main areas of research in this field.

1 *Learning or cognitive style*: habitual way of representing and processing information; innate to learner; not susceptible to change.
2 *Learning strategy*: way of approaching and tackling tasks; learned; capable of change.
3 *Learning approaches*: motivation for and attitude towards learning; largely stable but can change according to task or purpose.
4 *Learning preferences*: environmental preferences for learning, such as place, light, atmosphere.

The important principle which characterises each of these research areas is that learning is not better or worse depending on style, strategy, approach or preference but is *different*.

Whereas intelligence theory sets a limit on the capacity to learn, these theories describe the differences between learners' preferred or involuntary styles. This implies that a match between a learner's preference and the learning task will remove any such limits on learning potential.

LEARNING OR COGNITIVE STYLES

Individual differences are thought to underlie a whole range of more readily observable differences. Learners bring to their studies a stable, involuntary mode of representing information during their thinking. Riding (1991) proposed that two overarching dimensions can be identified which subsume the various constructs of previous researchers. These are *wholist-analytic style* – whether an individual tends to process information in wholes or parts – and *verbal-imagery style* – whether an individual represents information during thinking verbally or in mental pictures. Riding (1996) advocated advance organisers for wholists since they have difficulty seeing the structure and sections of learning material. A topic map indicating the hierarchically related separate areas would help them divide it into its parts. However, the wholist would have trouble disembedding particular information from tables and densely packed diagrams. For analytics an overview after the information has been presented would help learners to create an integrated picture of the topic. Analytics tend to focus on one part at a time, sometimes overemphasising an element of the whole. They are therefore likely to need help in seeing links and relationships between the parts of a topic and in establishing the appropriate balance between the significance of the parts. An overview in the form of a concept map would be highly relevant, as would tabulated information. Riding et al (2003) found that, for the overall learning behaviour of 206 13 year old secondary comprehensive Year 8 pupils, there was an interaction between working memory capacity and cognitive style. With the wholist-analytic style dimension, memory made a marked difference for analytics but had little effect for wholists, and with the verbal-imagery dimension verbalisers were affected but not imagers.

The predominant coding style of verbalisers suits them for tasks involving texts and definitions so verbal versions of pictorial and diagrammatic material are helpful to them. The greater use now of technology in schools means that it should also be possible, during teacher exposition and questioning, to use interactive techniques involving computers, cassette recorders and video equipment. Since imagers are found to achieve best on material which can be visualised in mental pictures, and which does not contain many acoustically complex and unfamiliar terms, it is suggested that verbal material should be converted into pictorial form for them. Imagers would also benefit from concrete analogies of abstract ideas. As they are superior to verbalisers on spatial and directional information, mapping tasks could be encouraged across subjects. Teacher exposition and questioning could be punctuated with pictures and artefacts or presented using computer graphics and video material.

Motivationally wholist-verbalisers will probably be less willing to focus for long periods on material or tasks which are not particularly stimulating, whereas imagers may well persevere with it. They are also likely to be happier working in groups while imagers usually prefer to work alone. Riding and Burton (1998) found that teachers rated the behaviour of wholist boys in Years 10 and 11 as significantly less good than that of analytic boys. They pointed out that a wholist style tends to be associated with a more sociable, outgoing personality which may, among some adolescent boys, present to teachers as deviant behaviour. Evans and Waring (2006) conducted research into the learning styles of 80 primary teacher trainees using Riding's construct. Whilst they found that many of the differences reported in the literature between the different cognitive styles were not evident in this study, the interpersonal and intrapersonal characteristics of wholists and analytics, respectively, were evident and perceived to impact on the teachers' planning and delivery in the classroom. For a full account of style constructs which can be grouped with Riding's dimensions, see Riding and Cheema (1991).

Integrating assessment of wholist-analytic and verbal-imagery dimensions

Riding (1991) developed a computer-presented test which directly assesses both ends of the wholist-analytic and verbal-imagery dimensions. The Cognitive Styles Analysis (CSA) comprises three subtests and uses response time to determine the subject's position on each dimension. The validity of the instrument is supported by the finding of significant relationships between style and a range of school learning performance (Riding et al, 2003). For pupils who exhibit learning difficulties a mismatch between their preferred learning styles and the learning tasks can affect their achievement more than a mismatch would for competent learners.

A huge body of research has been generated using the various available assessment instruments. A recent study using the Felder-Silverman Index of Learning Styles© (ILS) by Palou (2006) in Mexico found that an activity-based instructional approach improved the performance of 'actives' and 'sensors' found in previous studies to be disadvantaged in the science and engineering curricula. Conversely, a study in the USA by Smith et al (2006) using Gregorc's (1982) style delineator found no significant effect of learning style on graduate healthcare student performance when the medium of instruction in clinical skills was matched to style. For more information on these instruments see Riding and Rayner (1998).

LEARNING STRATEGIES

Kolb's work (1976; 1985) describes two dimensions: perceiving and processing. The dimensions are bipolar with abstract and concrete thinking at the ends of the perceiving dimension and doing (active) and watching (reflective) at the ends of the processing dimension. Kolb said that these dimensions interact so that four types of learner can be identified:

- 'divergers' who perceive information concretely and process it reflectively, needing to be personally involved in the task
- 'convergers' who perceive information abstractly and process it reflectively, taking detailed, sequential steps
- 'assimilators' who perceive information abstractly and process it actively, needing to be set pragmatic problem-solving activities

- 'accommodators' who perceive information concretely and process it actively, taking risks, experimenting and needing flexibility in learning tasks.

Kolb developed the notion of experiential learning as a cyclical sequence through the four areas of learning mode implied by the interaction of the two dimensions. His descriptions of learning styles are therefore not to be seen as static, but modifiable by the learner's training in the four sequences of the cycle. Learners will have a predilection for one of the stages, thus giving rise to the four styles. McCarthy pointed out that if learners are provided with experiences which ensure their use of stages in the cycle, in addition to their preferred one, their learning strategies may be extended (McCarthy, 1987).

Kolb's work both influenced workplace management training (Honey and Mumford, 1986) and found favour in the 1980s in educational settings. The Technical, Vocational and Educational Initiative (TVEI) funded by the Department for Employment (DFE) in the mid-1980s was very influential in developing 'flexible learning'; this used Kolb's work as its theoretical underpinning (Harris and Bell, 1990). Gibbs's (1992) work on adult learning was also influenced by Kolb. In further education, projects looking at the application of Kolb's learning styles to flexible, support-based pedagogy were developed (Fielding, 1994). Kolb's work continues to be influential and a recent study by Kayes (2005) confirmed the reliability and validity of his assessment instrument, the Learning Style Inventory. Jarvis et al (2003) report work adapted from Kolb with adult learners which demonstrated the influence of experience on learning and the role of this in andragogy, the science of adult teaching and learning. In Australia Mountford et al's (2006) study of 206 physiotherapy students found that most students preferred reflective rather than experiential learning modes. This might seem surprising given the practical nature of their vocation.

LEARNING APPROACHES

Biggs's (1978, 1987a, 1987b) work on approaches to study has been developed from Marton and Saljo's (1976) studies of 'deep' and 'surface' approaches to learning and Entwistle's (1981) work on learning orientations. Entwistle described four orientations to learning: 'meaning', 'reproducing', 'achieving' and 'holistic'. It was suggested that combinations of these orientations with extrinsic factors, such as the desire to pass examinations or a keen interest in a subject, generate certain approaches to study which employ different levels of thinking from 'deep' to 'surface'. Approaches to learning are thus a function of both motive and strategy and motives influence learning strategies (Biggs, 1993). An instrumental or surface motive engenders reproducing or rote-learning strategies. An intrinsic desire to learn is associated with deep motive and the use of learning strategies which emphasise understanding and meaning. An achieving motive might result from the need to pass examinations; from this can come strategies which stress time management and efficient organisation.

Students whose motives and strategies are compatible with the learning tasks are likely to perform well. Conversely, someone with a deep approach will be constrained by too superficial a task and a student who has an achieving motive will probably flounder if long-term, vague objectives are set. Ausubel (1985) showed that the need to compete in public examinations can lead to the adoption of rote-learning techniques resulting in temporary, peripheral learning. The type of learning orientation which has been encouraged in many countries, including the USA, the UK and Japan, by the increased emphasis on performance testing and school comparability is that of the achieving type (Darling-Hammond, 1994; Madeus, 1994). This militates against deep approaches which require learners to enjoy few time constraints and full learner autonomy. Clearly the short-term practices of schools to improve results serve to cultivate, at best, an achieving orientation and, at worst, a surface orientation to learning.

It has been suggested that there are cultural differences in motivation. However, the findings of many studies about the effects of competition and testing on motivation appear to hold true for both Eastern and Western education settings. Hardre et al (2006) investigated the relationships between 404 teachers' self-reported classroom goal structures, instructional self-perceptions, teaching efficacy and perceptions of students' motivation in a developing East Asian nation. The teachers reported that their students' motivation was primarily extrinsic and performance-oriented and was influenced by external factors, predominantly exam pressure and social expectations. Similarly, in Hong Kong, Lam et al's (2004) study with 52 grade 7 secondary pupils found that competition led students to focus narrowly on learning outcomes rather than learning opportunities.

LEARNING PREFERENCES

The *Productivity Environmental Preference Survey* (PEPS) (Price et al, 1991) derives from the work of Dunn et al (1979, 1989) and is widely used in the USA to measure the 'learning styles' of adults. Learners are thought to possess biologically based physical and environmental learning preferences which combine with emotional traits, sociological preferences and psychological inclinations to make up an individual style profile. Measures include preferences relating to sound, light, temperature, seating design, motivation, structure, persistence, responsibility, sociological needs, physical needs (auditory, visual, kinaesthetic and tactile), best time of day for learning, mobility, intake of food and drink, processing styles, impulsivity/reflectivity and hemispheric dominance (see the section on the brain on page 139).

The Learning Style Inventory (LSI) (Dunn et al, 1989), from which the PEPS was derived, uses similar factors to determine the preferences of younger learners. See Dunn and Griggs (2003) for a synthesis of the research into the LSI. An extensive website is also available at http://www.learningstyles.net. Dunn (1991) argued that instruction should be arranged which accommodates learners' preferences. The implications of this for a school classroom are quite profound since the potential range of factors a teacher would have to consider for a class of 30 pupils is enormous. Smith's (2006) research in Australia with 160 teachers and trainers of vocational learners found that teachers do make observations of learners' preferences, organising their ideas about preferences into those to do with mode of delivery and those to do with learning context differences. Smith notes, however, that the teachers responded to these differences pragmatically. It is clear that measuring preferences is better suited to adult self-use and, apart from possible application with small groups or with sixth form students, it is not easy to see how teachers could reconcile the extent of instructional matching which it implies with curriculum requirements within a school's resource base.

CROSS-CULTURAL STUDIES INTO LEARNING STYLES, STRATEGIES AND APPROACHES

Woodrow (1997) suggested that the style differences observed in different cultural groups are a function of environmental and cultural factors. Purdie and Hattie (1996) have compared the learning strategies employed by 16–18-year-old students in Australia and Japan, using the Self-Regulated Learning Interview Schedule of Zimmerman and Martinez-Pons (1986, 1988, 1990). They found that the range of strategies used by three culturally diverse groups was the same but that the pattern of use differed for each group. Significantly, the range of strategies used was broadest among high achievers irrespective of cultural group. This might suggest that, where learners are free to determine their own strategy use, high achievers are those who have used their habitual style traits without any mediation of culturally bound learning strategies. The Japanese students made far greater use of memorisation by rote than the Australian students, as did the Japanese students who had studied in Australia. Effort and willpower were seen to be closely associated with this use of strategy in a bid to succeed. The cultural determinant of this can be said to lie in the Japanese view that repetition is a route to understanding (Hess and Azuma, 1991). Kember and Gow (1990) reported the same tendency among the Chinese, and Lim (1994) among the students of Singapore. Two separate studies concerned with cross-cultural validation of Biggs's Study Process Questionnaire (Kong and Hau, 1996; Wong et al, 1996) revealed links between an achieving orientation and a deep approach to learning among Chinese secondary age pupils. Salili's (1996) investigation of achievement motivation among British and Chinese students, using McClelland's (1985) thematic apperception test (TAT), revealed the same tendency.

IMPLICATIONS OF RESEARCH INTO LEARNING STYLES, STRATEGIES, APPROACHES AND PREFERENCES FOR EDUCATION

Rayner and Riding have argued that a pupil's style profile will be 'a key consideration in curriculum design, assessment-based teaching and differentiated learning' (1997: 24), recognising, however, that such a profile needs to be manageable, accessible and geared to the real world of teaching. It is not necessary, even if it were possible within the constraints of organising and delivering a diverse curriculum, to know an individual's profile on the full range of style and strategy measures. Given that, unlike measurements of ability, learning styles, strategies and approaches are differentiated not by value but by function, acquiring a more definitive knowledge of individual style is less important than providing a diverse range of classroom approaches, resources, teaching styles and assessment media such that every learner has maximum access to the learning.

Reader reflection

Perhaps the fact that there are apparently so many learning style, strategy, approach and preference constructs should alarm us.

Is it feasible that there can be so many different ways of describing aspects of learners' processing or thinking styles?

Riding and Cheema (1991) claimed these were actually just different manifestations of (and labels for) the same construct or at least different aspects of the same construct.

How helpful is it anyway to determine whether a learner is an innovator or an adaptor, reflective or pragmatic, etc.?

Most of the theorists deal in polar opposites and they acknowledge that individuals may lie anywhere along a respective dimension and not necessarily at either end of it.

Does the fact that they deal only in linear descriptions suggest a failure to acknowledge the multi-faceted, context-bound nature of learning?

Situated cognition

'Situatedness', the study of cognition within its natural context, grew out of dissatisfaction with the disembedded approach of traditional cognitive psychology. Both information-processing and constructivist approaches essentially depicted knowledge as an object located within learners who are isolated from one another. They emphasised rational, individual, abstract thought processes, the study of which could reveal universal principles generalisable to all individuals in any circumstances. In contrast, situated cognition theory (Greeno et al, 1993; Lave and Wenger, 1991; Suchmann, 1987) stresses that learning cannot be studied in isolation from its context without destroying its defining properties. Situated learning casts the individual learner as a subsystem to a series of increasingly complex systems (classroom, school, neighbourhood, culture and humanity) wherein learning exists as a part of those contexts. This placement of learners within more complex systems is not new, having been described by Bronfenbrenner in his ecological model of human development. Bronfenbrenner (1979) conceptualised human development as 'the process of understanding and restructuring our ecological environment at successively greater levels of complexity' (Smith and Cowie, 1988: 10). His theory postulated four nested systems of development in context (see Figure 7.1):

- microsystem: the home, the classroom, friendships
- mesosystem: links between microsystems, for example no breakfast at home can lead to poor work at school
- exosystem: links between microsystems and settings in which the child does not participate but is affected by, for example a mother's stressful work environment may provoke intolerance with the child
- macrosystem: the ideology and organisations of society or subculture in which the child lives, such as unemployment levels, social taboos.

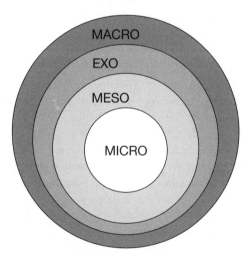

Figure 7.1 The four nested systems of development

Bronfenbrenner's model of ecological systems and subsystems helps explain the interconnectedness of environmental factors which impact on a child's learning, illustrating, for example, the effect of the interplay between a child's health, the state of the parents' relationship and a decision at national level to make budgetary cuts in education.

The impact of this 'development in context' on the growth and measurement of intelligence cannot be ignored. Baltes (1996) emphasised the life-span nature of development and the importance of historical influences stressing that age-related trends are but one of three important influences each determined by an interaction of biological and environmental factors:

- **Normative age-graded influences:** for example, the *advent of puberty (biological genesis) or starting school at 5 (environmental genesis)*.

- **Normative history-graded influences:** for example, famine *(biological impact) or China's one-child policy (environmental genesis)*.

- **Non-normative life events:** for example, *an accident causing brain damage (biological impact), divorce or job loss (environmental genesis)*.

Situated cognition theory goes further than Bronfenbrenner's and Baltes' analyses, espousing a collective knowledge which is embodied in 'the ongoing, ever-evolving interaction' between people (Davis and Sumara, 1997: 115) in real-life situations in the work or marketplace, social or educational settings. Whereas a cognitive approach to investigating adult performance in mental arithmetic showed poor results as it was in a laboratory setting, Lave (1988) argued that asking the same questions in the context of grocery shopping in the supermarket produces more realistic results (Seifert, 1999). Think, for example, of how quickly darts players sum their scores in the pub!

Situated explanations of cognition generally dispute the transference of knowledge between learning activities because the situative perspective does not allow that knowledge can exist as a 'substance' within the learner (Greeno, 1997). Instead, 'generality of knowing' is preferred as a phrase to describe a learner's 'participation in interactions with other people and with material and representational systems' (Greeno, 1997: 11). The situative perspective further claims that context-bound learning is more effective than the abstract representation of phenomena which constitutes much classroom teaching. Greeno calls for school learning to become more beneficial beyond the classroom, 'providing students with general resources for reasoning both in and with the concepts of subject-matter domains' (1997: 14). In recent years, the English school curriculum has increasingly adopted the use of 'authentic' learning activities which seek to replicate real-life situations. However, the idea that transference of learning is not possible is not generally embraced by teachers.

Clear parallels can be drawn with the work of Vygotsky, given his emphasis on interaction promoting cognition. However, some forms of situated cognition theory deny the possibility of individual cognition, suggesting instead that all learning is embedded within its interactive context and that there is therefore only collective cognition. It is difficult to see how cognition can be said not to be occurring in an individual's mind irrespective of any form of group cognition. Nevertheless, it is now widely accepted that much value comes from emphasising collaborative classroom activity. Cooperative group approaches to teaching and learning in which no one person has the monopoly on the direction of the learning are inferred by the situative perspective. Greeno has called for the arrangement of 'complex, social activities' with an emphasis on enquiry where pupils are given opportunities to formulate and evaluate 'problems, questions, conjectures, conclusions, arguments and examples' (1997: 10).

BRAIN FUNCTION

More is being learned all the time about the way the brain functions and this helps to eluci-date our understanding of mental processes. Many would claim, however, that such research is still in its infancy as there remains a great deal for us to find out. Neuroscientists revealed many years ago the physiology of mental functioning. The Spanish neuroscientist Cajal stud-ied the central nervous system, revealing the function of nerve cells (neurones) in transmitting information to and from the cerebral cortex (DeFilipe and Jones, 1991). The gaps between the neurones (synapses) are traversed and new connections made when think-ing occurs. Opportunities to grapple with ideas should therefore enable learners to 'grow' their brains by making new, strong connections. Information that is learned in a meaningful way will create longer-term connections that can be refreshed even after long periods of disuse, whereas rote learning is likely to lead to weak, temporary connections.

Research into hemispheric specificity indicates that the left side of the brain deals more with language and logic and the right side with spatial and visual awareness. It is also claimed that we can infer from electrical activity in the brain, measured using an EEG (electroen-cephalogram) while someone is asked to perform a variety of tasks, the different parts of the brain associated with the various processes of perception, attention, remembering, retrieval and language comprehension (Fodor, 1983; Hillyard, 1993). Brain scans have suggested that different brain patterns are activated when recalling facts learned by rote as opposed to in meaningful mode, which may explain why some rote learning, for example, of arithmetical tables, persists but why problem-solving strategies appear to be transferable to new problems only following meaningful learning. This theory contrasts with the ideas of developmental psychologists and information-processing theorists who argue that mental processes are domain-general not domain-specific. There is still doubt, however, about modularity or local-isation of brain functioning. Fodor (2000) queried his own claims for modularity and is sceptical about how much is actually known for certain about brain functioning.

Interest in how the brain works in relation to consciousness was revived by the publication and televising of Susan Greenfield's book, *Brain Story* (Greenfield, 2000). Greenfield cast doubt on the modularity theory, suggesting instead 'neuronal assemblies' in which millions of brain cells com-pete to create elements of consciousness. She did not provide robust evidence for this theory though. Blakemore and Frith (2005) explain that while the proliferation and pruning of brain cell connections in infancy encompasses most areas of the brain, the changes in the adolescent brain are specifically associated with regions of the cortex, including the prefrontal cortex. This is the area of the brain that deals with the higher order activities of planning, self-awareness, selecting behaviour and certain types of memory – sometimes referred to as executive functions.

Not only is there a dramatic reorganisation of connections related to the executive func-tions during this period, but there is also a significant increase in 'myelination'. Myelin is a white sheath of fat and protein that gradually develops around transmitter cells, insulating them and increasing the speed of interconnectivity. Myelination goes on into the twenties greatly increasing the speed of transmission between cells. These changes imply that there should be an improvement during the teens and early twenties in an individual's ability to focus attention, make decisions, exercise self-control and manipulate the memory to carry

Reader reflection

In acknowledging that the social world of the classroom is a crucial stage for learning, it is possible to consider two ostensibly competing perspectives on learning – the situated cognitive and the traditionally cognitive – coexisting as explanations of the learning process.

How might both be useful in their inferences for pedagogy?

The former could be said to be descriptive of the social contexts and interactions within which individual cognition, as explained from a cognitive perspective, occurs. The cognitive perspective can be used to explain phenomena about individual pupils' learning, personalities and behaviour implied by the analysis of empirical data.

But is it also helpful to do more than just describe these social, interactive contexts?

Learning environments can profitably be analysed from a situated perspective in order for researchers to understand, for example, the socio-political context and the educational, interactional settings within which the research takes place.

How could we make sense of the former without the latter?
It would be unbound by context and, as such, difficult to make sense of.

Can empirical validity and generalisability be claimed for a situated cognition research perspective?

The theoretical frameworks and constructs investigated within a traditional cognitive approach, for example the construct of learning style, intelligence or creativity, can be replicated but collectively constructed understandings which are bound by time and context are not replicable and therefore not amenable to empirical testing (Anderson et al, 1997).

out more than one task at a time. There are also likely to be subtle but significant developments in awareness both of oneself and of others, including the ability to understand another person's viewpoint – although these changes in social cognition may be temporarily obscured or confused by the effects of hormonal changes during puberty (see Palmer, 2006).

Thus the brain continues to grow and change over the first 20 years of life, which suggests that teaching methods at different stages in the educational process should be sensitive to these changes. Brain development seems to be more generalised the younger the learner. As students reach adolescence, neural connections in most areas become well established, but those in the regions associated with the executive functions continue to be fragile and malleable (Blakemore and Frith, 2005). Palmer (2006) suggests that it would make sense, therefore, for primary teachers to concentrate on a more general, holistic approach to education, helping to establish the overall architecture of the brain. They should also take into account that their pupils' attention span is likely to be shorter than adults', decision-making more difficult and working memory less efficient. Some tasks that seem negligible to adults are quite taxing for children. At secondary age, teachers should be able to assume that overall interconnectivity is established and concentrate on the still fragile areas in the prefrontal cortex, helping students become steadily more capable of selective attention, decision-making, planning and multitasking.

Psychologists are still trying to find an answer to the 'hard problem' of how subjective thought and streams of consciousness are derived from brain matter. In the meantime the most persuasive parts of neuro-scientific theory are cherry-picked for application within the classroom (see Chapter 9). To some extent work on brain functioning has impacted on education in a less superficial way, however, because of what it can tell us about specific learning disorders such as dyslexia, a reading disorder thought to derive from sensory-perceptual processing delays which impede the brain's phonological representation. Dyslexia is thought to affect 4–5 per cent of the school-age population, a not insignificant percentage. Problems about its definition and prevalence (more boys are reported to suffer from the condition but this may be because girls' better behaviour hides the problem) still abound (Elliott, 2005) but explaining the condition using 'brain science' has reduced the stigma which attached to it when the cause was attributed to lower intelligence.

Different views of intelligence

MULTIPLE INTELLIGENCES

Debate about whether a single intelligence can be identified or whether intellectual power is better characterised as multiple intelligences exercises contemporary theorists such as Nettelbeck and Wilson (2005) who reviewed past and current theories of intelligence. Those who favour an information-processing explanation of human understanding, Robert Sternberg in the USA, for example, describe intelligence in relation to its cognitive components. Thus Sternberg (1985) proposed a triarchic model of intelligence comprising three major aspects which interact with one another: analytical, creative and practical thinking. Analytical or *componential* intelligence is what is normally measured on IQ and achievement tests – planning, organising and remembering facts then applying them to new situations. Creative or *experiential* intelligence is the ability to see new connections between things and to develop original ideas. Practical or *contextual* intelligence is the ability to read situations and people, and manipulate them to best advantage. Neither experiential nor practical intelligence are measured in IQ tests according to Sternberg.

Much research effort has also been put into understanding genius, giftedness and creativity in relation to normal intelligence. Sternberg and O'Hara (1999) reviewed research into the relationship between intelligence and creativity, concluding that psychologists have still not reached a consensus about the relation between creativity and intelligence nor even a shared understanding of what these two constructs are. The very uncertainty of their work, however, should itself raise a critical awareness among educators of the complexity of their sometimes taken-for-granted assumptions about the measurement and fostering of 'ability' within learners. Sternberg's later work (2003b; 2005) argues for a model of intelligence that involves synthesising wisdom, intelligence and creativity (WICS). He bemoans the fact that Western society is organised around a closed system of selection that defines intelligence very narrowly. He counsels that giftedness is ultimately just expertise in development and that all measures of giftedness assess some kind of expertise to some extent.

Howard Gardner (1983; 1995) is well known for shunning a unitary explanation of intelligence, developing instead his theory of multiple intelligences (MI). Eight distinct intelligences are said to exist independently of one another: linguistic, spatial, logical-mathematical, musical, bodily-kinaesthetic, interpersonal, intrapersonal and naturalist. Gardner explained that individuals have different entry points to learning depending on the strength of their various intelligences. Sternberg (1999) pointed out that, although Gardner cited evidence to support his theory, he has not carried out research directly to test his model. Since we all recognise in ourselves some tendency to be better at some things than others, Gardner's theory seems intuitively to be relevant. However, if one sees cognition as the processing of information using fairly universal sets of mental strategies, it is difficult to conceive of separate, discrete intelligences. White (1998) has critiqued Gardner's theory in detail, questioning the criteria on which the designation of an intelligence is based and pointing out that much intelligent behaviour can often rely on more than one of Gardner's intelligences at once. Gardner's work has become very popular in educational circles, possibly because it offers an alternative to the view of intelligence as unitary and fairly stable, encouraging instead a focus on developing particular individual capabilities to their highest potential.

Silver et al (1997) advocated a synthesis of Gardner's MI theory with their own learning style theory, arguing that the former offers ideas about the content and context of learning while the latter elucidates the generalised processes of learning within which can be observed individual differences. Their integrated model of style and MI suggests how different combinations might translate into vocations, for example logical-mathematical intelligence within a person with a mastery learning style might lead to a job as an accountant or bookkeeper. Where it combines with an interpersonal learning style it is suggested the vocation might be a tradesperson or homemaker. There can be dangers in being overly enthusiastic about a theory or theories since a sceptic might argue that the integration of a different model of learning style with MI theory could elicit a whole range of other vocational trends.

The value of learning style theory, MI theory and other ideas we have looked at in this chapter is that they provide us with more questions with which to probe human behaviour and different ways of understanding it. Theoretical and empirical categorisations help us to make sense of our observations but attempting to characterise different types of learning or vocation too precisely can obscure our focus on the individual differences between people which make them unique.

A popular construct within the field of intelligence research is that of *emotional intelligence* (EI) (Goleman, 1995; Salovey and Mayer, 1990). While there is debate about the existence of discrete brain structures (the limbic system) for emotional experience and behaviour, there can be no doubt that an individual's emotional state and ability to deal with their feelings can impact on their educational performance. Traditionally this 'affective' domain of experience has been little more than acknowledged by educators with their main focus being on the 'cognitive' domain. It is now receiving more attention as a result of Goleman's popular work. He has related the ability to control impulses, motivate oneself and regulate moods to improved thinking and learning.

EI projects tend to combine common sense and neuroscience. Research has focused on the role of the prefrontal cortex, the part of the brain just behind the forehead, which develops most rapidly between the ages of 3 and 8. This mediates our emotional impulses, which come from the amygdala. The amygdala, part of the limbic system that controls and processes emotional experience and behaviour, takes over when someone is frightened or stressed (this is the well-known fight or flight mechanism that ensures survival) (OECD, 2005). It directs some of our most powerful and primitive feelings, such as fear, straight to all the major centres of the brain before the neocortex – the site of more rational reactions – has time to react. The amygdala thus controls the routing of information to the cortex, where it is stored as long-term memory; if a learner is frightened, perhaps of failure or reprisals, this transfer stops and long-term learning is prevented. The job of the prefrontal cortex is to manage some of these instinctive emotions, dampening some of the signals generated by the amygdala and weighing up appropriate reactions.

Hastings (2004) reported that a study was commissioned in 2002 by the DfES to look at all the literature about EI as well as the work of several English LEAs that were already committed to EI projects. The researchers found that schools developing programmes which fostered the emotional health of staff and pupils showed marked improvements in behaviour and learning, social cohesion, staff morale and confidence, and academic results. They did not, however, confirm a direct link between promoting emotional literacy and raising standards; this would be very difficult because isolating EI as the only variable making a difference would be almost impossible. Nettelbeck and Wilson (2005) concluded from their review of past and current intelligence theories that the existence of emotional intelligence cannot yet be confirmed.

Conclusion

Research into the ecology of development, suggestions about different types of intelligence, new understandings about the brain and the effect of underlying cognitive style on learning approaches and strategies, and an acknowledgement of the impact of social and emotional factors on motivation and achievement all contribute to a richer understanding of individual development through education.

Student activities

1 Find out what views your tutors and colleagues have about intelligence. Do they know anything about newer ideas of intelligence? Is there a tendency to think of intelligence as innate and fixed or do people conceptualise intelligence more fluidly? Try to explore this with any schoolteachers you know. How fundamental is their view of intelligence to the way they help pupils learn?

2 Think about your own learning style: do you write essays incrementally, piecing together the components one upon another or do you like to have a generalised idea of the whole essay before you start writing? Do you see pictures and images when you are thinking or reading, or do you find yourself thinking in words? Relate this to a review of some of the learning styles literature (see Riding and Rayner, 1998, for references).

The influence of social-constructivist ideas currently felt within institutions of education is very strong. These have built upon, rather than usurped, many of the ideas previously in favour. Even discredited notions of a single, measurable intelligence persist in our common-sense discourse of ability. The implications of more fluid ideas about intelligence, about the construction and site of knowledge and about the impact of greater learner autonomy through technologised forms of learning are beginning to impact on conventional wisdom about individual learning and achievement. Psychological research will continue to refine theoretical ideas about learning and, as students of education, you will enjoy a fascinating perspective on them. However, it is essential to adopt a critical stance when reviewing such research. This will be discussed further in Chapter 9.

Recommended reading

Blakemore, S-J. and Frith, U. (2005) *The Learning Brain. Lessons for Education.* London: Blackwell Publishing. This book reviews what we know about how and when the brain learns, and considers the implications of this knowledge for educational policy and practice. It covers studies on learning during the whole of development, including adulthood, and looks at what we can learn from brain research about children with learning difficulties.

Riding, R.J. and Rayner, S. (1998) *Cognitive Styles and Learning Strategies.* London: Fulton. This comprehensive text cites a huge range of research studies and explains clearly the many theoretical positions within style research. Well written and structured effectively, this book will be useful to those who want a deeper understanding of style constructs and their implications for education.

8

The influence of social factors, gender and ethnicity on achievement

This chapter explores the relationship between social factors and achievement in education. We have seen that factors such as intelligence and motivation are important in the success of individuals, but wider social influences are also highly significant. Research findings relating to class, ethnicity and gender are examined. The issue of equality of opportunity, which is so often taken for granted, is challenged. The assumption that schooling is one of the main determinants of a pupil's success is questioned in relation to the influence of wider social factors. The impact on education of discourses of class, gender and ethnicity is evaluated and current topical issues such as concerns about underachievement and school exclusion rates amongst African-Caribbean boys are discussed.

Introduction

The growth of concern with social factors and their relationship to educational achievement can be seen to correspond to the rise of policies of access and equality in Western nation states. Perhaps the most significant and enduring achievement of recent studies in relation to social factors in education has been to put questions of class, culture, gender and ethnicity at the centre of descriptions of educational processes and systems.

A number of questions arise. How might the specific practices of education be exclusive and excluding? In what ways do the everyday activities of the classroom, for instance, alienate children from various different types of background? What is the general culture of the school? How can it be described? How does it affect children from different backgrounds? At the centre of these lines of inquiry is the big question about whether education is doomed to replicate the inequalities in society or whether it can be an engine for challenging inequality and for promoting social justice. This chapter examines these questions by reference to class, gender and ethnicity issues in education.

The state of educational achievement

According to official statistics from the DfES overall educational achievement has increased steadily during the last two decades. End of key stage assessment has shown an increase in pupil attainment in the core subjects of English, mathematics and science (www.dfes.gov.uk). At every level of academic attainment more people hold qualifications and fewer people hold no qualifications. Over 76 per cent of young people between the ages of 16 and 18 are involved in full-time education or training (www.dfes.gov.uk/trends).

Educational achievement in higher education has also increased in the past decade with the number of English domiciled students in higher education rising by 25,000 between 1999/2000 and 2004/5 (www.dfes.gov.uk/trends). It might seem that the benefits of educational qualifications and access to higher education have been made available to the population as a whole. There is some truth in this, although what the figures mean in terms of patterns of inequality in society in general needs to be closely examined. More education for all does not necessarily mean more equal education. There are issues to confront about the distribution of education resources and benefits throughout the population. Inequalities in provision and achievement exist between individuals for a host of complex reasons but also, significantly, between social groups and 'population categories'.

Pupils at different types of school achieve different levels of success in public examinations. Selective schools, whether in the private sector or the maintained sector, have much higher percentages of their pupils achieving top grades than comprehensive (non-selective) schools. In selective schools in 2006, 98.3 per cent of pupils entered achieved 5 A* –C grades at GCSE whereas in comprehensive schools the figure was 56.4 per cent (www. dfes.gov.uk/rsgateway.) In addition, there are large, and fairly abiding, patterns of inequality associated with specific social groups. Social class, gender and ethnic group have been and remain key factors of inequality in education. The interaction between these three factors produces an even more powerful set of inequalities for many children. 'All pupils have a gender, class and ethnic identity – the factors do not operate in isolation' (Gillborn and Mirza, 2000: 23).

Social class and achievement

SOCIAL CLASS AND ECONOMIC BACKGROUND

Although social class is felt to be an important factor in educational achievement and has been on the 'agenda' of education studies for some time, it is not a category that is widely used in official statistics of education. As Hatcher (2004) points out, terms such as 'socio-economic status' and 'social advantage and disadvantage' are often used rather than class. Nevertheless, surveys which included class as a significant category have indicated that, by just about every criterion of achievement, middle-class pupils in maintained schools do better than working-class children. This imbalance was documented through a series of reports in the 1950s and 1960s when the question of class became a significant issue in education policy (Crowther, 1959; Gurney-Dixon, 1954; Newsom, 1963). These raised the issue of what kind of schooling was appropriate for a post-war democracy that created opportunities for all.

There has long been a relationship between wealth and education. In Victorian England the rich paid for the appropriate education of their sons as leaders and gentlemen at the expensive public schools. The poor and working class received little education at these times and what was given was largely provided by religious and capitalist benefactors in order to produce God-fearing, obedient and productive workers (see Chapter 4 for a history of the development of state schooling). Economic change led to the expansion of state education and greater social expectations of the people. This led to the liberal humanist view that Britain had become a meritocracy, in other words, that achievement in society was based upon effort and ability rather than position and power. From the liberal perspective education, whilst teaching us to live together, also offers the opportunity for individuals to develop in line with their ability and interests.

Studies of the earlier twentieth century pointed to the link between poverty and educational achievement (Halsey, 1978; 1995). It became clear that other social and cultural factors were linked to these economic conditions and these helped to explain why pupils from middle-class families continued to do better at school.

Although we may be tempted to assume that social change in the direction of equality has been significant, figures for Great Britain indicate that the link between social class, defined by parental occupation, and educational attainment remains strong.

According to DfES (2004a) figures, published and analysed in National Statistics Online (www.statistics.gov.uk), the gap in GCSE attainment levels by parental socio-economic group remains high and actually increased for a period in the 1990s.

The DfES figures show that 16 year olds with parents in higher professional occupations were far more likely to remain in full-time education compared with those with parents in routine occupations (www.statistics.gov.uk). Similarly, participation in further or higher education is strongly influenced by people's social and economic background. The HE sector expanded significantly in the early 1990s so more places became available. Statistics do not distinguish between institutions of different status but Oxford and Cambridge remain socially powerful and there exists an important social distinction between so-called new universities that were previously polytechnics (prior to 1992) and the established universities (Ward, 2006). The 'widening participation' agenda of the Labour government was intended to defray class inequalities in access to HE but lack of knowledge about what was available or possible led to disproportionate benefits for the middle classes (Blanden and Machin, 2004).

Even though educational provision has expanded there remains a strong correlation between the type of education received, success in school, progression to university and parental occupation. Children of the upper and middle classes continue to do better in the education system. Whitty (2002) suggests that class differentials will only be overcome if policies that address wider economic inequalities are addressed in addition to changes to the education system. Ball (2003) and Tomlinson (2005a) show how middle-class parents have been able to use their understanding of education systems and their social skills, since the end of the Second World War up to the present, to ensure that their children go to the 'best' schools and thus benefit from educational advantage (see Chapter 10 on the effects of political policy on educational opportunity).

Reader reflection

Inequality in achievement is recognised by the government in their five year strategy (DfES, 2004b) in which it is noted that in spite of all the recent reforms there remains:

a fundamental weakness in equality of opportunity. Those from higher socio-economic groups do significantly better at each stage of our system than those from lower ones – indeed … socio-economic group is a stronger predictor of attainment than early ability (DfES, 2004b, paragraph 20).

In what ways could you improve the achievement of those pupils from lower socio-economic groups in our society? Can you foresee any difficulties in implementing such ideas?

In order to understand how these inequalities work in education it is helpful to consider some theoretical explanations of how social factors influence achievement.

SOCIAL THEORIES OF ACHIEVEMENT

Social reproduction

Some theorists coming from a Marxist or social conflict perspective (see Chapter 2 for an outline of these), such as Bourdieu and Passeron (1977) and Bowles and Gintis (1976), portrayed the education system as being one of several mechanisms of social reproduction. By this they meant the way in which those groups in the more privileged and powerful social positions maintain their place from generation to generation. Thus the social inequalities in society are constantly being reproduced over time. Social reproduction theorists considered the education system played a very important part in this process.

For Bowles and Gintis (1976) the education received corresponds to the future working environments that these pupils can expect and as such prepares young people to take their 'appropriate' place in society. The children of the wealthy go to private schools where they 'learn' how to be successful. Schools in poor areas with predominantly working-class intakes are more likely to suffer from teacher shortages or to be housed in poorer buildings. They tend to be low attaining schools in terms of pupil achievements and most likely to be failing or put at risk by Ofsted in the current English education system. In state schools where there is more of a social mix the middle-class pupils tend to be concentrated in the higher academic groups whilst the working-class find themselves more likely to be placed in the lower teaching sets (Arnot and Reay, 2006). This reflects the future positions of pupils in society, which they come to see as 'normal' and expected as they replicate their positions within school.

How do pupils get separated onto different tracks like this? Officially they are grouped according to ability in order that they may be taught and learn more effectively. This grouping can begin at a very early stage in their school life with primary schools in England, for instance, being encouraged to teach pupils in ability groups at least in their literacy and numeracy lessons. However, Bowles and Gintis (1976) suggested that actually there is often very little measurable difference between pupils initially and that they are grouped on the basis of very little evidence. In fact grouping can result as much from teacher perceptions as actual academic difference. The pupils who teachers perceive as more able or likely to do well in the future are those that display middle-class characteristics. As time goes on the difference between groups of pupils may be seen to widen and this is due to the increasing effects of being taught differently, experiencing differential teacher expectations and being offered different opportunities through the curriculum.

The 'Hidden Curriculum'

If the 'official' curriculum is considered to be what is formally taught in school through subjects on the timetable, the 'hidden curriculum' is all that is taught and learned unofficially through the process of schooling. This is often as significant for the individual pupil as the formal learning. Bowles and Gintis originally coined the term as a result of a major study in the USA in which they noted the prevalence of regulatory practices: uniform, time keeping, rowed seating in classrooms, rules for corridor movement, the countless injunctions to maintain order and so on. They point out the training in boredom represented by the majority of school time, spent on passively being instructed or in actively performing tasks that have no obvious meaning or visible use. Effectively this is training in accepting relations of subordination, preparing the majority of pupils for a waged life working for a corporation or institution that will deploy similar tactics and practices for economic gain. What is fascinating is the similarities between the forms of control described in this study of 30 years ago and the rituals and routines that still prevail in schools today. A further form of control is exercised via the organisation of pupils into groups.

When pupils are put in different sets they are effectively being given a different 'value' depending upon whether they are in a top, middle or bottom group. Being placed in a high or low set is likely to be a very different experience for the individual pupil in terms of the enthusiasm and behaviour of their peers in the group, the attitude of the teachers, the type of work given and expectations of the amount and level of work they need to produce. The hidden curriculum message here is that pupils have a place in school (society) and the powers that be have mechanisms for keeping them in those places.

Finally, the hidden curriculum can be seen thriving within the apparently uncontrolled features of school life. Pupils learn how to survive on the corridors and in the toilets; they are aware of the pecking order that goes unnoticed by the official school system. There is a whole unofficial process of learning that these pupils go through. Thus school is good preparation for, and reflects, the communities that they will live in.

Social reproduction theory, then, demonstrates how the educational experiences of pupils correspond to their future employment. Schooling is in this way preparation for their future lives.

Cultural capital

Bourdieu and Passeron (1977) suggested that one main way in which education ensured the reproduction of society was by the passing on of cultural values from one generation to the next. Dominant culture is a set of properties, characteristics, behaviours, orientations that dominant class groups already have and that subordinate class groups must strive to acquire if they want to compete for educational success. As it is the dominant middle-class values that schools endorse it is the continued superior position of this group that is ensured. Middle-class children are already attuned to the codes and meanings of schooling, whereas for working-class children these are likely to be opaque.

Pupils who are used to these middle-class codes and 'live' them are able to take most advantage of the education system. Thus middle-class pupils are used, through their socialising experience as children in middle-class society, to conversing with adults in an appropriate manner. Middle-class children better understand how to speak, how to behave with books, how to sit at story-telling time and how to conduct themselves as good pupils in general. They have developed a wide, rich vocabulary, a social awareness and appropriate knowledge to a far greater degree than working-class pupils who have not had the same opportunities. Middle-class children are taught the importance of success at school for their future opportunities and have learned to practise deferred gratification at home (a belief that hard work now will lead to reward later) that is so important in creating this success. The whole process of schooling, as well as the institutional habits and demands, are likely to be much less amenable to working-class children's culture than to middle-class children's culture.

Social inequalities are not simply based on wealth. Bourdieu introduces the idea of cultural capital – the accumulation of cultural attributes that can be reinvested into education with a positive return for their holder. Bourdieu said that these cultural attributes possessed by middle-class children help them to progress at school and give them an advantage over their working-class peers. Their cultural values are in effect an economic advantage to be realised in the future. Thus they can be seen as a form of capital in the sense that an economist would use the term. They are cultural capital and of value to be invested in the same way as money is wealth to be invested for the future. As pupils progress through the various stages of schooling this cultural capital accumulates further and is ultimately high value currency to trade for a well-paid, high status role in society (Bourdieu and Passeron, 1977).

Reay (2006) notes that several contemporary theorists have been influenced by the work of Bourdieu in developing new conceptualisations of class processes and practices that embrace the influence of everyday, largely unacknowledged social class practices. Skeggs (2004), for instance, explained how class works as a form of property through race, gender, sexuality and nationality.

> Within such analyses class is seen as everywhere and nowhere, denied yet continually enacted, infusing the minutiae of everyday interactions while the privileged, for the most part, continue to either deny or ignore its relevance to lived experience. (Reay, 2006: 290)

Language

As language is such an important part of our means of communication the ability to use and understand language will be a significant factor in success in education. How we learn to read different genres and the range of vocabulary we develop will depend upon our exposure to different stimuli. This is particularly important in the early childhood years. The range of linguistic experience amongst children differs greatly, influenced largely by social background. Bernstein (1971, 1973) suggested that it was as though there are two different language codes in operation. The restricted code consists of short sentences with relatively simple words. This code gives basic description and relies on a tacit understanding of the area of conversation by all involved who make assumptions that are not verbalised. It relies on other communication apart from just verbal such as hand gestures and facial expressions. This is the sort of language that is used in brief everyday exchanges by everyone.

The elaborate code is, as the name implies, a much more sophisticated form of speech. It involves richer use of language with complex sentence construction and much more detailed explanation. This code does not rely on taken for granted assumptions or other non-verbal communication in transmitting the message. It is more applicable to polite social settings and gatherings. It may be portrayed as a more formal use of language. Due to its richness and more complex nature it is also more appropriate to formal learning situations. It is a form of language more familiar to the middle-class child who will have heard it in conversations between adults and also will have practised it with some of these adults as well as their own parents. Thus, whilst being the formal language of the middle-classes, it is also the language used in school by teachers and textbooks. Pupils who are more used to hearing and using such language will not notice any difference in a school setting. Those pupils not used to such language and unable to use it feel less easy in the formal school learning situation, are unlikely to express themselves in the expected manner at school and are more likely to be perceived as less able generally by their teachers. Bernstein suggested that working-class children were not used to hearing or using the elaborate code in their daily lives and so were at a disadvantage when they entered the formal learning environment of the primary school.

Bernstein proposed that language differences lead to different levels of achievement between class groups. In Bernstein's work language is an essential component for a description of the way that social structure and stratification works through education. Experience is organised through language but language differences are related explicitly to social systems. According to this position, language does not simply reflect the world but actively organises the world into categories of experience. Linguistic systems or dialects reflect different types of social experience, expressing the forms of life and dispositions particular to their social environments. Children therefore come to school from different linguistic environments that are not matched by forms of language used in schools. The acquisition of language and processes of socialisation could be said to be one and the same process producing cultural orientations. In effect, language differences represent different 'symbolic orders' for different groups (Bernstein, 1971 and 1973). In schooling, dominant forms of language may relate negatively or positively to the linguistic, symbolic legacies of sections of school populations.

The danger in the position expressed by Bernstein in relation to class, language and education was the attribution of *essential* qualities to the differences between working-class language and middle-class language, and the potential correlation of working-class culture with less expressive linguistic forms. The use of the distinction between working-class speech as 'restricted code' and middle-class speech as 'elaborated code' became infamous, as it seemed to imply a hierarchy of expressive power. This position was tackled positively in the work of Labov and in the development of sociolinguistics by Halliday, who refined Bernstein's thought with a more acute sense of the arbitrary nature of symbolic linguistic power (Halliday, 1979). Both Labov and Halliday were keen to shift the argument away from the taint of deficit models of working-class language implied by Bernstein. While Halliday reminds us of the *social* dimension of educational failure, he also flags up the *linguistic* aspect of educational failure: 'Educational failure is really a social problem, not a linguistic one; but it has a linguistic aspect ...' (Halliday, 1979: 24). This focus on language indicates how cultural difference may be a crucial factor in achievement in education.

Labov's work was significant as a radical departure in debates about language and education, insisting that 'the logic of non-standard English', the grammar and the expressive power of non-standard forms was in all ways comparable with the standard, dominant and educationally privileged forms (Labov, 1973). The effect was to deflate the myth of linguistic deprivation, while also indicating that the effect of the domination of standard English was to maintain existing inequalities of access.

In the USA, the question of language has consistently drawn much interest and analysis, especially in relation to the underachievement of large sections of the population, particularly African Americans who have consistently fared less well through state-funded education. Schools are constantly promoting ideas about language and linguistic norms. All pupils do not share these norms equally. Certain groups may actually have quite different linguistic norms as part of their upbringing or lived cultural heritage. This means that many children, black American children particularly, may experience the school as a linguistically and culturally alienating environment.

Rather than have their children and pupils suffer the kind of cultural negation that can come from being unrecognised by the official and unofficial language of the school, some activists adopted an alternative approach. They decided that the best way to ensure that the culture of the school was not alienating for the children from African-American background was to use the language of black Americans, called 'Ebonics', as a medium of instruction. They took positive measures to celebrate the linguistic heritage of their charges and to teach the characteristics of Ebonics and draw comparisons with so-called standard English. Delpit (1995) and Smitherman (2000) have written about the need to make schools user-friendly, cultural, linguistic environments for African-American pupils and have demonstrated how Ebonics may be used to effect changes in the rates of success for African-American children in state schools. The Ebonics movement has been politically contentious, partly because it challenges the given order of things and partly because it has been misread as an attempt to offer a non-academic curriculum to African-American children (Labov, 1997).

The Ebonics issue has many implications when examining the use of language in education, particularly concerning the school as a linguistic environment.

- It indicates the extent to which language is a significant factor in educational success and failure.
- It raises questions about the nature and social role of standard English in education, particularly in relation to practices of assessment.
- It highlights the tension between the cultures of pupils in schools and the culture expressed in the dominant practices of the school and the curriculum.

It is interesting to consider the development of the Ebonics movement in relation to the emergence of Saturday schools for black youth in the UK. Parents uneasy about what they perceive to be lax codes of discipline exercised in mainstream schooling have established these schools.

Labelling

Symbolic interactionists see individual existence as always being bounded and impinged on by external forces (see Chapter 2 for more details on this group of theorists). We are what we are by process rather than by fixed characteristics or identity. Identity is produced by the relation between your view of yourself and the way others view and react to you. Identity is always being worked on. It is in a state of flux and it may well vary considerably according to context. In addition, the institutions we inhabit impose social roles upon us like that of pupil or teacher. David Hargreaves' seminal study, *Social Relations in a Secondary School* (1967), indicates how the school effectively (and not always at a conscious level) defines pupils as conformist or non-conformist, successful or not successful. This sets up a dynamic of social relations that produces broadly differentiated subcultural groups in the pupil population. So pupils who find themselves being negatively defined in relation to the dominant values of the school in terms of behaviours, attitudes and academic work may themselves accept this definition. They may also transform it into a positive form of identity so that an alternative form of high status can be achieved by rule-breaking and general non-conformism. In *Deviance in Classrooms* (Hargreaves et al, 1975), factors such as appearance, attitudes to discipline, ability to work, 'likeability', relations with other pupils, personality and deviance rating were found to contribute to the way that teachers distinguish and define pupils.

Teachers 'size up' pupils using knowledge gained from their past experiences of teaching, i.e. whether a child is good, naughty, clever, low ability, a 'typical' boy or girl etc., and then react appropriately to a range of classroom situations. Teachers will tend to apply a range of stereotypical experiences that will help them interpret each situation in order to decide how to act. The use of labels and stereotypes is like using an adaptable template to overlay onto social settings to aid understanding and guide actions. Pupils also need to make sense of classroom life and to find themselves a place in this social setting. They become quickly aware of the teacher's position in the classroom and how this varies from teacher to teacher. They will also make initial decisions about classmates. The decisions made by the teachers and pupils about all of those others in the classroom are initially provisional and open to change and negotiation but over time become clearer and more agreed.

Early on in classroom life certain behaviours, however casual, become noted and a label is attached to the 'actor'. It may be to do with such things as (lack of) intellectual ability, temperament, lack of concentration, poor attitude to school, 'coolness'. The label becomes reinforced if the appropriate behaviour is repeated, especially if other associated characteristics are also present, such as physical appearance of the pupil, how the pupil speaks to others, who the child's friends are, i.e. whether they are associated with a 'nice' or a rough crowd. The person being labelled is often not aware of a negative label that is being placed upon them until it has actually happened. Subsequent behaviour serves to reinforce the label and the expectations of others. Thus we expect naughty boys to behave badly, watch out for any signs of misbehaviour and punish it immediately. This may cause resentment and further difficult behaviour from these boys as they feel they are being picked on and treated differently from others. This surly response from them will further serve to confirm our opinion of their difficult behaviour and bad attitude. Any 'normal' behaviour by the boys, even if it takes up the majority of their time in the classroom, is unlikely to be noticed. We only really 'pick up' on behaviour that confirms the label. Thus as labels become reinforced it becomes more difficult for the 'subject' to resist, escape, change, or amend them, though not impossible.

Labelling theory suggests that as types get imposed upon pupils this affects their sense of themselves and their identity. In the long run this will influence their performance and potential to achieve. Labels will mean that others treat them according to their label. Thus certain pupils are 'policed' around the classroom and the whole school more than others as they are instantly recognised by other teachers and pupils. It then becomes even harder for these 'leopards to change their spots' and they will tend to develop a self-image that matches the label. They come to accept that they are 'not very good at school things'. Consider the following case study of how labelling works:

A case study of a group of pupils with learning difficulties

A number of reception class pupils, due to a range of reasons, do not initially take to reading and writing. As they move to Year 1 their classroom teacher identifies these pupils as needing extra support. In the classroom they are put in a group with other pupils who have been similarly identified as needing help and their table has a teaching assistant working with them for most of the time. Sometimes their whole table works with another teacher away from the rest of the class in a small room in what is called the special learning unit.

Their classmates soon see these pupils as different. They begin to be called names associated with low ability, are easily mocked by peers when they make mistakes and are laughed at when they express their opinions in class discussion. In a short time they become very unsure of themselves. They come to accept that they are not very clever at school and that most of their classmates are better than they are at everything. They stop volunteering for things and wish to be left alone. They will begin to avoid writing, as this is where they can be further identified as failures. Thus pupils become labelled and in the end behave in a way expected. For the pupils in this example the label will be reinforced as they do badly in each assessment throughout their school life and ultimately end up in the bottom sets in the secondary school. The difference between these pupils and those in the top sets will become greater over time.

The chance of being labelled and the ability to resist labels varies depending upon circumstances and also upon the social ability of the subject, or what we explained earlier as their cultural capital. Rist (1970), looking at interaction in American kindergartens, found that teachers quickly labelled and defined pupils as soon as they entered school and that the crucial factor in determining positive and negative identities was social class. Becker (1971), in researching schoolteachers and councillors in Chicago, identified how they defined the 'ideal pupil' and how pupils from non-manual backgrounds most closely fitted this ideal whereas pupils from traditional working-class, manual backgrounds were furthest from it.

Thus middle-class pupils who are being naughty are more likely to be seen as high-spirited than be labelled as disruptive pupils. They do not have the associated attributes of someone usually seen as disruptive or anti-school. It is more likely that other reasons for this behaviour will be identified and the problem can be 'solved'. However, once a label, such as lacking in ability, disruptive and naughty, has been assigned to a pupil it is difficult to resist. In fact the more a pupil reacts against sanctions and authority the stronger the label of 'problem pupil' becomes.

How pupils are labelled can also influence the learning opportunities made available to them. Smith (2001) explains that the labelling of African-American boys in special education is influenced by a number of judgements. Access to knowledge by pupils depends on teachers' judgements about the ability of pupils to use it and about their readiness. Social class has been found to be strongly influential in how teachers make judgements about pupils' relative 'abilities'. So it is that 'appropriate' knowledge is directed towards 'appropriate' pupils (Ball, 1981; Keddie, 1973). From these studies it is clear that through a process of social construction pupils are classified and evaluated in schools. Chapter 9 deals with the issue of organising pupils for learning in more detail.

Related to the labelling process the concept of *self-fulfilling prophecy* indicates how the definitions that teachers make of pupils can powerfully influence how well they do and is a factor in determining their level of academic school success. Various studies have indicated how teachers react differently to pupils when given different types of information about them (Rosenthal and Jacobson, 1968).

Self-fulfilling prophecy

This concept was used by J.W.B. Douglas in his now classic study *The Home and the School* (1964) to describe the social process whereby working-class pupils came to underachieve. Douglas studied a sample of middle-class and working-class pupils and their progress through primary school.

There were material differences between middle- and working-class households that affected the schooling of the pupils noted by Douglas, such as the more overcrowded housing, fewer material possessions and poorer diet of many working-class pupils. He found that middle-class parents were more able to help their children achieve in the education system having been usually more successful themselves. They were able to 'push' their children and were more likely to contact the school and speak to the teachers about their children's progress. Working-class parents also wanted their children to do well at school but were less aware of how to achieve this. They were less confident when talking to the teachers about their children's progress not having been successful at school themselves and tended to ask more about their children's behaviour in lessons rather than academic progress. The teachers got to know their pupils quickly and formed expectations early on as to how well they could do. Douglas found that the teachers subconsciously expected more from the pupils with middle-class characteristics who, from their previous experience, were associated with success. It happened that it was these pupils that did in fact tend to do better. Douglas suggested that this could have been due to their ability and their better social circumstances but also to what he called a self-fulfilling prophecy.

This implied that if you expect students/pupils to do well then they will often fulfil expectations. This may be due to the teachers helping them and encouraging them more; also the student may work harder because they believe they are able to do what others expect of them. Conversely, if you don't expect pupils to succeed, as a teacher, you may not stretch them as much and will almost prepare them to do less well. As a pupil you will become resigned to others doing better than you. Douglas suggested that the expected low achievement of working-class pupils and the expected high achievement of middle-class pupils became effectively a self-fulfilling prophecy.

Reay claims that, despite government rhetoric on both sides of the Atlantic about equity, freedom and choice, very little progress has been made towards social justice and equality in education for the working-classes over the past hundred years (2006: 304). She cites evidence from a number of studies that indicate that social class continues to exert a significant influence upon the educational achievement of pupils and students but has little impact on educational policy. We now turn our attention to gender, another important influence on educational achievement.

Gender and achievement

SEX AND GENDER

Defining terms

It is important to first examine the terms 'sex' and 'gender' that are used to categorise and identify us all. Sex refers to our biological make up. It identifies us as male or female. Biological differences include chromosomes, hormones and physical sexual characteristics such as sexual organs, body hair, physique, etc. Gender refers to the social construction of masculine and feminine. It is what we expect males and females to be 'like' in terms of behaviour, appearance, beliefs and attitudes. There has been a continuing debate as to how much of our maleness and femaleness is biologically determined and how much is socially constructed.

A biological determinist, or essentialist position, as outlined by Kehily (2001) purports that, even though we are subject to social constraints, it is our biological make up that plays the major part in determining who we are and how we behave. This viewpoint suggests that even in modern industrial societies our biological sex still to a large extent determines our behaviour, so that the two sexes relate to each other in a way that maintains human survival. The functionalist perspective of some early sociologists such as Parsons (1959) and Davis and Moore (1967), whilst exploring the influence of cultural factors on the development of societies, still have a biological underpinning to their theories. The family was seen as a functional prerequisite to the maintenance of any society and the conjugal roles of the male breadwinner and the female homemaker/child rearer are presented as being the most appropriate. Though alternatives are seen as possible, there is a view promulgated by these functionalists that the 'normal' roles of men and women, with their biological basis, provide the best 'fit' for any kind of society. So, whilst in some, often traditional, communities these sociologists could point to large extended families and in others, usually modern industrial societies, to nuclear families, the role of women is seen essentially as domestically based in both.

The physical differences between males and females, whilst being less apparent in young children, become more obvious as we grow up and move through adolescence and into adulthood. However, there is a wide variation both within and across the genders in terms of individual physical characteristics. What is deemed as attractive to the opposite sex is different from society to society and changes over time with fashion. Clothing, diet and body building/reducing exercises to change our appearance are all used and with advances in medical science people can radically alter their physical characteristics and even biological sex. In modern societies and across a range of cultures any presentation of a clear uncomplicated sexual divide would constitute an oversimplification.

Differentiating between notions of sex and gender became more important when early feminist writers such as Oakley (1975) wished to highlight the significance of cultural as opposed to biological factors in explaining the ongoing socially inferior position of women in society. Their argument was that though there are biological differences between the sexes, it was social constructions of gender and sexuality that led to the oppression of women. The biological arguments were seen as part of the male hegemony that perpetuated the myth of male superiority. The whole notion of masculinity and femininity could be seen to be socially rather than biologically determined and could thus be challenged. What still remains unclear is the dividing line between biological and social influences on an individual's gender construction.

Influences upon the creation of gender

If we were to consider different societies in history and around the world we see many differences in gender roles. In her now classic anthropological account, Mead (1935) found great variation in the roles of men and women in a study of three tribes in New Guinea. In one tribe both men and women were gentle and submissive with little clear division between the sexes whilst in another men were more aggressive with women being more submissive. In the third, women were more involved in leadership of the group and were more aggressive whereas the males were responsible for domestic tasks, were more 'fussy' about their appearance and tended to gossip. For Mead this illustrated the significance of social expectations upon male and female behaviour.

The representation of gender as a binary split between masculine and feminine makes them appear as opposites with everyone falling either side of the sexual binary line. In this way stereotypes of male and female can be presented as diametrically opposed, for example male v. female, hard v. soft, rational v. emotional. Kehily (2001) suggests that the dualist creation of gender by society can have direct bearing on our sexuality and sexual identity. Thus from birth we begin to be male or female and to be mistaken for being of the opposite sex from that with which you identify is a significant concern as we seek to maintain our self-identity.

Gender characteristics that stereotype appropriate physical appearance and behaviour can cause pressure to conform, particularly on young people who are coming to terms with themselves as they develop. To be identified as different or 'other' can have a significant effect upon the self-image of young people. Kehily (2001) examines the issues of sexuality in school and how identities are negotiated and created. Pupil interaction and perceptions are significant in the 'othering' process. Labels become attached to pupils and some are more difficult to resist or counter than others. Language plays a very powerful part in this process and use of sexual insults such as 'queer' or 'slag' have lasting repercussions on the identities, future interactions and sexual behaviour of the young people involved. Use of such terms, whilst causing conformity amongst many for fear of being seen as different, may actually serve to distance and create outsiders of others. Vicars (2006), in an article entitled 'Who are you calling queer? Sticks and stones can break my bones but names will always hurt me', drew upon autobiographical accounts to show the implications of being identified as 'queer' within schools and the effects of homophobic language on such pupils.

Masculinities and femininities

If we carefully examine groups of young people and consider the broad range that exists in terms of behaviour, beliefs, values, preferred appearance, etc. we see that it becomes difficult to place them all into too rigid a definition of what constitutes female or male behaviour. The majority of boys are not disruptive in the classroom and all girls do not get on with their work quietly. For this reason some writers, such as Kenway and Willis (1998), Mac an Ghaill (1994), Paechter (1998) and Swain (2004), speak of masculinities and femininities that allow for greater variation. As Reay says, 'Femininity is not a unified discourse ... femininity is dynamic, various and changing and it is perhaps helpful to think in terms of multiple femininities rather than one femininity' (2001: 153). Swain says that pupils live within the context of their own communities and that these wider contexts influence the local school policies. 'Each school has its own *gender regime* which consists of ... individual personnel expectations, rules, routines and a hierarchical ordering of particular practices' (2004: 182). Whilst there is a great deal of commonality between schools there is also variation.

However, male dominance, or patriarchy, in many societies is clear. Theories of biological determinism may in fact help to maintain this supposedly 'natural' order of things. Feminists, in particular, point to the patriarchal hegemony that enables these explanations to persist.

Feminist perspectives

Feminism takes the ideological perspective that women are placed at a disadvantage to men in society by virtue of their gender. Feminists seek to study, explain and highlight these disadvantages with a view to creating change in future power/gender relationships. Wide variations in beliefs exist, from what could be termed moderate to extremist, under the general umbrella term of feminism. Taylor (1995), from the overview of different feminist groups conducted by Oakley, identified four main sub-categories as follows, though they accept that even this attempt at categorisation can only be considered as very generalised.

1 *Liberal feminists* believe that society can be reformed and equal opportunities achieved through peaceful protest and campaigning. They are basically using the democratic political process and education of the people to create change. They would argue that it is this strategy that has led to the social and economic reforms that have altered the position of women since Victorian times, securing the vote, equality in educational provision and better employment opportunities. However, the fight against prejudice is not completed and the campaigning needs to continue.

2 *Radical feminists* do not see change coming through liberal reform. They see the very ideas, values and belief systems that underpin society as reinforcing the domination by men of women, a system they call 'patriarchy'. Radical feminists believe that women need to gain independence from men and that this can only be achieved by separating from them.

3 *Marxist feminists* consider the capitalist system of production as being the cause of inequality and oppression in society. As well as social class, unequal gender relationships form part of the division and oppression created by this type of economic production. Thus Marxist feminists work for the overthrow of the capitalist system in order to destroy the existing class and gender divisions.

4 *Black feminists* stress the oppression they face that encompasses both ethnic and gender relationships. In effect they suffer from unequal relationships with both black and white men and also white women.

POLICY APPROACHES TO GENDER DIFFERENCES

Historical developments in gender relations and the schooling of boys and girls

The roles of men and women and their relationships are not fixed and have varied over time. This can be illustrated by considering the comparatively short period from Victorian England to the present day. In the early 1800s Britain was very much a patriarchal society. Women were not able to vote, own property or obtain a divorce. Within the middle classes it was considered essential for a young woman to become married and they effectively moved from being controlled by their father to being controlled by their husband. It was men who governed the empire and the society. Men ran businesses and supported the family. Women did not work and were confined to a life that revolved around the home. Boys from the more affluent classes would be educated at public and grammar schools but the education of girls would be primarily left to governesses, would be conducted in the home and would revolve around acquiring the skills and knowledge suitable for a lady. For the working classes life was much harder and both men and women worked, though women did the more menial factory work and were paid less than men. In the early educational provision for the working classes girls were able to attend school as well as boys, though both were taught appropriately to the social expectations of the time.

It took years of pressure and steady change in social attitude for women to gain legal equality with men. They gained the right to divorce and, importantly, to retain their own property upon divorce. After years of campaigning women gained the vote in 1918. However, this was only for those over 30. They did not gain it on equal age terms with men until 1928. It was still legally possible to discriminate in terms of gender. So women could be paid less than men for the same job, and it was possible to refuse someone employment because they were female and therefore considered unsuitable. It was possible to refuse entry to social gatherings on gender grounds. Thus many public houses had male only bars where women were only allowed at the weekends. The Sex Discrimination Act of 1975 outlawed discrimination on the grounds of gender.

From this date women, legally at least, had equality with men. However, whilst there had been these legal changes there were still economic and social differences that were strongly influenced by gender. In employment terms women remained very underrepresented in many, usually more highly paid professions and the average earnings of women remained well below that of men. It has actually been very difficult for women to 'break into' male dominated areas such as medicine, law and engineering. The term 'the glass ceiling' has been coined to illustrate the invisible but powerful constraints upon the progression of women upwards in society. It was also still largely accepted that a woman's place was really in the home and that the man was the breadwinner. In this way women's employment was largely seen as a temporary occupation before they raised children or as a way of supplementing the main income of the husband when the children were older. Changes in attitude have continued to take place and over the years women have increasingly taken up careers in many areas that previously they did not. Due to changes in employment rights, women and men are entitled to maternity and paternity leave that makes it more possible for a woman to pursue her career and have children. It is also significant that men are employed in some occupations that were previously considered suitable for women only such as nursing. However, whilst there has been a change in social attitudes and lifestyles, it is still not a level playing field. Whilst many women now have more demanding jobs, domestic responsibilities do not seem to have been equally shared and they still take most responsibility for running the household. Women's average earnings still lag behind those of men and they are still underrepresented in many areas of higher paid employment (www.statistics.gov.uk).

Social and political attitudes are reflected in education. State education has been provided since the end of the nineteenth century to all pupils regardless of gender. The introduction of the tripartite system saw the development of single sex grammar schools and often, though not always, single sex secondary modern schools. It was the development of new large comprehensive schools from the 1960s onwards that saw boys and girls taught together in their secondary education. However, being taught in the same school did not necessarily mean that they had equal opportunity, nor that gender did not have a significant effect upon a pupil's experiences. This was the time when the women's liberation movement was highlighting gender inequality in society. These inequalities were reflected in the classroom where teachers, peers and parents treated boys and girls very differently. At that time it was not considered politically incorrect to have gender specific stereotypical expectations of pupils so curricular activities were unashamedly contrived around them, for example needlework for girls and metalwork for boys.

In the 1970s and 1980s much feminist research in education was concerned with the perceived underachievement of girls and how the education process worked to maintain this through discrimination and marginalisation. The gender differences were maintained and highlighted through the processes of schooling that involved the separation of the genders, differences in uniform, a gender-specific curriculum and differential expectations of behaviour. This was further enforced through the attitude of teachers, peers, parents and later, their usually male, employers. Feminist researchers were interested to show how the ambitions of female students remained low and how they were discouraged in a variety of ways from choosing the 'hard' mathematical and scientific subjects so important to future employment prospects in favour of the more 'feminine' arts and humanities.

Oakley (1975) looked at the socialisation of young children and how they acquire their gender roles from home, school and peers. Children learn gender expectations from the society surrounding them and these lessons are reinforced through play. Whyte (1983) looked at gender stereotyping and bias in the primary school curriculum. This was displayed through reading schemes and lesson content that emphasised the different positions of men and women in society. Sharpe (1976) considered the influence of gender stereotypes in secondary schools and how this encouraged teenage girls to behave in 'feminine' ways and to develop gendered career aspirations. Spender (1982) investigated interaction in the classroom, language and the curriculum. She noted the marginal position of girls in the classroom and the message this gave about their future roles in society.

Curriculum changes

Strategies were developed to make the curriculum more girl friendly in response to such concerns and there have been many initiatives designed to raise the achievement of girls by raising awareness, altering attitudes, increasing ambition. Consideration was given to the curriculum and teaching methods. A seminal example is the Girls into Science and Technology Project (GIST), a four year project from 1979–83 that investigated the reasons for girls' underachievement in science and technology and encouraged teachers to develop classroom strategies to change this (Smail, 2000). Similarly, Genderwatch was a practical evaluation pack that enabled teachers to monitor gender in all areas of school life with a view to raising awareness and taking positive anti-discriminatory action (Myers, 1987). These initiatives tended to be individual rather than coordinated and Murphy and Gipps (1996) have suggested that although they have worked for many, mainly middle-class, girls, they have been singularly unsuccessful for a great many others and, in fact, have provoked a male backlash.

Whilst this research, raising of awareness and development work was based on the underachievement of girls relative to boys, the actual figures show that the reality was not that straightforward. Even in the 1970s girls were outperforming boys in English and modern foreign languages (MFL). Also, more girls were achieving five or more O level passes (equivalent to A*–C, GCSE) than boys. However, because these included subjects that were seen as low status such as home economics and because boys were doing better at maths and sciences, regarded as 'hard' subjects of high status, girls were perceived as underachieving (Francis, 2000). Also, it should be noted that the tripartite system, in operation before the widespread development of the comprehensive system, had favoured boys due to the larger number of places available in boys' grammar schools as opposed to those admitting girls. Thus boys did not need to score as highly as girls in the 11-plus to secure a grammar school education.

Dillabough (2001) suggests that much of the initial work in this area was a sustained attempt to expose patriarchal school structures, challenge sexist school practices and ultimately reform the process by which both boys and girls were educated. The social and cultural reproduction theories of Bourdieu and Passeron (1977) and Bowles and Gintis (1976) and the hegemony of the capitalist, patriarchal society (Gramsci, 1985, 1991) were used to explain the subjugation of women along with the working classes as part of preparation for their future roles in society. However, though these grand theories were useful tools of explanation as Arnot (2002) notes, they tended to be very deterministic and did not enable explanations of change or allow for personal agency by which women could begin to rise out of their inferior position. This led gender theorists to consider constructions of gender identity.

The Conservative government came to power in 1979 emphasising competition, individual achievement and success. The Tories did not trust the liberal education establishment and sought to reform the education system. Whilst not being concerned with the promotion of equal opportunities, one of their reforms, the introduction of the National Curriculum, had what is now often regarded as a significant impact on the achievements of girls (Francis, 2000). From its inception all pupils were required to take the whole curriculum. Thus it was no longer possible for boys or girls to 'drop' some subjects in favour of others.

The Conservatives were also responsible for the introduction of league tables at GCSE and A level that were used to judge overall school performance. These tables made the achievements of boys and girls more transparent than ever. Since the introduction of these tables it can be seen how the performance of both boys and girls has steadily improved. What has caught the public attention, though, is that the improvement in the results of girls has been greater than that of boys. Whilst continuing to outperform boys in language subjects, girls have caught up boys in maths and the sciences. Concern is now focused on the performance of boys.

RELATIONSHIP BETWEEN GENDER AND ACHIEVEMENT

GCSE and examination performance

In 2001/2, 58 per cent of girls in their last year of compulsory education achieved five or more GCSE grades A*–C, compared with 47 per cent of boys. In 2005/6, 63.9 per cent of girls achieved five or more GCSE grades A* –C, compared with 54.3 per cent of boys (www.dfes.gov).

Table 8.1 *Those pupils achieving A*–C in selected subjects at Key Stage 4 as a percentage of all pupils in schools at the end of 2005/06*

	Boys	Girls
English	51	67
Maths	52	55
Any science	49	51
Double science	38	41
Physics	8	6
Modern foreign language	26	39
Geography	20	18
History	20	22

Source: DfES (www.dfes.gov)

Whilst there is a need to be very careful when interpreting statistics such as these on gender and examination performance (Gorard, 2000; Hammersley, 2001), we can see from the figures that from 2001/2 to 2005/6 the percentage of all pupils gaining five or more GCSE grades at A*–C has increased. Girls have continued the trend that Francis (2000) had noted in relation to O level, that is, attaining a higher percentage of five or more passes at A*–C than boys. What is significant is when the achievements of males and females are compared for each subject. Girls are now doing better than boys in all the core subjects apart from the single sciences when taken separately, reflecting perhaps the continuing male bias in these subjects.

Explanations for boys' achievements

Elwood notes that over the last two decades we have shifted from debates about equal opportunities and improving the educational experiences of girls to those concerning notions of underachievement and male disadvantage (2005: 337). Moral panic developed over boys' underachievement, particularly in the popular press. Clearly this was rather an overreaction (Connolly, 2004). After all, overall results of both boys and girls improved. Girls' improvement has been greater but not by a great deal. The media has portrayed boys as falling behind. They have homed in on the apparent growth of a 'laddish' culture among teenage boys that is anti-study, against school values and leads to underachievement.

   Various explanations have been offered to explain why girls are performing better than boys.

(1) **Genetic differences** In previous times it has been the assumption, due to male hegemony, that women were the weaker and thus the inferior sex that needed to be protected. This was considered to be in all aspects, not just muscular strength. It is interesting that the consistently higher level of achievement by girls academically can now lead us to the conclusion that this is due to genetic differences, i.e. the intellectual superiority of women. Noble et al (2001) point out that, interesting though this notion is, the evidence is cur-

rently very thin. They also warn against the taking up of stereotypes that ignore the fact that difference in achievement between genders is not that large and more importantly that great variations in achievement occur within the genders. Feminist analysts would suggest that the 'moral panic' that has accompanied this perceived failure of boys and the demand to rectify the situation is a reflection of the fear within the male dominated political establishment that there may be some basis to the genetics argument.

(2) **Changes in society and the masculine image** There have in recent decades been enormous changes in the economy that have had repercussions on how people earn their living, the organisation of the family and the amount of leisure time and disposable income available. The traditional occupations based upon heavy industry dominated by male workers that involved strength and training in traditional skills have disappeared. This has had significant effects upon communities based around these industries such as mining, ship-building, steel and deep sea fishing (Noble et al, 2001). Newer forms of employment are service based and seen as being more traditionally female. The male is no longer the only, or even the major 'breadwinner'. Thus the traditional masculine image in working-class communities is no longer applicable as it was even twenty years ago. It is suggested that, whilst many families have more leisure time with more disposable income to spend upon home luxuries, holidays, clothes, etc. and women play more of an active role in society, many working-class boys see no particular role for themselves. They see no need to work hard at school as it will make little difference to their future. At the same time these boys emphasise and play out their masculinities at school where it is important to be seen as 'hard', 'cool', not a 'poof' or a 'swot' (Smith, 2003). Of course it can be argued that working-class boys could always get masculine jobs in the past and so have never really had reason to work hard at school. Perhaps, as Connolly suggests, forms of masculinities and femininities that exist are not just about gender alone but are combinations with social class and ethnicity that 'produce differing and enduring forms of identity' (2006: 15).

(3) **School culture** It is suggested that the school culture works against the achievement of boys and in favour of girls (Noble et al, 2001, and Smith, 2003, discuss these arguments). There are a number of strands to this point of view.

- It is assumed that the assessment regimes have developed to favour girls with more emphasis on coursework rather than final exams. However, this trend has reversed in recent years with no significant falling back of girls' performance.
- The curriculum is said to favour girls with little to excite boys and the type of learning is considered not to suit boys' learning styles. This point ignores the nature of many aspects of the curriculum where content is specifically chosen to attract boys. Also, learning styles do vary for girls as well as for boys. Arnot and Miles (2005) suggest that the increasing emphasis on a performative school system has led to greater resistance from working-class boys who have a history of low achievement. This, they say, is being misinterpreted as a new development termed 'laddishness'.
- Jones and Myhill (2004) noted how beliefs about identity can inform teachers' perceptions resulting in a tendency to associate boys with underachievement and girls

with high achievement. Elwood (2005) says that boys are now seen as 'poor boys' or 'boys will be boys' or, associated with this second stereotype, 'problem' boys. Proposed solutions to low achievement emanating from these stereotypes involve shifting classroom practices in order to engage boys' interests. She points to a whole raft of initiatives and policies and associated publicity involved in tackling the problem of boys' underachievement.

Reader reflection

After reading about the achievements of girls and boys, how helpful are the concepts of self-fulfilling prophecy and labelling in explaining differential achievement in terms of gender?

In summarising the arguments concerning gender and achievement at GCSE we can say that the performance of boys, and girls overall has improved throughout the 1990s and the 2000s, that girls have been improving faster than boys, and that they are now outperforming boys in many subjects and are at least performing more or less equally in all. However, to portray girls as achieving and boys as underachieving is too simplistic a view (Arnot and Miles, 2005; Gipps, 2006; Elwood, 2005). It should be noted that the differences in overall performance of boys and girls are not that great. It is the improvement in performance of girls from the more middle-class backgrounds in all subjects that has caused the rise in girls' performance overall. Boys from middle-class backgrounds continue to generally perform well. Boys and girls from the lower socio-economic groups continue to underperform when compared to their more affluent peers. Thus, as Connolly (2006) says, whilst gender does exert an influence on GCSE attainment, this is overshadowed by the effects of social class and ethnicity.

Ethnicity and achievement

'RACE' AND ETHNICITY

A further social factor that influences educational achievement is that of 'race' or ethnicity. It is important to consider what the terms 'race' and 'ethnicity' actually mean.

'Race'

'Race' is a form of classification whereby individuals are grouped according to certain genetically inherited physical characteristics. People are categorised by 'racial' groupings in matter of fact ways and in daily conversations the term 'race' is applied as though the labels given are straightforward. However, apart from being a socially loaded concept, the use of 'race' as a means of categorisation is fraught with problems.

Using the term 'race' assumes the existence of a number of clear physical 'types' into which all humans fall. It is these inherited physical characteristics that are then used to identify the races to which people(s) belong. Thus skin colour, hair type, body shape are racial characteristics and the idea of 'race' is firmly linked to the idea of physical type.

The concept of 'race' portrays certain groups of people as naturally different and represents a biologically determinist view of human development. It creates a justification for not treating 'them' the same as 'us' or not feeling guilty about such different treatments. Implicit in theories of 'race' is often an unstated belief that certain mental as well as physical characteristics can also be attributed to 'racial' groups.

Racial classification came to the fore as European powers expanded their colonial empires. Thus the Victorian English (British?) ruled many parts of the globe. This could be portrayed as a result of their national characteristics and moral fibre that were part of their racial superiority. In effect the empire was seen as the natural order of things. The colonists had a duty to guide and care for the colonial peoples that they ruled whom they regarded as inferior. This idea of 'racial' superiority has been used to justify the inhumane treatment and physical domination of one group over others throughout history. Consider how past empires have maintained their power over and treated their conquered peoples, for example, the Roman, British, Spanish and Portuguese empires; the apartheid system in South Africa; Hitler's Germany.

Reader reflection

Throughout history theories of 'racial' difference with the implication of superiority of one 'racial' group over another (eugenics), have been espoused. Jensen (1973) for example theorised about the difference in IQ of black and white Americans. Eysenck (1971) looked at differences between traits, physical and intellectual, of different racial groups. However, these theories fail to take into account social factors that led to differences in educational achievement, for instance sporting success was used as a major route out of poverty for black youth in educational regimes that assumed they were intellectually inferior. The same value was not placed on sporting prowess so black people were not fighting against the label they had been assigned by succeeding in sport. This, in turn, fed the stereotype that black people are good at sport.

How powerful do you think ethnic stereotypes are today in influencing people's attitudes and behaviour by comparison with the past?

Whilst 'race' was used as a means of social categorisation, scientists down the years have been unable to give a clear biological basis to the concept. Attempts to create lists of 'races' proved impossible due to the fact that mutually exclusive characteristics could not be identified. Even grouping everyone into one of three broad groups of Caucasoid, Negroid and Mongoloid has proved problematic. There is such a range of peoples within each category and also any physical characteristics identified are never totally exclusive to any group. Whatever categorisation for 'race' is used there is a great range of differences within each group and at the same time overlap between the categories. Thus the idea of 'race' is effectively a social construction based on prejudiced stereotypes. For that reason many writers, when they use it, put the term 'race' in inverted commas as we do in this text.

Ethnicity

Rather than 'race' the term 'ethnic group' is now more frequently used with ethnic minorities to refer to all groups making the minority. The term 'ethnicity' includes cultural and religious beliefs as well as physical similarities and so is felt to be a more appropriate term that is adaptable to social as well as physical variations. Tizard and Phoenix suggest that 'ethnicity refers to a collectivity or community that makes assumptions about shared common attributes to do with cultural practices and shared history' (2001: 128). As such they suggest that it is largely 'insider' defined. However, both of the terms 'race' and 'ethnic group' can be seen as social constructions whose meaning and applications change over time. They are often used as a means of boundary maintenance (Anthias and Yuval-Davis, 1992) and to categorise and emphasise the differences between groups of people (Stanley, 2004). The terms 'race' or 'ethnicity' should be seen as being used and evolving within the economic, political and social power relationships of any society at the time.

Confusion is maintained by the use of a range of racially/racist-based terms in any documentation or analysis. Thus a range of people(s) from many different origins are included, or conversely excluded, when categories such as 'Asian' are created. The same can be said of the use of the term 'black', which can be used to include African, African-Caribbean and sometimes Asian. What many official monitoring documents now encourage is self-categorisation whereby they include a wide range of categories and allow people to place themselves in the one in which they feel they belong or even to add one for themselves if it is not included.

Migration

Human history is one of continuous migration around the globe driven by a variety of causes – wars, trade, employment, escape from natural disasters such as flood, famine, earthquake, etc. The history of the British Isles certainly reflects this world picture with population movements of those born within the islands, both voluntary and forced, from rural areas to towns and cities and also away into other parts of the world; there have been peoples that have arrived as conquerors from the northern Scandinavian countries, Rome and France; many others have arrived as refugees fleeing political and economic persecution such as the Huguenots, Jews, Poles, Hungarians and Irish. Post-Second World War Britain, until recently, has largely been in an official position of net emigration, i.e. more people leaving the country to live than entering. There was immigration from the Caribbean in the 1950s and 1960s and from India, Pakistan and Bangladesh in the 1960s and 1970s. More recently there has been immigration from parts of Africa, Eastern Europe and the Near East from countries such as Afghanistan, Iran and Iraq. This is clearly driven by the linked forces of political instability and global economic pressures.

Gundara (2000) points out that though all of these communities and groups share common experiences of racism and have often struggled against this in similar ways, sometimes coming together in this process, they are very different communities and their diversity must be realised. Thus, though Indian, Pakistani and Bangladeshi communities are often classified as Asian and so regarded as the same by a cool white majority, they are very different in culture, religion, language and economic circumstances. Also, it should be realised how young people from these ethnic groups are further adapting. As with all young people they develop their own ambitions, lifestyles and leisure pursuits that at times cause conflict with their parents. Thus as adolescents they face the conflicts of striving for independence from their family yet seeking support and solidarity from their traditional communities in the face of racism. Gundara, in talking about multiple identities, suggests that black youth are engaged in 'defining themselves in the context of dominant British identity as well as their identity as Black persons in Britain' (2000: 44).

The ethnic make up of Britain has changed throughout its history and continues to do so. Thus it is an impossible task to identify a British culture. It also makes the use of the term 'ethnic' unsafe in any more than a very general sense.

POLICY APPROACHES TO COMBATING RACISM

Gillborn (2001), whilst warning against the dangers of making oversimplistic generalisations, expanded on an earlier typology of Tomlinson (1977) to show the recent history of policy on race since the Second World War up until the current Labour government.

Gillborn (2001) has divided the period up into six phases:

1 Ignorance and neglect (1945 to late 1950s)
2 Assimilation (late 1950s to mid 1960s)
3 Integration (mid 1960s to late 1970s)
4 Cultural pluralism and multiculturalism (late 1970s to late 1980s)
5 Thatcherism: The new racism and colour-blind policy (mid-1980s to 1997)
6 Naïve multiculturalism: New Labour, old inequalities (1997 onwards).

Ignorance, assimilation and integration

In the period of ignorance and neglect the official response to migration from the Caribbean and Indian subcontinent was to ignore it and do nothing. By default this was supporting the traditional colonialist views on racial inequality. The assumption was immigrants would do menial, low paid work that reflected their racial status.

The late 1950s to the mid-1960s was a period of assimilation followed by integration (mid-1960s to late 1970s). During the first part of this period it was assumed that any immigrants would become part of British society. It was expected that 'they' would dress, talk and live like 'us'. Thus over time migrants would become assimilated into British life. This was very much perceived as a one-way process of 'them' becoming more like 'us'. 'Racial incidents' were presented as part of a 'colour problem', i.e. the failure of 'coloured' people to fully assimilate. Clearly any issues were seen as emanating from the minority group and not the white majority whose home this had always been. The integrationists realised the impracticality of this policy and that differences in appearance could not be eradicated just by making migrant groups conform in social behaviour terms. They emphasised equal opportunity and began to call for more tolerance of cultural diversity. It is worth noting that the Race Relations Act was passed in 1976 outlawing discrimination on the basis of 'race'.

Multicultural education

The multiculturalism and anti-racist phase, from the late 1970s to the late 1980s, came about during a period of social unrest during which ethnic minority groups protested more openly about the social and economic oppression they faced – high unemployment, poor housing, lack of opportunity. The resistance of ethnic minority youth grew in the form of difficult and disruptive behaviour at school, increasing truancy and disturbance on the streets. The result, in the summer of 1981, was a period of significant rioting in a number of urban centres such as Handsworth in Birmingham and Toxteth in Liverpool.

In response to this growing urban unrest and based on the initial findings in the Rampton Report, the Conservative government set up the Swann Commission. The Swann Report (DES, 1985b) stressed the pluralistic make up of British society. This was seen as a strength and the cultural richness it brought needed to be recognised as leading to a vibrant developing society. However, the report also pointed to the inequality and prejudice that minority groups faced in all areas of their lives. Swann felt that, if not addressed, this inequality would lead to greater tension and civil unrest. The report wanted racism in all its guises to be addressed but particularly what it called institutional racism. This, it stated, was where the official institutions in society, such as the education system, the health service and the police, operate in a way that automatically discriminates against and disadvantages certain groups. The procedures and processes of such institutions needed to be monitored carefully for such practices. The Swann Report also stated that racism should not be seen as primarily a minority issue but rather a white problem. It was members of the white majority who were engaged in racism and discriminatory practices. It was this group that needed to be educated. Swann made the point that education about and against racism was as, if not more, important in areas that were predominantly white.

The report was largely ignored politically in favour of a bland summary accompanying it written by Lord Swann that failed to draw attention to the issues of racism raised in the actual report. This summary caused a split among different groups involved in writing the report. It was felt by some that Lord Swann had been influenced by the Conservative government of the day, which was seeking to avoid criticism. However, the sentiments of the actual Swann Commission could be seen in the notion of multicultural education that grew in schools and LEAs across Britain.

Multicultural education involved understanding and celebrating difference through education. Thus diversity was reflected in the curriculum by educating about different cultures through, for example, awareness of different forms of music, religious ceremonies and beliefs, languages and diet. This approach also involved the scrutinising of classroom texts to make them more representative. However, whilst being regarded as a move forward from assimilationism, the multicultural approach has been criticised for being condescending. Multicultural programmes came to be seen as naïve and inadequate, largely in terms of how they ignored institutional racism in education (Williams, 1981). Some even suggested multiculturalism was itself racist and a cause of disaffection (Mullard, 1981). It was argued that multiculturalism was nothing more than a form of social control, a misguided form of tokenism designed to integrate rather than to enable serious cultural differences to be properly expressed. In spite of these protests, multiculturalism remained (and remains) a position adopted by institutions at different levels of the education system.

Anti-racist education

The anti-racist movement, whose proponents believed that a more active stance needed to be taken to oppose racism, took a more radical approach. Racist attitudes needed to be vigorously opposed and policies that emphasised a belief in equality of opportunity clearly and forcefully stated. This approach was adopted by a number of LEAs and local authorities and became associated with left-wing administrations that were targeted for attack by the Conservative government of Margaret Thatcher in the 1980s. Thus this approach soon became discredited as extremist.

Gillborn (2001) labelled the Conservative premiership of Margaret Thatcher a period of new racism and colour-blind policy. He describes how the Conservative governments of Thatcher and later John Major (1979–97) emphasised individualism and the use of the market as a means to economic and social success. At the same time there was a resurgence in emphasis on national identity, seen clearly in the international conflict in the Falklands, and reaction against perceived high levels of immigration that were changing the 'British' way of life.

It was in the late 1980s and early 1990s that the National Curriculum was introduced along with policies that encouraged parents' choice of school for their children. Whilst the rhetoric was one of raising standards, Gillborn (2001) noted that this was a reform that was clearly 'colour-blind' taking no account of ethnic diversity. Differences in culture and language were not considered when imposing a rigid curriculum for all. The assumption that curriculum content was 'neutral' hid the bias towards traditional white British values. This can be seen when examining the content of the history, literature and modern foreign language (only

European languages were considered as appropriate at this time) parts of the National Curriculum programmes. Ethnic minority pupils, whilst not seeing themselves reflected in the curriculum they were taught, were further alienated by a rigid testing regime that took no account of language differences. Gillborn suggests that by stressing individualism, the market and choice, 'race' inequalities were effectively 'removed from the agenda' (2001: 99).

From 1997 onwards is a period Gillborn calls 'naïve multiculturalism' (2001: 19). In examining the policy of the Labour government from this time he suggests that whilst 'racial' inequality and achievement were acknowledged and recognised as needing to be tackled, there have been no policies that actually address this specific issue. The murder of a black teenager, Stephen Lawrence, in a racist attack in London and the lack of response by the police, fuelled by their initial assumptions that it was likely to have been the black boy's fault, led to accusations of institutional racism echoing those raised by Swann nearly 20 years earlier. The Macpherson Report (1999) that followed an inquiry into the murder highlighted a need for positive changes in education to tackle racism. Gillborn (2001) notes that the Labour government responded, as had the Conservative administration at the time of the Swann Report, with tokenistic gestures calling for greater tolerance and understanding. It was assumed that such issues could be 'covered' in the introduction of citizenship into the curriculum. It is this lack of an anti-racist approach and the will to change things that leads Gillborn to conclude that little has changed in terms of government policy towards 'race' over the last 20 years.

ACHIEVEMENT OF ETHNIC GROUPS

Much of the research in the second half of the twentieth century and the early years of the twenty-first century focused on the underachievement of black pupils in the education system. This was seen as largely influenced by the experiences of these pupils in a racist society and education system.

In the 1970s and early 1980s attention was drawn to the curriculum in which black faces did not appear except as part of topics involving slavery. Ethnic minorities were presented in the media and also the classroom in negative ways. Thus many areas of the world were portrayed as being 'primitive' and as jungle or desert and certainly in poverty. Large parts of the Indian subcontinent and Sub-Saharan Africa, for example, only appeared in the media when suffering famine. In this way young ethnic minority pupils could find few, if any, positive images of themselves or people like themselves. It was suggested in some early studies (Coard, 1971; Milner, 1975) that this may have led to lack of self-esteem and thus underperformance. Others said that this actually led to cultures of resistance and ethnic minority pupils forming their own, alternative, views of self that brought them into conflict with the establishment (Mac an Ghaill, 1988; Sewell, 1997).

The racism ethnic minority pupils faced in the education process has been pointed out by many studies (Majors, 2000; Wright et al, 1999). Black pupils, boys in particular, were more likely to get into trouble at school, to be labelled as 'difficult' pupils by teachers and to be excluded from school. Black pupils were seen as less academic and more likely to be in the lower academic sets. Attempts were made to address these issues during the multicultural and anti-racist movements that developed in the 1970s onwards. The curriculum was adapted to include more positive images of ethnic minorities and curriculum materials were made more inclusive in terms of the appearance of different ethnic groups in textbooks. However, the introduction of the National Curriculum from 1988 onwards and the colour-blind approach taken to education, which made no allowances for ethnic differences in curriculum content, assessment, or first language of the pupils, can be said to have put back the development of equality of opportunity for ethnic minority pupils to before the 1970s.

Whilst much of the literature explained the poor performance of black children in schools and related this to their experiences of schooling, Blair (2000), Gardner (2001) and Demie (2005) show how some schools can develop cultures that value all pupils in which all ethnic groups can be successful. However, Tomlinson (2005b) suggests that current policies that pro-mote market forces and encourage parents and pupils to compete for places at 'good' schools will continue to legitimate inequalities and ensure that ethnic minorities remain largely in those schools that are heavily criticised as underperforming. This, she says, will do little to promote social justice.

Whilst teachers have been made more aware of racism in schools and the importance of multiculturalism, their response to the behaviour of black pupils and the placing of these pupils in lower sets in disproportionate numbers has been defended by Foster (1990) as being a legitimate response to what they were presented with rather than racist action on their part. Whilst not denying the effects of racism, Foster is in fact defending teachers from being scapegoated as the main reason for these pupils' behaviours and achievements. Crozier (2005), however, suggests that institutional racism continues to have a significant impact upon the achievements of young black people who experience cumulative negative experiences throughout their education. She suggests that the school system holds a pathological view of the black child that works against his or her success. It has been suggested that the develop-ment of the pressures of league tables, together with a need to maintain an image of good discipline and high pupil performance, have led to the increase in the number of exclusions of pupils with behavioural problems and thus the number of black pupils excluded. According to National Statistics Online for 2004 the permanent exclusion rates for pupils from 'other' black groups was 42 pupils per 10,000, black Caribbean and mixed white groups 41 pupils per 10,000, black Caribbean groups 37 per 10,000 respectively. These were up to three times the rate for white pupils, which were 14 pupils per 10,000. It should be noted that Chinese and Indian pupils had the lowest exclusion rates, at 2 or less pupils excluded per 10,000. These fig-ures need to be considered alongside the GCSE performance for these groups below.

Table 8.2 *Achievement of pupils as a percentage in each ethnic group for 2006*

	Boys		Girls	
	5 GCSEs A*–C	5A*–C including Maths and English	5 GCSEs A*–C	5A*–C including Maths and English
White British	53.0	40.5	62.3	48.5
All Asian	55.5	41.4	66.9	51.1
Indian	67.1	54.3	76.6	64.3
Pakistani	45.4	30.6	57.9	39.0
Black	41.0	27.4	55.1	39.8
Black Caribbean	36.5	22.7	52.9	36.0
Black African	45.2	31.7	56.7	43.3
Chinese	75.5	59.7	84.8	72.2

Source: DfES (www.dfes.gov.uk)

These statistics for the achievement of pupils from different ethnic groups show a complex picture of differential achievement. Girls achieve better than boys in all categories. Chinese children perform particularly well as do Indian children. Of particular concern is the performance of black, particularly Caribbean, boys. What must be acknowledged, however, are the vast differences in the size of each ethnic group that make up these statistics. For example, whilst there are 253,257 boys in the white British category there are 4,191 black Caribbean boys, 7,015 Indian boys and only 1,137 Chinese boys. This variation in numbers will make any statistical interpretation of the statistics very provisional. Certainly ethnicity is a significant factor to be taken into account when explaining pupil achievement. However, as pointed out previously in our discussions of class and gender, in order to appreciate these social processes and how they affect the individual, we need to be aware of the complex inter-relationship between ethnicity, gender and economic circumstances in the form of social class (Arnot and Miles, 2005; Gillborn and Mirza, 2000; Gipps, 2006).

Conclusion

There is no doubt that the processes and effects of education can and do influence the life opportunities of individuals and particular social groups. In the past, alternative forms of education were openly provided for different social groups. It seemed reasonable to educate the children of the labouring classes to fulfil their future roles effectively. Likewise the sons of the middle classes needed to be equipped to take decisions fitting to their future station in life. Economic life and working conditions have changed greatly and today the emphasis is more on equality of opportunity and the adaptability of the workforce. But, as Reay (2006) points out:

> The most recent statistical data show that the educational gap between the classes has widened over the last ten years (ONS, 2005). We are all much more credentialled now than we were then … The attainment gap between the classes in education is just as great as it was 20, 50 years ago and mirrors the growing material gap between the rich and poor in UK society. Against a policy backdrop of continuous change and endless new initiatives it appears that in relation to social class the more things change the more they stay the same (2006: 304).

Rising GCSE and A level results, increasing percentages of pupils staying in full-time education post 16, improved performance at all levels by females and ethnic minorities, and greater participation in FE and HE all seem to point to the opening up of opportunity. But inequalities in education persist with the continued low achievement and effective exclusion of significant sections of the population. Class, gender and ethnicity remain significant factors that operate at different levels and in various ways to influence educational outcomes.

Student activities

1 Discuss with others your different experiences of growing up and the influence that social factors such as class, ethnicity and gender had upon you. Particularly consider:
   - when you were a young child
   - your life at primary and secondary school
   - any paid employment you have undertaken
   - your life as a student
   - your future aspirations.

2 Find the gender balance for a number of courses at your university/college. Has this changed over a number of years? Discuss the findings and reasons for any significant results.

3 Visit the Higher Education Statistics Agency website (www.hesa.ac.uk) and the UCAS website (www.ucas.ac.uk) and chart the number of places in HE taken by students according to socio-economic status, gender and ethnicity over the last five years. What trends, if any, can you identify from these statistics?

Recommended reading

Ball, S. (2003) *Class Strategies and the Education Market: The Middle Classes and Social Advantage.* London: RoutledgeFalmer. How the middle classes harness market forces to their advantage is a clear theme of this book. Stephen Ball examines the way in which the middle classes maintain their social position and how the education system supports them in doing this. This is a challenging but very important analysis.

Browne, N. (2004) *Gender Equity in the Early Years.* Maidenhead: Open University Press. This book examines policy, provision and practice for early years children and the extent to which these promote equity. This is a very useful text for those with a special interest in early years issues.

Kailin, J. (2002) *Antiracist Education: From theory to practice.* New York: Rowman and Littlefield. This book shows how covert racism is able to permeate all areas of social life and stresses the need to be aware of this in order to counteract it. It outlines the similarities and distinctions between multicultural and antiracist education. It then makes the case for adopting an anti-racist approach. The author gives rich ethnographic accounts of teaching anti-racist education in the US.

Kehily, M.J. (2002) *Sexuality, Gender and Schooling. Shifting agendas in social learning.* London: Routledge/Falmer. Using an ethnographic approach, this text examines how young people construct understandings of gender and sexuality. In doing so it considers key debates and issues in this area.

9 Organising teaching and learning: pedagogical trends

Our discussion in Chapter 4 demonstrated how historical narratives can shed light on different aspects of education. Some historical reflection will help us now to examine how current pedagogical trends have evolved. This historical narrative, informed by our overview of psychological research and information about how class, ethnicity and gender can impact on educational achievement, provides us with a set of perspectives with which to analyse issues about how pupils and other learners are grouped and taught and how learner attainment is conceptualised. The chapter will consider pedagogical trends since the 1950s from setting and streaming of learners through mixed ability teaching and differentiation, culminating with the current vogue for personalised learning and the growing influence of psychopedagogy.

Introduction

This chapter first embarks on a review of the different ways learning groups have been organised since the start of the comprehensive system, which is a key pedagogic issue. Tracing historical precedents and analysing them within their contemporary social, economic and political contexts allows us to better understand current developments in pedagogy. In recent years teaching and learning approaches have been influenced by what we might refer to as psychopedagogy – the basing of pedagogical approaches on popular ideas from psychological research. As with everything we have examined in this text, it is not possible to appreciate what this means without also looking at the ideological context that has spawned it. It is of fundamental importance that educators and students of education apply a questioning approach to the plethora of teaching and learning techniques that seem so easily to gain favour through our globalised, media-rich modern communication systems. This chapter explores some of these recent pedagogical trends, inviting readers to think back to their research bases discussed in Chapter 7 and the extent to which they might legitimately be applied in practice.

Grouping pupils for learning

The traditional notion that individual differences in how people learn can be explained by differences in a single intelligence as measured by IQ tests has been shown to be sterile. Commentary from the 1960s and 1970s (Ball, 1981; Hargreaves, 1972; Jackson, 1964) was very sceptical of the ceiling effect on pupil attainment that such a view implied. This was referred to as the self-fulfilling prophecy where pupils meet the expectations set of them and no more and has been discussed in Chapter 8. A look back at the various ways of organising learners demonstrates that the conditions responsible for encouraging this ceiling effect, namely setting by ability, are directly related to prevailing ideological forces, in particular to the strength of emphasis on conventional, publicly comparable assessment data.

STREAMED GROUPS

In 1964 a seminal study was produced by Brian Jackson (Jackson, 1964), who wrote from the heart as an experienced teacher disenchanted with an education system which he had taken for granted but later found to be wanting. His investigation into the effects of streaming children into groups, on the basis of mathematical or literacy competence, within primary schools was highly influential. It came at a time politically and economically ripe for consciousness to be raised about perceived social and educational injustices. Jackson found that 'A'-stream teachers were more experienced and better qualified, that children with autumn birthdays were overrepresented in 'A' streams, that working-class children were underestimated and relegated to the 'C' stream where they stayed and that over a third of parents had no idea what streaming meant.

Jackson adopted a teaching approach, as a result of his findings, that put no ceiling on his expectations of pupils which, in turn, liberated them from simply meeting specified goals. He also developed teaching resources which caught the interest and met the needs of his pupils. What Jackson was breaking down was the much discussed 'self-fulfilling prophecy' wherein teachers' expectations of pupils were said to limit their achievement. There was serious worry about this phenomenon when the Plowden Report (CACE, 1967) confirmed that, at as young an age as 7, a child's life chances were fixed because there was seldom any transfer between streams. This phenomenon may have drawn a spurious legitimacy from stage theories of development such as Piagetian theory (see Chapter 6). Widely adopted as applicable to an educational context, these theories did tend to spawn ideas about learning readiness which suggested that it was not sensible to expect certain capabilities from children until they were maturationally ready. Teachers may have considered that the concept of learning readiness could be applied to 'ability' equally well as to age, serving as a justification for the stability of streamed groups.

Hargreaves (1972) argued that believing in the child's potential for improvement, often in the face of contradictory evidence, and the communication of this belief to the child, was the key to releasing this potential. In 1967 he had studied the effects of streaming on pupils in a secondary modern school, pointing to the development of subcultures within the lower streams. Sporting norms and values at variance with those of the school, these groups became alienated from the mainstream aims. Disenfranchised from status positions within school, which were bound up in high achievement, pupils in the lower streams gained status instead from deviant behaviour. This perpetuated the lack of movement between streams.

MIXED ABILITY TEACHING

When comprehensive schooling was introduced in the late 1960s it was hoped that the problems created by using streaming as a form of differentiation would abate. Initially, however, a certain resistance to change and a lack of experience in teaching pupils of all abilities together simply led to a replication of the secondary modern/grammar groupings of pupils on a smaller scale within the comprehensives. The DES (1978a) stressed the social arguments for mixed ability groupings: for the individual there would be increased equality of opportunity, less rejection and classification; for the teacher there would be greater control since mixed grouping avoids the emergence of a sink mentality and promotes group cooperation, better relationships and a reduction in competitive/aggressive behaviour; and, for society, class differences would be counteracted helping to create a non-competitive, non-elitist society.

Keddie (1971), observing the introduction of a new humanities curriculum within a comprehensive school, found a relationship between perceived ability and social class. She argued that teachers classified children in terms of an ideal type of pupil even though the classes were of mixed ability. Pupils meeting the teachers' stereotype of an 'A'-stream type pupil were given access to higher-grade knowledge, even though all pupils were supposed to be taught the material in the same way. The result was the differentiation of an undifferentiated curriculum.

By the late 1970s mixed ability grouping had become widespread but neither research nor HMI reports could find evidence to support the strategy because the grouping, whether banded, setted, streamed or mixed, did not in itself appear to improve teaching and learning (Bourne and Moon, 1994; Slavin, 1990). The HMI findings (DES, 1978a) indicated that in the main teachers were teaching to the middle via whole class teaching with the needs of the less and more able pupils being ignored. Both HMI and a study by Kerry (1984) found little evidence of task differentiation. Where attempts had been made to cater for the range of abilities in one class, these had of necessity to be so teacher directed that they limited the extent to which the pupil could be intellectually challenged. 'Death by a thousand worksheets' is a phrase with which many teachers of the 1970s can identify. It describes the overuse of differentiated worksheets within mixed ability classrooms (Toogood, 1984).

Ball (1981) reported on the change from banding (where pupils are placed in broad ability bands on the basis of results in English and mathematics and then setted further into ability groups for each subject) to mixed ability grouping in one comprehensive school in the 1970s. Later, in 1987, he commented that:

> At Beachside the implementation of mixed-ability as a teaching problem was left almost entirely to the teaching departments to cope with. Each department was asked by the headteacher to produce a report outlining their intended responses, but there was no follow-up

to the reports, and in several cases the teaching strategies actually employed bore no resemblance to original stated intentions. (Ball, 1987: 40)

The political heat generated by the introduction of mixed ability methods was such that much energy was employed engineering and safeguarding them (Toogood, 1984). Clearly thought-out school policies for the teaching of these groups were rare; Toogood's text provides a retrospective explanation of the approach taken at one 'progressive' school and Kelly's (1975) collection of case studies describes the methods employed in five schools. Despite some innovative developments by individual teachers (Hart, 1996), there were few systematised approaches within either schools or LEAs to galvanise these strengths and disseminate good practice. Along with political pressure, this helped seal the fate of mixed ability teaching which declined in the 1980s, to be replaced by setting within each subject.

SETTING VERSUS COLLABORATION

There is evidence (Bourne and Moon, 1994) that the introduction of the National Curriculum with its differentiated attainment levels led to changes in grouping policy. The publishing of examination results forced the hand of many stalwart supporters of mixed ability teaching because of the risk of a perceived association between mixed ability teaching and poor examination results (Boaler, 1997). The very public arena in which schools increasingly functioned encouraged further abandonment of mixed ability teaching in favour of setting rather than efforts to develop more appropriate teaching strategies to support it (Weston, 1996).

Boaler's (1997) review of the research found that while there was a small, but not statistically significant, advantage for the most able pupils if they were setted, the losses for the less able were large if they were setted. Their attainment was significantly lower than the attainment of the less able who were in mixed ability groups. In recent years a number of studies have been conducted into the effects of mixed and setted ability groupings within both primary and secondary schools by Judith Ireson and Susan Hallam and their research team at the London Institute of Education (see, for instance, Hallam et al, 2004, and Ireson and Hallam, 2005). Boaler (1996) conducted her own three-year study comparing the GCSE mathematics results of 310 pupils in two schools, one of which set the pupils while the other taught pupils in mixed ability groups. She found that results were significantly better among the latter group even though test results from Year 7 indicated the pupils were performing at the same levels (Boaler, 1996). When Boaler asked Year 11 pupils in the setted school about mathematics lessons the responses revealed a dissatisfaction with the fixed pace of progress. Some pupils, especially girls, found the pace too fast which occasioned them to become anxious; more of the boys reported that the pace was too slow. This was the case across the eight sets which is a striking finding, given that one would assume a limited range of ability within each set. The pupils preferred the arrangements lower down the school when they had been able to work at their own pace in mixed ability groups because they gained a better understanding. Many of the pupils who were negatively affected by setting were the most able. Boaler concluded that 'a student's success in their set had relatively little to do with their ability, but a great deal to do with their personal preferences for learning pace and style' (1996: 585). A number of studies suggest that attempting to match tasks to learners' abilities may be less effective than providing differentiated, individualised teacher support to pupils working on the same task (see Burton, 2003, for a review).

Where pupils remained in mixed ability groups, for instance at primary level and in some 'progressive' comprehensives, the standard collaborative learning method was heterogeneous grouping. High ability pupils were felt to benefit from having to organise their thoughts in order to explain them to their less able partners and from having studied new material more carefully in order to explain it later. Low ability pupils were said to learn from these explanations, which were often more accessible than those given by a teacher. Conversely, Bennett and Dunne (1992) and Jones and Carter (1994) found that within setted systems for older pupils, lower ability groups were unable to collaborate or stimulate each other sufficiently to make progress. The academic rationale for a mixed approach is significantly different from the social benefits advocated for mixed ability grouping in the 1970s. Indeed social problems have been found to exist *within* mixed groups: Dowrick (1996) found evidence in Mulryan's (1992) study that low ability pupils were looked down on by their partners. In Japan, studies have indicated that ability is a much less central concern than effort (Purdie and Hattie, 1996). The Western notion of ability is turned on its head, hence 'intelligence is viewed as an expression of achievement; it results from experience and education' (p. 848).

Townsend and Hicks (1997) examined the relationship between academic task values (for mathematics and language) and perceptions of social satisfaction for 162 12- and 13-year-old pupils in New Zealand using a cooperative, interactive learning structure and in ordinary classrooms. Task values for engagement in learning activities were found to be higher in classrooms using a cooperative goal structure and to be associated with higher social satisfaction among pupils. The authors suggested that these findings imply a need to examine the coordination of multiple goals which extend beyond the academic domain. Brown, describing the learning communities she espouses, aims at: 'non-conformity in the distribution of expertise and interests so everyone can benefit from the subsequent richness of available knowledge. Teams composed of members with homogeneous ideas and skills are denied access to such richness' (1994: 10).

There seems, then, to be a complex relationship between grouping structures, pedagogical strategy, academic achievement and social satisfaction. It is possible to conclude that the classroom strategies employed are of greater significance to the quality of learning than is the organisation of the teaching groups. Slavin suggested that what is needed is a better understanding of how to choose teaching methods which work at appropriate times with particular pupils in different group structures, since 'it does not move the discussion forward at all to note that students differ and then to assume that all achievement differences must be dealt with through some sort of grouping' (1993: 13). Thus in the 1990s the common pedagogical approach was to differentiate learning experiences, tasks and materials for learners.

Differentiated learning

Two principles that informed the concept of a differentiated approach to learning can be identified. The first lies in changing notions of the rather nebulous term 'ability' which we see became 'abilities' in the National Curriculum Council's definition of differentiation: 'the matching of work to the abilities of individual children, so that they are stretched, but still achieve success' (NCC, 1993: 78). This suggested a shifting, wide-ranging set of skills, interests and talents rather than a singular ability which is stable across a range of contexts. The idea of responding to or matching work to this range of abilities was the natural corollary of adopting this definition of ability. Thus Visser defined differentiation as: 'the process whereby teachers meet the need for progress through the curriculum by selecting appropriate teaching methods to match the individual child's learning strategies, within a group situation' (1993: 15).

By this definition the common-sense notion of an all-embracing ability derived from IQ theory had been replaced by a more finely tuned, diagnostic assessment of what each child is capable of at a particular time, with a particular teacher, in a particular subject, using a particular learning strategy. This has echoes of Howard Gardner's explanations of the proclivities learners have for different aspects of their learning (Gardner, 1983). Chyriwsky (1996) emphasised the need for subject-specific identification of ability, eschewing the global IQ testing approach. Leo and Galloway (1996) highlighted the impact of children's own conceptions of ability on their goal orientations, citing the work of Dweck (1991) and Nicholls (1989). These studies indicated a tendency for adolescents to conceive of ability as stable and fixed, which led to performance-oriented goals which in turn affected the effort they made in class; if they felt their efforts would not have an effect on their achievement they reasoned there was no point. Younger children were found to be more likely to conceive of ability as changeable, something which is affected by effort; this can orient them towards learning goals. Leo and Galloway also suggested that teachers' conceptualisations of ability affect the way they teach pupils. Those holding a view of ability as a fixed, stable entity 'might behave in ways which impede effective development of mastery learners' (1996: 43).

The second principle of differentiated learning lay in the emphasis on process. Thus: 'Differentiation is a planned process of intervention in the classroom to maximise potential based on individual needs' (Dickinson and Wright, 1993: 1). Tubbs placed the teacher at the centre of this intervention, defining differentiation as 'the means by which a teacher intervenes in every pupil's education in order to provide effective and relevant access for them to the curriculum' (1996: 49). Stradling et al identified teacher–pupil dialogue as one manifestation of this intervention process: 'The commonest characteristics of differentiation between individual learners tend to be an emphasis on dialogue in the form of regular review between teachers and individual pupils about their progress and their learning needs' (1991: 11).

Groups of pupils, whether setted or mixed ability, will display differences in their interest in the topic, presentation skills, ability to work cooperatively or independently, listening skills, parental support, learning styles, gender, ethnic group, cultural background and so on. These differences have an impact on scholastic achievement (Maqsud, 1997). In responding to these differences by differentiating the learning the teacher's aim is itself to make a difference – the difference between where a pupil is now and where they have the potential to be. This resonates clearly with Vygotsky's (1978) work on zones of proximal development when he explained that what a child does at first in cooperation with others, they will then learn to do alone. The clear implication of this social constructivist approach is that the teacher's intervention will vary from child to child; as Warnock had explained in the seventies: 'The purpose of education for all children is the same; the goals are the same. But the help that individual children need in progressing towards them will be different' (DES, 1978b: 5).

> The two principles which characterised a differentiated approach to facilitating learning can be summarised as follows:
>
> 1 Pupil performance is not a function of a simply defined ability, but of a range of interrelated internal and external factors; it is more helpful to use the notion of contextually dependent sets of skills and aptitudes as the underpinning to achievement.
> 2 The teacher's focus will be on the learning process rather than on the learning product.

DIFFERENTIATION AND ATTAINMENT

These principles are manifestly more complex than those identified by the National Curriculum Council (NCC) (1990) which explained that the National Curriculum would help teachers to:

- assess what each pupil knows, understands and can do
- use their assessment and the programmes of study to identify the learning needs of individuals
- plan programmes of work which take account of their pupils' attainments and allow them to work at different levels
- ensure that all children achieve their maximum potential (Hart, 1996: 21).

While committed to the potential of individuals, the NCC, in linking differentiation to an assessment of attainment, placed the same ceiling on expectations as that occasioned by the streaming of the 1960s. In contrast, the two principles outlined above embrace the complex nature of attainment, and in pursuing process rather than product, encourage a liberation of learner potential.

In the 1990s the publication of examination results led to schools adopting tactics such as cramming sessions for pupils on the C/D grade boundary of GCSE to boost results. More recently this strategy has even extended to pupils in the final year of primary school in order to boost a school's percentage of level 4s in the core subjects end of key stage tests. The culture of national benchmarks based on assessment and other performance indicators along with parental and employer pressure are recurring features of school life. Since 1998 the Labour government have endorsed these ideas by publishing, annually through Ofsted, benchmarking data for schools to determine their examination targets in relation to the achievements of schools in similar situations. Thus, the ramifications of individual differences in attainment are more far-reaching than a single child's performance in examinations. This now goes hand in hand with the implications which that single child's performance has for the aggregated results of a school.

DIFFERENTIATION AND IDEOLOGY

In its broadest sense differentiation is a construct which describes a whole host of educational phenomena, from the ways in which schooling systems are organised within societies, how learners are divided up for teaching and assessment, the extent to which teachers observe policies of inclusion, right through to the particular teaching and learning strategies a teacher employs with individual pupils.

These various manifestations of differentiation are inextricably bound up with the socio-political and ideological contexts in which they exist. The 1960s was a time of largesse, economic boom and social conscience wherein the drive was for equality of treatment through comprehensive schooling, social opportunity, gender and ethnic rights. After difficult economic times in the 1970s, the late 1980s and early 1990s were again a time of economic progress but the prevailing ideological ethic was one of personal enterprise, endeavour and resourcefulness and not state responsibility (Thatcherism). Equality of opportunity in education was ostensibly provided by creating the appearance of choice of schools. This choice was promoted by an expectation that schools should be more publicly accountable for their 'performance' through comparative league tables of examination results. In fact the choice for pupils of low-income families had been reduced since high-income families could transport their children to schools with the best results.

As you will read in Chapter 10, a change of government did not alter the emphasis on choice although the New Labour rhetoric used to support it became one of 'social justice'. In 2001 the government white paper, *Schools achieving Success* (DfES, 2001), set out how diversity of provision would be achieved through different types of schools such as Specialist Schools, which demonstrated a particular subject competence, and Beacon Schools, chosen for their exhibition and dissemination of best practice (see Burton, 2003 for a fuller discussion of this). This was extended through a commitment to creating 'trust schools' in the Education and Inspections Act which would be independent of local authority control and would (ostensibly) create even greater choice for parents and pupils (DfES, 2006). The commitment to independent trust schools was a further step in Labour's strategy that emphasised how selective and differentiated provision could, in its view, meet everyone's needs.

Yet the political and popular backlash against the partial selective admissions processes for such schools took the government by surprise and this element of the Act's provision was changed. The key point here is that neither structural nor pedagogical change can be achieved if the appropriate political conditions do not pertain. So what changed in five years? A host of issues that were nothing to do with education, most significantly the war on Iraq, combined to erode confidence in the prime minister and his government such that the hitherto benign backbench and public acceptance of New Labour spin gave way to a healthier questioning of so-called 'social justice' education policies. The rhetoric that creating choice and diversity in schooling served to advance the opportunities for every pupil and not just those with the human, physical and cultural capital to access it lost its credibility.

At all levels of the education system, then, differentiation – of pedagogy, of assessment, even of school type – took hold throughout the 1990s and into the new century, buoyed along by Labour ideology of 'choice and diversity' and 'social justice'. Significant by its absence in government guidance towards the end of the 1990s, however, was any mention of *how* classroom learning was to be enhanced (Reynolds, 1997). Decisions about what strategies to deploy within a differentiated pedagogy were still the preserve of teachers. This changed with the implementation in England of what became known as the national strategies for literacy, for numeracy and later for primary education and key stage 3 more generally. These gave prescriptive guidance on the format and content of lessons and, although not compulsory, were adopted by the majority of schools because of the force of the official support and government documentation behind them. The strategies were criticised for their straitjacket approach to learning, which was thought to stifle creativity, and questions were raised regarding the rigour and provenance of the research underpinning them with several studies registering concern that they elicited limited learning gains (Brown et al, 2003; Kyriacou, 2005; Wyse, 2003). This entrée of government and its advisers into the very heart of the teaching and learning process continued so that by the middle of the first decade of the new millennium they were taking a great deal of interest in the methods that teachers and learners might employ to effect 'personalised learning' (Leadbeater, 2004). Thus the control of the curriculum exercised by a number of governments across the world via national curricula began to be further extended via an even more insidious form of control, that of pedagogical approaches. Bates (2005) confirms increasing control of pedagogy in Australia, for instance.

Personalised learning

Much of the psychological research described in Chapter 7 has been drawn on internationally in the development of psychopedagogic approaches embraced within the current trend for personalised learning (PL). Burton (2007) has argued that PL has its pedagogical and political roots in the 1990s vogue for differentiated learning. Weston (1996) described differentiation as a shorthand for the methods teachers use to enable each pupil to achieve their intended learning targets. The pedagogical discourse of the 1990s established 'differentiation' as a seminal term and this definition resonates with its successor, 'personalised' or 'tailored' learning, promoted by the UK government. The DfES (2004a) described personalised learning as having its roots in the best practices of the teaching profession. 'It has the potential to ensure that every child or young person reaches the highest possible standards by tailoring learning and teaching. Personalised learning by its very nature cannot be prescriptive and has to be developed within a given context' (http://publications.teachernet.gov.uk /personalised learning). Despite this lack of prescription five components of personalised learning were identified by the education minister David Miliband (2004b) as: assessment for learning; teaching and learning strategies; curriculum choice; school organisation and community links. To these were added ICT, advice and guidance, mentoring and student voice. PL would appear, then, to embrace most of what goes on in schools and is actually not terribly new or different. There is also an obvious policy tension in pursuing a personalised curriculum because personal choice does not sit easily with the notion of a broad and balanced curriculum entitlement enshrined within the National Curriculum.

The white paper referred to earlier (DfES, 2001) described a range of ways in which pedagogical diversity was to be pursued. These included the use of different types of adults in classrooms, for example classroom assistants and learning mentors, investment in ICT equipment, on-line curriculum 'catering for children of all abilities' (p.5) and the facility for the most able pupils to progress at a faster pace. These initiatives have since been implemented via an initiative known as 'workforce remodelling' in England (DfES, 2003). There is also much more emphasis in schools and colleges worldwide on developing the learning technologies and software to support personalised learning. Sophisticated hypermedia systems can identify learners' interests, preferences and needs and adapt the content of pages and the links between them to the needs of that user (Triantafillou et al, 2004). There is some evidence that blended learning, which involves a variety of instructional media, leads to better motivation to learn (Klein et al, 2006). We saw in Chapter 7, however, that social constructivist research (Bruner, 1983; Vygotsky, 1978) has repeatedly demonstrated the necessity for group interaction and adult intervention in consolidating learning and extending thinking. Many teachers are familiar with these key ideas but Kutnick et al (2002) caution that they may not think strategically about the size and composition of groups in relation to the tasks assigned, calling for educationalists once again to pay attention to the social pedagogy of pupil grouping. This is compounded in the UK by the requirement for whole class teaching within the national literacy and numeracy strategies. Whole class teaching tends to place the emphasis for talking with the teacher through whom all interactions are routed. Myhill's (2006) extensive research demonstrated that teacher discourse can sometimes impede pupil learning because cognitive or conceptual connections are not made sufficiently clear.

Personalised learning was further promoted in the subsequent white paper (DfES, 2005a) with an explicit call for the setting of pupils, the implicit assumption being that setting enhances personalisation. Yet, as we saw earlier, research provides no clear evidence that setting creates greater learning gains for pupils. In an extensive study that followed 6000 Year 9 pupils in 45 secondary comprehensive schools through to Year 11, Ireson et al (2005) found no significant effects of setting on GCSE achievement in English, mathematics or science.

Frith (2005) has made predictions about the implanting of microchips to enhance cognitive functioning and techniques to track an individual's learning within the developing brain in order to match teacher or teaching method to learner. Until such ideas come to fruition, teachers will continue to need a detailed knowledge of each learner's progress, strengths and challenges in a particular learning context. Whether we call it personalised learning, differentiation or a learner-centred approach, the issue is not one that can be simply dealt with by governmental injunctions to setting, since in both set and mixed ability groups the individualised nature of pupil learning and teacher response is paramount.

The drive towards personalised learning has been fuelled in the UK and beyond by an approach towards the professional development of teachers that has increasingly taken the form of 'edutainment'. Charismatic, high profile education consultants deliver courses on new pedagogies such as those embraced within Smith's accelerated learning (Smith, 1996; Smith and Call, 2002). High-energy presentations draw eclectically from a range of research findings thought to have practical benefits for learning. These are presented with a theatrical fervour and missionary zeal that is compelling. Teachers generally enjoy these stimulating sessions and the recipe approach to pedagogic techniques but they are seldom encouraged to look deeper into the research that underpins them. Many teachers are keen to trial these techniques, tending initially to accept them at face value rather than to question their theoretical or empirical validity (Bartlett and Burton, 2006b). In the UK, government money was directed at such trends so headteachers encouraged their staff to explore their application in what can be an overly simplistic, mechanistic way, where short-term gains, possibly in the form of end of term test results, were the goal. When teachers meet for professional purposes within local, national or virtual communities of practice the new trends are discussed and the shorthand terms used to describe these ideas become generic, passing into educational discourse with a legitimacy and authority borne of practitioners' enthusiasm and partial application of the constructs. Consequently, there is a danger that education dissertations focus on the practical application of an increasingly narrow set of the latest popular ideas where the construct itself is not the focus of the investigation for its legitimacy is taken for granted. In this way the corpus of pedagogical research work has become self-referential and based on taken-for-granted assumptions with little attempt made to refer back to the original psychological research on which those assumptions may have been loosely based.

Psychological research and pedagogical developments

This somewhat unscholarly approach to developing and justifying pedagogical techniques reveals why there is some scepticism about the robustness of the research bases underpinning new trends such as personalising learning. Examining further the context in which such psychopedagogy has grown up helps explain why this less than rigorous approach to the research and development of new ideas holds sway. Educational research had been criticised for its apparent lack of relevance to practical teaching and learning situations. As discussed in

Chapter 3, governments called for research that would have a direct impact on practice in classrooms and for teaching approaches to be supported by practitioners' own research into 'what works' with learners. The utilitarian value of research was sought and attempts made to define 'evidence-based practice' (EBP). The basic tenet of EBP, that is, without evidence we cannot trust professionals, has, however, been shown to be oversimplistic (Pring, 2004). Hammersley (2004) suggested EBP has the effect of undermining opposition to politically-favoured standpoints. This in turn, of course, serves to reinforce policy positions.

As we saw in Chapter 7, research that has been increasingly popularised within educational pedagogy includes studies on learning or thinking styles, learning strategies, approaches and preferences, metacognition, brain functioning and thinking skills, emotional intelligence and multiple intelligences. Accelerated learning (Smith and Call, 2002) is an umbrella term for a series of pedagogical approaches that draw from a range of theories including many of those listed above. It might be said to cohere a set of principles that have governed effective teaching and learning for some time. Motivating learners is a key precept as is the expectation that all learners can achieve at a level normally considered beyond them. It stresses the need to understand how learning happens rather than what is learned. An assurance is given that all suggestions are based on sound research but little time is given within in-service sessions to an examination of this research.

Within the accelerated learning approach reference is made to VAK (see Dryden and Vos, 2001), the construct that there are predominantly three learning styles – visual, auditory and kinaesthetic – that pupils can be categorised into, with appropriate tasks matched to their individual styles. The emphasis on this single style construct is an example of the tendency to adopt the easiest or most attractive construct on offer rather than to properly examine the range of ideas available and their respective research bases. In some educational circles VAK appears to have become synonymous with learning styles, virtually replacing it as the generic term (Burton and Bartlett, 2006b). As Chapter 7 demonstrates, this is simply inaccurate since a whole host of style constructs have been generated from a range of research, each predicated to differing degrees on empirical research. Yet teachers tend only to have heard of the VAK construct because it is easy to understand and internalise, easy to assess, useful as a labelling device to justify treating pupils in particular ways or having certain expectations of them. Such popular pedagogical ideas tend to be promoted through universal media on a global stage with one or two references to an original source providing the appearance of rigorous research legitimacy.

The power of government and global education media endorsement of VAK is plain in schools where pupils walk around with labels identifying their VAK style. This should concern us on many levels, from the lack of teachers' critical engagement in allowing such practice to the stultifying effect of labelling, and thereby limiting, learners' potential and opportunities. Certainly a great deal of money has been made from the commercial application of style instruments in schools. Coffield et al (2004) reviewed 71, concluding that most, including resources advocated by the DfES, were unreliable and of negligible pedagogical value. Teachers are probably better off providing varied pedagogy that reflects the host of ways in which learners interact with and process information rather than matching tasks to individuals that simply serve to reinforce the stereotypes assigned to them.

Reader reflection

It is interesting to consider how the exclusive use of kinaesthetic forms of learning could possibly facilitate pupils' learning of the curriculum.

If we labelled pupils in this way would it mean they would never be expected to interact with visual or auditory stimuli in the form of reading a book or listening to one another?

Emphasis on the identification of a single style attribute would certainly lead to this odd conclusion.

Is it actually possible, though, to use just one mode – don't we employ an interaction of seeing, hearing and doing in most things we learn?

Think about how your own learning requires the use of different strategies according to the task and the context.

Should teachers attempt to train learners not to use particular learning strategies or to need particular environmental preferences?

The business of basing pedagogy on learning styles in their more multifarious forms is complex.

Should educators define each learner across a range of style constructs and match tasks accordingly?

A similar tendency to oversimplification pertains to ideas about metacognition, which, as we saw, has a sound basis in research (Shayer and Adey, 2002, for instance). In our knowledge society it might be argued that there is a surfeit of information generated together with ever more technological ways of accessing it. This requires people generally and learners in particular to develop more sophisticated ways of finding things out and greater confidence in filtering them for relevance and reliability. Claxton (2002) has argued that learners need above all to learn to learn and that teachers' main focus should be teaching them how. This metacognitive approach has in some circles been dubbed 'learnacy', a product perhaps of the tendency to think that ideas are only accessible if they are reduced to sound bites or tabloid shorthand. This tendency is reinforced in some education texts by authors' preoccupation with gratuitous alliterative devices and metaphors to communicate their ideas as if they would not otherwise be understood. Thus Claxton talks about pupils needing to exercise their 'learning muscles' and to become 'resourceful, resilient, reflective learners', using these terms as organising vehicles for his arguments. This approach can lead to the publishing of polemic rather than detailed research accounts and can divert students of education from wrestling with the central research proposition.

Research into brain functioning, though relatively speaking in its infancy, has caught the imagination of both the general public and the education sector. There is a tendency to alight on elements of the research that appear to lend themselves to innovative pedagogic techniques. Novelty claims that are well known but not well substantiated by research include the beneficial effects of listening to music while learning, sipping water to 'hydrate the brain' and using neuro-linguistic programming to reveal how the brain codes experience in order to improve communication.

Brain gym is a popular brain improvement tool that has a longer legacy and was developed by the American, Paul Dennison, in the late 1960s who, as a dyslexic, was interested in the connection between physical activity and learning ability. It comprises a set of exercises designed to improve concentration, reading ability and hand–eye coordination. UK researchers have since found that using such simple movements improves learning. Exercise sessions usually last for a few minutes and are often used at the beginning of lessons to focus pupils' attention. They are sometimes related to the work that is being taught, for example letter sounds, arithmetical functions or hand-writing; they may be used to break up passive learning or to refresh pupils, particularly those with attention difficulties. It is suggested that brain gym can help children become calm, alert and ready to concentrate by stimulating neurological pathways so that both sides of the brain work together. Mind mapping is a strategy copyrighted by Tony Buzan to facilitate this dual hemispheric functioning, which in turn enhances problem solving, the generation of creative ideas and the organisation of thoughts. It has been suggested that stress causes people to overuse the right side of the brain leading to emotions obscuring understanding so attempts to balance this would be considered effective pedagogical strategy. Studies authenticating long-term benefits, however, are not well known.

In terms of pedagogic influence, emotional intelligence continues to be prevalent, with most professional development courses and management textbooks drawing on its maxims (see Killick, 2006; Zins et al, 2004). Goleman's popular work (Goleman, 1995) related the ability to control impulses, motivate oneself, and regulate moods to improved thinking and learning and to better self and people management. We can agree this is sensible enough but not all subscribe to the elevation of emotions within education. Ecclestone (2004) has criticised the trend, arguing that it detracts from risk-taking and pointing to a lack of systematic research evidence to support claims made about the damaging effects of poor emotional literacy. Subjecting emotional intelligence to research is indeed problematic because it is not easy to isolate such a nebulous variable within a research context.

Finally, we turn to the vexed subject of how intelligence theory influences pedagogy. We have seen that IQ theory had a far-reaching effect on pupil life chances within the tripartite selective secondary school system set up after the Second World War. Since then attention has turned to multiple forms of describing, developing and assessing intelligence. We considered Gardner's theory of multiple intelligences and Sternberg's work on triarchic categorisations of intelligences in Chapter 7. Clearly these models are significantly different from one another and although developed around the same time, fewer educators have heard of Sternberg's model than Gardner's. Sternberg (2003a) argued that schools undervalue creativity and think it is no different from general intelligence.

Reader reflection

It is easy to see how Gardner's model could gain currency at a common-sense level since people often display particular talents or tendencies. Indeed the school curriculum and Hirst's (1975) forms of knowledge use similar categorisations.

But can we really believe that these constitute discrete and differently processed forms of intelligence? Do we have evidence that learners use different thinking and processing techniques across eight areas of experience and activity in the way the existence of discrete forms of intelligence might suggest?

Think about how you might approach the understanding of an educational ideology within your course and contrast this with the processes you use to determine your weekly household finances. Does your brain employ different processing techniques to do these two things or is it just the context that is different?

White (1998, 2004) has heavily critiqued Gardner's work but his critique does not seem to have registered with educators as reliance on Gardner's problematic explanation of intelligence persists in schools in many countries.

Insufficient scepticism has been applied generally by the educational community to the provenance of psychopedagogic approaches so a thoroughgoing questioning of their theoretical and empirical bases is overdue.

Conclusion

Psychological research has for many years facilitated new understandings amongst educators about how people learn from which pedagogical implications have been derived. The varying influence of these theories is linked to shifts within both policy imperatives and pedagogical 'trends' and the extent to which these are championed by an increasingly sophisticated global media. Psychological research continues to develop and refine theoretical ideas about learning but educators must resist reductionist attempts to produce neat, digestible, commercialised chunks of pedagogy from them. Teachers, students and education professionals will enjoy a fascinating perspective on psychopedagogy as long as a critical, enquiring approach is taken to their theoretical or empirical basis and to their political provenance. Distinguishing between pragmatic arguments and the 'educational' – political? – rhetoric constructed to justify these strategies plays a key part in this. Harris and Ranson (2005), for instance, expose the contradictions in the UK government's linking of personalised learning and social justice.

Edgar Stones, an influential educational psychologist, railed against the ready adoption of populist terms (2000, 2002) and the increasingly fluid and amorphous perceptions of pedagogy. He argued for an unequivocal expression of the concept and alluded to the influence of fashion on the communication of educational ideas. It may be that you, as students of education, will be the ones that expose the 'emperor's new clothes' syndrome that currently besets education where constructs such as 'learnacy' and 'personalised', 'tailored' or 'brain-based' learning become accepted sound bites within the educational lexicon, having been used in ministers' speeches or government documents without anyone sharing an understanding of what they mean, much less a knowledge of their research basis.

Student activities

Think of examples to illustrate how the age of the students, their academic ability, the resources available and the number of students in the group may influence how a teacher plans a lesson.

Recommended reading

Capel, S., Leask, M. and Turner, T. (2005) *Learning to teach in the secondary school: a companion to school experience*, 4th edn. London and New York: Routledge. This is a comprehensive, up to date text outlining a wide range of pedagogical issues and approaches in an accessible way.

Tomlinson, P., Dockrell, J. and Winne, P. (eds) (2005) *Pedagogy – Teaching for learning*. British Journal of Educational Psychology, Monograph Series II: Psychological Aspects of Education – Current Trends. Leicester: The British Psychological Society. This text is a collection of papers taken from conferences organised by the British Psychological Society on aspects of education. Its aim is to disseminate the latest developments in psychological research amongst educators and also students of education. As such it links psychological theories to education practice aiming to counterbalance the often shallow approach that has been taken to such issues in recent years by practitioners.

Politics and policy in education

In Chapter 4 we gave a historical outline of the development of the modern English education system. Inevitably such developments are influenced by their political, social and economic context so it is important to examine the relationship between policy and political ideologies in education. This chapter provides an overview and commentary on the development of the state education system in England since the Second World War showing how policy in education is influenced by the constant interaction and struggle between differing sets of beliefs and wider political circumstances. The post-war political consensus during a period of reconstruction, the expansion in education and the influences on the growth of the comprehensive movement are outlined. The disillusionment that arose during the time of economic crisis in the 1970s is discussed. The development of a policy of market forces and, paradoxically, the increasing control of central government during the Conservative administrations of the 1980s and the first half of the 1990s is contrasted with the development of 'third way' politics by Labour from the second half of the 1990s and into the twenty-first century. The influence of political ideologies on education is well illustrated through this analysis.

Introduction

Previous chapters have indicated that the development and organisation of systems of education is not a straightforward matter. Education is not a neutral concept. We may wish for the development of 'the good society' but what this actually looks like and how we get there can be viewed very differently. A 'good society' may be based on the discipline and order shown by citizens or it may be a result of the freedom of all to develop themselves or more likely a combination and balance of both of these things. Consider how often pupils are subjected to punishments and controls to make them comply yet are also encouraged to question and explore. The purposes of education may be broadly agreed as developing minds, imparting significant knowledge, ensuring the continuation of social order, preparing young people for future employment. However, constructing the detail of an educational experience is a highly problematised, political activity.

Chapter 5 has shown how educators must grapple with issues of curriculum content and pedagogy. What must be taught and also, perhaps, what is best avoided? For instance, what do we tell young people about drugs and sex? Do we allow wide ranging discussion on such topics in our schools? Which teaching styles and techniques are most effective? Should the emphasis be on disciplined learning or freedom to explore? Drawing back from the detail, it is also necessary to engage with issues about the universal nature of education. What aspects should be for all citizens? Will they be compulsory? If so, for how many years shall people be expected to study? Is the education provided different for different sections of the population? If so, in what ways and how is the populace to be divided? Is it to be paid for by the state or the individual? The answer to this may depend upon whether society or the individual is deemed to be the beneficiary. The circumstances an individual is born into are clearly very important in determining subsequent educational experience.

Kelly suggests that education is a political activity whereby society prepares its young for adult life. Education and politics are 'inextricably interwoven' and it is not possible to discuss education without considering the political environment:

> The political context, then, is a major element in any scheme or system of education, and one without reference to which such a scheme or system cannot be properly understood. (2004: 161)

The history of the development of any education system illustrates competing views as to the purposes of education and how these are best met. These views are very much linked to how individuals would like to see their society develop (see Chapter 2 for a discussion of ideology in education). As education has to be paid for and may affect the quality of a future workforce, any system has to be seen in relation to the economy. Identifying who possesses the power to make decisions which bring about change is important and not always so clear cut.

The influence of different groups of people varies over time and, as education is clearly a central concern in our society, it is always an important national issue. Marsh (2004) suggests that the education received is a result of a complex relationship between decision-makers, stakeholders and other influences, in which no one group is in total control. We must not assume that because politicians pass a national curriculum as law that it will be interpreted in the same way by all of those operating at different levels of its delivery. He also suggests that it is naïve to assume that teachers have ever been in total control of the classroom. They are affected by forces outside of the classroom as well as by the pupils within.

When examining the development of education systems a significant question to be answered is who decides what is to be taught, how it is to be taught and to whom. To illustrate this we will look at the recent development of one part of the education system in England. In examining the compulsory sector (primary and secondary education) we will be able to see the effects of differing ideological beliefs and the pressure these bring to bear on the political process. Clearly any particular 'slant' placed on the telling of these developments may reflect the ideologies and backgrounds of the authors. Particular events may often be interpreted in various ways. We have made decisions, based on wider academic readings, about what to include as important in this brief historical analysis, and therefore what to leave out.

Towards post-war reconstruction and consensus

THE 1944 EDUCATION REFORM ACT

The account will start as politicians in the depths of the Second World War consider the peace to come. The vision was to create a prosperous, thriving society. How to do this and what it would look like was seen differently by politicians of the left and the right (McKenzie, 2001). Whatever the political perspective, education was to play an important part in realising the dream. In Chapter 4 we described the 1944 Education Act as a great political moment. As we saw, the Act enabled the introduction of the tripartite system of secondary education. In terms of the division of responsibility for the new national education system which the Act created there was a 'balance of control' (Coulby, 1989) between central government, local government and the schools. This system of checks and balances has been portrayed as a period of consensus or, alternatively, a triangle of tension between state, LEAs and teachers, which ensured that no one group obtained too much power in the running of the education system.

Apart from making religious education compulsory, the 1944 Education Act made no stipulations concerning the curriculum. This whole area was left to the discretion of the teachers and the individual schools. Barber (1996) gives two reasons why this may have been the case.

1 In the 1920s the government was concerned that teachers may have joined the growing labour movement and become affiliated to the trade union movement. This had occurred elsewhere in Europe and was seen as contributing to civil unrest in these countries. In order to keep teachers neutral they were incorporated to some extent as partners in the policy process and control over the curriculum was ceded to them.

2 At the time of the formulation of the 1944 Act Britain was still at war with the fascist powers. It was felt that controlling the education, as part of a wider control of people's minds, was how enemy totalitarian regimes had operated and so democratic governments would not seek to interfere with the curriculum. Teachers, by being allowed to exercise their professional educational judgements over the curriculum, were seen to be helping to safeguard democracy. Tropp (1957) gave an account of the steady rise in the status of the teacher as a professional after the Second World War. Lawton (1980: 22) refers to this period as the 'golden age' of teacher control of the curriculum.

THE GROWTH OF THE COMPREHENSIVE MOVEMENT

After the Second World War education was increasingly seen, in advanced industrial societies, as a key investment in the promotion of both economic wealth and social justice (Brown et al,

1997). This was a period of growth after the destruction of the war with full employment and a steady rise in living standards. According to Chitty (2004) both major political parties were committed to the principles of the welfare state, along with full employment and a mixed economy. In education throughout the 1950s and into the 1960s the emphasis was on expansion. The economy was changing to processes of mass production and the growth in white collar and professional employment meant that these new workers needed to have completed more education. Education became increasingly seen as an economic investment. A link was perceived to exist between an educated workforce and an expanding economy. The future labour force was regarded as human capital and as such it needed to be developed.

The 1960s was a time of rising standards of living. It could be summed up by the election slogan of Conservative Prime Minister, Harold Macmillan that: 'You've never had it so good.' Many factory workers were now earning high wages, and could be seen to be living a 'new lifestyle' (see Goldthorpe and Lockwood's thesis of the affluent worker, 1968). The structure of society was altering and more people were becoming middle-class due to increasing affluence. Certainly the majority was materially much better off and with these improved living and working conditions came raised expectations for the future. Thus the argument for increasing public expenditure on education became irresistible. The comprehensive school movement was born from an alliance of three groups:

- leading sections of the Labour Party keen to promote social reform through education
- the organised sectors of the teaching profession who favoured a more egalitarian system
- some key intellectuals in the new education-related academic disciplines (Silver, 1973) able to exert some influence on government thinking.

Comprehensive schooling was successfully sold to the electorate as an opportunity for making what was seen as valuable in grammar school education available to everyone. It was also presented as being essential for the needs of industrial modernisation which would enhance the wealth of all. In this it was related to Harold Wilson's rhetoric of a 'technological revolution' (CCCS, 1981). This revolution would involve the reshaping of the social infrastructure of the country accompanying industrial expansion. Schools and the new universities would be egalitarian powerhouses to effect this dual transformation – a powerful vision. The detail of how investment in education would be transformed into specific economic benefits was never actually clarified (Chitty, 1992) and the concept of human capital always remained at a general level of application.

According to Chitty (1992), Labour was able to put what were seen as the sound economic arguments of developing human capital alongside desires for social reform as justification for the comprehensivisation of state education. Anthony Crosland, the Labour Secretary of State for Education, issued circular 10/65 and then 10/66 which put pressure on LEAs to reorganise on comprehensive lines (see Lawton, 2005, for an outline of the arguments put forward by Crosland for this reorganisation). Halsey et al (1997) suggest that the focus on the link between education and social democracy at the time can be seen in the increasing movement for reorganisation of secondary education. It was felt that in these comprehensive schools pupils from varied social backgrounds would mix and tolerance and respect towards each other would be created. Comprehensives would provide greater opportunity as pupils would be allowed to develop rather than being separated out and discriminated against. This in turn would allow the development of social democracy:

> From the democratic-socialist perspective of the time it could be seen and still can be defended as a major advance in breaking down the barriers of class, gender, and ethnicity. (Halsey et al, 1997: 5).

The trend with new schools was to make them community schools so that there would be joint use of facilities. This was a more efficient use of resources and also helped promote the social democratic ideals of the Labour Party.

In some LEAs the reorganisation of the tripartite system into comprehensive schools did cause problems with amalgamations between traditional grammar and non-academic secondary modern schools. There were issues of split sites and clashes of school cultures. For many comprehensivisation did not have the auspicious start hoped for (Young, 1998).

The rise of conflict and dissent in policy

The post-war consensus has perhaps tended to be overstated. Though there was a move towards comprehensive education this was still not universally accepted. There was some opposition to these new forms of secondary school, particularly within the Conservative Party, where many saw a need to re-establish a Tory identity. Many Conservatives felt that they had gone along with the consensus for long enough and that it was damaging both to the electoral prospects of the party and to the country. They pointed to an insidious move to the left, which had gone largely unnoticed, under the auspices of a national consensus. Britain was felt to be in decline, both morally and economically, by many Conservative politicians from the mid-1960s onwards (see Lawton, 1994; Tomlinson, 2001).

ECONOMIC CRISIS

There was little concern amongst the general public with problems in education so long as there remained full employment. This appeared to be the case in the 'swinging 60s' with the increasing affluence, a football World Cup win and hope for even more prosperity in the future. Rising standards of living for all sectors of society, whilst not reducing inequality, created at least a semblance of unity, according to Chitty. Economic crisis, when it came in the 1970s, had a significant effect and 'fundamentally altered the map of British politics' (Chitty, 2004: 31). Education had been linked with the rebuilding of society after the Second World War, with secure employment, better living standards and the eradication of poverty. When there was recession, however, questions began to be asked about how effective education had been and the value gained from money previously invested. The whole of compulsory education came under scrutiny. Economic pressure to reduce spending focused attention back onto fundamental questions concerning the purposes of education.

PUBLIC OUTCRY

Throughout the 1970s there was growing public concern regarding education, which was actively fuelled by the media, the press in particular. There was a public perception, whether based on fact or not, that education was in crisis (Dale, 1983). Standards were felt to be falling. There are ideological issues here about standards of 'what' and how they are being measured (see Kelly, 2004, for a discussion of the use and meaning of the term 'standards').

'Progressive' and 'child-centred' approaches adopted in primary schools, which had been promoted particularly in the light of the Plowden Report and much sociological and psychological research of the 1960s, were now questioned. It was felt that these approaches had led to indiscipline, lack of direction in pupils' learning and a resulting lack of knowledge acquisition. Pupils were no longer being taught the basic skills of reading, writing and arithmetic in any systematic way. Classrooms were portrayed as chaotic with little learning taking place.

These public concerns were highlighted by the William Tyndale case which made the headlines in 1976 as being overly progressive and indisciplined. Here, despite the worries expressed by parents, the headteacher of William Tyndale Primary School claimed the professional expertise to continue with progressive teaching methods. The Auld report (1976), which was set up to investigate the case, found many faults with how the school was being run. This instance, by the media attention it drew, strengthened the public mistrust of teachers, teaching methods and teachers' control over the curriculum. In secondary schools, in particular, the curriculum was felt to be too academic for many young people. It was not practical and not relevant to their future and appeared to be out of touch with modern life. This was held to account for much pupil unrest which was perceived to be part of a growing discipline problem within schools and which was spilling over into the wider society. These new comprehensive schools now came under increasing criticism and teachers and teaching methods were seen as the prime cause.

MIXED ABILITY

Mixed ability teaching practices in secondary education had expanded throughout the late 1960s and early 1970s. Informed by child-centred ideologies which aimed to motivate pupils and encourage an individual approach to pupils' learning, they were increasingly criticised by traditionalists. Having to cope with such a wide range of ability in each class put a great deal of strain on many teachers, whole class teaching being inappropriate. Pupils still often felt labelled within their classes and disruption was made worse as the able were often not challenged whilst the less able could feel left behind. The perception was that comprehensives were producing mediocrity by teaching to the 'middle' with ability and potential being wasted as it had been in the tripartite system. Thus, as well as the secondary curriculum not being relevant, academic standards were also felt to be falling. By emphasising individual development and equality, it was felt that comprehensives and primary schools were discouraging the very competitive spirit that was needed to improve the economy. Comprehensives were at a further disadvantage in that they were often compared to, and in fact in some areas were in competition with, grammar schools that only taught able pupils.

THE CURRICULUM

The curriculum had changed in many comprehensive schools. Critics saw the traditional subjects and their content being diluted into themes or topics. History, geography and religious education were now often combined with aspects of sociology to form 'social studies' or 'integrated humanities'. Some felt this led to important traditional knowledge not being taught and being replaced by the transmission of what were portrayed as left wing egalitarian beliefs. Teachers were not felt to be upholding traditional stable values and were stereotyped as 'lefty', indoctrinating, longhaired and lazy. Thus schools and teachers could be seen to be to blame for many of the country's problems. In a seminal article in *The Times Educational Supplement* (Weinstock, 1976: 2) entitled 'I blame the teachers', key industrialist, Arnold Weinstock, blamed them for the economic and social problems of the time. These criticisms were cited and much of the growing unrest captured in a series of Black Papers written by a group of right wing politicians and thinkers published between 1969 and 1977 (Cox and Boyson, 1975, 1977; Cox and Dyson, 1969a, 1969b, 1970). They criticised falling standards and an associated moral decline and put both down to progressive teaching methods encouraged in the Plowden Report (Central Advisory Council for Education, 1967). The Black Papers claimed this ideology led to sloppiness, lack of rigour, decline in discipline and thus disruption in the education of all pupils.

THE 'GREAT DEBATE'

The Black Papers critique can be seen as a humanist backlash upon the prevailing progressive and social democratic ideologies of the time which had also been linked to the reconstructionists. The solution suggested in the later of the papers was to take control of the curriculum and the running of education away from the teachers and the educationalists and place them in the hands of the parents and employers. Thus a policy of market forces was proposed, where the power of the consumer, not the producer, determined the 'product'. These criticisms of the education system and those who had been running it reflected the growing importance of what became known as the 'New Right' within the Conservative Party. They raised questions about the purpose of education in society including issues of what and how pupils should be taught. As value for money came to be seen as increasingly important in the growing recession, these questions were also asked by the Labour Prime Minister of the time, James Callaghan.

Under increasing economic pressure and with growing public concern being expressed over education, a speech made by Callaghan at Ruskin College in 1976 marked a significant point in the history of recent education policy. Callaghan's intentions for the speech are still debated (see Lawton, 2005 and Phillips, 2001). It could be taken as a critique of a system in crisis or it could be interpreted as a desire to move to a more radical agenda. He did not openly condemn education, in fact he noted achievements, though this was done with faint praise.

Callaghan spoke of issues that caused him concern and that needed attention. He felt that the curriculum was not appropriate for the needs of a modern economy and that many of the brightest pupils were not being encouraged and were even being discouraged from taking up courses relevant to careers in industry. He noted the great strides in social aspects of education but was also worried that a number of pupils were not acquiring the basic academic skills needed in later life. Though teachers were professionally involved in the curriculum, he felt it should not just be left to them – others in society needed to be involved. To this end Callaghan proposed a 'great debate' concerning the curriculum. Certainly this can be seen as the first significant occasion since the 1944 Act on which teacher autonomy in curriculum matters was questioned by the government in power. What this speech signified was the growing public feeling stoked by politicians and the media that the education system needed to be more accountable. It was felt that teachers and LEAs needed to be responsive to the wider society which was, after all, paying for education. In ideological terms the focus was shifting away from the individual and more towards society and the importance of traditional knowledge.

When Labour lost the general election of 1979 there followed a substantial period of Conservative government up until 1997. The early Thatcher years were a time of economic and social upheaval. There was a change in emphasis from the social democratic policies of the consensus politicians to the rigours of monetarism and the free market. This was reflected throughout government policy and so too in education. Education had come to be seen as part of the national problem and it provided a convenient scapegoat for intractable economic and social issues. Education could also, whilst undergoing a process of reform, be seen as a future solution to many of the economic difficulties of the time. It could prepare suitable workers and instil social responsibility and respect for authority amongst the young. What had previously been an education programme for a new affluent society had come to be seen as politically biased and damaging to the nation's development. It was claimed there was a need to get back to basics, to eliminate political meddling in education, to return to traditional values and at the same time modernise education for the needs of a changing economy. There was an ideological shift taking place in public life from progressivism to classical humanism alongside instrumentalism and economic revisionism.

Conservative policy: ideology of the New Right

After the defeat of the Conservatives in 1974 there had arisen a movement for reform within the party. It was felt that for many years the two main parties, Labour and Conservative, had been similar in their 'centralist' approaches to government. The rhetoric of consensus which resulted had hidden a steady drift to the left which was illustrated by policies such as the comprehensivisation of education (Chitty, 2004). Certain right wing thinkers, such as the Black Paper authors, felt that it was this drift which had led to the decline in fortunes not only of the Conservative Party but also of the country. They argued that socialist policies had ignored traditional values and stifled the important characteristics of individual achievement and entrepreneurship. The stress on equality of opportunity had been at the expense of competitiveness and the developing welfare state had created a culture of dependency and conformity. These policies were considered inevitably to lead to a steady economic and moral decline.

THE RISE OF THE NEW RIGHT

The Conservative policy became influenced by groups within the party identified by the term the 'New Right'. This was not a coherent force but what Trowler (2003) labelled an amalgam of ideologies and associated groups. Their point of unity was a common enemy in socialism. The potential internal conflicts of the New Right were overcome and factions within the party were held together by the strong leadership of Margaret Thatcher. The origins of the new right can be seen in traditional strands of Tory thought stemming from the nineteenth century. These are a combination of a desire for order and stability in society along with the importance of individual freedom and enterprise. Both of these were seen as needed in the creation of a thriving economy (Lawton, 1994; Tomlinson, 2005a; Phillips, 2001). These two positions can be described as neo-conservative and neo-liberal.

Neo-liberalism (market forces)

Neo-liberals attest to the importance of a free market economy which involves freedom of choice for consumers and producers with minimum state interference (see Olssen et al, 2004, for a detailed account of the development of neo-liberalism). These ideas stem from the economic model of perfect competition. This assumes that in the running of an economy there are certain factors of production, these being labour, land and capital, which are pulled together by entrepreneurs. These factors will be used most effectively when supplying the goods which consumers demand. Producers will endeavour to provide what consumers want, to sell their products and make their profit. This profit enables them to expand and to be even more successful in the future. Those producers who do not make what the public want, or who cannot produce it as efficiently (cheaply) as competitors, will go out of business. Thus those who meet demand and are the most efficient will survive (Tubbs, 2006). The factors of production used by those who go out of business are released to be used by more efficient producers in this or other industries. Thus competition leads to the most effective use of resources which will ultimately benefit the whole society.

The neo-liberals advocate minimum interference by government in the market. They suggest that this only benefits the less efficient producers and allows the production of goods which the market has not demanded. Protected industries, like those which are nationalised, will never become truly efficient and will always need to be supported by taxpayers' money.

Thus protectionism means we all pay more for our goods and leads to a weak economy that will ultimately fail in world markets. Free competition benefits us all by creating efficiency of production and a strong economy. It was suggested that education could be seen as another product. Competition would, as in other industries, lead to more efficient use of resources whilst satisfying consumer demand. This would put a stop to the educational establishment forcing its own view of what should be supplied as education on everyone. This competition would in turn make the system more cost effective and be part of economic regeneration (see Tooley, 2001 for an explanation of how this could happen).

Neo-conservatism (traditional values)

Neo-conservatives believe in the importance of upholding standards and traditional values. Ball (1994) referred to this group as 'Cultural Restorationists'. This ideology stressed the importance of authority, a national identity and high standards. Economic decline could be traced to moral decline of which the education system was a major cause. The neo-conservatives felt that this was largely due to progressive teaching which lacked an important stress on values and discipline. There needed to be greater supervision over the work of teachers and LEAs alongside reform of the curriculum. Lawton (1992) noted that:

whereas the neo-liberals tend to talk about choice, competition and the market in education, the neo-conservatives are more likely to advocate traditional values, traditional subjects, and less educational theory in the training of teachers, but greater immersion into the traditional values of good schools (1992: 7.)

NEW RIGHT EDUCATION POLICY

Certainly these different ideological strands revealed dissatisfaction with the developments of education in the 1960s and 1970s. One ideology emphasised freedom of choice and markets, the other the need for control and a return to tried and tested methods. There is potential conflict between these groups but certainly a view that things needed to change. In spite of their differences neo-conservatives and neo-liberals both had a mistrust of state professionals who prevented the development of a free market and efficiency and were also seen as subversive (Carr and Hartnett, 1996). A policy developed which reflected both ideologies whilst stressing one and then the other at different times. The policy was not totally contradictory. Whitty (1990) suggested that it was necessary for central government to take control of the curriculum to allow the market to develop, thus preventing the producers, that is, the teachers and LEAs, from stifling the development of competition by their control.

The government's mistrust of teachers and suspicions as to their subversive motives were brought to a head in 1986 and 1987 in a prolonged industrial dispute over pay and conditions. This resulted in severe disruption in schools. By their actions the teachers lost much public support and the government became even more determined to reform schooling and to alter the balance of power in education (see Ball, 1988 for an account of the strike and its effects). The policies of many LEAs on equal opportunities, anti-racism and so on began to be seen as 'loony' by the Conservative government (Coulby, 1989). Increasingly it was felt that the producer control of the education system needed to be broken. The Conservative government did introduce some changes in the early 1980s with major reforms in education occurring from the 1988 Education Reform Act onwards. Perhaps most significant of these early changes was the setting up of the assisted places scheme, whereby able pupils from state schools were offered places at public school, with the state assisting the parents with the payment of fees. This can be said to show a mistrust of the state system and a belief that the private sector was superior. It also diverted public funds from the state to the private sector. The Education Reform Act of 1988 which followed was arguably the most significant piece of legislation since the 1944 Act and was the first of a series of acts that led to significant changes to the education system (DES, 1988).

Conservative policy: implementation

Conservative reforms should be seen in terms of how they were designed to create the market of the neo-liberals, to reinforce a more traditional morality of the neo-conservatives or in some cases achieve both of these potentially contradicting goals. They were to tip the balance of power away from the teachers and LEAs, sometimes towards the centre, at other times towards parents thus giving choice to the consumers.

ALLOWING PARENTAL CHOICE OF SCHOOL

Up to this time pupils were allocated to a school by their LEA and the number of pupils on each school roll was also decided by the LEAs. This enabled them to plan for the education of all pupils within their authority. It also meant that they could control intake for each school and thus balance the size of schools in the authority. Parents had comparatively little say in the schools their children were sent to by the LEA and it was usual for pupils to be allocated places at their local primary or secondary school.

Under the 1988 Education Reform Act parents were able to choose which school they wanted their children to attend. They could send them to schools which offered the kind of education they wanted rather than to a school chosen by the LEA. This meant that schools now had to start attracting parents and marketing themselves if they were to maintain a sufficiently high intake of pupils. This was particularly important in the secondary sector as parents were able to consider schools over a wider travelling distance for their children. The LEA was no longer able to protect undersubscribed schools by giving them extra funding to cushion the fall in pupil numbers due to the introduction of 'local management of schools'.

CREATING INCREASING AUTONOMY OF SCHOOLS (LOCAL MANAGEMENT OF SCHOOLS)

Previously the LEA was in control of the budgets for all maintained schools in its area and it allocated funds according to its own policy. Thus some schools may have been given more funds by the authority than others for a variety of reasons. In this way the LEA could protect schools from falling rolls and they could be given extra support if they were having particular problems. In effect this meant that some schools were subsidising others. From the point of view of the neo-liberals this meant that the efficient were paying for the inefficient and there was no financial incentive for schools to become more effective or to make an effort to be more attractive to parents and pupils.

The 1988 Education Reform Act gave headteachers more control over their own budgets and forced LEAs to pass on to schools a high percentage of the money allocated to them by central government. The money was to be allocated on the basis of the number of pupils on roll. Schools which were successful and growing, as more parents opted for them, would receive more money thereby enabling them to build upon their success. Those who were unable to attract pupils and were suffering from falling rolls would need to act quickly if they were to survive. Thus the consumer would reign supreme in the market and schools would need to offer the sort of education which attracted parents. The LEAs were no longer able to interfere as they had lost much of their financial power.

THE CREATION OF CITY TECHNOLOGY COLLEGES (CTCS), GRANT MAINTAINED (GM) SCHOOLS AND SPECIALIST SCHOOLS

For parents to be able to exercise choice there needed to be different types of school available. Greater diversity would stimulate competition and force existing state schools to change more quickly. A new type of school, a city technology college, was to be jointly funded by the government and industry. They were to be technology and industry oriented for pupils of secondary school age. This epitomised the link between education and economic development. They were designed to offer opportunities to pupils from inner city areas who were oriented towards technology. It was expected that these schools would provide models of good practice that other schools in the area would have to follow.

Schools that wanted the freedom to develop in their own way and to sever links with the bureaucratic LEAs could become grant maintained. This meant that they were funded directly from central government and were in total control of the whole of their budget.

Increasing diversity of schools was encouraged to further stimulate the market. Later the CTC concept was modified and widened, enabling more schools to join the City Technology Trust scheme, providing they were able to attract matching funding from industry. Towards the end of the Conservatives' third term of office the specialist secondary schools initiative was launched whereby secondary schools were able to apply to become specialist schools in a particular area of the curriculum – science, music, technology, modern foreign languages or sport. Once again the schools needed to attract sufficient private funding to support their application.

Though the Conservative government expected that the majority of schools would welcome the option to become grant maintained, they did not, and this category of school was later abolished by the Labour government. However, the concept of CTCs and specialist schools, though initially slow to 'take off' was later embraced by Labour in its desire to raise standards.

INTRODUCTION OF THE NATIONAL CURRICULUM

Politicians in the mid-twentieth century had not dared to prescribe the curriculum for fear of appearing similar to fascist or communist dictators and thus undemocratic. This fear had passed into history with the World Wars now so distant. With the increasing public concern over education, a national curriculum was now seen as a way of ensuring an appropriate schooling for all pupils. For the New Right it was a way of breaking the subversive control that teachers exerted over the curriculum. The National Curriculum was to be compulsory for all pupils aged 5 to 16. It was to be assessed and it was envisaged that test results at the end of the four key stages would be made public in the form of league tables. The results would show how pupils were progressing, how schools were achieving, and how standards were being raised.

The subjects and their content were traditional and thus reflected clearly the influence of the neo-conservatives. The neo-liberal element of the party perhaps did not favour this traditional approach since it had no element of choice for the consumer. However, they did go along with it in that future changes in content could be made and it would certainly encourage competition with the publication of National Curriculum test results. These would provide large amounts of information about the 'output' of each school for the consumer.

REGULAR INSPECTIONS OF SCHOOLS

In 1993 a rigorous inspection service was set up under the newly created Office for Standards in Education (Ofsted). As well as checking on the running of each school, inspection reports were made public giving the consumer information on which to make informed choices. Schools deemed to be 'failing' would have to improve rapidly or be severely dealt with.

THE INTRODUCTION OF LEAGUE TABLES OF SCHOOLS

League tables of school performance were developed in the first instance to show GCSE results. These would provide consumer information and encourage competition amongst producers. The aim was to expand the tables to include end of key stage results.

The concept of an education system driven by market forces was becoming more and more influential towards the end of the Conservative administration in all sectors of education and it was proposed to extend this further had they won the 1997 general election. There was also, paradoxically, a move to allow schools greater powers to select pupils. This was part of the neo-conservative ideal of schools for an academic elite as had existed before comprehensivisation. The high status selective schools would perhaps naturally be formed from those that were already oversubscribed.

Reader reflection

As noted above the Conservative reforms were designed to create the market of the neo-liberals, to reinforce a more traditional morality of the neo-conservatives or in some cases achieve both of these potentially contradicting goals.

How did each of the policies implemented by the Conservatives over this period (outlined above) actually work towards these different goals?

Conservative policy: a critique

It was not all plain sailing for the Conservative government and its education policy. The National Curriculum encountered a number of problems during its introduction. Large amounts of prescribed content implemented over a very short timescale, coupled with the fear of untried assessment methods, placed great strain on teachers and schools. This was exacerbated by government reforms on school management being introduced simultaneously.

This caused confrontation between teachers and the government and resulted in the boycotting of the early end of key stage tests. In response to increasing public disquiet the government set up the Dearing Commission to look into the curriculum. Whilst its brief was to make a complex system more 'workable' the ideological basis of the curriculum was not open to question. The Dearing Report, published in January 1994, did recognise the unwieldy nature of the curriculum. There was far too much content and the assessment was very complex and time consuming. It proposed a streamlining of the curriculum which would give greater flexibility to the individual schools and teachers in their planning. This allowed more time to be spent on mathematics and English in the early years and the possibility of subject choice and vocational options in the later years. The subjects were to be reviewed for September 1995 with a promise of no further changes for five years. Only the core subjects of English, mathematics and science were to be nationally tested though teachers were expected to monitor pupil progress in the other subjects in relation to the National Curriculum levels.

A list of the Conservative achievements in education by the end of their term might include the following:

- The balance of power had changed with LEAs having lost much of their power to central government and individual schools.
- Control of the curriculum was still an area of contention but certainly was no longer clearly the preserve of teachers. It was now quality controlled and monitored by government agencies.
- A market had developed with the introduction of greater parental choice and financial control delegated to schools. This had a great effect on how schools were run. There was an increasing emphasis on management training, cost effectiveness and efficiency. Schools now operated much more on the lines of individual businesses. The producers, in this case the headteachers running the schools, were able to respond to the wishes of the consumers, that is, the parents.

A list of Conservative disappointments in education by the end of their term could include the following:

- Only a handful of CTCs were created. This was due partly to the difficulty in attracting funding from industry and partly to strong local opposition in some areas from parents and politicians (Brooks, 1991).
- Nowhere near as many schools opted for grant maintained status as the government had hoped. The anticipated flood of applications to leave LEA control did not materialise.
- Allowing parental choice actually caused problems for many parents. In each LEA certain schools, usually with good examination results and in the more affluent areas, became oversubscribed. This led to problems whereby increasing numbers of parents living outside of the immediate area could not get their children into the school of their choice because it was full. Schools with poor reputations often had difficulty in improving their image as middle-class parents living in their area tried to send their children to schools further away. These undersubscribed schools, often serving poor neighbourhoods, had to accept a number of pupils who for whatever reason could not get into other schools. In this

way they came to be seen as sink schools and remained low in the performance league tables. This is a form of market failure and illustrates how free markets may actually fail to satisfy supply and demand. As pupil places were limited in oversubscribed schools the choice again became that of the school (the producer). This was often based on set catchment area criteria and neither the school nor consumer had a free choice in reality.

- The status of teaching had changed. Teachers had suffered criticism for many years, had come under scrutiny from Ofsted and retained little professional control over the curriculum. Many education theorists talked of the proletarianisation and deprofessionalisation of teachers (see Apple, 1988; Bartlett and Burton, 2003; Furlong, 2005; McCulloch, 2001; Ozga, 1995). In the labour market teachers' salaries were not competitive with alternative employment and subsequently problems of teacher recruitment emerged. By the end of the Conservative period of office the teaching force was ageing with fewer young teachers coming forward to replace them.

When the Conservatives came to office in 1979 there were mounting problems with an economy that was undergoing a major restructuring in terms of employment and production. Under their stewardship education policy shifted towards stressing traditional forms of knowledge, the needs of the workplace and the promotion of enterprise through competition. This was reflected in the policy of the New Right which was a combination of neo-conservatism and neo-liberalism. Towards the end of their term of office public opinion began to swing against the tyrannies of tradition and a free market in favour of modernism and governmental restraint of market excesses. Thus there was a move back towards liberal humanism and social democracy.

New Labour policy: ideology and perspectives on education

After the defeat of the Callaghan administration in 1979 and in their first years out of office Labour moved to the left with the growing influence of the Militant Tendency within the party (McKenzie, 2001). It was presented in the media as a party of extremists and the Conservatives were able to portray Labour as unelectable. During the next twenty years the 'modernisers' set about altering the image and policies of the party. These efforts finally bore fruit with the victory in the 1997 general election. Lawton (2005) outlines the mixed ideological origins of the Labour Party having been formed from a combination of socialist groups and the declining Liberal Party. Many people considered the Labour Party's prime task as representing the working classes on issues of employment, housing and social conditions but there was little discussion of a socialist view of education. As Lawton explains:

> The Labour Party has usually merely taken the existing education system and suggested minor adjustments to it in order to make it serve the interests of working class children more fairly (1992: 23).

Labour had supported the development of the tripartite system, believing that the 11-plus would provide equal chances to all children of obtaining a grammar school education. Grammar schools were seen as a route whereby working-class children could improve their futures. Labour politicians did not acknowledge the inequalities of the selection process and its effects on maintaining social disadvantage at this time (see Chapter 8 on how social factors can influence achievement in education). In the 1960s the Labour policy on comprehensive education was never made compulsory. Many LEAs ignored their instructions and maintained the tripartite systems. Though wishing to use education for the benefit of all sections of society, Labour had no real image of how comprehensive schools should operate and no view on the curriculum. These important areas were left to educationalists to decide. The Labour feeling, as expressed by Wilson when Prime Minister, was that comprehensive schools should aim to provide a grammar school education for all.

Labour ideology rests on the social democratic principles of ensuring equality of opportunity and individual freedom within a strong state framework. The state protects us and thus allows us to become free. This is freedom with responsibility involving fellowship and cooperation. Under New Labour this is expressed as a partnership between individuals and the state. Both are seen as having duties and responsibilities to each other if, ultimately, we are all to benefit from economic and social development (Avis, 1999). According to Tony Blair, (Wintour, 1994: 8) New Labour is not so much:

> a set of rigid economic ideological attitudes, but a set of values and principles. The simple case for democratic socialism rests on the belief that individuals prosper best within a strong, active society whose members acknowledge they owe duties to each other as well as to themselves, and in part at least depend upon each other to succeed.

New Labour saw a need to modernise Britain even if this meant questioning traditional Labour beliefs. The 'modernisation project' was how Prime Minister Blair was able to embrace the wider electorate. It was by calling for a pragmatic approach to the solving of Britain's problems, rather than so-called dogma, that New Labour appealed to the 'middle ground'. It was this 'common'-sense attitude, and not being tied by traditional allegiances of left and right, that Labour presented as the 'third way'. This was seen to be for the benefit of the whole country and thus it became the Tories and anyone else who disagreed with the government who were now presented as the intolerant extremists. To understand Labour's third way modernisation policies we need first to consider the societal changes that provided the context for them.

TECHNOLOGICAL AND SOCIAL CHANGE

Since the middle of the twentieth century, there has been rapid and continuous change in our society affecting all areas of our lives. Patterns of employment, housing conditions, health care, leisure activities, individual mobility and forms of transport have all changed. If we consider forms of information and communication technology (ICT) used in the home we can see the extent of these changes. Fifty-five years ago few households had a television. Those sets that existed were black and white with only one channel. Twenty years ago very few households had a personal computer (PC) and these were large and very slow. Ten years ago few houses had internet access. If they did it was often through a shared phone landline. Broadband did not yet exist. Video recorders will have appeared in most homes and disappeared again over a twenty year period. These advances and developments are taking place in all areas of our lives. As we look through modern large, often multinational, chain stores and retail outlets we can see how commodities that service all parts of our lives are continually being updated or replaced as being redundant (Bartlett and Burton, 2006b).

This rapid and accelerating pace of change can be seen as a result of a combination of developments in economic production, ICT and globalisation. These are very much interlinked forces.

Development of economic production

Methods of production have changed rapidly over a comparatively short time from labour intensive to mass production to automation, requiring few people, if any, in the actual making process. Goods can be produced more quickly and cheaply than previously. A greater variety of products are made, in larger numbers, than ever before and consequently the standard of living for the majority of people has risen.

Development of ICT

Whilst the development of factories that employed early mass production techniques of machines linked by conveyor belt revolutionised industry, the development of modern computer and robotic driven systems has produced a further revolutionary leap forward. IT now plays an important part in all areas of our lives. This has meant that new skills and knowledge are required by us all, both in our daily lives and at work. At the same time many of the old working skills have become rarer and even obsolete, as they are no longer in demand as part of the production process. Weavers, wheelwrights and coopers all disappeared years ago but now even skills that were developed and prized in the past fifty years have already become redundant. Many tasks that required engineering skills, for instance, are now done by machines and much of the manual and mental dexterity required by some jobs is no longer needed, for example typewriting was superseded by word processing but even this skill is already redundant in some businesses which use voice recognition software to enable information to be dictated.

The technology is advancing so quickly that it becomes very difficult to keep up and the need for workers to be able to update becomes more important than the skills they currently possess. One of the key factors in creating such rapid change is the revolution in communications that has taken place. It is now possible to access information and communicate instantly and at any time via the internet and the World Wide Web. It is as though the earth has shrunk and time has been compressed into smaller units (Edwards and Usher, 2000). This is clearly a fundamental element of the globalisation process.

DEVELOPMENT OF GLOBALISATION

Burbules and Torres (2000) suggest that globalisation can be seen as having a range of meanings. If by globalisation one means movement of people, ideas and products around the world then it has always existed. From the earliest of times there have always been migrations of people. There have been voyages of exploration, wars of conquest and the development of trade over land and by sea. What has changed is the speed and ease with which labour and goods can now be transported in response to fluctuations in supply and demand around the world. Thus markets have been able to expand until we have what can be termed a global economy.

Whilst there are many benefits that can derive from globalisation, such as greater choice of goods at lower prices resulting from market forces, there are also many potential problems (see Nederveen Pieterse, 2000). Competition may benefit the wealthier parts of the globe but those who are poor and forced to sell their labour and economic assets cheaply remain disadvantaged. There is the distinct possibility that the market will result in the dominance of the culture of the rich at the expense of the rest, i.e. the 'McDonaldisation' of the world as Western, predominantly US, tastes spread and the demand for their products increases globally whilst smaller cultures and languages are lost (Ritzer, 2000).

THE RISK SOCIETY

Beck (1992) saw these forces of the market, modern technology and globalisation as creating changes in the very nature of society, an evolution from modernity to reflexive modernity. This reflexive modernity is characterised by an increased lack of certainty in our lives and consequently individuals have to make constant decisions on how they act in their daily lives. Their choices concern how they work, what they spend their money on, personal relationships with family, friends and others. We will benefit or not according to the decisions we make and so each choice involves an element of risk. Beck said we are now living in a 'risk society' where, due to the rapidly changing social environment, we can no longer be sure of our social structures, such as the family, work or even the government itself, as they are in a state of constant flux. Market forces, which are beyond individual or state control, are seen to have increasing power; in tandem with this is the stronger emphasis on individualisation. Beck notes a growing variation in the ability of individuals to manage their positions in this risk society. Some sections of the population benefit from greater choice, wealthier lifestyles and the latest technology. For others – those who do not have the marketable skills required for regular employment – this increasing choice brings the risk of them losing out even more, resulting in widening social division. These divisions occur within countries but can also be seen as happening globally with great differences between the wealthy and poor areas of the world.

THE THIRD WAY

The impact of these global markets and the profound social changes that have accompanied them led many social commentators, such as Giddens (1998 and 2000), to suggest that the policies of the traditional left with their emphasis on state control were no longer feasible. However, whilst there appears little doubt as to the power of the global market and the inability of governments to maintain total control over their own economies, Giddens makes the point that we should not assume that governments now have nothing to offer against the forces of globalisation. He suggested that there is a complex two-way interaction between the global and the local. Whilst global forces influence nations, governments can operate to promote, protect and support where appropriate. Rather than withering away under the growth of the global market, governments can play an active part in helping their people respond. Thus Giddens suggests a third way that lies between the old forms of state socialism and the tyranny of totally free markets. It involves the state promoting competitiveness and efficiency whilst encouraging inclusion by ensuring the provision of services such as education, health and social security. These structures will provide individuals with the support they need to operate freely in the global 'knowledge' economy. Governments also have an important part to play in the development of the civil society that gives individuals identity, security and belonging in an increasingly uncertain world.

For the Labour government this third way ideology manifests itself in the desire to provide vital services such as health and education for every individual, the creation of opportunity for all to succeed in life whilst at the same time stressing the duty of everyone to play their part in society. There is a strong emphasis on social justice and the rights and responsibilities of each citizen (Lawton, 2005). The language of partnership is used to describe the relationship between government and citizen. It is this third way ideology that has influenced the thinking of a number of world governments at the beginning of the new millennium.

THE RESPONSE OF THE LABOUR GOVERNMENT – LIFELONG LEARNING

The Fryer Report (NAGCELL, 1997), building on discussions provoked by Beck and Giddens, agreed that the UK is going through a period of profound social change that characterises it as a risk society.

Fryer identifies twelve key aspects of the changes taking place within our society:

- accelerating change in many dimensions of life, from work to the family, driven in part by powerful and often remote global forces
- increasing diversity and fragmentation of experiences and institutions and a greater willingness to tolerate, even celebrate, such features of the modern world
- changing identities, loyalties and aspirations
- much greater emphasis upon consumption and its pleasures, including too some democratisation of inventiveness and creativity
- more focus upon choice, lifestyle and individuality
- the increasing variety and pluralism of popular culture
- the pervasive and growing role of information and knowledge in many arenas of economic, social, political and working life
- the growing importance of communications and information technology to many aspects of our lives
- the development of new dimensions of political participation, in the realms of constitutional reform and active citizenship
- the emergence of new agendas in politics, concerned with issues as diverse as race and gender equality, disability rights, the environment, food and transport
- a widening of key social divisions, experienced in fields of income, employment, housing, health and education, including access to information;
- evidence of the growth of social exclusion, despair and even a sense of hopelessness, resulting from the impact of multiple deprivations.

The report noted changes in employment through the introduction of new work practices, the application of new technologies, the production and delivery of new products and services, and the reduced size of workplaces (NAGCELL, 1997: 11). These changes have significant effects upon the type of worker required and it suggested that in the future there will be diminishing opportunities for unskilled and semi-skilled employment and those with only 'one industry' or task-specific skills will be increasingly at risk. Thus we are in the midst of changes in the time, location and forms that work takes.

New Labour policy: implementation

Arnove (2003) suggests that the development of a global economy and the increasing interconnectedness of societies pose common problems for education systems around the world.

The Labour government placed education as a central plank in their policy agenda of modernisation, with the concept of lifelong learning as an important element in that policy. Taylor suggests that 'New Labour's policy on lifelong learning can be divorced neither from its general education policy nor from its broader human capital approach to education, within an ideology of 'marketised welfarism' (2005: 101). Labour felt a need to build on existing strengths of the education system but also to overcome the spiral of disadvantage whereby 'alienation from, or failure within, the education system is passed on from generation to generation' (DfEE, 1997b: 3). Thus the importance of education, both in the compulsory years and throughout life, has been stressed. The theme that runs through government policy is once again the developing of human capital in order to compete in the knowledge economy.

THE LEARNING AGE

The Labour government after coming to power in 1997 published its green paper 'The Learning Age, A Renaissance for New Britain' (DfEE, 1998b) in response to the Fryer Report. It saw the greatest challenge for the country as the need to equip ourselves with new skills, knowledge and understanding. To remain competitive in this new world required the modernising and reform of many of our traditional social and economic institutions. Labour politicians spoke of the need for a 'can do' culture which was central to the modernisation project. To succeed they needed:

> the commitment, imagination and drive of all those working in our schools and colleges, if we are to set aside the doubts of the cynics and the corrosion of the perpetual sceptics. We must replace the culture of complacency with commitment to success. (DfEE, 1997: 3)

They wished to heal the atmosphere of hostility created by the Conservative years of confrontation and the mistrust of government that had developed among those working in education.

> Education is the key to creating a society which is dynamic and productive, offering opportunity and fairness to all. It is the Government's top priority. We will work in partnership with all those who share our passion and sense of urgency for higher standards. (DfEE, 1997: 9)

Education, lifelong learning and the creation of a learning culture were seen in Labour policy (DfEE, 1998b) as a key part of the wider process whereby individuals work together, with the help of government, in forging a better and more inclusive society. Thus education and lifelong learning is important on two levels. On the individual level, if people are not to be excluded from society they will need to be educated to obtain employment in the modern economy. Those in work will need to continually upskill to maintain their employability. At a national level, if our economy is to compete in the new global market we need to develop a 'flexible' labour force that is adaptable and able to respond immediately (Bartlett and Burton,

2006c). Continuous learning is portrayed as of central importance in the context of a transformed, globalised economy (Taylor, 2005: 103).

EXCELLENCE IN SCHOOLS

The white paper *Excellence in Schools* (DfEE, 1997) outlined Labour's strategy for raising standards. It espoused six policy principles:

- Education will be at the heart of government.
- Policies will be designed to benefit the many, not just the few.
- Standards matter more than structures.
- Intervention will be in inverse proportion to success.
- There will be zero tolerance of underperformance.
- Government will work in partnership with all those committed to raising standards (DfEE, 1997: 5).

The following challenges and agenda for action were set out:

- to ensure that every child learns the basics of literacy and numeracy early and well
- to increase levels of achievement and opportunities in schools for all pupils
- to challenge schools to improve and take responsibility for raising their own standards
- to tackle truancy and reduce exclusions from school
- to reduce social exclusion by equipping all children to be active citizens and by encouraging young people to stay in learning after 18
- to modernise comprehensive secondary education for the new century
- to improve the quality of teaching and leadership in schools
- to involve parents and local communities in the education of children, to reduce social exclusion and to develop effective partnerships at a local level to raise standards (DfEE, 1999b: 3).

When analysing Labour's education policy we need to consider its main objectives. These are both social and economic. Their aim is to improve the educational experiences and raise educational standards for all thus creating a high quality, flexible labour force able to compete in the global knowledge economy. Those sections of society that have traditionally been excluded need to be involved to ensure that no group is left behind in the social changes taking place. Thus Labour espouses a belief in social justice and opportunity for all combined with an individual responsibility to play one's part. To achieve this inclusive and prosperous society New Labour is pursuing an ideology of the third way that involves traditional Labour policies of state support and social welfare combined with the benefits of individualism and the market.

EVERY CHILD MATTERS

During the 1990s and early 2000s a number of child abuse cases had caused public concern. Investigation into the death of a young girl, Victoria Climbié, led to the setting up of the Laming Inquiry. The Laming Report (2003) found that key services responsible for the welfare of children and young people were operating separately with no coordination between them. It was this lack of a cohesive approach that had prevented the sharing of significant information and decisive action being taken that could have prevented the death of this child. The resulting Children Act of 2004 and the publication of *Every Child Matters: Change for Children* (DfES, 2004c) had a significant impact on services working with children. From this time the child was to be put at the centre and services built around their needs rather than the other way around.

In each authority, local education and social services were now combined into an integrated children's services approach under a Director of Children's Services. This enabled the creation of multi-agency teams bringing together school nurses, social workers, educational psychologists and the police. Education, social and health care services would be provided on the same site in extended schools thus making them the centre of local communities.

LABOUR'S FIVE YEAR STRATEGY FOR CHILDREN AND LEARNERS

In July 2004 Labour published its five year strategy (DfES, 2004b). Acknowledging the overall improvement in standards of teaching and pupil performance, the need to go even further was identified. Significantly it was noted that:

> We have opened up opportunity at every stage of life. But we have not yet broken the link between social class and achievement. No society can afford to waste the talent of its children and citizens. So major challenges at each key phase of life remain. (DfES, 2004b: 4)

Thus, whilst there had been reforms aimed at raising educational achievement in Labour's first two terms of office, those in lower socio-economic groups continued to perform less well and the differences in performance between the lower and higher socio-economic groups widened as pupils got older. The links between poor health, disadvantage and low educational outcomes were seen as remaining 'stark' (p. 12). It was also noted that, in terms of attainment, there was a large 'middle group' of pupils who were not being challenged and whose performance also needed to be improved. Now was seen as the time to modernise the traditional comprehensive system of state education in order to meet these further challenges. A monolithic state system of standardised comprehensive schools was no longer regarded as appropriate to meeting modern needs. Different groups apart from the state, such as businesses, voluntary bodies and religious groups, also needed to be involved in the running of schools where appropriate. On the basis of the experience of their two previous terms in office Labour identified five key principles of reform (see the reader reflection box below) underpinning the drive for a step change in children's services, education and training.

Reader reflection

What do you think each of the five key principles of reform will mean in practice?

- Greater personalisation and choice, with the wishes and needs of children, parents and learners centre-stage.
- Opening up services to new and different providers and ways of delivering services.
- Freedom and independence for frontline headteachers, governors and managers with clear simple accountabilities and more secure streamlined funding arrangements.
- A major commitment to staff development with high quality support and training to improve assessment, care and teaching.
- Partnerships with parents, employers, volunteers and voluntary organisations to maximise the life chances of children, young people and adults (DfES, 2004b: 5).

These five key principles fitted the multi-professional approach involving health, education and social service professionals when placing the child at the centre. Thus schools were to become the centres of the community with health care, before and after school clubs and wider social activities also taking place there. The emphasis on personalised learning allowed schools and education professionals to concentrate much more on the needs of individual pupils and how to improve their learning. It was expected that this would help to reduce the disaffection felt by many pupils through the standard curriculum. Within this strategy Labour also took the opportunity to expand the specialist schools programme and to promise the introduction of 200 independently managed academies. These moves amount to a significant distancing from the existing comprehensive system of secondary education.

The strategy was further developed in the white paper 'Higher Standards, Better Schools for All' (DfES) where the Secretary of State for Education stressed the need to:

> tailor education around the needs of each individual child, … give parents greater choice and active engagement in how schools are run … empower schools and teachers to respond to local and parental demands. (2005a: 2)

The creation of a range of independent providers of education and a decreasing reliance on the state was taken further in the Education and Inspections Act (2006) that enabled the creation of trust schools and changed the role of local authorities. Key provisions of the Act include:

- enabling all schools to become trust schools by forming links with external partners such as universities, companies, parent groups and voluntary sector organisations. Trust schools will own their own assets, employ their own staff and set their own admission arrangements.

- giving local authorities a more strategic commissioning role rather than being a direct provider of education. (Eurydice, July 2006: 9)

The Act also launched the development of specialised vocational diplomas outlined in the 14–19 Education and Skills White Paper (2005b). These will have a significant impact on the curriculum for many pupils at key stage 4. Schools and FE colleges will need to cooperate to deliver these diplomas, which will constitute a major change in their traditional relationships. One of the dilemmas with this could be a tendency to guide pupils onto either an academic or a vocational track rather than to facilitate a mix and match approach. The former is easier to facilitate but would take the system back several years to a traditional academic/vocational divide with all of its related value judgements and parity problems.

POLICY SUMMARY

We might list the key Labour policies as follows.

- Quality assurance measures have been developed which are aimed at monitoring perform-ance in all phases of education such as testing of pupils and compiling league tables of performance with regular inspection of all educational institutions. Since the 2005 Education Act these inspections are now 'lighter touch' for institutions performing well. However, those deemed to be unsatisfactory must improve rapidly or risk being closed down, taken over or reopened as an academy.

- The integrated approach to children's services (DfES, 2004c) now links the different agen-cies working with children and parents more closely.

- The 'remodelling' of the teaching profession means that teachers liaise more with other professionals working with children. Other adults apart from teachers are employed in the classroom, such as teaching assistants and learning mentors, as part of improving the teaching and learning process.

- The rapid expansion of nursery provision is based upon the presupposition that a good start is more likely to lead to a positive view of learning throughout the compulsory phases of education and beyond.

- In primary education there has been a drive to reduce class sizes for the youngest children. There is an emphasis on what are regarded as essential basic skills for the whole learning process, hence the development of literacy and numeracy strategies and an emphasis on the use of ICT in the classroom.

- In secondary schools there is now an emphasis in key stage 3 on literacy, numeracy and ICT skills and the development of personalised learning.

- Secondary comprehensive education has been modernised. This has involved a rapid increase in the number of secondary specialist schools as well as the introduction of acade-mies and trust schools. These changes are designed to develop the secondary curriculum and raise standards across the sector by increasing parental choice and competition between schools.

- The National Curriculum has been reformed for all pupils. It has become more flexible and relevant to vocational needs of pupils at key stage 4 particularly.

- Citizenship has been introduced into the curriculum to help address rapid social change and the potential fragmentation of established communities.

- The reforms in post-16 education have seen a dramatic increase in the number of pupils who now stay on in education after 16. A levels have been modernised and vocational A levels have been introduced. Specialised vocational diplomas for 14–19s will be introduced from 2008. These will be an alternative to the traditional curriculum since they are a combination of general education and applied vocational learning. They will be comparable to GCSE and A level and can be used as a means of entry into specific forms of vocational employment or more generally as a stepping-stone to further and higher education. It is expected that these diplomas will involve schools and FE colleges working together on the educational provision for pupils of 14 plus.

- The number of students taking first degrees in higher education has increased with the expansion of higher education. The aim is that ultimately 50 per cent of young people in the 18 to 25 age group will take part in higher education. The development of foundation degrees has emphasised a vocational application of higher education and helped make higher education accessible to a wider range of the population. Whilst the sector has expanded the system of funding has changed with the introduction of tuition fees for students, the abolition of student grants and the introduction of student loans. Those from poorer economic backgrounds will be able to apply for greater financial support. The justification for these changes is that higher education is expensive to provide, and as the individual benefits from higher education they should bear a proportion of the costs themselves.

- A range of measures has been introduced to improve education and training opportunities in the workplace. There are programmes in place to develop the basic literacy, numeracy and ICT skills of those in low paid jobs, the long-term unemployed and young offenders. The need to update older workers in ICT skills and other new forms of working is also recognised. Those on welfare benefits are provided with suitable skills training after an assessment of their needs. Financial support is also available for the low paid.

These policies do not just involve the domain of education and training. They are part of wider social policies that are aimed at inclusion. Thus there is an overlap between social, economic and education policy in what supporters of the third way would portray as 'joined up government'. Strategies that take a broader approach to child and family welfare, such as Surestart, have aimed at improving the future chances of children and their parents by involving health, social and education agencies.

New Labour policy: a critique

SCHOOLS

It has been suggested (Lawton, 2005; Taylor et al, 2005; Tomlinson, 2005a) that whilst Labour has introduced many policies aimed at monitoring and raising standards in schools, it has dispensed with very little of what the Conservatives initiated. Walford (2005) points to contradictions with policy initiatives that on the one hand are aimed at reducing inequality and providing better opportunities for the disadvantaged and on the other at encouraging diversity and the development of markets. As noted earlier in the chapter, rather than presenting a radical view of education, Labour continues to tinker with what exists. Thus Labour politicians wish to improve standards but there is no questioning of the nature of these standards. They are taken as accepted. The term 'modernisation' is used but it is modernisation based on old images of what is important.

Provision that appears to be taken from the Conservatives includes:

- choice and competition – the commodification and consumerisation of education
- autonomy and performativity – the managerialisation and commercialisation of education.
- centralisation and prescription – the imposition of centrally determined assessments, schemes of work and classroom methods (Ball, 2001: 46).

These three main strands of Labour policy are not separate. They work together and are interwoven throughout the developments in education introduced by the government. Ball (2001) suggests that these policies are part of a globalisation process where all educational policy is moving in this direction.

Extensive use of target setting has been developed at all levels to plan and monitor change. Targets set at every level of the education system mean that greater control over priorities, and the monitoring of progress towards them, can be exerted by the centre. Each school is required to set challenging targets for improvement with LEAs monitoring the progress of schools and helping them to meet their targets. LEAs must prepare an educational development plan, also with targets, showing how they intend to promote school improvement.

Fielding (2001) explains how the setting of targets may be helpful when used by individuals to guide their development but may become tyrannical when the target becomes the overriding reason for action. If these specific targets are met at the expense of other important development needs this may be detrimental to a teacher's performance. Measurement by targets can encourage subversion of the results and teachers and heads may become adept at hiding damaging information and boosting favourable figures. This is a practice common in industries which rely on checking up on the workforce through such targets (Deming, 1986). For instance, by concentrating on small numbers of pupils to improve test results, such as raising those just below a GCSE C grade to just above it, other pupils or different aspects of school life may be neglected. The effort and expenditure to achieve one specific target may not be the best use of resources. Thus a great deal may be spent on bringing truants back into school, simply to reduce the rate, when the actual cause of truancy and what may be best for all involved may not have been considered.

Harris and Ranson suggest that the government's school improvement policy emphasises performativity and is 'founded upon the twin pillars of accountability (inspection, test scores, league tables) and standards (target setting, monitoring, raising achievement plans)' (2005: 573). This assumes that the causes for low performance lie essentially within the school and result from poor leadership or ineffective teaching and that these faults can be rectified. Thus through a range of school improvement initiatives all schools will be able to improve on the 'accepted' measures of performance. For reasons outlined below Harris and Ranson suggest that this is not necessarily the case and that many poorly performing schools in deprived areas have great difficulty in raising their performance for perfectly legitimate reasons beyond their control.

> In short, a combination of market individualism and control through constant and comparative assessment (i.e. league tables) has demoted certain schools to the lower echelons of performance, indefinitely. The reason for this partly resides in the neo-liberal world of competition and marketisation where affluent parents have the informal knowledge and skill to be able to use marketised forms to their own benefit through sets of informal cultural rules. (2005: 574)

Though equality of opportunity may remain part of the Labour rhetoric, the policies which encourage differentiation and specialisation do not match this. Though Labour abolished grant maintained schools and the assisted places scheme there was no proposal to do away with grammar schools and there has followed the rapid expansion of the specialist schools programme and the development of new city academies and trust schools. However, such choice tends to reinforce the very social inequalities that Labour is trying to eliminate (Ball, 2001, 2003). Clark (2006) suggests that just making the same opportunities available for all when some pupils start from a disadvantaged position will allow inequality to persist. Thrupp and Tomlinson (2005a) do not doubt Labour's commitment to social justice but feel that there exist contradictions between this ideal and the pursuit of market policies that promote competition, diversity and privatisation, thus maintaining the advantages of 'privileged' choosers. Such markets do not create schools with a social balance or help to promote equal opportunities. Thrupp and Tomlinson (2005) suggest that 'the creation of a competitive market state in which there is no level playing field for the disadvantaged to take part is not socially just' (p. 552).

Middle-class parents are able to operate the system to their advantage to ensure that their children receive the 'best' from the system (Ball, 2003; Gewirtz et al, 1995; Tomlinson, 2005). Schools in the areas chosen by large numbers of middle-class parents tend to perform well and are oversubscribed. Those who cannot make the choices that help them to escape the poorer more deprived geographical areas remain in the schools deserted by the middle-class. These become sink schools, less likely to attract extra resources and teachers. They remain underperforming and less able to rise from this position. Lupton (2005) suggests that these high-poverty contexts exert downward pressures on quality that are very difficult to overcome. For these reasons Thrupp and Lupton (2006) highlight the significance for daily school life and pupil achievement of the particular social context in which each school operates.

In these ways the development of an education market helps to reproduce social inequalities (Ball, 2003). The five-year strategy (DfES, 2004b), the Higher Standards White Paper (2005) and the Education and Inspections Act (2006) re-emphasise this policy. In promoting different forms of school that are run by external partner bodies and thereby providing choice to parents, the effect is to further emphasise social differences in achievement rather than to resolve them (Harris and Ranson, 2005; Taylor et al, 2005). Such measures will increase rather than diminish social segregation, leaving working-class students stranded in predominantly working-class schools (Reay, 2006, citing Taylor, 2006, and Webber and Butler, 2006).

ADULT EDUCATION AND TRAINING

Biesta comments that 'the dominant policy discourse nowadays sees adult education first and foremost as a lever for economic growth and global competitiveness' (2005: 688). The very instrumental approach to education taken in recent decades involves a narrow view of the purposes of education and can lead to a restricted curriculum with an unhealthy emphasis on measurable outcomes. Rather than raising educational standards and encouraging involvement of students this may actually lead to the increasing alienation of certain groups from the education system.

This human capital approach assumes that educating the workforce to a higher level will lead to increased economic performance. However, any causal link between educational qualifications and production has never been clearly established (Bartlett and Burton, 2006b). In fact whether increasing educational provision, particularly in HE, does have a significant economic impact has been increasingly questioned (Wolf, 2002). Gorard et al (2002) have suggested that government strategies for the retraining and upskilling of the workforce, with the emphasis on basic low-level skills, have so far had very little impact in spite of the media hype that has surrounded them. Work-based training does not appear to be rising in uptake (Gorard, 2003).

It may be that the existence of a risk society and the need to develop an adaptable workforce have been greatly exaggerated and are really little more than social myths encouraged by those with vested interests in capitalist production (Hughes and Tight, 1998). Why might this myth be perpetuated? Crowther (2004) portrays lifelong learning as a 'deficit discourse'. By this he means that responsibility for retraining is placed upon the individual rather than government. Thus any failure is seen as individual rather than systemic. It is individuals who need to adapt to a lifetime of increasing occupational insecurity due to changing employment conditions with more part-time and temporary work. The political rhetoric of lifelong learning involving individuality, adaptability and operating in the 'knowledge economy' may be drawing attention away from real structural inequalities in society by emphasising the importance of individual action.

Furthermore, the current emphasis by government, educationalists and employers on acquiring formal qualifications through education whether part- or full-time, and the requirement of enrolment in vocational or skills training as a prerequisite of entitlement to welfare benefits, means that lifelong learning may actually be a form of compulsion and control over the workforce (Coffield, 2002; Minter, 2001; Tight, 1998). Crowther sees it as 'a new disciplinary technology to make people more compliant and adaptable for work in the era of flexible capitalism' (2004: 125).

This ideology of lifelong learning does not inevitably have to be the dominant discourse. There are calls for individuals and local communities to have greater involvement in the development of a broader approach to lifelong learning that would encourage informal as well as formal networks (see Crowther, 2004; Taylor, 2005; Tight, 1998). This would allow learning to move from being for instrumental purposes alone to becoming an enriching experience for individuals and their communities. In the same way Harris and Ranson (2005) call for the return of true local democracy and control of schools rather than their increasing corporativisation and control by independent groups as the only way to truly raise the quality of education.

Conclusion

The post-1944 period began with what has been portrayed as a general consensus in terms of the desirability of development and expansion in education. There was hope for the future and for the development of a better society. By the early 1970s there had been rapid curriculum development, an increase in the 'pupil-centred approach' to learning and the implementation of the first wave of comprehensive schools. By the mid-1970s there was an economic downturn and education increasingly became a focus of national concern through the 'great debate' on education. In some quarters it was felt that there had been a fall in academic standards and that schools had played a major part in the nation's moral decline. Teachers and their progressive teaching methods were depicted as being largely responsible.

With the election of the Conservatives in 1979 education policy was strongly influenced by the New Right. This was a mixture of neo-liberalism, which proposed the creation of the free market involving consumer choice and competition to raise standards, and neo-conservatism, which advocated a return to the traditional values that had allegedly made Britain successful in the past. Disillusionment with this combination of traditionalism and a free market, lacking in adequate constraints, led to a move back towards the centre in terms of ideologies with the development of Labour's third way. With their 'modernised' form of social democracy Labour seems to be attempting to combine the benefits of a free market whilst ensuring the exercise of social constraint and state support.

In education Labour says its aim is to open access and raise standards for all sections of society by emphasising partnership and the involvement of all concerned. This is said to involve recognising the professionalism of teachers and increasing public spending on education. Conversely it also means the setting of targets and emphasising the accountability of those working in education. At the same time the competition between schools, the traditionalist curriculum and the diversity of provision to maintain consumer choice will remain.

Third way politics can be characterised as a mixture of ideologies and an attempt at compromise, which has been able to flourish, some would argue, because of the desire for conciliation following the confrontational approach of the Conservative years in government. However, many would claim that this eclectic approach to education policy is not very significantly modified Thatcherism and likely to fracture when put under pressure. There is clearly a dichotomy, for instance, between the rhetoric of professional recognition for teachers and greater accountability and control through performance management systems that emphasise targets. There is also a contradiction between policies that promote market forces and a desire to develop social justice for all. Thus education is riven with ideological splits even if government and policy makers have political motives for presenting educational practices as derivative of a consensus position.

This brief analysis has considered important developments in education since the Second World War. Brevity can breed oversimplification and the emphasis of some points at the expense of others. Nevertheless we have at least highlighted how beliefs about the nature of education, the possession of political power, and economic and social circumstances all help to shape policy and lead to change in the education system. It is important to realise that there is no one objective, unchanging vision of how education should be that is superior to all others. What should be taught, how it should be taught, issues of measurement and standards remain, as ever, dependent upon ideological belief. Successive governments develop their views of education in relation to their vision of society. To those in power, therefore, their proposals are generally not seen as contentious since they are for the good of society. Governments do find it difficult, at times, to do all they would wish because of opposition from those with alternative ideologies. This continuous political process leads to the evolution of the education system. Public opinion about the type of education that is desirable also changes with time and circumstances so the resulting development of education is a product of the struggle between competing ideologies.

Student activities

1 Visit the DfES website (www.dfes.gov.uk). Look up current publications on educational developments. Read through several of these and try to identify the key parts of Labour education policy. How do these key parts relate to the ideologies discussed in Chapter 10?
2 Obtain the current education policies of several political parties. Try to differentiate between the policies and identify the ideological basis for them.
3 Visit the Eurydice website (www.eurydice.org). This site is run by the European Commission and provides information on the organisation of the education systems and current policy developments of member states. Compare the current reforms and priorities in education for several different countries in Europe. Try to account for similarities and differences between them. Draw on information you compiled when doing question 3 in Chapter 1.

Recommended reading

There are many interesting texts that examine contemporary developments in education. They do tend to be for the more advanced student as they are based on at least some awareness of the ideological nature of education and how this interrelates with politics.

Chitty, C. (2004) *Education Policy in Britain*. Basingstoke: Palgrave Macmillan. In this very useful book for the education studies student Chitty considers the nature of education before giving a historical overview of education policy from the 1944 Education Act onwards. He then looks at developments in certain key areas such as the compulsory school curriculum, pre-school provision, higher education, citizenship.

Lawton, D. (2005) *Education and Labour Party Ideologies 1900–2001 and beyond*. Oxon: RoutledgeFalmer. This book analyses the development of the Labour Party from the 1900s to the present. It pays particular attention to the developing political ideologies in the party and how these have impacted upon Labour policy when in and out of office.

Tomlinson, S. (2005) *Education in a Post-Welfare Society*. 2nd edn. Maidenhead: Open University Press. Tomlinson provides a critical overview of education policy since 1945. She discusses the relationship of policy to the economy, class, race and gender over this time during both Conservative and Labour administrations.

Olssen, M., Codd, J. and O'Neill, A. (2004) *Education Policy: Globalisation, Citizenship and Democracy*. London: Sage. This text outlines theories of globalisation, liberalism and social democracy. This is a very useful volume indeed and will aid the development of a more detailed understanding of these significant influences upon policy.

11 Education – a contested enterprise

It is argued in this chapter that to study education in any meaningful way requires an awareness of the interrelationship between the different disciplines involved, that is, it requires a multidisciplinary approach. Education is presented as the result of continual conflict and interaction between competing ideologies at many levels. The chapter suggests that, inevitably, the ideologically charged area of education will always be at the heart of the development of any society and will remain a focus of political debate and struggle. Some reference is made to broader areas of education study that readers should also investigate which are beyond the remit of this book.

Introduction

The aim of this book has been to introduce the study of education. The approach has highlighted the value laden nature of education and how both its policies and practices are informed by different sets of beliefs. These ideologies can be seen to permeate every part of the education process. Their various proponents bring them to bear on the principles and practices of education through the often politicised processes of developing theory to determine practice and extrapolating theory out of practice. Education Studies is able to apply an eclectic range of research questions and analytical tools to reveal and explore these theories from a number of perspectives.

Theory and practice in education

Common-sense perceptions often represent theory as being quite distinct from practice. This is sometimes the case in education where the classroom or 'chalk-face' is perhaps set against what are felt to be the vague irrelevancies of the world of theory. In fact, this common-sense view is itself a theory of how things are and – as with all theories – represents a particular way of looking at the world. We all approach the social world in a theoretical way and develop our own theories to help us understand it. In accepting that we are all interpretively situated Carr suggests that actually education theory itself is 'the product of the educational theorist's own interpretive assumptions; that educational theory is just one more discursive practice' (2006: 155). He sees such theory as not necessarily causing educational change but being used to justify it.

EDUCATION AS THE FOCUS OF STUDY

We have seen the impact of disparate ideological perspectives on education as an area of study:

- from the functionalist view of education existing to prepare citizens for society to the Marxist view of education acting as an agency of the state in the reinforcement of class differentials;
- from the view of education as ensuring social order to Rousseau's view that humans can, through the development of society, rise above their natural state.

We also looked at how, in using particular educational ideologies, the emphasis can be on the development of the individual, the significance of particular knowledge or the importance of inculcating economic and social skills. Sometimes the emphasis is clear, as in the case of certain vocational courses and practical instruction. Often, however, the aims and objectives of a curriculum are broad, involving all three of the above educational ideologies, as we saw in the case of the National Curriculum. This inevitably leads to difficult decisions and compromises in terms of appropriate content, pedagogy and assessment.

Whilst in daily classroom life the complexity of competing ideologies which seek to influence education may not be very apparent, there are tensions and conflicts inherent in even the simplest curriculum and educational policy decisions. These are a consequence of the different belief systems which pervade the education system at every level. We have referred to the compulsory sector when analysing the relevance of these ideologies to education but the analysis is of course applicable to other sectors of education. Lifelong learning, early childhood education, post-compulsory education, citizenship education, for example, can all be interpreted in terms of these ideological influences.

There remains a deep conflict in ideas about knowledge, the curriculum and the school. Acknowledging the power of the curriculum to be a purveyor of beliefs and values raises important issues about the purpose and nature of education. Although a number of Western nation states have adopted national curricula that are similar in content and structure, there remain big questions about the utilitarian value of curriculum knowledge and its cultural authority. Also significant is the way the curriculum acts as a vehicle for socialisation and the different motives ascribed to this by competing ideologies of education. Pertinent to these issues is a consideration of the structural features of the curriculum. In the case of the English National Curriculum this would include an examination of, for example, the value of testing of standard attainment targets and prescribed forms of teaching and learning such as the literacy and numeracy hours, and the means of communication and control. The 'story' surrounding the implementation of the National Curriculum is a fascinating example of ideological power struggles. We have only been able, in Chapter 5, to briefly introduce its development but an indepth study would facilitate an analysis from philosophical, psychological, sociological and historical perspectives. The kind of learning promoted and cultivated by any curriculum reveals much about a society's fundamental premises and culture.

The attention paid to the planners', researchers' and teachers' views of the curriculum might suggest that the pupils/students are passive recipients in the education process. However, that is certainly not the case. Learners of all ages may be subject to various forms of teacher control. Frightened by the ogre, mesmerised or motivated by the raconteur or enthusiast, they generally accept the power differential between themselves and the teacher and agree to conform at least to a certain extent. However, it should not be assumed that they have no say. Their power varies and depends upon a number of factors in the relationship between themselves and their teachers. Learners of any age can use different strategies to cause disruption during the teaching session. They may even leave the lesson and not come back. At least one of the authors has found it particularly disconcerting to find a student doing an essay for another subject during a lecture. When challenged the student simply replied that the essay was more important. Learners are thus able to exercise at least some degree of autonomy in many ways. In some situations the learner is granted 'legitimate' autonomy. For example, in higher education it is usual for students to design their own projects and independent programmes of learning with supervised help as part of their degree course. In pursuing 'off-task' behaviour in school or university learners are, of course, exercising 'unlegitimated' forms of autonomy which often involve resisting the official goals of the curriculum, school or college.

When considering the individual in education and influences upon their achievement we face a number of complex issues which are only resolvable from different perspectives. When we measure success in education what factors are we looking at? Achievement could be seen in academic terms measured in examination scores, it could be physical ability assessed by coordination and strength or it could be social skills in terms of being able to cooperate with others or demonstrate leadership. Ultimately different institutions and agencies, including government, schools, colleges and universities, determine what should be measured and this is based upon what attributes are valued most highly.

Thus, as researchers of education, we are still interested in whether education develops individuals and gives them the opportunity to progress or whether it perpetuates inequalities. In Britain the question remains about the extent to which the education system is a meritocracy or whether such a concept is a myth designed to legitimate and help maintain inequality. Paradoxically, the education system can be shown to reproduce existing inequalities whilst simultaneously extending opportunities and access for all.

Reader reflection

Education is a central force within society and is likely to play a significant part in the shaping of future generations. Being such a contested enterprise it is at the heart of the public political process. This process is played out at national level in law making and parliamentary debate and at the local level of the school and individual teacher in terms of the day-to-day classroom-based decisions. An understanding of how different sets of beliefs and values compete in this process is central to the analysis. At any one time a number of ideological influences can be identified as seeking to influence policy.

Consider how frequently education issues appear prominently in the media and the controversies surrounding them.

Education, then, draws on particular disciplines to provide explanations and to inform research. In this book we have emphasised philosophy, sociology, psychology and history, but sometimes it is difficult to determine which of these discourses of knowledge is most relevant to the question in hand. In recent times the strict divisions of the curriculum and of different areas of knowledge, study and research have been challenged. Claims for official forms of knowledge and truth have been challenged by such discourses as feminism, deconstructionism and post-modernism, which have deliberately sought to problematise the nature of truth and knowledge. They have begun to influence the way that theorists of education think about and define systems, institutions, practices and effects (Parker, 1997). Education as a focus of study offers opportunities for the interaction between discourses and this can give rise to 'hybrid' forms of knowledge – as with gender studies and social geography, for example. This often means that the boundaries of education study are not fixed, which can have highly beneficial effects in terms of the construction of interdisciplinary forms and examples of knowledge.

Thus, a number of traditional and emerging disciplines contribute to our understanding of education. We contend that the disciplines individually would be unable to deal with the issues in such a cohesive manner. Whilst drawing on the theories and research of the traditional disciplines, education studies is an increasingly significant area of study in its own right which can benefit too from analyses drawn from newer discourses. What remains to the fore of any study is the contested nature of education itself and how beliefs and values permeate every aspect of it.

The breadth of education studies

In this volume we have been unable to examine the full range of topics covered within education studies courses. Instead we have concentrated on outlining some of the major questions and issues with which education studies is concerned, using schools and the compulsory education sector to illustrate where appropriate. Readers will be aware that this is just one sector of formal education and that even this could be examined in greater depth. Some of the other important areas which warrant further study as significant topics within the field of education studies are outlined below. The fundamental questions raised in this volume concerning beliefs, values and purpose remain appropriate in respect of these topics.

FURTHER AND HIGHER EDUCATION

The post-16 sectors of further and higher education have expanded rapidly since the late 1980s. Whilst the great majority of the readers of this book have attended school, an increasing proportion will also have attended some form of further education institution. Most will currently be attending, or intending to enter, higher education. These post-compulsory sectors have become increasingly significant arenas for education as greater numbers of students remain in some form of education after the age of 16. It has now become unusual, as opposed to the norm of a few years ago, to leave school at 16 rather than continue with some form of post-compulsory education or training. At the end of 2005, over 76 per cent of 16–18 year olds were participating in some form of education and training, made up of 89 per cent of 16 year olds, 80 per cent of 17 year olds and 59 per cent of 18 year olds (DfES, 2006, http://www.dfes.gov. uk/trends/index).

Traditionally, higher education was regarded as an elitist sector for public school and grammar school pupils. Universities were for a minority of academically successful pupils. The 1960s saw the development of polytechnics run by LEAs which were designed to give an alternative to the traditional subject approach. They were to provide more applied courses at degree level that would be appropriate to meeting the needs of industry. However, over time, they also began to offer degree courses similar to those run by the traditional universities. In the Education Reform Act (1988) polytechnics were given their independence from LEAs. The binary line, which separated them from the traditional universities, was later abolished altogether and they became full universities in 1992 (Ward, 2006). The Robbins Report (1963) had suggested that as society benefits from the quality of university graduates then society should pay the cost of their education. This was affordable when only a small proportion of the population partook of higher education. As the numbers entering higher education rapidly expanded a new view emerged – that since graduates benefit most from higher education they should bear at least some of the cost.

A study of higher education might focus attention on the expansion of student numbers, funding the increased provision and the quality of degree study. The desire to expand access to higher education was confounded by the perennial problem of paying for the expansion. Higher education suffered from a funding crisis as the number of students rapidly expanded whilst central funding per student decreased. Total spending on higher education increased but it had to be spread across far more students. These 'efficiency savings' or 'cuts', depending upon one's point of view, had a significant impact upon the sector. This funding shortfall became unsustainable so government legislated for 'top-up fees' of just over £1000 per annum which students had to pay up-front annually, raising this in 2006 to £3000. Although students do not pay these fees until they are earning a sufficient amount to pay through salary deductions, this represented a momentous shift in the ethos of free access to higher education for all. Student grants, originally provided for the majority of students by the government, became available only to very low income households. Students generally support themselves through loans, part-time work and savings. For many, these pragmatic policy decisions were difficult to reconcile with the stated government intention to widen participation in HE to 50 per cent of 18–30 year olds by 2010 in the interests of social justice since it was clearly going to affect worst those from lower socio-economic groups.

Funding shortfalls also led to a focus on the nature of teaching and learning by the Higher Education Funding Council for England (HEFCE) and within the higher education institutions themselves. Students were encouraged to be more self-directing with a growing emphasis on independent study and distance learning. This was presented as increasing student autonomy but it can be viewed more sceptically as a means of reducing the quality of provision as students' contact time with tutors decreased. At the same time lecturers were given greater teaching loads and larger groups. This might be considered ironic in the context of higher fees for courses. The quality of higher education became an issue with the government promising to maintain standards whilst increasing student numbers and reducing costs. Universities are monitored by the Quality Assurance Agency and increasingly by the media, which compiles university league tables based on a range of indicators including employment rates of students, staff–student ratios, library spend, research income and so on. As universities are forced to compete even harder in the marketplace for students such comparative tables take on greater significance for them and the notion of students as customers forces them into a new service culture.

The newly created market for students and research funding in the HE sector has threatened to widen the gulf between the traditional Russell group of universities (the established 'old' prestige universities including, for example, Oxford and Cambridge), who may in the future demand greater fees from students, and the newer less established institutions. The divide dispensed with by the abolition of the binary line is re-emerging between the elite universities and mass higher education institutions. Thus, issues of student access, individual achievement, teaching and learning methods, and the nature of the curriculum apply just as much to higher education as to the compulsory sector. Ideological conflict is, as it always has been, an important part of developments in higher education.

The experience of further education in many ways mirrors that of higher education. Further education institutions have faced similar changes since they were given their 'independence' from LEAs and have become responsible for their own finances. This development was an important part of creating the market within further education provision. The introduction of this demand-led approach, coupled with a decline in central funding, meant colleges had to become more flexible with increasing proportions of staff employed on part-time and temporary contracts.

Both further and higher education have witnessed the development of management cultures in a similar form to that of business and industry. Education is considered a product which the consumer pays for up front. The emphasis is on outcomes which may be linked to organisational inputs. The market has perhaps been quicker to develop in post-compulsory education where its customers, the students, choose to 'buy' the product. The analysis of the compulsory sector in Chapters 4 and 10 helps us to understand these developments as both further and higher education have become subject to similar policies of market forces and competition. The exercise of central control through inspection and monitoring also became tighter as LEA involvement was eroded in the former polytechnics and further education institutions. The Learning Skills Councils fund FE institutions with joint inspections by Ofsted and the Adult Learning Inspectorate (ALI) impacting on that funding. As the post-16 sector expands, issues of accountability come into sharper focus, especially at a time when the government is promoting entitlement to a wide range of 14–18 vocational courses.

LIFELONG LEARNING

The whole issue of lifelong learning and the development of a learning society has become increasingly high profile in political debate and links to our earlier discussions concerning appropriate educational experiences. It is suggested that changes in the economy with the development of modern communications technology and the obsolescence of traditional skills mean that, rather than having one job for life, employees may follow several different careers during their working lives. They will need to be adaptable, continually learning and updating their skills (DfEE, 1998b). This concept of lifelong learning does not only apply to the workforce. Prolonged life expectancy means that citizens will remain active for longer and will want to develop a wide range of interests and skills throughout their lives. Thus lifelong learning is promoted as a continuous process.

There are interesting issues to consider when thinking about how this lifelong learning will take place. Whilst it may involve traditional forms of teaching and learning in the classroom, this approach is unlikely to be appropriate for all, or even the majority, of the adult population. The emphasis is likely to be on information and communications technology with the development of flexible and distance learning modes. There is debate, however, as to whether we are actually moving towards a learning society or if the whole concept is political rhetoric linked to images of creating opportunity. Whilst some would see lifelong learning as a liberating process, increasing learner autonomy and helping to create a more socially democratic society, others portray it as just another, though perhaps more sophisticated, form of control being developed through modern technology (Bartlett and Burton, 2006a; Crowther, 2004). The relationship between lifelong learning and modern modes of employment is certainly open to question.

EARLY CHILDHOOD EDUCATION

At the other end of the educational spectrum early childhood studies is rapidly becoming an area of study in its own right (Maynard and Thomas, 2004). Early childhood studies considers physiological, psychological, sociological and legal aspects of child development. Interest in this area has increased with the expansion of educational provision for younger children in schools, nurseries and playgroups. Hotly debated issues about the appropriateness of particular educational early years experiences, coupled with differing theories of child development, create a rich source of study (Moylett, 2003). Sylva and Pugh (2005) argue that early years education has been transformed in recent years. The growth of early years provision forms a central policy plank of the current Labour government. A significant development in this area was the incorporation of the foundation stage into the National Curriculum and the creation of early learning goals. The Children Act of 2004 and the publication of *Every Child Matters: Change for Children* (DfES, 2004c) also had a significant impact on services working with children. We can only gesture to the ideological tensions inherent in these policies but they are worthy of thorough exploration.

SPECIAL NEEDS AND INCLUSION

Special needs has also become an important area of study in its own right and is of particular interest in education studies. Issues of access, equality and inclusion are significant in the current political climate (Clough and Garner, 2003). They relate to individual and social factors which influence success in education. Armstrong suggests that 'New Labour has placed inclusion at the centre of its educational agenda' (2005: 135). A study of special needs considers the different forms in which learning difficulties are manifested and the way they impact upon individuals and society. There is also an imperative to consider how far social inclusion is actually developing or, whether conversely, much of the rhetoric is merely masking a lack of change.

CITIZENSHIP AND SOCIAL JUSTICE

Rapid social change in society due to, amongst other things, advances in technology and developing global economic pressures has led to concern about increasing social fragmentation. This has resulted in emphasis being placed upon the importance of citizenship education which involves, variously, consideration of individual rights and responsibilities, notions of active involvement by citizens in society, the promotion of social justice and an understanding of global and environmental issues. The concept of citizenship is open to varying definitions and is ideologically loaded (Garratt, 2003). A tension can be seen between citizenship education being an empowering experience for students and, through emphasising social cohesiveness, a form of social control. Faulks (2006) argues that there is a strong case for including citizenship in the curriculum but that diversity of secondary school provision, social exclusion, changing conceptions of what counts as political and lack of consideration of appropriate forms of delivery have all meant that provision of citizenship education 'remains in a precarious state'.

Consideration of the global economy and its implications for environmental and social justice might be said to be proper elements of a citizenship curriculum for the twenty-first century. The environmentally unfriendly practices of the past are now a source of real concern in most societies, particularly as their consequences are visited differentially on individuals depending on where in the world they live and how rich they are. Since the United Nations made education one of four priorities in the quest for sustainable development, there has been increasing pressure for issues of sustainability to secure a central place in the curricula of schools, colleges and higher education (Shallcross et al, 2006).

ORGANISATION THEORY

All sectors of education are made up of organisations of various sizes: schools, colleges, universities, local education authorities. Organisation theory and the study of behaviour in organisations constitute important elements in education studies courses. As many post-graduate students of education work in the field there is a particular interest in theories of management and their application as part of professional and academic study (see Bush and Middlewood, 2005; Hargreaves and Fink, 2006). By considering organisations which are primarily people centred an emphasis is placed on theories related to performance management or management by objectives, human relations management and also quality management. The whole area of institutional effectiveness, touched upon in Chapter 3, also falls within this remit.

Other aspects of organisational theory treat the nature and purposes of educational organisations as much more problematic when examining them. They are concerned with life in these organisations from different perspectives (Ball, 1981). Thus some studies consider the nature of being a pupil (Willis, 1979). Others examine the labour process of teaching and how this may be seen in relation to concepts such as professionalism, deskilling, proletarianisation, resistance and renegotiation (Apple, 2004; Bartlett and Burton, 2003). These approaches often characterise educational organisations as being less predictable, more unstable and micropolitical than do more traditional management approaches.

COMPARATIVE EDUCATION AND GLOBALISATION

This book has limited itself to a consideration of the English education system. This, of course, can make us blind to alternatives and may lead us to assume that other parts of the world have had similar experiences to our own. It also encourages a distorted view of our own significance. We introduced the idea of comparative education in Chapter 1, and if we had space in the book to take in a wider range of education systems similar issues about how purpose and ideology shape curriculum design and models of learning would arise. The importance of comparing different systems and the significance of particular cultural influences to each system should be acknowledged (Alexander, 2002; Hankin, 2006). In addition the impact and pressures of globalisation on education systems and their pedagogy has generated a great deal of interest amongst educators. Bottery (2006), for example, has considered the effects of living in a globalised age and how this has influenced the perceptions of school principals and heads on the challenges that face them professionally, in both the United Kingdom and Hong Kong, regardless of existing cultural differences. Globalisation is a significant factor in shaping both policy and practice across the world as systems 'interfere' with one another and ideas, research, ideologies and institutions take on different shape and form.

It is interesting to see how the impact of fashions and trends is as keenly felt in education as on the high street. The power of the media to advertise, promote and interpret these trends is as significant in relation to 'new' educational phenomena as it is to consumer goods. Populist newspapers, predictably, tend to take a reductionist and sensationalised approach to educational issues that they feel will interest the general public, such as 'synthetic phonics' in reading (Goswami, 2005) or whether dyslexia exists or not (Elliott, 2005). They avoid an examination of the research issues underpinning them but latterly this 'tabloiding' of education policy, pedagogy and practice has led to ideas becoming popularised and even sensationalised within the education media itself. The backdrop for this is an increasingly 'media-ised' and 'celebretised' notion of success within society in general and education in particular. Many countries have annual teacher and lecturer awards ceremonies, often fronted by a media celebrity and sponsored by quality newspapers. Teachers and educators become the consumers of, and the audience for, this mediated expression of pedagogical or policy developments, whether through the educational press, dedicated teachers' television channels or via a proliferation of government websites.

As a manifestation of globalisation this social phenomenon is fascinating but it is important to understand the impact of it. The speed with which the internet and television can transmit ideas and information and appear to afford them (often spurious) validation should concern us as educators. We need to be interested in the way in which these ideas are researched and justified and not just in their utilitarian application. A sociological interpretation of this phenomenon is likely to lie in constructs of power and control wherein sections of society are enabled to sustain and reproduce themselves through the control and packaging of what people are taught and how they are taught it.

Conclusion

This volume has argued for a critical multidisciplinary approach to the study of education. It also demonstrates the importance of treating education as a field of study in its own right. This enables us to look at the major issues, structural features and sources of controversy in education and to ask critical questions. The last question we would put to you is the same as the first,

    'What exactly is education?'

To answer this question we need to go back to the beginning.

Bibliography

Adey, P. (1992) 'The CASE results: implications for science teaching', *International Journal of Science Education*, 14: 137–46.

Albert, R.S. and Runco, M.A. (1999) 'A history of research on creativity', in R. Sternberg (ed.), *Handbook of Creativity*. Cambridge: Cambridge University Press.

Alexander, R. (2002) *Culture and Pedagogy*. Oxford: Blackwell.

Althusser, L. (1984) *Essays on Ideology*. London: Verso.

Altrichter, H., Posch, P. and Somkeh, B. (1993) *Teachers Investigate their Work: An Introduction to the Methods of Action Research*. London: Routledge.

Anderson, G. with Arsenault, N. (1998) *Fundamentals of Educational Research*. London: Falmer Press.

Anderson, J. and Bower, G. (1973) *Human Associative Memory*. Washington, DC: Winston.

Anderson, J.R., Reder, L.M. and Simon, H.A. (1996) 'Situated learning and education', *Educational Researcher*, 25: 5–11.

Anderson, J.R., Reder, L.M. and Simon, H.A. (1997) 'Situative versus cognitive perspectives: form versus substance', *Educational Researcher*, 26: 18–21.

Andrews, R. (ed.) (1996) *Interpreting the New National Curriculum*. London: Middlesex University Press.

Anthias, F. and Yuval-Davis, N. (in association with H. Cain) (1992) *Racialized Boundaries: race, nation, gender, colour and class and the anti-racist struggle*. London: Routledge.

Apple, M. (1988) 'Work, Class and Teaching', in J. Ozga (ed.), *Schoolwork: Approaches to the Labour Process of Teaching*. Milton Keynes: Open University Press.

Apple, M. (2004) *Ideology and Curriculum*, 3rd edn. London: RoutledgeFalmer.

Aries, P. (1962) *Centuries of Childhood: A Social History of Family Life*. London: Cape.

Armstrong, D. (2005) 'Reinventing "inclusion": New Labour and the cultural politics of special education', *Oxford Review of Education*, 31 (1): 135–51.

Arnot, M. (2002) *Reproducing Gender?* London: RoutledgeFalmer.

Arnot, M. and Miles, P. (2005) 'A Reconstruction of the Gender Agenda: the contradictory gender dimensions in New Labour's educational and economic policy', *Oxford Review of Education*, 31 (1): 173–89.

Arnot, M. and Reay, D. (2006a) 'The framing of performance pedagogies: pupil perspectives on the control of school knowledge and its acquisition', in H. Lauder, P. Brown, J. Dillabough and A.H. Halsey (eds), *Education, Globalisation and Social Change*. Oxford: Oxford University Press.

Arnove, R. (2003) 'Introduction: Reframing Comparative Education', in R. Arnove and A. Torres (eds), *Comparative Education: The Dialectic of the Global and the Local*. Oxford: Rowman and Littlefield Publishers.

Aronowitz, S. and Giroux, H.A. (1986) *The Conservative, Liberal and Radical Debate over Schooling.* London: Routledge and Kegan Paul.

Assessment of Performance Unit (1986) *Speaking and Listening, Assessment at Age 11.* Windsor: NFER-Nelson.

Assessment Reform Group (2002) *Assessment for learning: 10 principles – Research based principles to guide classroom practice.* www.assessment-reform-group.org/ASF-report1.html.

Atkinson, J. and Shiffrin, R. (1968) 'Human memory: a proposed system and its control processes', in K. Spence and J. Spence (eds), *The Psychology of Learning and Motivation*, 2: London: Academic Press.

Atkinson, J.W. (1964) *An Introduction to Motivation.* Princeton, NJ: Van Nostrand.

Auld, R. (1976) *William Tyndale Junior and Infant Schools Public Inquiry: A Report of The Inner London Education Authority* (The Auld Report). London: ILEA.

Ausubel, D.P. (1968) *Educational Psychology: A Cognitive View.* New York: Holt, Rinehart and Winston.

Ausubel, D.P. (1985) 'Learning as constructing meaning', in: N. Entwistle (ed.), *New Directions in Educational Psychology: 1. Learning and Teaching.* Lewes: Falmer Press.

Avis, J. (1999) 'Shifting identity: new conditions and the transformation of practice – teaching within post-compulsory education', *Journal of Vocational Education and Training*, 51 (2): 245–64.

Avis, J. (2001) 'Educational Research, the Teacher Researcher and Social Justice', Education and Social Justice, 3 (3): 34–42.

Baddeley, A.D. (1997) *Human Memory: Theory and Practice*, 2nd edn. Hove: Psychology Press.

Ball, S.J. (1981) *Beachside Comprehensive: A Case Study of Secondary Schooling.* Cambridge: Cambridge University Press.

Ball, S.J. (1987) *The Micro-Politics of the School: Towards a Theory of School Organisation.* London: Methuen.

Ball, S.J. (1988) 'Staff relations during the teachers' industrial action: context, conflict and proletarianisation', *British Journal of Sociology of Education*, 9 (3): 289–306.

Ball, S.J. (1990) *Politics and Policy Making in Education.* London: Routledge.

Ball, S.J. (1993) *The Micro-Politics of the School.* London: Routledge.

Ball, S.J. (1994) *Education Reform: A Critical and Post-Structural Approach.* Buckingham: Open University Press.

Ball, S. (2001) 'Labour, learning and the economy: a "policy sociology" perspective', in M. Fielding (ed), *Taking Education Really Seriously: Four Years' Hard Labour.* London: RoutledgeFalmer.

Ball, S. (2003) *Class Strategies and the Education Market: The Middle Classes and Social Advantages.* London: RoutledgeFalmer.

Baltes, P.B. (1996) *Interactive Minds: Life-Span Perspectives on the Social Foundations of Cognition.* Cambridge: Cambridge University Press.

Bandura, A. (1977) *Social Learning Theory.* Englewood Cliffs, NJ: Prentice-Hall.

Barber, M. (1996) *The National Curriculum: A Study in Policy.* Keele: Keele University Press.

Bartlett, F.C. (1932) *Remembering.* Cambridge: Cambridge University Press.

Bartlett, S. and Burton, D. (eds) (2003) *Education Studies: Essential Issues.* London: Sage.

Bartlett, S. and Burton, D. (2006a) 'The Growth of the "New Education Studies"', *Escalate Newsletter*, Issue 5 Summer 2006: 6–7.

Bartlett, S. and Burton, D. (2006b) 'Practitioner Research or Descriptions of Classroom Practice? A Discussion of Teachers Investigating Their Classrooms', *Educational Action Research*, 14 (3): 395–405.

Bartlett, S. and Burton, D. (2006c) 'Lifelong Learning' in J. Sharp, S. Ward and L. Hankin (eds), *Education Studies: An issues based approach.* Exeter: Learning Matters.

Bash, L. and Coulby, D. (1989) *The Education Reform Act: Competition and Control.* London: Cassell.

Bassey, M. (1990) 'On the nature of research in education (Part 2)', *Research Intelligence*, 37 Summer: 39–44.

Bates, R. (2005) 'On the future of teacher education: challenges, context and content', Journal of Education for Teaching: International Research and Pedagogy, 31 (4): 301–5.

Beck, U. (1992) *The Risk Society: Towards a New Modernity.* London: Sage.

Becker, H.S. (1971) 'Social class variations in the teacher pupil relationship', in B.R. Cosin, I.R. Dale, G.M. Esland and D.F Swift (eds), *School and Society.* London: Routledge and Kegan Paul.

Bee, H. (1985) *The Developing Child,* 4th edn. New York: Harper & Row.

Bee, H. (1992) *The Developing Child,* 6th edn. London: HarperCollins.

Bee, H. and Boyd, D. (2007) *The Developing Child,* 11th edn, Pearson International Edition. Boston, USA: Pearson Education.

Bee, H.L., Barnard, K.E., Eyres, S.J., Gray, C.A., Hammond, M.A., Speitz, A.L., Snyder, C. and Clark, B. (1982) 'Predication of IQ and language skill from perinatal status, child performance, family characteristics, and mother–infant interaction', *Child Development*, 53: 1135–56.

Bell, J. (2005) *Doing Your Research Project: A guide for first-time researchers in education, health and social science,* 4th edn. Maidenhead: Open University Press.

Bennett, N. and Dunne, E. (1992) *Managing Classroom Groups.* Hemel Hempstead: Simon and Schuster.

Bernstein B. (1971) *Class, Codes and Control.* London: Routledge and Kegan Paul.

Bernstein B. (ed.) (1973) *Class, Codes and Control,* 2. London: Routledge and Kegan Paul.

Bernstein, B. (1995) *Pedagogy, Symbolic Control and Identity.* London: Taylor and Francis.

Biesta, G. (2005) 'The Learning Democracy? Adult Learning and the Condition of Democratic Citizenship', *British Journal of Sociology of Education*, 26 (5): 687–703.

Biggs, J.B. (1978) 'Individual and group differences in study processes', *British Journal of Educational Psychology*, 48: 266–79.

Biggs, J.B. (1987a) *The Study Process Questionnaire (SPQ) Manual.* Hawthorne, Victoria: Australian Council for Educational Research.

Biggs, J.B. (1987b) *Student Approaches to Learning and Studying.* Hawthorne, Victoria: Australian Council for Educational Research.

Biggs, J.B. (1993) 'What do inventories of students' learning processes really measure? A theoretical review and clarification', *British Journal of Educational Psychology*, 63: 3–19.

Black, P., Harrison, C., Lee, C., Marshall, B. and Wiliam, D. (2002) *Working inside the black box: Assessment for learning in the classroom.* London: King's College, University of London.

Blair, M. (2000) 'The education of Black children: why do some schools do better than others?', in R. Majors (2001) *Educating our Black children. New directions and radical approaches.* New York: Routledge.

Blakemore, S.-J. and Frith, U. (2005) *The Learning Brain. Lessons for Education.* London: Blackwell Publishing.

Blanden, J. and Machin, S. (2004) 'Educational Inequality and the Expansion of UK Higher Education', *Scottish Journal of Political Economy*, 51 (2): 230–49.

Blaxter, L., Hughes, C. and Tight, M. (2001) *How to Research*, 2nd edn. Buckingham: Open University Press.

Blaxter, L., Hughes, C. and Tight, M. (1996) *How to Research*. Buckingham: Open University Press.

Bloom, B. S. (1956) *Taxonomy of Educational Objectives,* 1. London: Longman.

Boaler, J. (1996) 'A case study of setted and mixed ability teaching', paper presented at the British Education Research Association Conference, Lancaster University, September.

Boaler, J. (1997) 'Setting, social class and survival of the quickest', *British Educational Research Journal*, 23: 575–95.

Bottery, M. and Wright, N. (1999) 'The directed profession: teachers and the state in the third millennium', a paper given at the Annual SCETT Conference, Dunchurch, November.

Bottery, M. (2006) How different are we? Globalisation and the perceptions of leadership challenges in England and Hong Kong. Keynote lecture at BESA Conference, Bishop Grossteste College, Lincoln, 30 June.

Bouchard, T.J. and McGue, M. (1981) 'Familial studies of intelligence: a review', *Science*, 212: 1055–9.

Bourdieu, P. (1991) *Language and Symbolic Power*. Cambridge: Polity Press.

Bourdieu, P. and Passeron, J. (1977) *Reproduction in Education, Society and Culture*. London: Sage.

Bourne, J. and Moon, B. (1994) 'A question of ability?', in B. Moon and A. Shelton-Mayes (eds), *Teaching and Learning in the Secondary School*. London: Routledge.

Bowles, S. and Gintis, H. (1976) *Schooling in Capitalist America: Educational Reform and the Contradictions of Economic Life*. London: Routledge and Kegan Paul.

Brewer, W.F. (1999) 'Bartlett, Frederic Charles', in R.A. Wilson and F.C. Keil (eds), *The MIT Encyclopedia of the Cognitive Sciences*. Cambridge, MA: MIT Press.

British Educational Research Association (BERA) (2003a) 'Ethical Guidelines for Educational Research: consultation of members', *Research Intelligence*, 82. Southwell: BERA.

Broadbent, D. (1958) *Perception and Communication*. London: Pergamon Press.

Bronfenbrenner, U. (1979) *The Ecology of Human Development*. Cambridge, MA, Harvard University Press.

Brook, A. (1999) 'Kant Emmanuel', in R.A. Wilson, and F.C. Keil (eds), *The MIT Encyclopedia of the Cognitive Sciences*. Cambridge, MA: MIT Press.

Brooks, R. (1991) *Contemporary Debates in Education: A Historical Perspective*. London: Longman.

Brown, A.L. (1994) 'The advancement of learning', *Educational Researcher*, 23: 4–12.

Brown, P., Halsey, A.H. and Stuart Wells, A. (1997) 'The transformation of education and society: an introduction', in A.H. Halsey, H. Lauder, P. Brown and A. Stuart Wells, *Education: Culture Economy Society*. Oxford: Oxford University Press.

Brown, M., Askew, M., Millett, A., Rhodes, V. (2003) 'The key role of educational research in the development and evaluation of the national numeracy strategy', *British Educational Research Journal*, 29 (5): 655–667.

Browne, N. (2004) *Gender Equity in the Early Years*. Maidenhead: Open University Press.

Bruner, J. (1966) *Towards a Theory of Instruction*. New York: Norton.

Bruner, J. (1983) *Child's Talk: Learning to Use Language*. Oxford: Oxford University Press.

Bruner, J.S. (1972) *The Relevance of Education*. London: Allen and Unwin.

Bryant, I. (1996) 'Action research and reflective practice', in D. Scott and R. Usher (eds), *Understanding Educational Research*. London: Routledge.

Bryman, A. (2001) *Social research methods*. New York: Oxford University Press.

Bullock Report (1975) *A Language for Life*. London: HMSO.

Burbules, N. and Torres, C. (eds) (2000) *Globalisation and Education: Critical Perspectives*. London: Routledge.

Burden, R. and Williams, M. (1998) *Thinking Through the Curriculum*. London: Routledge.

Burgoyne, J. (1994) 'Stakeholder analysis', in C. Cassell and G. Symon (eds), *Qualitative Methods in Organisational Research: A Practical Guide*. London: Sage.

Burt, C. (1955) 'The evidence for the concept of intelligence', *British Journal of Educational Psychology*, 25: 158–77.

Burton, D. (2003) 'Differentiation of schooling and pedagogy', in S. Bartlett and D. Burton, *Education Studies: Essential themes and Issues*. London: Sage PCP, 42–71.

Burton, D. (2007) Psycho-pedagogy and personalised learning, *Journal of Education for Teaching*, 33 (1).

Burton, D. and Anthony, S. (1997) 'Differentiation of curriculum and instruction in primary and secondary schools', *Educating Able Children*, 1 (1): 26–34.

Burton, D. and Bartlett, S. (2005) *Practitioner Research for Teachers*. London: Paul Chapman Publishing.

Burton, D. and Bartlett, S. (2006) 'Shaping pedagogy from psychological ideas', in D. Kassem, E. Mufti and J. Robinson (eds) *Education Studies*. Maidenhead: Open University Press.

Burton, D. and Bartlett, S. (2007) 'The Evolution of Education Studies in Higher Education in England', *Curriculum Studies*.

Burton, D.M. and Robinson, J. (1999) 'Cultural Interference: clashes of ideology and pedagogy in internationalising education', *International Education*, 28 (2): 5–30

Bush, T. and Middlewood, D. (2005) *Leading and Managing People in Education*. London: Sage.

Buzan, T. http://www.buzanpluseducation.com accessed October 27 2006.

Canter, L. and Canter, M. (1977) *Assertive Discipline*. Los Angeles: Lee Canter Associates.

Capel, S. and Gervis, M. (2005) 'Motivating pupils', in S. Capel, M. Leask and T. Turner, *Learning to teach in the secondary school*. London: Routledge.

Capel, S., Leask, M. and Turner, T. (2005) *Learning to teach in the secondary school: a companion to school experience*, 4th edn. London and New York: Routledge.

Carr, W. (2006) 'Education without theory', *British Journal of Educational Studies*, 54 (2): 136–59.

Carr, W. and Hartnett, A. (1996) *Education and the Struggle for Democracy: The Politics of Educational Ideas*. Buckingham: Open University Press.

Carr, W. and Kemmis, S. (1986) *Becoming Critical: Education, Knowledge and Action Research*. London: Falmer.

Carter, K. (1998) 'School Effectiveness and School Improvement', in Halsall, R. (ed), *Teacher Research and School Improvement: Opening Doors from the Inside*. Buckingham: Open University Press.

Carter, K. and Halsall, R. (1998) 'Teacher Research for School Improvement', in HALSALL, R. (ed), *Teacher Research and School Improvement: Opening Doors from the Inside*. Buckingham: Open University Press.

Cattell, R.B. (1963) 'Theory of fluid and crystallized intelligence: a critical experiment', *Journal of Educational Psychology*, 54: 1–22.

Cattell, R.B. (1970) *The Technical Handbook to the 16 PF.* Illinois: Institute for Personality and Achievement Tests.

Central Advisory Council for Education (CACE) (1967) *Children and their Primary Schools* (Plowden Report). London: HMSO.

Centre for Contemporary Cultural Studies (CCCS) (1981) *Unpopular Education.* London: Hutchinson.

Centre for Contemporary Cultural Studies (CCCS) (1991) *Education Limited.* London: Unwin Hyman.

Child, D. (1986) *Psychology and the Teacher,* 4th edn. London: Cassell.

Child, D. (2004) *Psychology and the Teacher,* 7th edn. London: Continuum.

Chitty, C. (1992*) The Education System Transformed.* Manchester: BaselineBooks.

Chitty, C. (2004) *Education Policy in Britain.* Basingstoke: Palgrave Macmillan.

Chitty, C. and Dunford, J. (1999) *State Schools: New Labour and the Conservative Legacy.* London: Woburn Press.

Chomsky, N. (1965) *Aspects of the Theory of Syntax.* Cambridge, MA: MIT Press.

Chyriwsky, M. (1996) 'Able children: the need for a subject-specific approach', *Flying High,* 3: 32–6, Worcester: The National Association for Able Children in Education.

Clark, C. (2005) 'The structure of educational research', *British Educational Research Journal,* 31 (3): 289–308.

Clark, J. (2006) 'Social Justice, Education and Schooling: Some philosophical issues', *British Journal of Educational Studies,* 54 (3): 272–87.

Claxton, G. (2002) *Building Learning Power: helping young people become better learners.* Bristol:TLO.

Clough, P. and Garner, P. (2003) 'Special Educational Needs and Inclusive Education: Origins and Current Issues', in S. Bartlett and D. Burton, *Education Studies: Essential Issues.* London: Sage.

Clough, P. and Nutbrown, C. (2002) *A Student's Guide to Methodology.* London: Sage.

Coard, B. (1971) *How the West Indian Child is Made Educationally Subnormal in the British School System.* London: New Beacon Books.

Coffield, F. (2002) 'Breaking the consensus', in R. Edwards, N. Millar, N. Small and A. Tait (eds), *Supporting Lifelong Learning.* London: RoutledgeFalmer.

Coffield, F., Moseley, D., Hall, E. and Ecclestone, K. (2004) *Learning Styles: a systematic and critical review.* London: Learning and Skills Development Agency.

Cohen, L. Manion, L. and Morrison, K. (2000) *Research Methods in Education,* 5th edn. London: Routledge.

Cole, M. and Scribner, S. (1974) *Culture and Thought.* New York: Wiley.

Collins, A.M. and Quillian, M.R. (1969) 'Retrieval time from semantic memory', *Journal of Verbal Learning and Verbal Behaviour,* 8: 240–8.

Connolly, P. (2004) *Boys and Schooling in the Early Years.* London: RoutledgeFalmer.

Connolly, P. (2006) 'The effects of social class and ethnicity on gender differences in GCSE attainment: a secondary analysis of the Youth Cohort Study of England and Wales 1997–2001', *The British Educational Research Journal,* 32 (1): 3–21.

Cooley, C.H. (1902) *Human Nature and the Social Order.* New York: Scribner.

Cooper, C. (1999) *Intelligence and Abilities.* London: Routledge.

Cooper, D. (2001) 'Plato, 427–347 BCE', in J. Palmer (ed.), *Fifty Major Thinkers on Education: From Confucius to Dewey.* London: Routledge.

Copeland, I. (1999) *The Making of the Backward Pupil in Education in England 1870–1914*. London: Woburn Press.

Corbetta, P. (2003) *Social Research: Theory, Methods and Techniques*. London: Sage.

Coulby, D. (1989) 'From Educational Partnership to Central Control', in L. Bash and D. Coulby, *The Education Reform Act. Competition and Control*. London: Cassell.

Covington, M. (1998) *The Will to Learn: A Guide for Motivating Young People*. Cambridge: Cambridge University Press.

Cowley, S. (2004) *Getting the Buggers to Think*. London: Continuum.

Cox, C.B. and Boyson, R. (1975) *Black Paper 1975: The Fight For Education*. London: Dent.

Cox, C.B. and Boyson, R. (1977) *Black Paper 1977*. London: Maurice Temple Smith.

Cox, C.B. and Dyson, A.E. (eds) (1969a) *Fight for Education: A Black Paper*. Manchester: Critical Quarterly Society.

Cox, C.B. and Dyson, A.E. (eds) (1969b) *Black Paper Two: The Crisis in Education*. Manchester: Critical Quarterly Society.

Cox, C.B. and Dyson, A.E. (1970) *Black Paper Three: Goodbye Mr. Short*. London: Critical Quarterly Society

Craik, K. (1943) *The Nature of Explanation*, Cambridge: Cambridge University Press.

Craik, F. and Lockhart, R. (1972) 'Levels of processing: a framework for memory research', *Journal of Verbal Learning and Verbal Behaviour*, 11: 671–84.

Creemers, B. (1994) 'The History, Value and Purpose of School Effectiveness Studies', in D. Reynolds, B. Creemers, P. Nesselrodt, E. Schaffer, S. Stringfeld and C. Teddlie (eds), *Advances in School Effectiveness Research and Practice*. Oxford: Pergamon Press.

Crowther Report (1959) Ministry of Education, *15 to 18*. London: HMSO.

Crowther, J. (2004) '"In and against" lifelong learning: flexibility and the corrosion of character', *International Journal of Lifelong Education*, 23 (2): 125–36.

Crozier, R. (1997) *Personality Differences in Education*. London: Routledge.

Crozier, G. (2005) 'There's a war against our children: Black educational underachievement revisited', *British Journal of Sociology of Education*, 26 (5): 585–98.

Cuff, E. and Payne, G. with Francis, D., Hustler, D. and Sharrock, W. (1984) *Perspectives in Sociology*, 2nd edn. London: Allen and Unwin.

Curry, L. (1983) 'An organisation of learning style theory and constructs', in L. Curry (ed.), *Learning Style in Continuing Education*. Halifax, Nova Scotia: Dalhousie University.

Dadds, M. and Hart, S. (2001) *Doing Practitioner Research Differently*. London: RoutledgeFalmer.

Dale, R. (1983) 'Thatcherism and Education', in J. Ahier and M. Flude (eds), *Contemporary Education Policy*. London: Croom Helm.

Darling-Hammond, L. (1994) 'Performance-based assessment and educational equity', *Harvard Educational Review*, 64: 5–30.

Darwin, C. (1859) *On the Origin of the Species by Means of Natural Selection*. London: Murray.

Davies, J. and Brember, I. (1999) 'Reading and mathematics attainments and self-esteem in Years 2 and 6 – an eight year cross-sectional study', *Education Studies*, 25: 145–57.

Davies, I. and Hogarth, S. (2004) 'Perceptions of Educational Studies', *Educational Studies*, 30 (4): 425–39.

Davis, B. and Sumara, D.J. (1997) 'Cognition, complexity and teacher education', *Harvard Educational Review,* 67: 105–21.

Davis, K. and Moore, W.E. (1967) 'Some principles of stratification', in R. Bendix and S.M. Lipset, (eds), *Class, Status, and Power.* London: Kegan Paul.

Dearing, R. (1994) *The National Curriculum and its Assessment: Final Report* (Dearing Report). London: School Curriculum and Assessment Authority.

Dearing, R. (1994) *A Review of the National Curriculum.* London: School Curriculum and Assessment Authority.

DeFelipe, J. and Jones, E.G. (1991) *Cajal's Degeneration and Regeneration of the Nervous System.* New York: Oxford University Press.

Delpit, L. (1995) *Other People's Children: Cultural Conflict in the Classroom.* New York: New Press.

Demie, F. (2005) 'Achievement of Black Caribbean pupils: good practice in Lambeth schools', *British Educational Research Journal,* 31 (4): 481–508.

Deming, W. (1986) *Out of the Crisis: Quality, Productivity and Competitive Position.* Cambridge: Cambridge University Press.

Denscombe, M. (2003) *The Good Research Guide,* 2nd edn. Maidenhead: Open University Press.

Denzin, N. (1970) *The Research Act,* Chicago: Aldine.

Department of Education and Science (DES) (1965) *Circular 10/65: the Organisation of Secondary Education.* London: HMSO.

Department of Education and Science (DES) (1978a) *Mixed Ability Work in Comprehensive Schools,* HMI Matters for Discussion 6. London: HMSO.

Department of Education and Science (DES) (1978b) *Report of the Committee of Enquiry into the Education of Handicapped Children and Young People* (Warnock Report). London: HMSO.

Department of Education and Science (DES) (1981) *West Indian Children in our Schools* (Rampton Report), London: HMSO.

Department of Education and Science (DES) (1983) *Teaching Quality. London:* HMSO.

Department of Education and Science (DES) (1985a) *The Curriculum from 5 to 16.* London: HMSO.

Department of Education and Science (DES) (1985b) *Education for all* (Swann Report). London: HMSO.

Department of Education and Science (DES) (1985c) *Better Schools.* London: HMSO.

Department of Education and Science (DES) (1987) *Statistical Bulletin 10/87: The Secondary Schooling Staffing Survey – Data on the Curriculum in Maintained Secondary Schools in England.* London: HMSO.

Department of Education and Science (DES) (1989a) *National Curriculum: From Policy to Practice.* London: HMSO.

Department of Education and Science (DES) (1988) *The Education Reform Act,* London: HMSO.

Department of Education and Science (DES) (1989b) *The Task Group on Assessment and Testing: A Report.* London: HMSO.

Department of Education and Science/Welsh Office (DES/WO) (1989) *Records of Achievement: Report of the Records of Achievement National Steering Committee.* London: DES/WO.

Department for Education and Employment (DfEE) (1997) *Excellence in Schools.* London: The Stationery Office.

Department for Education and Employment (DfEE) (1998a) *The National Literacy Strategy: Framework for Teaching.* London: DfEE.

Department for Education and Employment (DfEE) (1998b) *The Learning Age: A Renaissance for a New Britain.* London: The Stationery Office.

Department for Education and Employment (DfEE) (1999a) *The National Numeracy Strategy: Framework for Teaching.* London: DfEE.

Department for Education and Employment (DfEE) (1999b) *Meet the Challenge. Education Action Zones.* Sudbury: DfEE Publications.

Department for Education and Employment (DfEE) (2001) *Schools Building on Success.* London: DfEE.

Department for Education and Skills (DfES) (2001) *Schools achieving Success.* London: DfES Publications.

Department for Education and Skills (DfES) (2003) *Every Child Matters.* London: The Stationery Office/Department for Education and Skills.

Department for Education and Skills (DfES) (2004a) *A national conversation about personalised learning.* Online Publications.

Department for Education and Skills (DfES) (2004b) *Five year strategy for children and learners.* London: Department for Education and Skills.

Department for Education and Skills (DfES) (2004c) *Every Child Matters: Change for Children.* London: HMSO.

Department for Education and Skills (DfES) (2005a) *Higher Standards, Better Schools for all.* Norwich: The Stationery Office.

Department for Education and Skills (DfES) (2005b) *Education and Skills.* Norwich: HMSO.

Department for Education and Skills (2006) Education and Inspections Act, Norwich: The Stationery Office.

Derrida, J. (1987) *Positions.* London: Athlone.

Dickinson, C. and Wright, J. (1993) *Differentiation: a Practical Handbook of Classroom Strategies.* Coventry: NCET.

Dillabough, J. (2001) 'Gender theory and research in education: modernist traditions and emerging contemporary themes', in B. Francis and C. Skelton (eds), *Investigating Gender: Contemporary Perspectives in Education.* Buckingham: Open University Press.

Donald, J. (1992) *Sentimental Education.* London: Verso.

Donaldson, M. (1978) *Children's Minds.* London: Fontana.

Douglas, J.W.B. (1964) *The Home and the School.* St Albans: Panther.

Dowrick, N. (1996) '"But many that are first shall be last": attainment differences in young collaborators', *Research in Education,* 55: 16–28.

Driver, R. and Bell, J. (1986) 'Students' thinking and learning of science: a constructivist view', *School Science Review,* 67 (240): 443–56.

Driver, R., Leach, J., Millar, R. and Scott, P. (1996) *Young People's Images of Science.* Buckingham: Open University Press.

Dryden, G. and Vos, J. (2001) *The Learning Revolution: to Change the Way the World Learns.* Stafford: Network Educational Press in association with Learning Web.

Dunn, R. (1991) 'How learning style changes over time', presentation at the 14th Annual Leadership Institute: Teaching Students Through Their Individual Learning Styles, 7–13 July, New York.

Dunn, R., Dunn, K. and Price, G. (1979) 'Identifying Learning Styles', in J.W. Keif (ed.), *Student Learning Styles: Diagnosing and Prescribing Programmes*. Reston, VA: National Assocation of Secondary School Principles.

Dunn, R., Dunn, K. and Price, G.E. (1989) *The Learning Style Inventory*. Lawrence, KS: Price Systems.

Dunn, R. and Griggs, S. (2003) *Synthesis of the Dunn and Dunn learning styles model research: who, what, when, where and so what – the Dunn and Dunn learning styles model and its theoretical cornerstone*. New York: Learning Styles Network/St. John's University.

Durkheim, E. (1947) *The Division of Labour in Society*. New York: Free Press.

Durkheim, E. (1970) *Suicide: A Study in Sociology*. London: Routledge and Kegan Paul.

Durkheim, E. (1964) *The Rules of Sociological Method*. New York: Free Press.

Dweck, C.S. (1991) 'Self-theories and goals: their role in motivation, personality and development', *Nebraska Symposium on Motivation*, 38, University of Nebraska Press.

Eagleton, T. (2000) *The Idea of Culture*. Oxford: Blackwell.

Ebbinghaus, H. (1885) *Memory: a Contribution to Experimental Psychology Refurbished*, 1964 edn. New York: Dover.

Ecclestone, K. (2004) 'Learning or therapy?: the demoralisation of education', *British Journal of Educational Studies*, 57 (3): 127–41.

'Education and Inspections Act 2006: Elizabeth II. Chapter 40'. Norwich: The Stationery Office.

Edwards, R. and Usher, R. (2000) *Globalisation and Pedagogy: Space, Place and Identity*. London: Routledge.

Elliott, E.S. and Dweck, C.S. (1988) 'Goals: an approach to motivation and achievement', *Journal of Personality and Social Psychology*, 54: 5–12.

Elliott, J. (1991) *Action Research for Educational Change*. Milton Keynes: Open University Press.

Elliott, J. (1993) 'What have we learned from action research in school-based evaluation?', *Education Action Research*, 1 (1): 175–86.

Elliott, J. (1996) 'School Effectiveness Research and its Critics: Alternative Visions of Schooling', *Cambridge Journal of Education*, 26 (2): 199–223.

Elliott, J. (1998) *The Curriculum Experiment. Meeting the Social Challenge*. Buckingham: Open University Press.

Elliott, J. (2001) 'Making Evidence-based Practice Educational', *British Educational Research Journal*, 27 (5): 555–74.

Elliott, J. (2003) 'Interview with John Elliott, December 6, 2002', *Educational Action Research*, 11 (2): 169–180.

Elliott, J. (2005) 'Dyslexia myths and the feel-bad factor', *Times Educational Supplement*, 2 September, London: Times Newspapers.

Elwood, J. (2005) 'Gender and Achievement: what have exams got to do with it?' *Oxford Review of Education*, 31 (3): 373–93.

Engestrom, Y. (1993) 'Developmental studies of work as a testbench of activity theory', in S. Chaiklin and J. Lave (eds), *Understanding Practice: Perspectives on Activity and Context*. Cambridge: Cambridge University Press.

Entwistle, N.J. (1981) *Styles of Learning and Teaching*. Chichester: Wiley.

Erikson, E.H. (1980) *Identity and the Life Cycle*. New York: Norton.

Eurydice, July 2006, p. 9.

Evans, C. and Waring, M. (2006) 'Towards Inclusive Teacher Education: Sensitising individuals to how they learn', *Educational Psychology*, 26 (4): 499–518.

Evans, K. and King, D. (2006) *Studying Society: The Essentials*. Oxon: Routledge.

Eysenck, H.J. (1947) *Dimensions of Personality*. London: Routledge.

Eysenck, H.J. (1967) *The Biological Basis of Personality*. Springfield IL: Thomas.

Eysenck, H.J. (1971) *Race, Intelligence and Education*. London: Temple-Smith.

Fallan, L. (2006) 'Quality Reform: Personality type, preferred learning style and majors in a business school', *Quality in Higher Education*, 12 (14): 193–206.

Faulks, K. (2006) 'Education for citizenship in England's secondary schools: a critique of current principle and practice', *Journal of Educational Policy*, 21 (1): 59–74.

Fazey, J.A. and Marton, F. (2002) 'Understanding the space of experiential variation', *Active Learning in Higher Education*, 3 (3): 234–50.

Festinger, L. (1957) *A Theory of Cognitive Dissonance*. Evanston, IL: Row, Peterson.

Feuerstein, R., Klein, P. and Tannenbaum, A. (eds) (1991) *Mediated Learning Experience*. London: Freund.

Fielding, M. (1994) 'Why and how learning styles matter: valuing difference in teachers and learners', in S. Hart (ed.), *Differentiation and the Secondary Curriculum: Debates and Dilemmas*. London: Routledge.

Fielding, M. (2001) 'Target setting, policy pathology and student perspectives: learning to labour in new times', in M. Fielding (ed.), *Taking Education Really Seriously: Four Years' Hard Labour*. London: RoutledgeFalmer.

Flavell, J.H. (1979) 'Metacognition and cognitive monitoring', *American Psychologist*, 34: 906–11.

Flavell, J.H. (1982) 'Structures, stages, and sequences in cognitive development', in W.A. Collins (ed.), *The Concept of Development: The Minnesota Symposia on Child Psychology*, 15: 1–28.

Flick, U. (2002) *An Introduction to Qualitative Research*. London: Sage.

Fodor, J. (1975) *The Language of Thought*. Cambridge, MA: Harvard University Press.

Fodor, J. (1983) *The Modularity of Mind*. Cambridge, MA: MIT Press.

Fodor, J. (2000) *The Mind Doesn't Work That Way: The Scope and Limits of Computational Psychology*. Cambridge, MA: MIT Press.

Foster, P. (1990) *Policy and practice in multicultural and anti-racist education: a case study of a multi-ethnic comprehensive school*. London: Routledge.

Foucault, M. (1977b) *The Archaeology of Knowledge*. London: Tavistock.

Foucault, M. (1988a) *Technologies of the Self*. London: Tavistock.

Foucault, M. (1988b) 'What is an author?', in D. Lodge (ed.), *Modern Criticism and Theory*. London: Longman.

Francis, B. (2000) *Boys, Girls and Achievement. Addressing the Classroom Issues*. London: Routledge.

Freud, S. (1901) 'The psychopathology of everyday life', republished in 1953, in J. Strachey (ed.), *The Standard Edition of the Complete Psychological Works of Sigmund Freud*, vol 6. London: Hogarth.

Frith, U. (2005) 'Teaching in 2020: the impact of neuroscience', *Journal of Education for Teaching: International Research and Pedagogy*, 31 (4): 289–91.

Furlong, J. (2005) 'New Labour and Teacher Education: the end of an era', *Oxford Review of Education*, 31 (1): 119–34.

Gagne, R.M. (1977) *The Conditions of Learning*. New York: Holt International.

Galton, F. (1869) *Hereditary Genius*. New York: Macmillan.

Garaigordobil, M. and Perez, J.-I. (2005) 'Creative Personality Scale: An exploratory psychometric study', *Estudios de Psicologia*, 26 (3): 345–64.

Gardner, H. (1983) *Frames of Mind: The Theory of Multiple Intelligences*, New York: Basic Books.

Gardner, H. (1995) 'Reflections on multiple intelligences: myths and messages', *Phi Delta Kappan*, 77: 200–3, 206–9.

Gardner, P. (2001) *Teaching and Learning in Multicultural Classrooms*. London: David Fulton.

Garratt, D. (2003) 'Education for Citizenship', in S. Bartlett and D. Burton, *Education Studies: Essential Issues*. London: Sage.

Gavin, H. (1998) *The Essence of Cognitive Psychology*. London: Prentice Hall Europe.

Gessell, A. (1925) *The Mental Growth of the Preschool Child*. New York: Macmillan.

Gewirtz, S., Ball, S. and Bowe, R. (1995) *Markets, Choice and Equity in Education*. Buckingham: Open University Press.

Gibbs, G. (1992) *Improving the Quality of Student Learning*. Bristol: Technical and Educational Services.

Gibson, J. (1979) *The Ecological Approach to Visual Perception*. Boston, MA: Houghton Mifflin.

Giddens, A. (1985) *The Constitution of Society*. Cambridge: Polity Press.

Giddens, A. (1998) *The Third Way: the renewal of social democracy*. Cambridge: Policy Press.

Giddens, A. (2000) *The Third Way and its Critics*. Cambridge: Policy Press.

Gillborn, D. (2001) Racism, policy and the (mis)education of Black children. In R. Majors (ed.) *Educating our black children: new directions and radical approaches*, London: RoutledgeFalmer.

Gillborn, D. and Mirza, H. (2000) *Educational Inequality: Mapping Race, Class and Gender: A Synthesis of Research Evidence*. London: Office for Standards in Education.

Gillies, R.M. and Ashman, A.F. (2003) *Co-operative Learning: The Social and Intellectual Outcomes of Learning in Groups*. London: RoutledgeFalmer.

Gipps, C. (1993) 'The structure for assessment and recording', in P. O'Hear and J. White (eds), *Assessing the National Curriculum*. London: Paul Chapman Publishing.

Gipps, C. (2006) 'Gender, Performance and Learning Style'. Public Lecture, University of Wolverhampton, 10 May.

Gipps, C. and Pickering, A. (2006) 'Assessment for learning', in J. Arthur, T. Grainger and D. Wray (eds), *Learning to teach in the primary school*. London: Routledge.

Gipps, C. and Stobart, G. (1993) *Assessment*. London: Hodder and Stoughton.

Glaser, B. and Strauss, A. (1967) *The Discovery of Grounded Theory*. Chicago: Aldane.

Goldthorpe, J.H., Lockwood, D., Bechhofer, F. and Platt, J. (1968) *The Affluent Worker: Industrial Attitudes and Behaviour*. Cambridge: Cambridge University Press.

Goleman, D. (1995) *Emotional Intelligence*. New York: Bantam.

Goodson, I.F. (1994) *Studying Curriculum: Cases and Methods*. Buckingham: Open University Press.

Gorard, S. (2000) *Education and Social Justice: The Changing Composition of Schools and its Implications*. Cardiff: University of Wales Press.

Gorard, S., Rees, G. and Selwyn, N. (2002) 'The "conveyor belt" effect: a reassessment of the impact of national targets for lifelong learning', *Oxford Review of Education*, 28 (1): 75–89.

Gorard, S. (2003) 'Patterns of Work-based Learning'. *Journal of Vocational Education and Training*, 55 (1): 47–63.

Goswami, U. (2005) 'Synthetic Phonics and Learning to Read: A Cross-language Perspective', *Educational Psychology in Practice*, 21 (4): 273–282.

Gramsci, A. (1985) *Selections from Cultural Writings*, London: Lawrence and Wishart.

Gramsci, A. (1991); *Prison Notebooks*, New York: Columbia University Press.

Green, A. (1990) *Education and State Formation*. London: Macmillan.

Greenbank, P. (2003) 'The Role of Values in Educational Research: The Case for Reflexivity', *British Educational Research Journal*, 29 (6): 791–801.

Greenfield, S. (1997) *The Human Brain: A Guided Tour*. London: Weidenfeld and Nicolson.

Greenfield, S. (2000) *Brain Story*. London: BBC Worldwide.

Greeno, J.G. (1997) 'On claims that answer the wrong questions', *Educational Researcher*, 26: 5–17.

Greeno, J.G., Smith, D.R. and Moore, J.L. (1993) 'Transfer of situated learning', in D.K. Detterman and R.J. Sternberg (eds), *Transfer on Trial: Intelligence, Cognition and Instruction*. Norwood, NJ: Ablex.

Gregorc, A. R. (1982) *Style Delineator*. Maynard, MA: Gabriel Systems.

Guilford, J.P. (1950) 'Creativity', *American Psychologist*, 5: 444–54.

Guilford, J.P. (1967) *The Nature of Human Intelligence*. New York: McGraw-Hill.

Gundara, J. (2000) *Interculturalism, education and inclusion*. London: Paul Chapman Publishing.

Gurney-Dixon Report (1954) *Early Leaving*. London: HMSO.

Hadow Report (1926) Board of Education, *The Education of the Adolescent*, London: HMSO.

Hall, E., Leat, D., Wall, K., Higgins, S. and Edwards, G. (2006) 'Learning to Learn: teacher research in the Zone of Proximal Development', *Teacher Development*, 10 (2): 149–66.

Hall, K. and Sheehy, K. (2006) 'Assessment and Learning: Summative approaches', in J. Arthur, T. Grainger and D. Wray (eds), *Learning to teach in the primary school*. London: Routledge.

Hallam, S., Ireson, J. and Davies, J. (2004) 'Primary pupils' experiences of different types of grouping in school', *British Educational Research Journal*, 30 (4): 515–33.

Halliday, M.A.K. (1979) *Language as Social Semiotic*. London: Arnold.

Halsall, R. (2001) 'School Improvement: An Overview of Key Findings', in Halsall, R. (ed). *Teacher Research and School Improvement: Opening Doors from the Inside*. Buckingham: Open University Press.

Halsey, A.H. (1978) *Change in British Society*. Oxford: Oxford University Press.

Halsey, A.H. (1995) *Change in British Society from 1900 to the Present Day*, 4th edn. Oxford: Oxford University Press.

Halsey, A.H., Heath, A.F. and Ridge, J.M. (1980) *Origins and Destinations*. Oxford: Clarendon Press.

Halsey, A.H., Lauder, H., Brown, P. Wells, A. (1997) *Education: Culture Economy Society*. Oxford: Oxford University Press.

Halliday, M. (1979) *Language as Social Semiotic*. London: Arnold.

Hammersley, M. (2001) 'Obvious all too obvious? Methodological issues in using sex/gender as a variable in educational research,' in B. Francis and C. Skelton, *Investigating Gender Contemporary Perspectives in Education*. Buckingham: Open Universtity Press.

Hammersley, M. (2002) *Educational Research, Policymaking and Practice*. London: Paul Chapman Publishing.

Hammersley, M. (2004) 'Some questions about evidence-based practice in education', in G. Thomas and R. Pring (eds). *Evidence based Practice in Education*. Maidenhead: OU Press. pp. 133–149.

Hammersley, M. (2006) 'Philosophy's Contribution to Social Science Research on Education', *Journal of Philosophy of Education*, 40 (2): 273–86.

Hammersley, M. and Atkinson, I. (1995) *Ethnography: Principles in Practice*, 2nd edn. London: Routledge.

Hammersley, M. and Gomm, R. (2000) 'Introduction', in R. Gomm, M. Hammersley and, P. Foster (eds), *Case Study Method*. London: Sage.

Hankin, L. (2006) 'Comparative Education', in J. Sharp, S. Ward and L. Hankin, *Education Studies: An Issues Based Approach*. Exeter: Learning Matters.

Hardre, P., Huang, S., Hua, C., Ching, H., Chiang, C., Ting, J., Fen, L. and Warden, L. (2006) 'High School Teachers' Motivational Perceptions and Strategies in an East Asian Nation', *Asia-Pacific Journal of Teacher Education*, 34 (2): 199–221.

Hargreaves, A. and Fink, D. (2006) *Sustainable Leadership*. San Francisco, California: John Wiley/Jossey-Bass.

Hargreaves, D. (1967) *Social Relations in a Secondary School*. London: Routledge and Kegan Paul.

Hargreaves, D. (1972) *Interpersonal Relations and Education*. London: Routledge and Kegan Paul.

Hargreaves, D. (1996) 'Teaching as a research based profession: possibilities and prospects', Teacher Training Agency, Annual Lecture, Birmingham.

Hargreaves, D., Hestor, S. and Mellor, F. (1975) *Deviance in Classrooms*. London: Routledge and Kegan Paul.

Harris, A. and Ranson, S. (2005) 'The Contradictions of Education Policy: Disadvantage and Achievement', *British Educational Research Journal*, 31 (5): 571–87.

Harris, D. and Bell, C. (1990) *Evaluating and Assessing for Learning*. London: Kogan Page.

Hart, S. (ed.) (1996) *Differentiation and the Secondary Curriculum: Debates and Dilemmas*. London: Routledge.

Harter, S. (1985) 'Competence as a dimension of self-evaluation: toward a comprehensive model of self-worth', in R.L. Leay (ed.), *The Development of the Self*. Orlando, FL: Academic Press.

Hartley, D. (1997) *Re-Schooling Society*. London: Falmer Press.

Harvey, D. (1991) *The Condition of Postmodernity*. Oxford: Blackwell.

Hastings, S. (2004). 'Emotional intelligence', *Times Educational Supplement*, Friday 15 October.

Hatcher, D. (2004) 'Social Class and School', in D. Matheson (ed.), *An Introduction to the Study of Education*, 2nd edn. London: David Fulton.

Hayes, D. (2000) *The Handbook for Newly Qualified Teachers*. London: David Fulton.

Hayes, D. (2006) *Primary Education: Key Concepts*. London: Routledge.

Hayes, N. (1993) *A First Course in Psychology*, 3rd edn. Walton on Thames: Nelson.

Hayes, N. and Orrell, S. (1998) *Psychology: An Introduction*, 3rd edn. London: Longman.

Hebb, D.O. (1949) *The Organisation of Behaviour*. New York: Wiley.

Helsby, G. (1999) *Changing Teachers' Work: The 'Reform' of Secondary Schooling*. Buckingham: Open University Press.

Henderson-King, D. and Smith, M. (2006) 'Meanings of Education for University Students: Academic Motivation and Personal Values as Predictors', *Social Psychology of Education*, 9 (2), 195–221.

Her Majesty's Inspectorate (HMI) (1977) *Curriculum 11–16: A Contribution to Current Debate*. London: HMSO.

Her Majesty's Inspectorate (HMI) (1994) 'The entitlement curriculum', in B. Moon and S. Mayes, *Teaching and Learning in the Secondary School*. London: Routledge.

Herrnstein, R.J. and Murray, C. (1994) *The Bell Curve: Intelligence and Class Structure in American Life*. New York: Free Press.

Hess, R.D. and Azuma, M. (1991) 'Cultural support for schooling: contrasts between Japan and the United States', *Educational Researcher*, 20: 2–8.

Hillage, J., Pearson, R., Anderson, A. and Tamkin, P. (1998) *Excellence in Research on Schools*. London: Department of Education and Employment.

Hillyard, S.A. (1993) 'Electrical and magnetic brain recordings: contributions to cognitive neuroscience', *Current Opinion in Neurobiology*, 3: 217–24.

Hirst, P.H. (1975) *Knowledge and the Curriculum*. London: Routledge and Kegan Paul.

Hitchcock, G. and Hughes, D. (1993) *Research and the Teacher*. London: Routledge.

Hitchcock, G. and Hughes, D. (1995) *Research and the Teacher*, 2nd edn. London: Routledge.

Honey, P. and Mumford, A. (1986) *Using Your Learning Styles*. Maidenhead: Honey.

Hopkins, D. (2001) *School Improvement for Real*. London: RoutledgeFalmer.

Hopkins, D. (2002) *A Teacher's Guide to Classroom Research*, 3rd edn. Buckingham: Open University Press.

Hopkins, D. and Harris, A. (2000) *Creating the Conditions for Teaching and Learning*. London: David Fulton.

Horn, P. (1989) *The Victorian and Edwardian Schoolchild*. Gloucester: Sutton.

Hough, J. R. and Ogilvie, D.T. (2005) 'An Empirical Test of Cognitive Style and Strategic Decision Outcomes', *Journal of Management Studies*, 42 (2): 417–48.

Hoyle, E. (1980) 'Professionalisation and deprofessionalisation in education', in E. Hoyle and J. Megarry (eds), *World Yearbook of Education 1980: Professional Development of Teachers*. London: Kogan Page.

Hughes, C. and Tight, M. (1998) 'The Myth of the Learning Society', in S. Ransen (ed.) '*Inside the Learning Society*. London: Cassell.

Hughes, M. (1975) 'Egocentricity in children', unpublished PhD thesis, Edinburgh University.

Hunter, I. (1994) *Rethinking the School*. Sydney: Allen and Unwin.

Hurt, J.S. (1979) *Elementary Schooling and the Working Classes*. London: Routledge and Kegan Paul.

Husbands, C. (2004) 'Models of the curriculum', in V. Brooks, I. Abbott and L. Bills (eds), *Preparing to teach in secondary schools: A student teacher's guide to professional issues in secondary education*. Maidenhead: Open University Press.

Ireson, J. and Hallam, S. (2005) 'Pupils' liking for school: Ability grouping, self-concept and perceptions of teaching', British Journal of Educational Psychology, 75 (2): 297–311.

Ireson, J., Hallam, S. and Hurley, C. (2005) 'What are the effects of ability grouping on GCSE attainment?', *British Educational Research Journal*, 31 (4): 443–458.

Jackson, B. (1964) *Streaming: An Education System in Miniature*. London: Routledge and Kegan Paul.

Jackson, B. and Marsden, D. (1962) *Education and the Working Class*. Harmondsworth: Penguin.

James, W. (1890) *The Principles of Psychology*, 2 vols, Dover reprint 1950. New York: Dover.

Jarvis, P., Holford, J. and Griffin, C. (2003) *The Theory and Practice of Learning*, 2nd edn. London: Kogan Page.

Jenkins, D. and Shipman, M.D. (1976) *Curriculum: an Introduction*. London: Open Books.

Jensen, A.R. (1969) 'How Much Can we Boost IQ and Scholastic Achievement?', *Harvard Educational Review*, 33: 1–23.

Jensen, A.R. (1973) *Educational Differences*. London: Methuen.

Jones, D. (1990) 'The genealogy of the urban schoolteacher', in S. Ball (ed.), *Foucault and Education: Disciplines and Knowledge*. London: Routledge.

Jones, G. and Carter, G. (1994) 'Verbal and non-verbal behaviour of ability-grouped dyads', *Journal of Research in Science Teaching*, 31: 603–19.

Jones, K. (2003) *Education in Britain: 1944 to the Present*. Oxford: Polity Press.

Jones, S. and Myhill, D. (2004) '"Troublesome boys" and "compliant girls": gender identity and perceptions of achievement and underachievement', *British Journal of Sociology of Education*, 25 (5): 547–61.

Kailin, J. (2002) *Antiracist Education: From Theory to Practice*. New York: Rowan and Littlefield.

Kavanagh, S. (2000) 'A Total System of Classroom Management: Consistent, Flexible, Practical and Working', *Pastoral Care in Education*, 18 (1): 17–21.

Kayes, D. (2005) 'Internal Validity and Reliability of Kolb's Learning Style Inventory Version 3 (1999)', *Journal of Business and Psychology*, 20 (2): 249–57.

Keddie, N. (1971) 'Classroom knowledge', in M.F.D. Young (ed.), *Knowledge and Control*. London: Collier-Macmillan.

Keddie, N. (1973) 'Classroom knowledge', in J. Young (ed.), *Tinker, Tailor: The Myth of Cultural Deprivation*. Harmondsworth: Penguin.

Kehily, M. (2001) 'Issues of gender and sexuality in schools', in B. Francis and C. Skelton, *Investigating Gender: Contemporary Perspectives in Education*. Buckingham: Open University Press.

Kehily, M. J. (2002) *Sexuality, Gender and Schooling. Shifting agendas in social learning*. London: RoutledgeFalmer.

Kelly, A.V. (1975) *Case Studies in Mixed Ability Teaching*. London: Harper and Row.

Kelly, A.V. (2004) *The Curriculum: Theory and Practice*, 5th edn. London: Sage.

Kelly, G.A. (1955) *The Psychology of Personal Constructs*. New York: Norton.

Kember, D. and Gow, L. (1990) 'Cultural specificity of approaches to learning', *British Journal of Educational Psychology*, 60: 356–63.

Kemmis, S. and Wilkinson, M. (1998) 'Participatory action research and the study of practice', in B. Atweh, S. Kemmis and P. Weeks (eds), *Action Research in Practice*. London: Routledge.

Kenway, J. and Willis, P. (1998) *Answering Back*. London: Routledge.

Kerry, T. (1984) 'Analysing the cognitive demands made by classroom tasks in mixed ability classes', in E.C. Wragg (ed.), *Classroom Teaching Skills*. Beckenham: Croom Helm.

Killick, S. (2006) *Emotional Literacy at the Heart of the School Ethos*. London: Paul Chapman.

Klein, H.J., and Noe, R.A. and Wang, C. (2006), 'Motivation to Learn and Course Outcomes: The Impact of Delivery Mode, Learning Goal Orientation, and Perceived Barriers and Enablers', *Personnel Psychology*, 59 (3): 665–702.

Koffka, K. (1935) *Principles of Gestalt Psychology*. New York: Harcourt Brace.

Kohlberg, L. (1976) 'Moral stages and moralization: the cognitive-developmental approach', in T. Lickona (ed.), *Moral Development and Behaviour: Theory, Research, and Social Issues*. New York: Holt, Rinehart and Winston.

Kohler, W. (1940) *Dynamics in Psychology.* New York: Liveright.

Kolb, D.A. (1976) *The Learning Style Inventory: Technical Manual.* Boston, MA: McBer and Company.

Kolb, D.A. (1985) *The Learning Style Inventory: Technical Manual,* revised edn. Boston, MA: McBer and Company.

Kong, C.K. and Hau, K.T. (1996) 'Students' achievement goals and approaches to learning: the relationship between emphasis on self-improvement and thorough understanding', *Research in Education,* 55: 74–85.

Kozulin, A. (1998) *Psychological Tools. A Sociocultural Approach to Education.* Cambridge, MA: Harvard University Press.

Kramarski, B. and Mevarech, Z.R. (1997) 'Cognitive-metacognitive training within a problem-solving based Logo environment', *British Journal of Educational Psychology,* 67: 425–45.

Krnel, D. Watson, R. and Glazar, S. (2005) The development of the cencept of 'matter': a cross-age study of how children describe materials, *International Journal of Science Education,* 27 (3): 367–383.

Kubow, P. and Fossum, P. (2003) *Comparative Education: Exploring issues in international context.* Columbus, Ohio: Merrill Prentice Hall

Kutnick, P., Blatchford, P. and Baines, E. (2002) 'Pupil Groupings in Primary School Classrooms: sites for learning and social pedagogy?', *British Educational Research Journal,* 28 (2): 187–206.

Kyriacou, C. (2005) 'The impact of daily mathematics lessons in England on pupil confidence and competence in early mathematics: a systematic review', *British Journal of Educational Studies,* 52 (2): 168–86.

Labov, W. (1973) 'The logic of nonstandard English', in J. Young (ed.), *Tinker, Tailor: The Myth of Cultural Deprivation.* Harmondsworth: Penguin.

Labov, W. (1997) Testimony submitted by William Labov, Professor of_Linguistics at the University of Pennsylvania', 23 January (http://www.ling.upenn.edu/~labov/L102?Ebonics_test.html; + Winterson).

Lacey, C. (1970) *Hightown Grammar: The School as a Social System.* Manchester: Manchester University Press.

Lam, S., Yim, P., Law, J.S.F. and Cheung, R.W.Y. (2004) 'The effects of competition on achievement motivation in Chinese classrooms', *British Journal of Educational Psychology,* 74 (2): 281–96.

Laming, S (2003) *The Victoria Climbie Inquiry Report.* London: DfES.

Lave, J. (1988) *Cognition in Practice: Mind, Mathematics and Culture in Everyday Life.* Cambridge: Cambridge University Press.

Lave, J. and Wenger, E. (1991) *Situated Learning: Legitimate Peripheral Participation.* Cambridge: Cambridge University Press.

Lawrence, D. (2006) *Enhancing Self-Esteem in the Classroom,* 3rd edn. London: Paul Chapman Publishing.

Lawson, J. and Silver, H. (1973) *A Social History of Education in England.* London: Methuen.

Lawton, D. (1975) *Class, Culture and the Curriculum.* London: Routledge and Kegan Paul.

Lawton, D. (1980) *The Politics of the School Curriculum.* London: Routledge.

Lawton, D. (1992) *Education and Politics in the 1990s: Conflict or Consensus?* London: Falmer Press.

Lawton, D. (1994) *The Tory Mind on Education 1979–1994.* London: Falmer Press.

Lawton, D. (1999) *Beyond the National Curriculum.* London: Hodder and Stoughton.

Lawton, D. (2005) *Education and Labour Party Ideologies 1900–2001 and Beyond.* Oxon: RoutledgeFalmer.

Lawton, D. and Chitty, C. (eds) (1988) *The National Curriculum*, Bedford Way Paper 33. London: Institute of Education, University of London.

Leadbeater, C. (2004) *Personalisation through participation: a new script for public services.* London: DEMOS/DFES Innovations Unit.

Leedy, P. and Ormrod, J. (2001) *Practical research: planning and design.* New Jersey: Merrill Prentice Hall.

Leo, E.L. and Galloway, D. (1996) 'Evaluating research on motivation: generating more heat than light?', *Evaluation and Research in Education*, 10: 35–47.

Lewin, K. (1946) 'Action Research and Minority Problems', *Journal of Social Issues,* 2: 34–6.

Lim, T.K. (1994) 'Relationships between learning styles and personality types', *Research in Education*, 52: 99–100.

Long, M. (2000) *The Psychology of Education.* London: RoutledgeFalmer.

Lowe R. and Seaborne, M. (1977) *The English School: Its Architecture and Organization*, vol. 2. London: Routledge and Kegan Paul.

Luiselli, J., Putnam, R., Handler, M., and Feinberg, A. (2005) 'Whole-school positive behaviour support: effects on student discipline problems and academic performance', *Educational Psychology,* 25 (2–3): 183–198.

Lupton, R. (2005) 'Social Justice and School Improvement: Improving the Quality of Schooling in the Poorest Neighbourhoods'. *British Educational Research Journal*, 31 (5): 589–604.

Lyotard, J.-F. (1986) *The Postmodern Condition*, 2nd edn. Manchester: Manchester University Press.

Mac an Ghaill, M. (1988) *Young, Gifted and Black*. Milton Keynes: Open University Press.

Mac an Ghaill, M. (1994) *The Making of Men: Masculinities, Sexuality and Schooling.* Buckingham: Open University Press.

Madeus, G.F. (1994) 'A technological and historical consideration of equity issues associated with proposals to change the nation's testing policy', *Harvard Educational Review*, 64: 76–95.

Maehr, M.L. and Midgley, C. (1991) 'Enhancing student motivation: a school-wide approach', *Educational Psychologist*, 26: 399–427.

Majors, R. (2000) *The Black Education Revolution: 'Race' and Culture in Britain and America.* London: Routledge.

Maqsud, M. (1997) 'Effects of metacognitive skills and non-verbal ability on academic achievement of high school pupils', *Educational Psychology*, 17: 387–97.

Marsh, C.J. (2004) *Key Concepts for Understanding Curriculum,* 3rd edn. Oxon: Routledge Falmer.

Martin, G. (2004) 'A Brief History of State Intervention in British Schooling', In D. Matheson (ed), *An Introduction to the Study of Education.* London: David Fulton.

Marton, F. and Saljo, R. (1976) 'On qualitative differences in learning, 1: Outcome and process', *British Journal of Educational Psychology*, 46: 4–11.

Maslow, A.H. (1954) *Motivation and Personality.* New York: Harper.

Maybin, J., Mercer, N. and Stierer, B. (1992) 'Scaffolding learning in the classroom', in K. Norman (ed.), *Thinking Voices: The work of the National Oracy Project.* London: Hodder and Stoughton.

Mayes, A.S. and Moon, B. (eds) (1994) *Teaching and Learning in the Secondary School,* London: Routledge.

Maykut, P. and Morehouse, R. (1994) *Beginning Qualitative Research.* London: Falmer Press.

Maynard, T. and Thomas, N. (2004) *An Introduction to Early Childhood Studies.* London: Sage.

Mboya, M.M. (1995) 'Perceived teachers' behaviours and dimensions of adolescent self concepts', *Educational Psychology*, 15: 491–9.

McCarthy, B. (1987) *The 4MAT System.* Barrington: Excel.

McClelland, D.C. (1955) *Studies in Motivation.* New York: Appleton-Century-Crofts.

McClelland, D.C. (1985) *Motives, Personality and Society.* New York: Praeger.

McCulloch, G. (2001) 'The reinvention of teacher professionalism', in R. Phillips and J. Furlong (eds), *Education, Reform and the State: Twenty-five Years of Politics, Policy and Practice.* London: RoutledgeFalmer.

McCulloch, G. (2002), 'Disciplines Contributing to Education? Educational Studies and the Disciplines', *British Journal of Educational Studies,* 50 (1): 100–119.

McGarrigle, J. and Donaldson, M. (1974) 'Conservation accidents', *Cognition,* 3: 341–50.

McGregor, D. (1960) *The Human Side of Enterprise.* New York: McGraw-Hill.

McKenzie, J. (2001) *Changing Education: A Sociology of Education Since 1944.* Harlow: Prentice Hall.

McLean, M. (1992) *The Promise and Perils of Educational Comparison.* London: Tuffnell Press.

McNeill, P. and Chapman, S. (2005) *Research Methods,* 3rd edn. London: Routledge.

McNiff, J. (1988) *Action Research. Principles and Practice.* London: Macmillan.

McNiff, J. with Whitehead, J. (2002) *Action Research: Principles and Practice,* 2nd edn. London: RoutledgeFalmer.

McNiff, J. and Whitehead, J. (2006) *All you need to know about action research.* London: Sage.

Macpherson, W. (1999) (The Macpherson Report) *The Stephen Lawrence Inquiry,* CM 4262-I. London: The Stationery Office.

Mead, G.H. (1934) *Mind, Self and Society.* Chicago: University of Chicago Press.

Mead, M. (1935) *Sex and Temperament in Three Primitive Societies.* London: Routledge and Kegan Paul.

Meighan, R. and Siraj-Blatchford, I. (2003) *A sociology of Educating,* 4th edn. London: Cassell.

Merret, F. (1998) 'Helping readers who have fallen behind', *Support for Learning,* 13 (2): 59–63 (5).

Miles, M. and Huberman, M. (1994) *Qualitative Data Analysis.* London: Sage.

Miliband, D. (2004a) 'What does personalised learning mean to you?' Speech delivered at *North of England Conference,* January.

Miliband, D. (2004b) *Personalised Learning: Building A New Relationship With Schools,* Speech given at North of England Education Conference, Belfast, 8th January 2004.

Miller, G. (1956) 'The magical number seven plus or minus two: some limits on our capacity for processing information', *Psychological Review,* 63: 81–97.

Milner, D. (1975) *Children and Race.* Harmondsworth: Penguin.

Minter, C. (2001) 'Some flaws in the common theory of widening participation'. *Research in Post-Compulsory Education,* 26 (3): 303–19.

Mitchell, R. (1994) 'The communicative approach to language teaching: an introduction', in A. Swarbrick (ed.), *Teaching Modern Languages.* London: Routledge/Open University.

Montgomery, D. (1996) 'Differentiation of the curriculum in primary education', *Flying High,* 3: 14–28 (Worcester: The National Association for Able Children in Education).

Moon, B. (2001) *A Guide to the National Curriculum,* 4th edn. Oxford: Oxford University Press.

Morrison, K. and Ridley, K. (1989) 'Ideological contexts for curriculum planning', in M. Preedy (ed.), *Approaches to Curriculum Management.* Milton Keynes: Open University Press.

Mountford, H., Jones, S. and Tucker, B. (2006) 'Learning styles of entry-level physiotherapy students', *Advances in Physiotherapy,* 8 (3): 128–36.

Moylett, H. (2003) 'Early Years Education and Care', in S. Bartlett and D. Burton (eds), *Education Studies: Essential Issues*. London: Sage.

Mullard, C. (1981) *Racism in School and Society*. London: University of London, Institute of Education Centre for Multicultural Studies.

Mulryan, C. (1992) 'Student passivity during co-operative small groups in mathematics', *Journal of Educational Research*, 85: 261–73.

Munn, P. and Drever, E. (2004) *Using Questionnaires in Small-Scale Research: A Teachers Guide*, 2nd edn. Edinburgh: The Scottish Council for Research in Education.

Murphy, P. and Gipps, C. (1996) *Equity in the Classroom: Towards Effective Pedagogy for Girls and Boys*, Lewes: Falmer Press and UNESCO Publishing.

Myers, K. (1987) *Genderwatch: Self-Assessment Schedules for Use in Schools*. London: Schools Curriculum Development Council.

Myers Briggs, I., Kirby, L.K. and Myers, K.D. (1998) *Introduction to TYPE. A Guide to Understanding Your Results on the Myers-Briggs Type Indicator*, 6th edn. Oxford: OPP.

Myhill, D. (2006) 'Talk, talk, talk: teaching and learning in whole class discourse', *Research Papers in Education*, 21 (1): 19–41.

NAGCELL (1997) *Learning for the twenty-first century: first report of the National Advisory Group for Continuing Education and Lifelong Learning (the Fryer report)*. London: NAGCELL.

Namrouti, A. and Alshannag, Q. (2004) 'Effect of using a metacognitive teaching strategy on seventh grade students' achievement in science', *Dirasat*, 31 (1): 1–13.

National Curriculum Council (1990) *The Whole Curriculum: curriculum guidance three*. York: NCC.

National Curriculum Council (NCC) (1993) *Teaching Science at Key Stage 1&2*. York: NCC.

Naylor, S. and Keogh, B. (1999) 'Constructivism in the classroom: theory into practice', *Journal of Science Teacher Education*, 10 (2): 93–106.

Neisser, U. (1976) *Cognition and Reality*. San Francisco: Freeman.

Nettelbeck, T. and Wilson, C. (2005) 'Intelligence and IQ: What Teachers Should Know'. *Educational Psychology*, 25 (6): 609–30.

Newsom Report (1963) Ministry of Education, *Half our Future*. London: HMSO.

Nguyen, P.-M., Terloum, C. and Pilot, A. (2006) 'Culturally appropriate pedagogy: the case of group learning in a Confucian Heritage Culture context', *Intercultural Education*, 17 (1): 1–19.

Nicholls, J.G. (1989) *The Competitive Ethos and Democratic Education*. London: Harvard University Press.

Noble, C., Brown, J. and Murphy, J. (2001) *How to Raise Boys' Achievement*. London: David Fulton.

Norman, K. (ed.) (1992) *Thinking Voices: The Work of the National Oracy Project*. London: Hodder and Stoughton.

Norwood Report (1943) Board of Education, *Curriculum and Examinations in Secondary Schools*. London: HMSO.

Oakley, A. (1975) *Sex, Gender and Society*, London: Temple Smith.

Office for National Statistics (ONS) (2005) *Focus on Social Inequalities: 2005 edition*. London: The Stationery Office.

Office for Standards in Education (Ofsted) (2000) *The Annual Report of Her Majesty's Chief Inspector of Schools. Standards and Quality in Education 1998/99*. London: The Stationery Office.

O'Hagan, T. (2001) 'Jean-Jacques Rousseau, 1712–78', in J. Palmer (ed.) *Fifty Major Thinkers on Education: From Confucius to Dewey*. London: Routledge.

Oliver, P. (2003) *The Student's Guide to Research Ethics*. Maidenhead: Open University Press.

Olssen, M., Codd, J. and O'Neill, A. (2004) *Education Policy: Globalisation, Citizenship and Democracy*. London: Sage

Organisation for Economic Cooperation and Development (OECD) (2005) *Learning sciences and brain research project*. www.teach-the-brain.gov.org.

Ozga, J. (1995) 'Deskilling a profession', in H. Busher and R. Saran (eds), *Managing Teachers in Schools*. London: Kogan Page.

Paechter, C. (1998) *Educating the Other: Gender, Power and Schooling*, London: Routledge.

Palmer, S. (2006) 'All in Their Minds', *Times Educational Supplement*, 9 June.

Palou, E. (2006) 'Learning Styles of Mexican Food Science and Engineering Students', *Journal of Food Science Education*, 5 (7): 51–7.

Parker, S. (1997) *Reflective Teaching in the Postmodern World*. Buckingham: Open University Press.

Parsons, T. (1959) 'The Social Structure of the Family', in R.N. Anshen (ed.), *The Family: Its Functions and Destiny*. New York: Harper and Row.

Parsons, T. (1964) *Social Structure and Personality*. New York: Free Press.

Parsons, T. (1970) 'Hobbes and the problem of order', in P. Worsley (ed.), *Modern Sociology: Introductory Readings*. Harmondsworth: Penguin Education.

Patmore, M. (2006) 'Mathematics for the future', in J. Sharp, S. Ward and L. Hankin (eds), *Education Studies: An issues based approach*. Exeter: Learning Matters.

Patrick, F., Forde, C. and McPhee, A. (2003) 'Challenging the new professionalism: from managerialism to pedagogy', *Journal of In-Service Education*, 29 (2): 237–53.

Pavlov, I.P. (1927) *Conditioned Reflexes: An Investigation of the Physiological Activity of the Cerebral Cortex*. New York: Dover.

Peters, R.S. (1966) *Ethics and Education*. London: Allen and Unwin.

Peters, R.S. (1967) 'What is an educational process?', in R.S. Peters (ed.), *The Concept of Education*. London: Routledge and Kegan Paul.

Petty, G. (2004) *Teaching Today: A Practical Guide*, 3rd edn. Cheltenham: Nelson Thornes.

Phillips, R. (2001) 'Education, the state and the politics of reform: the historical context', in R. Phillips and J. Furlong (eds) *Education, Reform and the State: Twenty-five Years of Politics, Policy and Practice*. London: RoutledgeFalmer.

Phillips, N. and Lindsay, G. (2006) 'Motivation in gifted students', *High Ability Studies*, 17(1): 57–73.

Piaget, J. (1932) *The Moral Judgment of the Child*. New York: Macmillan.

Piaget, J. (1952) *The Origins of Intelligence in Children*. New York: International University Press.

Piaget, J. (1954) *The Construction of Reality in the Child*. New York: Basic Books.

Piaget, J. (1959) *The Thought and Language of the Child*. London: Routledge and Kegan Paul.

Pole, C. and Lampard, R. (2002) *Practical social investigation: Qualitative and quantitative methods in social research*. London: Prentice Hall.

Pollard, A. (2005) *Reflective Teaching*, 2nd edn. London: Continuum.

Porter, J. (1999) *Reschooling and the Global Future: Politics, Economics and the English Experience*, Oxford: Symposium.

Postman, N. and Weingartner, C. (1969) *Teaching as a Subversive Activity*. Harmondsworth: Penguin.

Price, G.E., Dunn, R. and Dunn, K. (1991) *Productivity Environmental Preference Survey (PEPS Manual)*. Lawrence, KS: Price Systems.

Pring, R. (1989) *The New Curriculum*. London: Cassell.

Pring, R. (2004) *Philosophy of Educational Research*. London: Continuum.

Punch, K. (1998) *Introduction to Social Research*. London: Sage.

Purdie, N. and Hattie, J. (1996) 'Cultural differences in the use of strategies for self-regulated learning', *American Educational Research Journal*, 33: 845–71.

Quality Assurance Agency (QAA) (2007) *Benchmarking Academic Standards: Education Studies*. (www.qaa.ac.uk).

Quicke, J. and Winter, C. (1996) 'Kevin doesn't know owt: teaching the language of learning', Topic 15, No. 7. Slough: National Foundation for Educational Research.

Ravenette, A.T. (1999) *Personal Construct Theory in Educational Psychology: A Practitioner's View*. London: Whurr.

Rayner, S. and Riding, R.J. (1997) 'Towards a categorisation of cognitive styles and learning styles', *Educational Psychology*, 17: 5–27.

Reay, D. (2001) 'The paradox of contemporary femininities in education: combining fluidity with fixity', in B. Francis and C. Skelton (eds), *Investigating Gender: Contemporary Perspectives in Education*. Buckingham: Open University Press.

Reay, D. (2006) 'The Zombie Stalking English Schools: Social Class and Educational Inequality'. *British Journal of Educational Studies*, 54 (3), September: 288–307.

Reynolds, D. (1997) 'Now we must tackle social inequality not just assess it', *Times Educational Supplement*, 21 March: 23.

Reynolds, D., Creemers, B., Bird, J., Farrell, S. and Swint, F. (1994) 'School effectiveness: the need for an international perspective', in D. Reynolds, B. Creemers, P. Nesselrodt, E. Schaffer, S. Stringfield and C. Teddlie (eds), *Advances in School Effectiveness Research and Practice*. Oxford: Pergamon Press.

Riding, R.J. (1991) *Cognitive Styles Analysis*, Birmingham: Learning and Training Technology.

Riding, R.J. (1996) *Learning Styles and Technology-Based Training*, Sheffield: DfEE.

Riding, R.J. and Burton, D. (1998) 'Cognitive style, gender and behaviour in secondary school pupils', *Research in Education*, 59, May: 38–49.

Riding, R.J. and Cheema, I. (1991) 'Cognitive styles: an overview and integration', *Educational Psychology*, 11: 193–215.

Riding, R.J., Grimley, M., Dahraei, H. and Banner, G. (2003) 'Cognitive style, working memory and learning behaviour and attainment in school subjects', *British Journal of Educational Psychology*, 73 (21): 149–69.

Riding, R.J. and Rayner, S. (1998) *Cognitive Styles and Learning Strategies*. London: Fulton.

Rist, R. (1970) 'Student social class and teacher expectations; the self-fulfilling prophecy in ghetto education', *Harvard Educational Review*, 40: 441–51.

Ritzer, G. (2000) *The McDonaldization of Society*. Thousand Oaks, CA: Pine Forge Press.

Robbins Report (1963) *Higher Education: A Report of the Committee Appointed by the Prime Minister Under the Chairmanship of Lord Robbins, 1961–63* (Cmnd 2154). London: HMSO.

Rogers, C.R. (1983) *Freedom to Learn for the 80s*. New York: Macmillan.

Rogoff, B. (1990) *Apprenticeship in Thinking: Cognitive Development in Social Context*. Oxford: Oxford University Press.

Rogoff, B (1998) 'Cognition as a collaborative process', in D. Kuhn and R.S. Seigler (eds). *Cognition, Perception and Language*, vol. 2 of W. Damon (ed.), *Handbook of Child Psychology*, 5th edn. New York: John Wiley.

Rosenthal, R. and Jacobson, L. (1968) *Pygmalion in the Classroom*. New York: Holt, Rinehart and Winston.

Rotter, J.B. (1966) 'Generalised expectancies for internal versus external control of reinforcement', *Psychological Monographs*, 80 (609).

Rumelhart, D.E. and McClelland, J.L. (1986) *Parallel Distributed Processing: Explorations in the Microstructure of Cognition*. Cambridge, MA: MIT Press.

Rutter, M., Maughan, B., Mortimore, P. and Oulston, J. (1979) *Fifteen Thousand Hours: Secondary Schools and their Effects on Children*. London: Open Books.

Salili, F. (1996) 'Achievement Motivation: a cross-cultural comparison of British and Chinese students', *Educational Psychology*, 16: 271–9.

Salovey, P. and Mayer, J.D. (1990) 'Emotional intelligence', *Imagination, Cognition, and Personality*, 9: 185–211.

Salthouse, T. (1999) 'Aging and cognition', in R.A. Wilson and F.C. Weil (eds), *The MIT Encyclopedia of the Cognitive Sciences*. Cambridge, MA: MIT Press.

Sammons, P. Hillman, J. and Mortimore, P. (1995) *Key Characteristics of Effective Schools: a review of school effectiveness research*. London: Office for Standards in Education.

Schon, D. (1983) *The Reflective Practitioner: How Professionals Think in Action*. New York: Basic Books.

Scott, D. (1996) 'Ethnography and education', in D. Scott and D. Usher (eds), *Understanding Educational Research*. London: Routledge.

Scott-Baumann, A. (1995) *Review of the Learning Process*. Cheltenham: Cheltenham and Gloucester College of Higher Education.

Scrimshaw, P. (1983) *Educational Ideologies. Unit 2 E204. Purpose and Planning in the Curriculum*. Milton Keynes: Open University Press.

Seifert, C. (1999) 'Situated cognition and learning', in R.P. Wilson and F.C. Keil (eds), *The MIT Encyclopedia of the Cognitive Sciences*. Cambridge, MA: MIT Press.

Selman, R.L. (1980) *The Growth of Interpersonal Understanding*. New York: Academic Press.

Sewell, T. (1997) *Black Masculinities and Schooling*. Stoke on Trent: Trentham.

Shallcross, T., Loubser, C., Le Roux, Cheryl, O'Donoghue, R. and Lupele, Justin (2006) 'Promoting sustainable development through whole school approaches: an international, intercultural teacher education research and development project', *Journal of Education for Teaching: International Research and Pedagogy*, 32 (3): 283–301.

Sharpe, S. (1976) *Just Like a Girl: How Girls Learn to be Women*. Harmondsworth: Penguin.

Shayer, M. and Adey, P. (eds) (2002) *Learning Intelligence: cognitive acceleration across the curriculum from 5 to 15 years*. Buckingham, Philadelphia: Open University Press.

Silcock, P. (1999) *New Progressivism*. London: Falmer.

Silver, H. (1973) *Equal Opportunity in Education: A Reader in Social Class and Educational Opportunity*. London: Methuen.

Silver, H., Strong, R. and Perini, M. (1997) 'Integrating learning styles and multiple intelligences', *Educational Leadership*, September: 22–7.

Skeggs, B. (2004) *Class, Self, Culture*, London: Routledge.

Skilbeck, M. (1994) 'The core curriculum: an international perspective', in B. Moon and A. Shelton-Mayes (eds), *Teaching and Learning in the Secondary School*. London: Routledge/Open University.

Skinner, B. (1957) *Verbal Behavior*. New York: Appleton-Century-Crofts.

Slavin, R.E. (1990) 'Achievement effects of ability grouping in secondary schools: a best evidence synthesis', *Review of Educational Research*, 60: 471–99.

Slavin, R.E. (1993) 'Students differ: so what?', *Educational Researcher*, 22: 13–14.

Smail, B. (2000) 'Has the Mountain Moved? The Girls Into Science and Technology Project 1979–83', in Myers, K. (ed.) *Whatever Happened to Equal Opportunities in Schools? Gender Equality Initiatives in Education*. Buckingham: Open University Press.

Smith, A. (1996) *Accelerated Learning in the Classroom*. London: Network Educational Press.

Smith, A. (2001) 'The labelling of African-American Boys in special education: a case study in G. Hudak and P. Kihn (eds), *Labelling, Pedagogy and Politics*. London: RoutledgeFalmer: pp. 109–14.

Smith, A. and Call, N. (2001) The alps approach resource book. Stafford: Network Educational Press.

Smith, A. and Call, N. (2002) *The ALPS Approach*. London: ALITE.

Smith, A.R., Cavanaugh, C., Jones, J., Venn, J., and Wilson, W. (2006) 'Influence of Learning Style on Graduate Student Cognitive and Psychomotor Performance', *Journal of Allied Health*, 35 (3): 182–203.

Smith, E. (2003) 'Failing Boys and Moral Panics: Perspectives on the Underachievement Debate', *British Journal of Educational Studies*, 51 (3), 282–95.

Smith, P. (2006) 'Identifying learning preferences in vocational education and training classroom settings', *Journal of Vocational Education and Training*, 58 (14): 257–70.

Smith, P.K. and Cowie, H. (1988) *Understanding Children's Development*. London: Blackwell.

Smitherman, G. (2000) *Talkin' That Talk: Language, Culture and Education in African America*. London: Routledge.

Spada, M., Nikcevic, A., Moneta, G. and Ireson, J. (2006) 'Metacognition as a Mediator of the Effect of Test Anxiety on a Surface Approach to Studying', *Education Psychology*, 26 (5): 615–24.

Spearman, C. (1927) *The Abilities of Man*. London: Macmillan.

Spender, D. (1982) *Invisible Women: The Schooling Scandal*. London: Writers and Readers.

Stanley, J. (2004) '"Race" and education', in D. Matheson (ed), *An introduction to the study of education*. London: David Fulton.

Stenhouse, L. (1975) *An Introduction to Curriculum Research and Development*. Oxford: Heinemann Educational.

Stenhouse, L. (1983) *Authority, Education and Emancipation*. London: Heinemann.

Sternberg, R.J. (1985) *Beyond IQ: A Triarchic Theory of Human Intelligence*. New York: Cambridge University Press.

Sternberg, R.J. (1999) 'Intelligence', in R.A. Wilson and F.C. Keil (eds), *The MIT Encyclopedia of the Cognitive Sciences*. Cambridge, MA: MIT Press.

Sternberg, R.J. (2003a) 'Creative Thinking in the Classroom', *Scandinavian Journal of Education Research*, 47 (3): 325–38.

Sternberg, R.J. (2003b) 'WICS as a Model of Giftedness'. *High Ability Studies,* 14 (2): 109–37.

Sternberg, R.J. (2005) 'WICS: A Model of Positive Educational Leadership Comprising Wisdom, Intelligence, and Creativity Synthesised'. *Educational Psychology Review,* 17 (3): 191–262.

Sternberg, R.J. and O'Hara, L.A. (1999) 'Creativity and intelligence', in R.J. Sternberg (ed.), *Handbook of Creativity.* Cambridge: Cambridge University Press.

Stones, E. (2000) 'Iconoclastes: poor pedagogy', *Journal of Education for Teaching: International Research and Pedagogy,* 26 (1): 93–95.

Stones, E. (2002) '*JET*: directions for the future', *Journal of Education for Teaching: International Research and Pedagogy,* 28 (3): 207–10.

Stradling, R., Saunders, L. and Weston, P. (1991) *Differentiation in Action: A Whole School Approach for Raising Attainment.* London: NFER/HMSO.

Sugai, G., Horner, R.H., Dunlap, G., Heineman, M., Lowis, T.J. and Nelson, C.M. (2000) 'Applying positive behaviour support and functional behavioural assessment in schools', *Journal of Positive Behavior Interventions,* 2: 131–43.

Swain, J. (2004) 'The resources and strategies that 10–11-year-old boys use to construct masculinities in the school setting', *British Educational Research Journal,* 30 (1), 167–85.

Sylva, K. and Pugh, G. (2005) 'Transforming the early years in England', *Oxford Review of Education,* 31 (1), 11–27.

Taylor, C., Fitz, J. and Gorard, S. (2005) 'Diversity, specialisation and equity in education', *Oxford Review of Education,* 31 (1): 47–69.

Taylor, M. (2006) 'It's official: class matters', *Education Guardian,* 28 February: 1.

Taylor, P. et. al. (1995) *Sociology in Focus.* Ormskirk: Causeway Press.

Taylor, R. (2005) 'Lifelong: Learning and the Labour Governments 1997–2004', *Oxford Review of Education,* 31 (1): 101–18.

Teacher Training Agency (1996) *Teaching as a Research-based Profession.*(Prepared by the TTA and the Central Office of Information 3/96. TETR J036294JJ) London: The Teacher Training Agency Information Section.

Teddlie, C. and Reynolds, D. (2000) *International Handbook of School Effectiveness Research.* London: Falmer Press.

Terman, L.M. (1924) 'The mental tests as a psychological method', *Psychological Review,* 31: 93–117.

Thorndike, E.L. (1911) *Animal Intelligence: Experimental Studies.* New York: Macmillan.

Thrupp, M. (2001) 'Recent School Effectiveness Counter-critiques: problems and possibilities', *British Educational Research Journal,* 27 (4): 443–58.

Thrupp, M. and Lupton, R. (2006) 'Taking school contexts more seriously: The social justice challenge', *British Journal of Educational Studies,* 54, (3): 308–28.

Thrupp, M. and Tomlinson, S. (2005) 'Introduction: Education Policy, Social Justice and "Complex Hope"', *British Educational Research Journal,* 31(5): 549–56.

Thurstone, L.L. (1938) *Primary Mental Abilities.* Chicago: University of Chicago Press.

Tight, M. (1998) 'Lifelong Learning: Opportunity or Compulsion?', *British Journal of Educational Studies,* 46 (3): 251–63.

Tizard, B. and Phoenix, A. (2001) *Black, white or mixed race?: race and racism in the lives of young people of mixed parentage.* London: Routledge.

Tomlinson, S. (1977) 'Race and education in Britain 1960–77: an overview of the literature', *Sage Race Relations Abstracts*, 2 (4): 3–33.

Tomlinson, S. (2001) *Education in a Post-Welfare Society.* Buckingham: OUP.

Tomlinson, S. (2005a) *Education in a Post-Welfare Society.* 2nd edn. Maidenhead: OUP.

Tomlinson, S. (2005b) 'Race, Ethnicity and Education Under New Labour', *Oxford Review of Education*, 31 (1): 153–71.

Tomlinson, P., Dockrell, J. and Winne, P. (eds) (2005) 'Pedagogy – Teaching for learning', *British Journal of Educational Psychology*, Monograph Series II: Psychological Aspects of Education – Current Trends. Leicester : The British Psychological Society.

Toogood, P. (1984) *The Head's Tale.* Ironbridge: Dialogue Publications.

Tooley, J. and Darby, D. (1998) *Educational Research: A Critique.* London: Ofsted.

Tooley, J. (2001) 'The good, the bad and the ugly: on four years' Labour education policy', in M. Fielding (ed.) *Taking Education Really Seriously: Four Years' Hard Labour.* London: Routledge Falmer.

Townsend, M.A.R. and Hicks, L. (1997) 'Classroom goal structures, social satisfaction and the perceived value of academic tasks', *British Journal of Educational Psychology*, 67: 1–12.

Triantafillou, E., Pomportsis, A., Demetriadis, S. and Georgiadou, E. (2004) 'The value of adaptivity based on cognitive style: an empirical study', *British Journal of Educational Technology*, 35 (1): 95–106.

Tropp, A. (1957) *The School Teachers: The Growth of the Teaching Profession in England and Wales.* London: Heinemann.

Trowler, P. (2003) *Education Policy*, 2nd edn. London: Routledge

Troyna, B. and Carrington, B. (1990) *Education, Racism and Reform.* London: Routledge.

Tubbs, N. (1996) *The New Teacher: An Introduction to Teaching in Comprehensive Education.* London: Fulton.

Tubbs, N. (2006) 'Education and the Free Market', in J. Sharp, S. Ward and L. Hankin (eds), *Education Studies: An issues based approach.* Exeter: Learning Matters.

Tulving, E. (1972) 'Episodic and semantic memory', in E. Tulving and W. Donaldson (eds), *Organisation of Memory.* New York: Academic Press.

Tulving, E. and Craik, F. (eds) (2000) *The Oxford Handbook of Memory.* Oxford: Oxford University Press.

Verma, G. and Mallick, K. (1999) *Researching Education. Perspectives and Techniques.* London: Falmer Press.

Vicars, M. (2006) 'Who are you calling queer? Sticks and stones can break my bones but names will always hurt me', *British Educational Research Journal*, 32 (3): 347–61.

Visser, J. (1993) *Differentiation: Making it Work; Ideas for Staff Development*, Stafford: NASEN.

Vygotsky, L.S. (1978) *Mind in Society: The Development of Higher Psychological Processes.* London: Harvard University Press.

Walford, G. (1994) *Choice and Equity in Education.* London: Cassell.

Walford, G. (2001) *Doing Qualitative Educational Research: A Personal Guide to the Research Process.* London: Continuum.

Walford, G. (2005) 'Introduction: education and the Labour Government', *Oxford Review of Education*, 31(1): 3–9.

Walton, R. (2006) 'Science and society', in J. Sharp, S. Ward and L. Hankin (eds), *Education Studies: An issues based approach*. Exeter: Learning Matters.

Ward, S. (2006) 'The Nature of Higher Education', in J. Sharp, S. Ward and L. Hankin, *Education Studies: An Issues Based Approach*. Exeter: Learning Matters.

Wardle, D. (1970) *English Popular Education, 1780–1970*. Cambridge: Cambridge University Press.

Watson, J. (1913) 'Psychology as the behaviorist views it', *Psychological Review*, 20: 159–77.

Watts, J. (ed.) (1977) *The Countesthorpe Experience*, London: Allen and Unwin.

Weber, M. (1958) *The Protestant Ethic and the Spirit of Capitalism*. New York: Charles Scribner's Sons.

Weber, M. (1963) *The Sociology of Religion*. Boston, MA: Beacon Press.

Webber, R. and Butler, T. (2006) *Classifying Pupils by Where they Live: How well does this Predict Variations in their GCSE Results?* CASA working Paper 99. London: University College, London University.

Weinberg, R.A. (1989) 'Intelligence and IQ: landmark issues and great debates', *American Psychologist*, 44: 98–104.

Weiner, B.J. (1972) *Theories of Motivation*. Chicago: Markham.

Weiner, B.J. (1979) 'A theory of motivation for some classroom experiences', *Journal of Educational Psychology*, 71: 3–25.

Weiner, B.J. (1992) *Human Motivation: Metaphors, Theories and Research*. London: Sage.

Weinstock, A. (1976) 'I blame the teachers', *Times Educational Supplement*, 23 January: 2.

Wertheimer, M. (1923) 'Untersuchungen zur Lehre von der Gestalt', *Psychologische Forschung*, 4: 301–50.

Weston, P. (1996) 'Learning about differentiation in practice', *TOPIC*, 16 (4). London: NFER.

Wheldall, K. and Merrett, F. (1985) *The Behavioural Approach to Teaching Package*. Birmingham: Positive Products.

White, J. (2004) 'The Myth of Howard Gardner's Multiple Intelligences', *Lecture at the London Institute of Education*, 17 November. London.

White, J. (1998) *Perspectives on Education Policy: Do Howard Gardner's multiple intelligences add up?* London: Institute for Education.

White, J. (ed) (2003) *Rethinking the School Curriculum: Values, Aims and Purposes*. London: Routledge.

Whitty, G. (1990) 'The New Right and the National Curriculum: state control or market forces?', in B. Moon (ed.), *New Curriculum – National Curriculum*. Sevenoaks: Hodder and Stoughton.

Whitty, G. (2002) *Making Sense of Education Policy*. London: Paul Chapman Publishing.

Whyte, J. (1983) *Beyond the Wendy House: Sex-Role Stereotyping in Primary Schools*. York: Longman.

Williams, J. (1981) 'Race and schooling', *British Journal of Sociology*, 2 (2): 221.

Willis, P. (1979) *Learning to Labour*. Aldershot: Gator.

Willmott, R. (1999) 'School effectiveness research: an ideological commitment?', *Journal of Philosophy of Education*, 33 (2): 253–67.

Wilson, R.A. (ed.) (1999) *Species: New Interdisciplinary Essays*. Cambridge, MA: MIT Press.

Wintour, P. (1994) 'Blair gives "modern voice to Labour views"', *Guardian*, 24 June: 8.

Withers, R. and Eke, R. (1995) 'Reclaiming "Match" from the critics of primary education', *Educational Review*, 47: 59–73.

Wolf, A. (2002) *Does Education Matter? Myths About Education and Economic Growth*. Harmondsworth: Penguin.

Wong, N.Y., Lin, W.Y. and Watkins, D. (1996) 'Cross-cultural validation of models of approaches to learning: an application of confirmatory factor analysis', *Educational Psychology*, 16 (3): 317–27.

Wood, D. (1988) *How Children Think and Learn*. Oxford: Blackwell.

Woodrow, D. (1997) 'Social construction of theoretical beliefs', in D. Woodrow, G.K. Verma, M.B. Rocha-Trinidada, G. Campani and C. Bagley (eds), *Intercultural Education: Theories, Policies and Practices*, Aldershot: Ashgate.

Woods, P. (1999) *Successful Writing for Qualitative Researchers*. London: Routledge.

Wright, C., Weekes, D. and McGlaughlin, A. (1999) *'Race', Class and Gender in Exclusion from School*. London: Routledge.

Wyse, D. (2003) 'The National Literacy Strategy: a critical review of empirical evidence', *British Educational Research Journal*, 29 (6): 903–16.

Yates, S. (2004) *Doing Social Science Research*. London: Sage, Open University Press.

Yin, R. (2003) *Case Study Research: Design and Methods*. 3rd edn. Thousand Oaks, CA: Sage.

Young, M.F.D. (1971) *Knowledge and Control*. London: Collier-Macmillan.

Young, M.F.D. (1998) *The Curriculum of the Future: From the 'New Sociology of Education' to a Critical Theory of Learning*. London: Falmer Press.

Zimmerman, B.J. and Martinez-Pons, M. (1986) 'Development of a structured interview for assessing student use of self-regulated learning strategies', *American Educational Research Journal*, 23: 614–28.

Zimmerman, B.J. and Martinez-Pons, M. (1988) 'Construct validation of a strategy model of student self-regulated learning', *Journal of Educational Psychology*, 80: 284–90.

Zimmerman, B.J. and Martinez-Pons, M. (1990) 'Student differences in self-regulated learning: relating grade, sex, and giftedness to self-efficacy and strategy uses', *Journal of Educational Psychology*, 82: 51–9.

Zins, J.E., Weissberg, R.P., Wang, M.C. and Walberg, H.J. (2004) *Building Academic Success on Social and Emotional Learning. What does the research say?* Teachers College, Columbia University.

Index

Note: the letter 'f' after a page number indicates a figure